Ellen Price Wood

St. Martin's Eve

A Novel

Ellen Price Wood

St. Martin's Eve
A Novel

ISBN/EAN: 9783337025878

Printed in Europe, USA, Canada, Australia, Japan

Cover: Foto ©Thomas Meinert / pixelio.de

More available books at **www.hansebooks.com**

ST. MARTIN'S EVE.

A Novel.

BY

MRS. HENRY WOOD,

AUTHOR OF

"EAST LYNNE," "THE CHANNINGS," "JOHNNY LUDLOW,"
ETC.

Sixtieth Thousand.

LONDON:
RICHARD BENTLEY AND SON,

Publishers in Ordinary to Her Majesty the Queen.

1895.

CONTENTS.

ST. MARTIN'S EVE.

CHAPTER I.

THE LITTLE HEIR.

THE dull sombre light of a November afternoon was rapidly giving place to twilight. The day had been wet and cold; and the sodden leaves that strewed the park of one of England's fair domains did not contribute to the cheerfulness of the scene. The mansion belonging to it stood on a gentle eminence, well open to view, and looking boldly down on its lands: a long but not high house of red brick, with many windows; a cheerful house, rising behind a wide and gently sloping lawn, which on this ungenial day gave out as wretched an apppearance as did all else of outward nature.

But if the weather was rendering the demesne desolate, it seemed not to affect the house itself. Lights were gleaming from many of its numerous windows, were passing from room to room, from passage to passage; and fires added their red glow to the general brightness. A spectator might have said that some unusual excitement or gaiety was going on there. Excitement in that house there indeed was, but of gaiety none; for grim Death was about to pay it a visit: not to call any waiting for him in weary old age, but to snatch away the young and lovely.

Had you entered the hall, so bright with light, what would have struck you most was the hushed, unusual silence. Nearly all the servants of the establishment were gathered there; but so still were they, so motionless in their repose, that it had something unnatural about it. They stood in small groups, for the most part only half showing themselves, and gazing towards a closed dining-room, sorrow and consternation imprinted on their faces. Two physicians, almost as hushed in manner just now as the servants themselves, were partaking of refreshment within it. The butler himself waited on them; and as he came out and crossed the hall with noiseless tread, he repeated an ominous opinion he had heard hinted at. One of the women-servants, her tears streaming, started up the broad, carpeted staircase with impulsive but soft footfalls, and a younger girl, looking frightened to death, followed her. They stole along the corridor to the right, and halted at a door there. Why, or for what purpose, they could not have told, since they might not presume to enter the chamber; for their lady was lying there at the point of doom.

A handsome, spacious bed-chamber, opening into a dressing-room, but the door was almost closed between them now. Over the dressing-room fire was a tall, upright, middle-aged woman, more intelligent and respectable-looking than are some of her class. She wore a clean print gown, and a close white cap shaded a cheerful countenance. The fire shone full on her brown eyes, and on the tears that glistened in them. Strange sight! for the continuous scenes of sickness, some-times of death, in which these hired nurses' lives are passed, tend to render them callous to outward emotion.

Pacing the carpet slowly and sadly, his eyes cast down in thought, was a little man of ruddy complexion, sharp, thin features, and hair going grey with years. It was Mr. Pym, the family medical attendant. His hands were clasped behind him, as he walked, and his gaze, worn and anxious, was never lifted from the ground.

"This will make the second case we have lost this year," suddenly observed the woman, whose name was Dade, in whispered tones. "What can make it so unlucky a year?"

The surgeon gave no answer. Perhaps he did not like the "we" in her remark. But he knew that his duty was always performed to the very utmost of his skill and power; that it had been so in the two cases to which she alluded; and his con-science, so far, was at peace before God.

"There are no further means that can be tried?" resumed the nurse, using the words as an assertion, more than a question, and she glanced towards the partially-open door connecting the two apartments.

"None," was the conclusive reply. "She is sinking rapidly."

A long pause. The nurse stood motionless, the surgeon

pursued his slow and noiseless tread. Suddenly he stopped and turned his head, speaking in quick tones.

"Where's the baby, Mrs. Dade?"

"He's in the cradle, sir, by her side. She looked as if she wanted him left there."

And then the doctor remembered, and paced on as before. He had spoken in momentary forgetfulness.

The silence within the sick chamber was as great and more painful: the moments of bustle and anxiety had passed away. The fire in the grate had burnt down to embers; a pale light was emitted from the shaded lamp; the air was redolent, almost to faintness, of perfume. Essences had been sprinkled about in profusion, as if they would make pleasant the way to death! The heavy blue velvet curtains were drawn back from the bed; and, lying there, was a form young and fair, with a pale, exhausted face. Everything in the chamber spoke of wealth, comfort, luxury: but not all the wealth and luxury of the whole world combined, had they been brought together, could have arrested the fast-fleeting spirit already on its wing. On the far side of the bed stood a pretty cradle, ornamented with blue silk and lace: the little child so quietly and unconsciously sleeping in it, had seen the light but yesterday.

Leaning over the bed was a young man bowed down with grief, of attractive features and gentlemanly bearing. Not long had they been man and wife; but a year at most; and now it was hard to part; doubly hard with this new tie which had been born to them. Yet they both knew it must be so, and he had thrown his arm lightly across her, and laid his cheek, wet with tears, against hers, vainly wishing, perhaps half hoping, that his heart's bitter prayers might avail to renew her life. The silence between them had been long and agonizing: each heart was aching with painful thoughts; yet it seemed in that last hour as if they could not give them utterance. May Heaven shed its balm on all such partings!

He raised his face and pushed his hair from his brow as he looked at her, for she had moved restlessly, as if in sudden pain. It was not pain of body: of that she was free in this, the passing: but pain of mind. An anxious care, one of the many she must leave on earth, was pressing upon that lady's brain.

"When the months and the years go by," she murmured, breaking the silence, and clasping her hands in feeble supplication to him, "and you think of another wife, oh choose one that will be a *mother* to my child. Be not allured by beauty, be not tempted by wealth, be not ensnared by specious deceit; but take one who will be to him the loving mother that I would have been. Some one whom you know well and can trust. Not a stranger, not a—— "

" I shall never marry again," he interrupted in impassioned tones, when his first surprise allowed him to speak. " You, my first and only love, shall be the sole wife ever taken to my bosom. Never shall another woman usurp your place. And here I swear—— "

" Hush! hush!" she panted, laying her hand upon his lips to stay the incautious words. " It were cruel of me to exact such a promise from you : and it would be useless for you to make it, for you would never keep it, save with self-upbraiding. The remembrance of this scene will pass away; the remembrance of me will pass; and then you will ask yourself why should your life be condemned to solitude. No, no. To remain faithful to the dead is not in man's nature."

He thought in his own heart, honestly thought it then, that her opinion was a mistaken one, and he marvelled that she should so speak. He felt as sure as he could feel of anything in this world, that he should prove a living refutation of it. Dying though she was, partially oblivious already to earth and earth's interests, she yet saw clearer into human nature than he.

" Yet oh, forget me not wholly!" she whispered. " Let there be brief moments when the remembrance of me shall return to you; when you will dwell upon me as having been the one you once best loved on earth!"

Another deep silence from words, for he could not answer: his sobs were choking him; the pulses of his anguished heart were beating wildly. *She* spoke not from exhaustion; and several minutes passed on.

" What will you have him named?" he asked abruptly, pointing towards the cradle.

" Call him Benjamin," she replied, after a minute's thought, and she spoke now with difficulty. " He cost Rachel her life, as this child has cost mine. And oh, may he be to you the solace that Benjamin was to old Jacob; and may you love and cherish this child as he did his!"

Her voice gradually failed her, a spasm smote her features, and she lay more heavily on the pillow. Her husband raised her: he clasped her fluttering heart to his; he wildly kissed

her pallid face. But that face was losing its look of consciousness, and no tenderness could arrest the departing spirit. In
a paroxysm of alarm : as if, now that the moment had come,
it took him by surprise, a thing that had not been looked for :
he cried out to the medical man in the adjoining chamber.

Mr. Pym came in, followed by the nurse. He gave one
glance at the bed, and then whispered the woman to summon
the physicians. He knew their presence would be utterly
useless, but at such times man deems it well to fulfil these
outward forms.

They hastened up the stairs. They remained but a few
minutes in the room, and then left it ; soon left the house.
The better part of that lovely lady had quitted it before they
did.

And it was only the previous day that the joybells had rung
out in the adjacent village on account of the birth ! Only this
same morning that the local newspaper, wet from the press,
had given forth the festal news to the world !

" On the 10th inst., at Alnwick Hall, the wife of George
Carleton St. John, Esquire, of a son and heir."

And the journal went its way, as journals do go their way,
into many a neighbouring home, whose inmates made their
comments on the one piece of news that was of more interest
to them than all the rest, and congratulated each other on the
birth of Alnwick's heir, little conscious of the tragedy that was
supervening upon it.

Amongst the houses to which the journal penetrated was one
on the other side the village of Alnwick. A small, unpretend-
ing dwelling, this house, standing a little away from the high-
road, but a pretty place withal, hidden amidst its surrounding
shrubs and trees. It was called " The Cottage." Its mistress
had named it so with a sort of affectation of humility, for it was
superior to a cottage, even to an elegant one.

Lying back in a lounging chair, in one of the pretty sitting-
rooms, where she had just thrown herself, not from illness but
from fatigue, was the owner of the house, when the newspaper
was taken in. A woman of nearly fifty years, but looking a
great deal younger, with her still bright blue eyes and her
auburn hair. She was a widow ; a widow for the second time.
Barely twenty years of age when her first husband, Mr. Norris,
died, she had soon espoused another, Colonel Darling. In ten
years after that she was a widow again, and had remained so.

She chose to retain the name of Norris, without any right to it, and her cards were printed "Mrs. Norris Darling," so that people, especially strangers, hardly knew by which to address her, and sometimes called her Norris and sometimes Darling. The fact is, Mrs. Darling was a little given to pretension, as ladies will be, when conscious of a want of dignity in themselves or their surroundings. She had been packing things all the morning; she, her maid, and two of her daughters; for they were summoned from home unexpectedly; and she was falling into a doze when the footman entered.

"What is it?" she asked in peevish accents; and the man looked up in surprise at hearing it from his usually easy-tempered mistress.

"It is only the newspaper, ma'am."

"Put it down, Tomkins," she answered, too idle to take it. "I think I was asleep. I am very tired."

The man laid it on the table and quitted the room, meeting a staid-looking, rather old-fashioned young lady who was entering it, for whom he made way It was Miss Darling, and she looked thirty years of age if she looked a day. But she was only five-and-twenty.

"Well, Mary Anne, is it all done?"

"It is all done, mamma. Prance is waiting for Tomkins to cord the boxes."

Mrs. Darling closed her eyes again, and her daughter took up the unopened newspaper, when another young lady, very much resembling the first, and looking quite as old, came in. She gave a slight shiver as she passed the window, and began to stir the fire.

"What a miserable day it is! I wish we could put off our journey."

"Where's the use of wishing that, Margaret?" said Miss Darling. "But it *is* miserable. Has Charlotte found the cover of her desk?"

"I don't know. I don't suppose Charlotte has looked for it. I heard her tell Prance that none of her things must be forgotten."

"True. When did Charlotte ever trouble herself to look for anything?" was Mary Anne Darling's response; but she spoke it more in soliloquy than as a reply.

Margaret Darling—she was one year younger than her sister —drew her chair in front of the fire, and put her feet upon the fender.

"Is that the newspaper? Is there any news, Mary Anne?"

"Yes, there's news," was the quiet answer: but Miss Darling's manner was always quiet. "A baby is born at the Hall."

"What?" exclaimed Mrs. Darling, starting up as she caught the words, and all her lethargy was gone. "Is the baby born, Mary Anne?"

For answer, Miss Darling read out the words: "On the 10th inst., at Alnwick Hall, the wife of George Carleton St. John, Esquire, of a son and heir."

"I am glad it's a boy!" exclaimed Mrs. Darling. "How proud they will be of it! On the 10th—that was yesterday. Then rely upon it those bells Charlotte said she heard ringing, were for this. And now, how can I manage it? I must contrive to see Mrs. St. John before we go away."

"But why, mamma?"

"Why?" repeated Mrs. Darling, turning rather sharply on her daughter Mary Anne, who had asked the question. "Because I should like to do so; because it's neighbourly to go to her, poor young mother; because it may be months before we are back here, and I have the opportunity of seeing her again; and because I'm curious to hear all the interesting particulars. That's why, Mary Anne: and I shall go."

Mrs. Darling allowed no interference with her will—at least from *these* daughters, and Mary Anne was dutifully silent. "I was only thinking, mamma, what an unpleasant day it would be for you to walk over," she presently said. "And I don't see how you will have time for it."

"Plenty of time; and for the unpleasantness I don't care; you never yet knew me to stop indoors for weather. Pretty Mrs. St. John! Let me read the announcement for myself."

She took the paper in her hand, and was gazing at the words with a pleased smile, when the door again opened, and some one else entered the room. A tall, elegant girl of apparently only three or four-and-twenty, an imperious, regal, haughty girl, whose raven-black hair was braided over pale, regular features, and whose rich silk attire glistened and rustled as she walked. Who would have believed that she was older by some three or four years than the Miss Darlings?—who would have believed that they were even half-sisters?—she, with her stately beauty, her costly attire, and they with their homely faces, old-fashioned look, and plain green merino gowns.

Mrs. Darling had two daughters who absorbed all the money that she could spare for dress; the eldest, Charlotte Norris, and the youngest, whom you will meet by and by; no wonder that these two middle ones, Mary Anne and Margaret, with their meek spirits and quiet tastes, were obliged to dress in plain merinos.

"Charlotte, here's news in the paper," Mary Anne was beginning, but Mrs. Darling drowned the words: and Mary Anne saw with some momentary surprise, that her mother had crushed the paper in her hand, as if not caring that it should be seen.

"Charlotte, my darling, *would* you mind telling Prance that I shall want my black silk cloak taken out of the hair-trunk again? Go to her now, dear, before she has it corded."

Miss Norris, who had still the door-handle in her hand, quitted the room again. Mrs. Darling turned to her daughters.

"Say nothing to Charlotte of this announcement. I will tell her of it myself. It is my pleasure to do so."

"I beg your pardon, mamma," said Mary Anne. "Of course you know best."

Mrs. Darling did know best. At any rate, the two daughters before her were taught to think so. Mary Anne and Margaret Darling had been reared to implicit obedience in one respect —never to question the line of conduct pursued by Mrs. Darling to their half-sister; never to comment on it in the slightest degree. Mrs. Darling folded the newspaper as small as she could, crammed it into her pocket, and followed Charlotte upstairs.

Later in the day she set out to walk to Alnwick Hall. It was growing dark, and she had not intended to be so late as this, but one thing or another had detained her. The Hall was nearly three miles distant from her own home, through the village of Alnwick; but the road was by no means lonely in any part of it. She walked quickly, not stopping to speak to any one she met, and had left the village behind her some time, and was nearing the Hall, when the death-bell of Alnwick church rang out suddenly, but not very distinctly, on the heavy air. It was quite dark then.

"Poor old Mother Tipperton must be gone!" Mrs. Darling exclaimed to herself, standing for a moment to listen. "Pym told me she could not last long. Well, it was time: I suppose she was eighty."

Not another thought, except of old Mother Tipperton, entered her mind; not the faintest suspicion that the bell was tolling for one younger and fairer. She went on, over the broad winding way through the beautiful park, and gained the door of Alnwick Hall.

It might have struck her—but it did not—that besides the man who opened the door to her, other servants came peeping into the hall, as if in curiosity as to the visitor. She stepped over the threshold out of the gloomy night.

"How is your mistress, Haines? Going on all right?" she asked, rubbing her shoes on the mat.

"Oh, ma'am, she's dead!"

Mrs. Darling certainly heard the words, but they appeared not to penetrate her senses. She stared at the speaker.

"She is just dead, ma'am; not an hour ago. Two physicians were had to her, besides Mr. Pym, but nothing could be done."

Down sat Mrs. Darling on the hall bench. Perhaps only once before, in her whole life, had she been so seized with consternation.

"*Dead!* Good Heavens! I came to sit half-an-hour with her before leaving Alnwick, for I may not be back for months. What an awful thing! Poor Caroline Carleton!"

Drawing her cloak around her, Mrs. Darling crossed the hall towards the housekeeper's room, unconsciously calling the deceased by her maiden name, the one she had longest known her by. "I should like to see the nurse," she said, "if she can spare a moment to come to me."

The housekeeper, a stout, very respectable woman, who had come to the hall a year ago with its now dead mistress, was at the table writing a note as well as she could for her tears, when Mrs. Darling entered. Laying down her pen, she told all she knew of the calamity, in reply to the low and eager questions. But Mrs. Darling grew impatient.

"A fine beautiful baby, you say—never mind the baby, Mrs. Tritton. What can have caused the death?"

The stout old lady shook her head. "She died from exhaustion, they say, ma'am. But she had a fall a few days ago, and I believe that had something to do with it. I can't bear to *think* of it just yet. Alive and well and merry but a day or two since; and now dead! It seems like a dream."

Her sobs deepened. The ready tears filled Mrs. Darling's

eyes. She wiped them away, and inquired what would be done about bringing up the child. Mrs. Darling was a practical woman, and had never allowed feeling to interfere with business.

"That's the first great care," was the reply of the house-keeper. "Mr. Pym does not know of any one just now that could come in. I suppose it will have to be brought up by hand: and the master, I believe, wishes that it should be. As Mr. Pym says, the boy's so big and strong, that he'd bring him-self up almost, if you put him outside the street-door. And it's true."

"Does Mr. St. John take it much to heart?"

"Ay, that he does," was the emphatic reply. "He is shut up in his own room where he keeps his business papers and things. But, ma'am"—and the tone was suddenly subdued—"a body going by, and pausing a moment, may hear his sobs. If any young husband ever loved a wife, Mr. Carleton St. John loved his. Poor child! she's gone early to join her parents!"

Mrs. Darling, who had her full share of curiosity—and what woman has not, in a case like this?—stole upstairs to see the baby; to see the baby's poor young mother; to talk for a minute or two with the nurse, Mrs. Dade, who could not come to her. And then she stole down again; for time was getting on. The housekeeper asked her to take some refreshment, but she declined, explaining that a summons to her sick mother, who was very old, was taking her and her daughters away from home. They were starting that evening by the seven-o'clock night train.

"And they are at the station already, I am sure," she said; "and I must run all the way to it. Sad news this is, to cheer me on my journey!"

Sad indeed. And the public thought so as well as Mrs. Darling. The same week the newspapers put forth another announcement.

"On the 11th inst., at Alnwick Hall, in her twenty-third year, Caroline, the beloved wife of George Carleton St. John."

CHAPTER II.

"To remain faithful to the dead is not in man's nature."

Such were the words spoken by Mrs. Carleton St. John in dying; and a greater truth was never recorded by Solomon.

The seasons had gone on; spring had succeeded to winter; summer to spring; autumn was succeeding to summer. Nothing like a twelvemonth had passed since the death, and yet rumour was whispering that George Carleton St. John had begun to think of a second wife.

The baby had thrived from its birth. Mr. St. John appeared to have an invincible repugnance to any woman's supplying the place of its mother; and so they fed the child upon the next best food that was proper for it, and it had done well. The housekeeper strongly recommended Mr. St. John a niece of her own to take care of it, and the young woman arrived from a distance; a comely, fair-complexioned, nice-looking young woman, named Honoria Tritton; and she entered upon her charge. All things went smoothly; and Mr. St. John's first grief yielded to time and change: as all griefs must so yield, under God's mercy.

Friends had come to visit Mr. St. John during the summer. Relatives, they were, indeed, but distant ones. Gay people they proved to be; and they stayed on, and gradually the Hall held its festal gatherings again, and its master began to go out amongst the county families. Whether it might be to escape the sorrow left on him by his great loss, or to make things pleasanter for these visitors, certain it was that George St. John no longer eschewed gaiety, whether in his own house or abroad. Mrs. Tritton's opinion was, that he had invited his relatives to stay with him, because he found his life now at the Hall so monotonously dull. If so, their advent had had the desired effect, and had taken him out of himself and his trouble.

It is surprising, when once an effort of this sort is made, and we awaken from a prolonged grief, how *easily* that grief is laid aside. Unconsciously it seems to slip away from us, and is forgotten. From that eleventh day of November down to June,

Mr. St. John had done nothing but indulge his sorrow. It had grown calmer, of course, by degrees; but he had not in the least striven to lift from himself its bitterness. No very long term, some may say, this seven months; but let me tell you that it *is* long when given wholly to tears and solitude. A reaction must succeed to all violent emotion, even to that caused by the death of one dearly beloved; and it came to George St. John; came with the sojourn of his visitors. A fortnight's association with them, and he was not the same man. As host, he had to exert himself, and with the exertion came the pleasure in it. Ere June was ended, he had forgotten three-parts of his sorrow. It seemed, as he might have described it himself, to have slipped away from his heart, leaving healing and semi-forgetfulness in its place. He would have told you that he regretted his wife as much as ever; but he did not do so; for other interests were reasserting their sway within him. Sorrow had nearly spent itself, and was dying out. Do not blame him: man cannot act against his nature; least of all when in the heyday of youth.

He could not offer a churlish reception to his visitors, who had journeyed far to sojourn with him. They were of the world, and expected to be entertained. Mr. St. John invited people to the Hall to meet them; and went out with them in return. In July the county families began to seek their homes after the whirl of the London season, bringing their guests with them, and gay parties were the rule of the hour. Archery, boating, lawn dances, dinners; never a day but something more agreeable to the rest succeeded to the other. Mr. Carleton was pressed to attend all, and did attend a great many. Can you wonder at it? Of great prospective wealth, heir-presumptive to a baronetcy, and withal an attractive man—the world knew how to estimate him. But the prize was not as great as it had been, since no other woman who might succeed in gaining him, or whom he might choose himself irrespective of any seeking on her own part, could reasonably hope to give birth to the heir that should succeed. That heir was already in the world—the little child whose advent had cost a precious life.

It could not be said that Mr. St. John had very much right, especially now, to the name of Carleton. His name had been simply George St. John, until he married the rich heiress, Caroline Carleton: and with her property he had to assume her name, for her dead father had so enjoined it in his will. But for that expectant baronetage, he might have added the new name *after* his own.   As it was, he did not do so.   The new name was rather a convenience : there were several branches of the St. John family, one of them far higher in the world's social scale than George St. John of Alnwick, or even his uncle the baronet ; and people fell into the habit of calling him Mr. Carleton, as a distinction.   The little child had also been christened Carleton.

And so George Carleton St. John, yielding to the soothing hand of time, forgot in a degree her who had lain on his bosom and made the brief sunshine of his existence.   He went out in the world again, and held gatherings of his own, and was altogether reinstated in social life.

On a lovely day in September, Alnwick Hall was filled with guests.   Chiefest of all the fêtes by which that autumn and the neighbourhood had been distinguished, was this last one held at the Hall.   Mr. St. John had spared neither pains nor money to render it attractive : and he certainly succeeded.   Brilliant groups were in the park, in the temporary marquee on the lawn, and in the house itself ; a sort of *fête-champêtre*.   Was it out of place, all that glittering gaiety, with the closing scene of only ten months before ?—the young life so suddenly sacrificed ? Perhaps so : but the idea did not once occur to George St. John.   It was not likely to do so now, when *another* was casting her spells upon his heart.   I have told you that rumour had already whispered of a second mistress at Alnwick.

In a pleasant room, opening on one side to the conservatory, its front windows looking to the park, several ladies were assembled.   They were of various ages, of various degrees of beauty.   One stood conspicuous amidst the rest.   Not for her beauty, though that was great ; not for her dress, though that was all that can be imagined of costly elegance ; but for a certain haughty, imperious air, and a most peculiar expression that would now and again gleam from her eyes.   An expression that many had observed and that none could fathom ; a sort of wild expression of absolute *will*.   It was not often noticed ; but it was apparent just now.   You have seen that tall, finely-formed girl before, her well-set head, her swan-like neck ; you have seen the pale features, regular as any ever carved in sculpture, the thin lips so firmly closed, the luxuriant raven hair. Quiet to a degree in bearing and manner, in spite of her haughty air there was an indisputable attraction about her. Could the rumour be true—that the greatest match of the county was about to be laid at Charlotte Norris's feet? If so, what a triumph for her mother; what a triumph for herself, so proud and portionless.

Mrs. Norris (she was Mrs. Darling, you know) stood by her side. Very pretty still, but not half as grand a woman as her daughter. Charlotte looked well to-day; never better; in her pretty white gossamer bonnet and sweeping white bernouse, you could not have thought her to be much past twenty. And the ladies around looked on her with envious eyes, and repeated over to themselves, what a triumph for Mrs. Norris Darling!

Perhaps so; but that lady was as yet unconscious of it. She had no more idea that that particular triumph was in store for her, or that Charlotte had, even in rumour, been given to Mr. St. John of Alnwick, than had Alnwick's little heir, who was crowing before her eyes at that moment. This was the first time Mrs. Darling had been to the Hall since that melancholy evening visit in the past November. Only the previous day had she returned to her cottage home.

In the centre of the ladies stood a young woman, holding the baby. That he was a fine baby none could dispute. He was not indeed what could be called a pretty child, but a rather unusual look of intelligence for one so young distinguished his features and his clear grey eyes, rendering his face excessively pleasing. And had he possessed all the beauty that since the creation of man has been said or sung, those fair women, displacing one another around him, could not have bestowed more praise upon him—for he was the heir of Alnwick, and Alnwick's possessor was there to hear it.

George St. John's cheeks were flushed with pleasure, and his eyes shone as he listened to the flattery; for he fondly loved his child. The little boy wore a broad black sash on his white frock, black ribbons tied up his sleeves, and his pretty round fat arms were stretched out to any one who would notice him.

"Yes, he is a fine little fellow," observed Mr. St. John, more gratified as the praises increased. "He will walk soon."

"Pray is that his nurse?" inquired Mrs. Norris Darling,

scanning the maid through her eye-glass. "What is your name, young woman?"

"My name is Honoria, madam," replied the girl, looking pleased and curtseying, "but they call me Honour. Honoria Tritton."

"And what is the name of this dear child?" asked Miss Norris, drawing nearer. "I have always heard him called Baby."

"Well, his name gets abbreviated for the same reason that we shorten Honour's," laughed Mr. St. John. "He was christened Benjamin, but is universally known amongst us as Benja."

Mrs. Norris Darling (let us give her both names once in a way!) continued to examine the nurse by the help of the glass. She needed a glass just as much as you or I, reader; and had she not been surrounded by that fashionable crowd, would as soon have thought of looking at Honour through the ring of her parasol. But pretentiousness is given to many little ways pertaining to pretentiousness, and that is one of them. Mrs. Norris Darling possessed an idea that an eye-glass added immensely in some way to her dignity. She turned her glass on Honour from top to toe, in the same cool manner that other glasses are turned; and she saw a sensible-looking young woman, with a clear, fair skin, a good forehead, and truthful light blue eyes.

"Honoria Tritton?" she repeated. "You must be a relative of Mr. Carleton St. John's housekeeper! Have you had sole charge of the baby?"

"Oh yes, madam, the sole charge."

"It is a great responsibility," remarked Mrs. Norris Darling, dropping the glass, and speaking, not to Honour, but to the ladies around.

Mr. St. John had taken his child from the nurse's arms, and was fondly caressing it. His very actions, his movements, betrayed the depth of his affection, and a sharp feeling of jealousy shot through the heart of the beautiful Miss Norris as she watched him. "Will he ever love another child as he loves this one?" was the thought that arose unbidden to her mind. No, never, Miss Norris; you need not ask or wish it: man does not love another as he loves his first-born.

But her beautiful features were smooth as polished crystal as she drew near to Mr. St. John. He glanced at her with a welcoming smile.

"Do let me nurse him!" she said in low tones. "I adore children; and his one seems made to be loved."

Mr. St. John resigned the boy to her. She carried him away into the conservatory, to a remote bench out of sight, sat down, and amused him with her gold neck-chain. The little fellow sat confidingly on her knee; one hand enclosing her fore-finger, the other grasping the glittering coil. Mr. St. John followed her.

"Look at him!" she said, her quiet face changed to rapture as she glanced at Mr. St. John. "Look at his nimble little fingers and bright eyes! How happy he is!"

"Happy in all things save one," whispered Mr. St. John, leaning over the child, but gazing at herself. "He has no mother to love and guide him."

Those unfathomable eyes of hers were cast down, so that the eyelids concealed them, and a crimson flush mantled to her usually pale cheeks.

"He wants a mother," proceeded Mr. St. John; "he *must* 'ave a mother. Not now will I urge it, when so many are near; but, Charlotte, you know whom I would entreat to be that mother and my beloved wife."

A strange whirl of agitation shook her, impeding instant utterance. Mr. St. John saw the signs, and laid his hand upon her with a smile.

"Ought you to talk to me of a *beloved* wife?" she asked, in an impassioned tone, as she glanced momentarily up at him. "She who lies buried in her grave was yours."

"I did not love her as I shall love you," he hastened to avow —and in the moment's fervour it may be that he thought he spoke truth. "Had I known *you* better then, I might never have chosen her."

"Yet see how you love her child!"

"And I will passionately love any that may be born to you, Charlotte," he whispered. But the very remark, had Mr. St. John been cool enough or wise enough to analyze it, might have told him that her heart, even now, before she was anything to him, was shaken by jealousy of the child. He was neither cool nor wise just then.

He bent his head lower and lower; he murmured vows of everlasting tenderness; he suffered his face to rest against hers, as it had once rested against that of his dying wife. She resisted not. But when a host of intruders came flocking in, she raised her haughty head, and swept on with a scornful step, as she resigned the infant into the arms of its nurse.

George St. John had loved his wife with the fresh, rapturous feelings that he could never know again; and he loved her memory. Yet, here he was, ere ten short months had elapsed, willing to swear to another that she was the first who had awakened true passion in his heart! But Caroline Carleton had faded from his sight, and Charlotte Norris stood before him in all her beauty. It is the way of man; a,, and often of woman. *To remain faithful to the dead is not in man's nature.*

The fête was over, and they were driving home—Mrs. Darling and her daughter. To judge by the manner of the two ladies, one might have thought it was the mother who had received so momentous a proposal; not the daughter. Charlotte sat quiet and calm, leaning back in her corner of the chariot; Mrs. Darling was flushed, restless, evidently disturbed. Mr. St. John had said to her a word of enlightenment in parting, and it startled her out of her equanimity.

"Charlotte," she began—and not until they were drawing near the end of their homeward road, and the village of Alnwick was left behind them, did she speak—"Charlotte, I hope I misunderstood Mr. St. John?"

Charlotte lifted her eyes. "I do not know to what you allude, mamma. In what do you hope you misunderstood Mr. St. John?"

"He hinted to me that he should call to-morrow to speak to me about you. Charlotte, it will be of no use: I cannot let you marry Mr. Carleton."

"Please not to call him by that name," was the quiet rejoinder.

"Mr. St. John, then—what does it matter? I should not like you to marry him. Has he really asked you to be his wife?"

"Yes."

"It must have been very sudden!"

"Not so. I think we have understood each other for some little time past."

"Then he has been in the habit of coming to the cottage?"

"Oh yes."

Mrs. Darling, who had raised herself in some commotion as she asked the last question, sank back again, and a look of mortification, of mental trouble, settled on her face. The carriage was approaching their door ere she spoke again, her tones betraying an agitation that was ill suppressed.

"I cannot spare you, Charlotte! Charlotte, my darling, I cannot spare you! How often have I hoped, and urged, and prayed that you would never leave me—that you would be the one to stay and cheer my old age!"

Charlotte shook her head with a smile. Had her mother been less agitated, less evidently in earnest, she might have enlarged on the unreasonableness of such a wish. As it was, she only answered playfully, that her mother need not think of old age these twenty years.

"Are you marrying him for his money—his position?" resumed Mrs. Darling.

"I am tired, mamma; I wish you wouldn't question me. Really I can't exactly particularize why I am marrying him."

"*You* a second wife! Have you reflected, Charlotte, that Caroline Carleton was his first choice ; that there's already an heir to Alnwick who will inherit all ; that George St. John has hardly a shilling beyond his entailed estates——"

"Don't mamma!" was Charlotte's interruption, and her brow had contracted as if in pain. "It is quite useless your saying this. I should marry George St. John, though I knew that I must beg my bread afterwards from door to door."

A moan, as of ohe in sorrow too great for utterance, broke from the lips of Mrs. Darling, and she sank back in the carriage and clasped her hands in pain.

CHAPTER III.

THE UNEXPLAINED REASON.

NOT a word was spoken by either mother or daughter as they entered their home. The little French clock in the drawing-room pointed to eleven—for the festivities at the Hall had been prolonged into evening—and Charlotte, perhaps afraid of further contention, said good night, and went up at once to her chamber. Mrs. Darling threw off her cloak and bonnet and began to pace the room. It was rather a habit of hers when disturbed or vexed.

Never had she been so disturbed as now. Her ordinary crosses had been but light ones, which she scolded or talked away; *this* seemed to be too deep, too real, for any talking.

It might be unreasonable; every one who knew of it said it was so; but Mrs. Darling had lived in the ardent hope that her eldest daughter—more fondly cherished by her than all the rest—would never leave her, never marry. She had planned and schemed against it. Some two or three years ago, a suspicion arose in her mind that Charlotte was falling in love with George St. John, and she checked it by carrying off Charlotte, and keeping her away until the danger was over. He had married Caroline Carleton before they came back again. No one living had suspected this manœuvre on the mother's part, or that Charlotte had been in danger of loving the master of Alnwick—if she had not loved him—except Margaret Darling. Surely it must have been unreasonable. Mr. St. John was a free man then in every sense of the word, and Charlotte's son, had she married him and borne one, would have been the heir!

That Mrs. Darling's love for Charlotte had always been inordinate, those about them knew. But, as a woman of the world, she might have foreseen how utterly powerless would be a mother's love to keep her daughter always by her side. Charlotte once said to her in a joking way, that she had better put her into a convent, and make a nun of her: and indeed that would have been about the only way of preventing it. And now, in spite of her precaution, Charlotte was about to marry; to be a second wife. That fact alone brought some gall to Mrs. Darling.

She had deemed Charlotte so secure. She had never dreamt of the treason that was afloat. Their visit to her old mother in Berkshire had been prolonged until June, and all that time Charlotte had been safe under her own eye. In June, old Mrs. Darling (it was the same name, for Mrs. Darling's second husband had been a distant cousin) grew so convalescent that they had no scruple in quitting her; and Mrs. Darling had despatched Charlotte to Alnwick under convoy of Mary Anne, who was so much older than her years, and might be thoroughly trusted. Margaret remained behind with her grandmother, and Mrs. Darling went to France to see her youngest daughter Rose, who was at school there. She only intended to be absent a fortnight; by the end of that time she meant to be at

Alnwick; but ere it was concluded, she was summoned back in haste to her old mother, who had had a relapse. So that it was September before Mrs. Darling really returned to Alnwick. She arrived just in time to attend the fête at Mr. St. John's, and she went to it without any more prevision of what was to happen than a child unborn.

It was the first time that Charlotte had been away from her, and she was blaming herself bitterly. Perhaps self-reproach was never sharper than Mrs. Darling's as she paced the drawing-room this night. It seemed to her, now, that she might have foreseen something of the sort; that she should have kept her attractive daughter under her own eye. But she thought she had taken every precaution. She had charged Mary Anne not to admit gentlemen as visitors during her absence—unless, she had added, they were of a certain standing as to age, and married. Some few she had especially interdicted by name. Above all others would she have interdicted Mr. St. John of Alnwick, had she supposed that this would be the result; and she mentally heaped the most bitter reproaches on Mary Anne, and felt that she should like to shake her.

She turned to the bell with a sudden impulse, and rang it; indeed, Mrs. Darling was always an impulsive woman. All the servants had gone upstairs on Mrs. Darling's entrance, except the lady's-maid; hours were early in the quiet household. Mary Prance came in: a slender woman of five-and-thirty, with dark eyes and brown marks on her thin face; she wore a neat grey alpaca gown and small white linen wristbands and collar. A woman devoted to her mistress's interests, but disliked by the servants, who went so far as to call her a "deceitful cat." But Mary Prance was a clever woman, and not deceitful on the whole. She gratefully liked Mrs. Darling, who was always kind to her, and she loved the eldest daughter; but she cared for no one else in the wide world. She had entered the service as housemaid, a young girl, but her mistress had called her "Prance" from the first. Mrs. Darling—you remember the hint I gave you—could not call her servants by their simple Christian names. She turned sharply as the door opened.

"Where's Miss Darling?"

"Miss Darling has been in bed some time, ma'am. She went at eight o'clock. Her sore-throat was painful, though a trifle easier."

"Prance, who has visited here during my absence?" interrupted Mrs. Darling, impatiently drowning the words. "What gentlemen?"

The lady's-maid considered for a moment, recalling the visitors. "Dr. Graves, ma'am; he has come the oftenest, I think. And Mr. Pym, and old Sir William——"

"Not those old people, Prance; I don't care to hear about them," said Mrs. Darling, peevishly. "I mean young men—single men."

"Not any, I think," answered Prance, after a pause. "Miss Darling was denied to them."

"Mr. St. John of Alnwick has come?"

"Oh yes, Mr. St. John has come. He has come often."

With the answer, Mrs. Darling quitted the room for the chamber of her unconsciously offending daughter. The poor girl woke up, hot and startled at the unexpected entrance; at the sharp questions that so rudely assailed her ear. Not for some few moments did she understand sufficiently to answer.

Mr. Carleton St. John? Yes, he had been there rather frequently in the past few weeks. Had Charlotte had opportunities of seeing him alone? Yes, very likely she had; it might be so.

"Did you know," resumed Mrs. Darling, suppressing the storm of reproaches so ready to break from her lips, "that any attachment was arising between her and Mr. St. John?"

"No, mamma, I never knew it," replied Mary Anne, fully awake now. "I did not think of such a thing. *Has* it arisen?"

"Yes, it has arisen, you unhappy, careless creature, and I fear that she's going to marry him," retorted Mrs. Darling. "You are a hundred years older than Charlotte in staid experience. I entrusted her to your charge here as I might a younger sister, and you have suffered her to meet George St. John, and this is the result! I shall never forgive you, Mary Anne. Did I not warn you that I would have no single men calling here during my absence?"

"But—but—Mr. St. John is not a single man," returned the unfortunate Mary Anne, too bewildered to collect her senses. "I'm sure I did not think of him as anything but a widower steeped in grief. It seems only the other day that his wife died. I did not think of him at all as a marrying man."

Neither, in point of fact, had Mrs. Darling, or she might have expressly interdicted his visits by name, as she had those of others.

Mary Anne Darling was collecting her wits. She sat up in bed, thinking possibly that might help her. "Mamma, you *cannot* really expect to keep Charlotte unmarried! Remember her beauty. If it were me or Margaret, you might—— "

"You or Margaret!" screamed Mrs. Darling, excessively incensed at something or other in the words. "I wish you were both going to be married to-morrow! or to-night, for the matter of that."

"I was going to ask you, mamma," pursued Mary Anne, meek still in spite of the covert sneer, "what objection you can possibly have to her marrying Mr. St. John?"

"That's my business and not yours," said Mrs. Darling, tartly.

Mary Anne had never heard her mother altogether so cross, never seen her so vexed, and the girl wondered excessively. Hitherto, she had supposed the objection which existed to Charlotte's marrying, and which she had not failed to detect, arose from an exalted idea on her mother's part that no one likely to present himself was worthy of Miss Norris in a worldly point of view. But surely this could not apply to Mr. St. John of Alnwick! She spoke again, pursuing her train of thought.

"He will be Sir George St. John sometime, mamma; he will be more wealthy than he is now. It is really a better match than even Charlotte could have hoped for."

"I would give every shilling I possess in the world, rather than Charlotte should marry him!" spoke Mrs. Darling, in low, determined tones. "I would sacrifice half the years I have yet to live to keep her with me always! I shall never forgive you, Mary Anne. When you found that George St. John was taking to come here, you ought to have sent me word."

"Mamma, listen. I have told you that I never thought of such a thing as that Mr. Carleton St. John came, or could come, with any such idea; he, who has only just lost his wife. But if I had thought of it, if I had known it, what would have been my will against Charlotte's? It might have pleased her that he should be admitted; and you know you have taught us to give way to her in all things."

"Then you might have written to me. I repeat to you, Mary Anne, that I shall never forgive you."

"It must be, that he was previously married—that Charlotte's children will not inherit," cried Mary Anne, speaking aloud in her wonder, as she strove to find reasonable grounds for the objection to Mr. St. John. "But——"

"Hold your tongue," interrupted Mrs. Darling. "You have done mischief enough, without seeking for reasons that may not be disclosed."

More and more surprised grew Mary Anne. The last words were not spoken in reproach or anger, but in a tone of deep, bitter pain. They bore a sound of wailing, of lamentation; and she could only stare after her mother in silence, as Mrs. Darling quitted the room not less abruptly than she had entered it.

Mary Anne Darling lay down again, and curled the clothes round her with a pettish movement, feeling excessively aggrieved. But that was nothing new. She and Margaret had suffered all their lives through Charlotte, and had never rebelled. Miss Norris had been first and foremost; had received all the love, all the consideration, all the care; the house had only seemed to go on in reference to the well-being and convenience of its eldest daughter.

Brought up to this from their earliest years, Mary Anne and Margaret Darling had accepted it as one of life's obligations. But the young lady was feeling now that she was being unjustly censured. If there did exist any objection to Mr. Carleton St. John, Charlotte should be blamed for falling in love with him, or else be made to relinquish him. But Miss Darling did not believe in any objection : she thought her mother only wished to keep Charlotte to herself in her jealous affection—that she could not bear to part with her.

"I never knew anything so unreasonable," grumbled the young lady, giving the pillow a fierce poke upwards. "Charlotte was sure to marry sometime, and but for her mother's great watchfulness, she'd have been married before this. I *cannot* understand mamma. What though Charlotte *is* the apple of her eye, ought she to wish to prevent her fulfilling woman's proper destiny? The love of most mothers causes them to wish their daughters to marry; some to go the length of scheming for it : in this case it is schemed against. It is very selfish, very inconsistent; and yet mamma is not a selfish woman ! I can't understand her."

Mrs. Darling's opposition was not yet over. She sat the next day in her own room, thinking what an ill-used woman she was, calling up every little remembered cross of her past life; as many of us are prone to do in moments of annoyance, when things wear a gloomy aspect. She had married—a girl not out of her teens—Mr. Norris, of Norris Court, a gentleman whose standing in the county was almost as good as that of the St. Johns of Alnwick. But ere she had well realized her position as the wife of a wealthy man, the mistress of a place so charming as Norris Court; almost ere her baby was born, Mr. Norris died, and the whole thing seemed to pass from her as a dream. Had the child proved a boy she had been well off, and Norris Court still been hers as a residence; proving a girl, it lapsed from her to the next male heir in the entail. She turned out of it with her baby, the little Charlotte, and a small income of a few hundreds a year. These hundreds, at her own death, would be Charlotte's. The pretty house she had since called her home was in point of fact Charlotte's, not hers. It had come to Charlotte on her father's death, but she had it to reside in for her life. Norris Court was two miles distant from Alnwick; and Mrs. Norris in her young widowhood had quarrelled with its new possessors. The breach had never been healed, so that Charlotte was a stranger to her forefathers' home. Except for this cottage and the few hundreds a year, all in expectation, Charlotte Norris had nothing. How Mrs. Norris had bewailed these past untoward circumstances, her own heart alone knew.

Her own subsequent marriage with Colonel Darling had not greatly improved her circumstances in the long-run. At the Colonel's death, the chief portion of what he had passed to their son. A little was settled on the daughters, and Mrs. Darling had a certain benefit for life. But altogether her income was not a large one, especially considering her many wants, and that she was not one who could make a sovereign go as far as most people; and Mrs. Darling was in the habit of thinking that fate might have been kinder to her. In the lost glories of Norris Court, present benefits, real though they were, were overlooked. But for these comparisons, bred of discontent, some of us would get on better in the world than we do.

She sat in her own room, glancing back at these past grievances, dwelling on others that were more recent. It was the day following the fête. The interview with Mr. Carleton St. John was over, and Charlotte was his promised wife. Mrs. Darling had done what she could to oppose it—to the secret

surprise of Mr. St. John; but her opposition was untenable,
and had broken down. "If you have any tangible objection
to me, name it, and let me combat it as I best may," said Mr.
St. John. But apparently Mrs. Darling could bring forward
none, save the foolishly fond one that she could not part with
Charlotte; and the engagement took place. As Mrs. Darling
sat now, alone, her mind was still busy with a hundred wild
schemes for its frustration.

But she saw clearly that they would all be worse than useless; that unless there was some special interposition of
Providence, Charlotte would go to Alnwick. What was the
secret of her opposition? Ah, my reader, you must turn over
many pages ere you arrive at that. She had one very great and
good reason for dreading the marriage of her daughter with
George St. John of Alnwick.

Charlotte happened to come into the room as she sat there.
Mrs. Darling held out her hand; and Charlotte—who might
have looked radiant with happiness but that she and her
countenance were of an undemonstrative nature in general—
came and sat on a stool at her feet, her dress, bright mauve
muslin, floating around, her delicate hands raised from their
open lace sleeves to her mother's knee.

"I must say a few words to you, Charlotte. Promise to hear
me patiently and calmly."

"Of course I will, mamma."

"There's no of course in the matter, I fear. Times have
been, Charlotte, when—— "

"Oh mamma, never mind all that. I'm going to be good.
Tell me what it is."

"Do you remember, some three years ago—yes, it must be
quite three years now, for we did not leave London that year
until August—that we saw a good deal of George St. John?
We had met him in London that season; we met him on
our return here; and he fell into the habit of calling on us
often."

"I remember," replied Charlotte.

"The beginning of October we left home for Paris; a sudden
resolution on my part, you girls thought; which was true.
Charlotte, I must tell you now why I went. I was taking
you from danger; I was carrying you away from George St.
John."

A momentary glance upwards of Charlotte's eyes. Did Mrs.

Darling read anger in them? That something made her quail, there was no doubt, and she laid firm hold of both those slender wrists resting on her knee.

"For your sake, Charlotte; it was for your sake. I feared you were growing to love him."

"And if I were?" retorted Charlotte.

There was a long pause. Mrs. Darling appeared to be weighing some question with herself: she looked anxious, troubled, undecided: but she still held the hands with a firm grasp.

"Charlotte, I want you to trust me. There is a reason, why you should not become the wife of Mr. Carleton of Alnwick; but I cannot tell you what it is. I cannot so much as hint at its nature. I want you to trust me that this cause does exist; and to act upon it."

"To act upon it?"

"By declining to become Mrs. Carleton St. John."

"No," said Charlotte, very quietly. "What is the cause?"

"My darling, I have said that I cannot tell you: and that is why I ask you to trust me as confidently as you did when a little child. The thought came over me just now, while Mr. Carleton was here, to speak openly to him. The next moment I felt faint and sick with dread at the bare thought. I may not tell Mr. Carleton; I will not tell you—— "

"I do wish you wouldn't call him by that name! " Charlotte interrupted.

"My dear, it is that I have fallen into the habit of it," murmured Mrs. Darling.

"It's like a scene in a play," exclaimed Charlotte. "I may not marry George St. John for some reason, and I may not know what the reason is! He is not going to turn out my brother, or cousin, I suppose? Rather romantic, that, for these matter-of-fact days!"

"Oh, Charlotte, be serious! Do not indulge in nonsense now. You know that you are Charlotte Norris, and that he is George St. John; and that you never were related yet. It is not that: I wish it were nothing else."

"What is it?"

"I cannot tell you, Charlotte. I cannot; I cannot."

"Have you heard anything against him, that you are concealing?"

Mrs. Darling lifted her hand to her face, partially hiding it. She did not answer the question.

"Charlotte, you know how I love you. Well, I would almost rather see you die, than married to George St. John. No mother ever schemed to get her daughter a husband, as I schemed three years ago to keep you from one, when my suspicions were aroused that you were in danger of loving George St. John."

"The danger had ripened," said Charlotte, in low tones. "I did love him."

"My poor girl! And *his* love, though I did not know it then, was given to Caroline Carleton——"

"Don't say it!" interrupted Charlotte: and for the second time during their interview Mrs. Darling quailed, the tone was so wild, so full of pain. "I do not wish to be spoken to of his first wife," she added calmly, after a pause.

"You will not, surely, be his second, Charlotte! Charlotte, my Charlotte! You will not break my heart!"

"You will break mine, if you forbid me to marry Mr. St. John," was the whispered answer. "But indeed, mamma, I think we are talking nonsense," broke off Charlotte. "I am no longer a child. I am nearly nine-and-twenty; and that's rather too old to be told I may not marry, when there's no real cause why I should not do so."

"No real cause! What have I been saying, Charlotte?"

"I think there is none. I think what you are saying must be a chimera."

Mrs. Darling let fall the hands she held; she had only hoped against hope. Charlotte rose and bent over her mother to kiss her, whispering a few decisive words. Cruel words to her mother's heart.

"It is of no use trying to separate us, mamma. You did enough mischief in separating us before—but until this hour, I knew not that you acted intentionally. But for that, I might have been his first wife, chosen before all."

Charlotte Norris was wrong, so far: Mr. St. John's love had never before been given to her: it never would be given to her as it had been to Caroline Carleton. The first fresh green of the heart's spring had had its day, and was gone for ever.

A few more days; another attempt or two, futile as this one; a short, sharp battle with her secret wishes, and Mrs. Darling gave up opposition, and grew apparently reconciled to what she could not prevent. And in mid-winter, just after the new

year came in, the newspapers had another piece of news to
relate, concerning Mr. St. John.

"On the 2nd of January, at the church of St. Mary, Alnwick,
by the Reverend Dr. Graves, George Carleton St. John, Esquire,
of Alnwick Hall, to Charlotte Augusta, only child of the late
Herbert Norris, Esquire, of Norris Court."

CHAPTER IV.

A NEW MISTRESS AT ALNWICK.

THE mourning habiliments hitherto prevailing at Alnwick Hall
were put aside during the wedding-tour of its master, and the
servants appeared in gayer colours.   Master Benja's grey
merino frock was exchanged for a scarlet, and the black sash
and sleeve-knots were replaced by white ones.   Benja was a
sturdy little fellow of fourteen months now, sufficiently forward
in walking to get about the room and bring himself into all
manner of mischief.

A second marriage, a new mistress suddenly brought to an
established home, rarely gives pleasure to its inmates.   This
applies in an especial degree to its women-servants.   Whatever
the cause may be, or whence the feeling in the jealous human
heart takes its rise, it is an indisputable fact, that the second
marriage of a master is rarely liked, and the new bride is regarded with anything but love.   The case was such at the
Hall.   Tritton, the housekeeper, had lived in the family of
Miss Carleton before she was Mrs. St. John; had come with
her to the Hall when she married; and it was only natural,
perhaps that she should look upon her successor somewhat in
the light of a usurper.   Honour shared the feeling.   Ardently
attached to her young charge, having been *trusted* with him,
possessing almost full control over him, the prospect of a new
mother for the boy and a mistress for herself could not be
palatable.   But both Tritton and Honour were conscientious,
good women; and there is no doubt this feeling would have
soon worn itself out, but for circumstances that occurred to
increase it.

Mrs. Darling was not wise.   Her intentions no doubt were
good, but her judgment was not so.   From the day following

that of the ceremony, when Mr. and Mrs. St. John were fairly
away, Mrs. Darling haunted the Hall. Anxious for the comfort of Charlotte as she had never been for anything in her life,
she fell into the mistake of interfering with Charlotte's future
home before she entered upon it. She went about the house,
peering here, peeping there; she had changes wrought in the
rooms, in the furniture; she found fault with the arrangements
made by the servants, who had done their best, and superseded
them at will. She changed the position of beds, she examined
linen, she turned Benja and Honour from their day-nursery
into another; she ordered this to be done, she countermanded
that. This might have been tolerated in Mrs. Darling; indeed
it must have been; but what the servants could not and would
not tolerate, was a second edition of it in Prance. Prance
generally accompanied her mistress to the Hall; one or two
nights was left to sleep there; Mrs. Darling's worrying orders
were often transmitted through Prance; and Prance, as unwise
as her mistress, assumed a supercilious superiority (which indeed was partly her natural manner) excessively distasteful
to Mr. St. John's rather indulged but most respectable household.

It was a sad mistake. It was perhaps the first link in a
heavy chain, whose fetters would have to be worn for ever.
Mrs. Darling ought to have waited until her daughter came
home, she could then have suggested these alterations privately
to her if she deemed them so essential, and suffered Charlotte's
own authority to carry them out. How Mrs. Darling, a shrewd,
sensible, easy woman in general, fell into the error, must remain
a marvel. It caused the servants to look upon her as a
meddling, underbred woman, who was interfering most un-
justifiably in what did not concern her. She was really nothing
of the sort; it all arose from her surpassing anxiety for Charlotte's comfort.

This, I say, must have been borne from Mrs. Darling; but
when that unfortunate Prance came in, all the resentment was
turned upon her. Prance ordered after her mistress. Worse
still, she did not order as from her mistress, but as from herself; and her cold, you-must-obey-me tones, exasperated, the
maids at the Hall almost to rebellion. Putting present ill-
feeling apart, the result was unfortunate: for it created a prejudice against their new mistress, which Mrs. St. John would
have to live down. Altogether, what with the advent of the

new wife, the perpetual visitation of Mrs. Darling, and the hatred to Prance, Alnwick Hall was kept in a state of internal commotion.

In the midst of this, the day came round for the return of Mr. St. John and his bride. In the afternoon, Master Benja, in apple-pie order, the short scarlet frock and the white ribbons —for they were expected to arrive every hour—was toddling about the nursery, drawing a horse. Honour, in a new cap with white satin trimming, sat watching him, and talking to one of the housemaids, Edy, who had looked in for a gossip.

It may be as well that you should notice how these nurseries were situated. They were at the *side* of the house facing the east. Mr. St. John's bedroom was at the end, looking on to the park, and forming as it were an angle on that side the house. You saw the room once; some one was dying in it. His room opened to two others, one on either side of it. The one looking to the front was his own dressing-room; the other looking to the side, had been called the dressing-room of the late Mrs. St. John; and all three rooms opened to the gallery. It was this last room that had been Benja's nursery, and out of which Mrs. Darling had turned him. The next room to this, which opened to no other room, was the new day-nursery. Honour and Benja are in it now. And beyond it, the last room on this side the house, was the one in which Honour and Benja slept. The next to this, the first one looking to the north at the back of the house, was Mrs. Tritton's—but it is unnecessary to mention that. The passage in which the doors of these nurseries were situated was narrow, not like the wide front corridor or gallery. Immediately opposite the door of Benja's bed-chamber was the back staircase used by the servants. Honour, with her charge, was the only one who assumed the privilege of passing up and down the front stairs. It was as well to mention this : you will see why, later. Honour bitterly resented being turned from the nursery. It was unreasonable that she should do so (though perhaps not unnatural), as the room would be required for the new Mrs. St. John.

She was gossiping with the housemaid in the manner that servants like to gossip, when a voice in the next room startled them both. It was the voice of Prance; and the servants had not known she was in the house.

"There's that woman here again!" exclaimed Edy, in a whisper.

Honour had her finger to her lip in an attitude of listening. She wondered to whom Prance was talking. Tones that could not be mistaken for any but Mrs. Darling's, answered her. In point of fact, Mrs. Darling had come over to receive her daughter, bringing Prance to carry a few last trifling belongings of Charlotte's.

"Of course!" ejaculated Honour. "I knew *they'd* be here."

Honour was good in the main; sincere, thoroughly trustworthy; but she was not exempt from the prejudice to which her class is especially prone. You cannot help these things. It was her custom, whenever she found Mrs. Darling and her maid appeared upstairs, to catch up Benja and dart down to the housekeeper's room, with a vague feeling, arising from resentment, of carrying Benja out of their reach. She took him up now, horse and all, and was making her way to the back-stairs when Mrs. Darling suddenly looked out of a chamber and called to her.

There could be no pretending not to hear. She had been seen, and therefore was obliged to arrest her steps. It had not come to open rebellion against Mrs. Darling.

"I want you, Honour. Step here a minute."

"Carry the baby down, Edy," whispered Honour, giving her the child. "Tell Mrs. Tritton that they are up here, if she does not know it," she added, as a parting fling.

When Edy reached the housekeeper's room, she found it empty, except for the presence of a woman in black, who sat there with her things on, and who laid siege to the baby as if she had a right to him. It was the nurse, Mrs. Dade, who came occasionally to see the child, as she had opportunity. Edy, only a few months in the service, did not recognize her. Edy willingly resigned the charge, and made her way to the hall as fast as her feet could carry her: for a bustle in it warned her that their new mistress had arrived, and all her woman's curiosity was aroused.

She was crossing the hall on Mr. St. John's arm, a smile of greeting on her pale face as she glanced to the right and left. Mr. St. John laughed and talked, and mentioned two or three of the principal servants by name to his wife. Edy stood in a nook behind the rest, and peeped out; and just then Mrs. Darling, having become aware of the arrival, came down the stairs with loud words of welcome.

The bustle over, Mrs. Tritton went back to her own room,

shutting the door upon Edy. Nurse Dade had the boy on her knee, talking to him; and Honour, a privileged visitor, came in. Honour's tongue could be rather a sharp one on occasion; but the unexpected sight of the nurse arrested it for the moment.

"I should not have come up to-day, had I known," Nurse Dade was saying to the housekeeper. "It must be a busy day with you."

"Middling for that : not very. You heard of the marriage, I suppose?"

"I saw it in the newspapers. I had not heard of it till then. I have been away for six months, you see, and news came to me slowly. How well this little fellow gets on, Honour! You have done your part by him, that's certain."

Honour gave a sort of ungracious assent to the remark.

"What do you think she wanted with me?" asked she, turning to the housekeeper, alluding to Mrs. Darling. "You know that pretty sketch that master drew of Benja in the straw hat, one day in the garden, and hung it up in his bedroom? Well, she called me in to say she thought it had better be taken down and put elsewhere. I told her I must decline to meddle with my master's things, and especially with that, though it was done only on the leaf of a copy-book; and I wouldn't touch it. She first looked at me and then at the sketch; but just then there was a bustle in the hall; she ran down and I came away."

"And it's left hanging?"

"It's left hanging. Ah!"—and Honour drew a long breath—"Nurse Dade, we have changes here."

"There's changes everywhere, I think," responded the nurse. "But I must say I was surprised when I read it in the papers. So soon! and to recollect what his grief was *then !* But law ! it's the way of the world."

Honour took Benja, carried him to the far end of the room, and began amusing him with his horse. They made a considerable amount of noise, almost drowning the voices of the two women by the fire.

"Do you happen to know her?" the housekeeper had asked, and the nurse knew by intuition that she spoke of the bride.

"I've known her ever since she was a baby. My mother was nursing at Norris Court, and I went there for a day and a night, and they let me hold the baby on my lap, to say I had had it. I was quite a young woman then; a growing girl, as one may say."

"I don't know anything of her, hardly," said the housekeeper. "I've not chosen to ask questions of the servants, and I and Honour, as you are aware, are strangers in the neighbourhood. Her father was a colonel, was he not?"

"A colonel! No; it was Mrs. Norris's second husband that was a colonel—Colonel Darling. Miss Norris's father was Mr. Norris of Norris Court. Very grand, rich people they were: but as there was no boy, it nearly all went from the widow when Mr. Norris died. She married Colonel Darling when the first year was out."

"She must have been very young," remarked the housekeeper. "She does not look old now."

"Very young. I remember the first time I saw her in her widow's cap. I began wondering how *I* should look in a widow's cap, for she did not look much older than I was. She was very pretty. People said what a pity it was Mr. Norris should have died so soon and left her."

"What did Mr. Norris die of?"

"I can't tell you. I have never known. There was some mystery about it. My mother always said she did not know: and I don't think she did, she was so curious over it. He was ill about a week or ten days, but nobody was let go near him, except Mr. Pym and the valet, and a man-nurse they had. Some of the servants thought it was some infectious disorder: but nobody knew."

"And he died?"

"He died. The little baby, Miss Charlotte, as she was named afterwards, was born whilst he lay ill. My mother said Mr. Pym took her in to show her to her father; which was very wrong if it was fever; and when Mr. Pym came out his face was white, as if he had gone through some painful scene."

The housekeeper, who was by no means one to deal in mysteries, stared at the nurse. She had hushed her voice to that tone we are apt to use when speaking of things that must not be openly discussed. She sat gazing at the fire, as if recalling the past, the black strings of her bonnet hanging down.

"How do you mean, Mrs. Dade?"

" Mean ? "

" You speak as if you were scared."

" Do I ? I suppose I caught the tone from mother : she used to speak so when she talked of it. It was her way, when there was any sort of mystery in her places. Whether she came to the bottom of it herself, or whether she didn't, she always used a tone in speaking of it that partly scared you and partly sent you rampant to know more."

" But what mystery could there be in regard to Mr. Norris ? "

" That's just what I am unable to tell you. There *was* a mystery : everybody knew that ; but I don't believe anybody fathomed it. Whether it lay in his illness, or in his death, or in neither, mother never knew. Sometimes she thought it was connected with his wife. They had been a loving couple until one night, when some dispute occurred between them, and there ensued an awful quarrel : one of those dreadful disturbances that terrify a household. Mrs. Norris, a gentle, loving, merry young girl, as she had seemed until then, dashed her hand through a cheval glass in her passion, and cut it terribly. It all took place in their own room. Mr. Pym was fetched ; and altogether there was a fine hullabaloo."

" Were you there ? "

" I was not there ; nor mother either. It was not for some days afterwards that she was sent for to Mrs. Norris : but the servants told her of it. Mr. Norris had been ill ever since ; and three days later he was dead. The butler said—and he no doubt had it from the valet, for they were great friends— that it was that night's quarrel that killed his master."

" How could the quarrel kill him ? " cried the wondering housekeeper.

Nurse Dade shook her head. " I don't know. All sorts of things were said—as things in such cases often are, and per- haps not a word of truth in any of 'em. At any rate, Mr. Norris died, and nobody knew for certain how he died or what was the matter with him, or what could have given rise to the dreadful quarrel that led to it. There were but two persons who could have told the truth—Mrs. Norris and Mr. Pym."

" Mr. Pym must have been a young man then," observed the housekeeper, after a pause.

" About thirty, I suppose. He must be sixty now."

" Mr. Pym's not sixty ! "

" He is hard upon it. Nobody would take him for it,

though, he is so active. Mrs. Norris had to leave the Court
when she got well, for the new people to come to it; she went
straight to the house she's in now, which of right belongs to
Miss Charlotte—I should say Mrs. St. John."

"I hope she's amiable?" observed the housekeeper.

"She is when she likes, I believe. I don't know much of
her myself. She has a temper, they say—but then she has
been so much indulged."

"She is very handsome. But she's not in the least like Mrs.
Darling."

"She is very much like her father. Mrs. Darling's fair, Mr.
Norris was—— "

A clear, sonorous voice, calling "Benja," interrupted the
words. Honour heard it, for it penetrated even above the
shouts of the boy and the creaking of the steed. It was a call
she was accustomed to. Often and often, in passing through
the hall, going out or coming in, had Mr. St. John thus
summoned his child.

"Not the horse," said Honour to the boy, as she picked him
up. "Papa's calling. Benja shall come back to the horse by-
and-by."

Mr. St. John was in the hall, waiting. He took the child
from Honour, kissed him lovingly many times, and then carried
him into the drawing-room. Honour followed. She had not
been told to go down, and there was an irrepressible curiosity
in her mind to see Mrs. St. John.

She was seated alone, near the window, with a work-box
before her and some embroidery in her hand, looking as much
at home as though she had always lived there. Her raven hair
was partially turned from her forehead, showing off the finely-
cut but very thin features. Turning her head quickly at the
opening of the door, she saw her husband enter.

"I have brought you Benja, Charlotte. He must make
acquaintance with his mamma."

She rose with a smile, her dark-blue silk dress gleaming brightly
from its ample folds, met them midway in the room, and took
Benja. The boy, rather astonished perhaps at the summary
proceeding, stared at her from his wide-open great grey eyes.

"You will love mamma, Benja?" she said, kissing him
tenderly; and she placed him on her knee and held up to
him her shining gold chain, as she had done some two or three
months before. "Mamma means to love Benja."

But Benja was impervious to bribes to-day, and would have nothing to say to the gold chain. Suddenly, in the midst of his prolonged stare, he burst into tears, with a great deal of unnecessary noise.

"I am strange to him," said Mrs. St. John. "He will know me better in a day or two. See! what have I here for Benja!"

She took up a sweet biscuit from a plate that happened to be on the table. What with the biscuit, and her persuasive words, her kisses, Benja suffered himself to be coaxed, hushed his sobs, and kissed his new mamma.

"Friends from this minute," she said triumphantly, glancing up at her husband, who had stood by, smiling. "I will try and be a good mother to him, George."

"I shall like her better than I thought," decided Honour from the door, who could find no fault, even in her prejudice, with her new mistress. "I shall like her much if she will only love the child."

And thus the future lady of Alnwick had entered on her home.

CHAPTER V.

ON ST. MARTIN'S EVE.

"At Alnwick Hall, on St. Martin's Eve, the wife of George Carleton St. John, Esquire, of a son."

This was the next announcement in the local papers; some ten months, or a trifle more, having elapsed since the last one. And I hope you will have patience with these notices, and not find fault with their frequency: they are not yet over.

"On St. Martin's Eve!" Was Mr. Carleton St. John a Roman Catholic, that he should chronicle the birth of his children by the saints' days? No. And it was not by Mr. St. John's wish that it had been so worded, but by Mrs. Darling's.

It was no doubt a somewhat singular coincidence that this second child should have been born on the same day as Benja, the 10th of November. Mrs. Darling, who was temporarily sojourning at Alnwick Hall, and was naturally a little inclined

to be superstitious, regarded it as a most ominous event.
What, she thought, if the advent of this child should be
succeeded by the dreadful tragedy that had so fatally characterized the last? And it would perhaps hardly be believed,
but that some of you may have had opportunities of witnessing
these foolish fancies, that she dreaded the announcement
being made in the newspapers in the same words as the last.

"I cannot bear it," she said to Mr. St. John, "I could not
look at it without a shudder. Put anything else you like, but
don't put 'On the 10th of November!'"

Mr. St. John laughed outright; he could not help it.
"Charlotte is as well as she can be," he rejoined.

"I know; but a change might take place at any moment.
Pray do not laugh at me, Mr. St. John. Call it folly; superstition; what you will; only don't word this announcement as
you worded the last."

"But how am I to word it?" he asked. "If the child
was born on the tenth, I can't put it the ninth or the
eleventh. I won't send any notice at all, if you like; I don't
care about it."

"Not send any notice of Charlotte's child!" she echoed in
displeasure. "That would be a slight indeed."

"As you please. But you see the little fellow has chosen to
come on the tenth, and we can't send him back again to await
a more convenient day."

"Put 'On St. Martin's Eve,'" said Mrs. Darling, after a
pause of somewhat blank consideration.

"St. Martin's Eve!"

"Yes; why not? It *is* St. Martin's Eve, you know."

"Indeed I don't know," returned Mr. St. John, very much
amused. "I'm not sure that I knew we had a St. Martin at
all in the calendar."

"That comes of your having lived so little out of England.
The English pay no attention to the saints' days. I have been
abroad a good deal with my children, and know them all.
St. Martin's is a great day in some parts of France. Please let
it be so worded, Mr. St. John."

He took a pen and wrote it as she desired, laughing much.
"I should like to see Dr. Graves's eyes when he reads this,"
quoth he, as he put it into the envelope.

"A rubbishing old Low Churchman!" slightingly spoke
Mrs. Darling. "He's nobody."

So the notice was sent off; and in due time returned to the house in the newspapers. Mrs. Darling carried one upstairs proudly to her daughter. "See, Charlotte! How well it looks !"

Mrs. St. John took the paper in her delicate hand and read it in silence; read it twice. "How came George to put it in like that—'St. Martin's Eve?'"

"Because I requested it. You are quite well now, darling, as may be said: but I would not have the announcement made to the world in the same words as the last."

"It never could have been so made, mamma."

"Yes it could. Were not the two children born on the same day of the year?"

"Oh, that," coldly returned Mrs. St. John, as if the fact were not worth a thought. "The other had an addition which this must lack. It ran in this way: 'the wife of George Carleton St. John, of a son *and heir.*'"

Mrs. Darling made no rejoinder. But she cast a keen, stealthy glance at Charlotte from time to time, as she busied herself with some trifle at a distance.

Things had gone on very smoothly at the Hall during the past few months. Mrs. St. John had been at least kind to Benja, sufficiently loving in manner; and Honour liked her new mistress tolerably well. The girl's feeling towards her may best be described as a negative one; neither like nor dislike. She did not dislike her as she had formerly believed she should do; and she did not very much like her.

Perhaps if there had been a characteristic more prominent than another in the disposition of Charlotte Norris, it was jealousy. Mrs. Darling had been obliged to see this—and to see it exercised, too—during the course of her daughter's past life; and *one* of her objections to the master of Alnwick Hall, as a husband for Charlotte, was the fact that he had been once married and his heir was already born. That Charlotte would be desperately jealous of the little Benja, should she bear a son of her own, jealous perhaps to hatred, Mrs. Darling felt sure of: she devoutly hoped there would be no children; and an uncomfortable feeling had been upon her from the hour she learnt of the anticipated arrival. So long as Charlotte was without a son, there could be no very formidable jealousy of Benja. But there might be afterwards.

Certainly, there existed a wide difference between the future

of the two-year-old boy, sturdily stamping about the gravel-
path underneath, the great St. Bernard's dog, "Brave," har-
nessed with tape before him; and that of the young infant
lying in the cradle by the fireside. Many a mother, far more
gentle and self-forgetting than was Charlotte St. John, might
have felt a pang in contemplating the contrast. Benja had a
title in prospective; he would be rich amidst the rich. George
(by that name the infant was already registered) might count
his future income by a few hundreds. The greater portion of
the Alnwick estate (not a very large one) was strictly entailed;
and the large fortune brought to Mr. St. John by his first wife,
was now Benja's. Mr. St. John would probably have wished
to do as well by one child as by the other, but he could not
help himself; he could not alter the existing state of things.
The settlement he had been enabled to make on Miss Norris
was very, very small; but he intended to redeem this by
putting by yearly some of his large income for her and her
children. Still the contrast was great, and Mrs. Darling knew
that Charlotte was dwelling upon it with bitterness, when she
laid that emphasis just now on the "son *and heir.*"

That Mrs. St. John would inordinately love this child of hers,
there was no doubt about—far more so than might be well for
herself or for him. Mrs. Darling saw it as she lay there—lay
looking with eager, watchful eyes at the little face in the
cradle; and Mrs. Darling decided within herself—it may have
been from experience—that such love does not bring peace
in its wake. "I wish it had been a girl!" thought Mrs.
Darling.

Charlotte Norris had all her life been subject to taking likes
and dislikes—occasionally violent ones ; and she took a strong
dislike to the nurse that was now in attendance upon her,
barely suffering her in the room, and insisting on Prance's seeing to the baby instead, for Prance was at the Hall with her
mistress. The result was, that when, at the end of a fortnight,
Mrs. Darling quitted the Hall, Prance was transferred to Mrs.
St. John's service, and remained as nurse to the infant.

Some months went on, and spring came round. Mr. Carleton St. John, who was in parliament, had to be in London;
but his wife remained at Alnwick with her baby, who seemed
delicate. Not to have brought to herself all the good in the
world, would she have stirred without him. The frail little
infant of a few days had become to her the greatest treasure

earth ever gave; her love for him was of that wild, impassioned, all-absorbing nature, known, it is hoped, but to few, for it never visits a well-regulated heart.

And in proportion to her love for her own child, grew her jealousy of Benja—nay, not jealousy only, but dislike. Mrs. Darling had foreseen correctly: the jealousy and the dislike had come—the hatred would only too surely follow. Charlotte strove against this feeling. She knew how wrong it was, how disloyal to her husband, how cruel to Benja; and she fought against it well. She would take Benja on her knee and fondle him; and the child grew to love her, to run into her at all moments when he could triumphantly escape from Honour, and she would take him and pretend to hide him, and tell Honour to go into the woods and see if the little wild boy had flown thither. It is true that once or twice, upon some very slight provocation, she had fallen into a storm of passion that literally rendered Honour motionless with alarm, seizing the child somewhat after the manner of a tiger, and beating him furiously. Honour and Benja were alike frightened; even Prance looked on aghast.

Matters were not improved by the conduct of the two nurses. If dislike and dissatisfaction had reigned between them when Prance was only an occasional visitor at the house, how much · more did it reign now! They did not break frequently into a quarrel, but a perpetual system of what the other servants called "nagging" was kept up between them. Fierce and fiery was the disposition with which each regarded the other; a war of resentment, of antipathy—call it what you will—smouldering ever in their hearts.

It did not want fuel. Honour naturally wished Benja to be regarded as first and foremost in right of his seniority and position as the heir. Prance held up the infant as the chief; and it need not be said that she was tacitly, if not openly, supported by Mrs. St. John. It was doubly unfortunate. The squabbles of the nurses need not have done harm, but their rivalry in regard to the children enhanced the feeling in their mistress. To do Mrs. Darling justice, she absolutely discouraged any difference being made, even in thought, between the children, if such came under her notice in her temporary visits at the Hall; and once, when she heard a sneer given by Prance to Honour and Benja, she had called the woman to her privately, and taken her sharply to task.

Well, the time went on to Easter. On the Thursday in Passion-week Mr. St. John was expected home; and his wife, who loved him much, anticipated his return in a sort of impassioned eagerness, not the less strong because it was controlled under her usual cold and calm demeanour. The pony-carriage went to the station in the afternoon to meet the train; and Alnwick's mistress took her place at an open window that overlooked the approach, long and long before the carriage could return.

It was a warm, brilliant day; one of those lovely days that sometimes come in spring, presenting so great a contrast with the past winter, and raising many a heart to Heaven. As she sat there, Benja darted in. The door was not firmly closed, and the child pushed it open triumphantly and flew to Mrs. St. John, black as any little tinker: hands, face, dress, a sight to be seen. She wore a charming gown of apple-green figured silk, and a coquettish little lace head-dress, fastened with large gold pins.

"Benja, what have you been doing to yourself?"

Benja laid his little black hands on her gown, and told her a tale not very easy to be understood—his grey eyes laughing, his pretty teeth glistening. Brave had run somewhere, and Benja had run after him, and the two—or perhaps only Benja—had fallen down by the cocks and hens, where it was dirty. And they had *stayed* down apparently, and rolled about together.

"Then Benja's a naughty boy to get himself into such a state," she cried, having quickly interposed her handkerchief between the silk and the dirty hands. "Where's Honour?"

Benja broke into a merry laugh. He had contrived to double upon Honour and evade her, while she was looking for him.

The child kept his place at her knee, and chattered on in his imperfect language. Mrs. St. John did not give herself further trouble to understand it; she fell into a reverie, her fingers unconsciously rambling amidst the child's fair curls.

"Oh! so you are here, sir!" exclaimed Honour, looking in. "My goodness! I've been all over the house after you."

"Me wid mamma," chattered Benja.

"And a fine pickle you are in, to be with your mamma, naughty child!"

"You should not let him get into this state, Honour."

"It's not my fault, ma'am; he ran away from me after the dog."

"Take him into the nursery," concluded Mrs. St. John, turning her eyes again to the window and the winding road.

Honour carried him away, talking lovingly to him—that he was a sad little boy to make himself so dirty, and dirty little boys never went to heaven, unless they got clean again. And Mrs. Carleton St. John sat on, dreamily watching.

The first thing that aroused her from it was the sound of voices outside. She looked out and saw Honour and Benja. Master Benja was now dressed in a handsome green velvet tunic, and looked as if he had just come out of a bandbox. Honour had her things on for walking.

"Where are you going?" inquired Mrs. St. John.

"Me going to see papa," responded Benja, before Honour could speak, his eyes bright, and his cheeks glowing.

"I am taking him to meet the carriage, ma'am."

"But——" Mrs. St. John was beginning, and then suddenly stopped; and Honour was half scared at the blank look and the momentary flash of anger that succeeded each other on her face. "Why should you take him there?" she resumed. "He will see his papa soon enough at home."

"Why should I not take him, ma'am?" rejoined Honour, quite respectfully, but in a bold spirit.

And Mrs. Carleton St. John could not say why; she had no plea for refusal at hand. Honour waited a minute, but no words came.

"It's as well to walk that way as any other, ma'am," she said, taking Benja's hand. "His papa might be disappointed, else. When he used to return home last year, and did not meet Master Benja in the avenue, he'd cry out for him before he got well inside the doors."

"Oh, very well," said Mrs. St. John. "Keep in this upper part, within view."

They turned away slowly, Honour secretly rebelling at the mandate; and the mistress of Alnwick looked after them. She had been lost in a reverie, anticipating the moment of her husband's entrance, when, after her first welcome to him was over, she should summon her child and place it lovingly in his arms. It seemed that another child was to be first in those arms; and she had not bargained for it. One wild, unhealthy longing was ever haunting, half-unconsciously, the mind of Mrs. St. John— that her husband should love *her* child better than that other one.

She ran upstairs to Prance. She bade Prance hasten to attire the baby, and take him out to meet his papa. The child was asleep. Prance glanced at it as if she would have said so; but her mistress's tone was imperative, evidently admitting neither contradiction nor delay.

"Oh, so *you've* come!" was Honour's salutation, not very graciously expressed, when she found herself joined by Prance. "What's the matter with him?"

The question applied to the crying baby, fractious at being awakened out of its sleep. Prance, who rarely condescended to quarrel in words, went on with her quiet step and supercilious manner, her head in the air.

"I've as much right here as you," she said: "and Master George as the other. Mind your own business, and don't talk to me."

Presently the carriage came in view, Mr. St. John driving. He pulled up when he found himself near the children, gave the reins to the groom, and leapt out. Little Benja danced about his papa in an ecstasy of joy, and Mr. St. John clasped him in his arms.

Two minutes at the least elapsed before he remembered Prance, who had stood perfectly still, she and her charge. He turned to the baby to caress it, but his voice and face were strange, and of course it set up a loud cry, the more loud that it had not recovered its temper. Mr. St. John left it and walked across the grass with Benja, his whole attention absorbed by his first-born. The boy was sometimes caught up in his arms for a fresh embrace, sometimes flitting along by his side on the grass, hand in hand, the steel buttons on the child's green velvet tunic flashing in the sun. He had taken off his cap, throwing it to Honour, and his pretty curls blew away from his brow with every movement, displaying that winning expression of feeling and intelligence of which his features had given promise in his infancy.

Mr. St. John waved his hat to his wife at the open window. She had seen it all; the loving meeting with the one child, the neglect of the other. Passion, anger, jealousy, waged war within her. She could no more have controlled them than she could control the wind that was making free with her husband's hair. All she saw, all she felt, was that he had betrayed his ardent love for Benja, his indifference to *her* child. In that one moment she was as a mad woman.

What exactly occurred upon his entrance, George St. John could not afterwards remember; he was too much scared, too terrified, it may be said, to receive or retain any correct impression. A strange, wild look on his wife's face, telling, as it seemed to him, of madness; a wail of reproaches, such as had never been addressed to him from woman's lips; Benja struck to the ground with a violent blow, and his cheek bleeding from it, passed before his eyes as in a troubled vision. It appeared to last but a moment; but a moment: the next, she had sunk on a sofa; pale, trembling, hysterical.

George St. John collected his scattered senses, and picked up the child. He wiped his poor little outraged face with a handkerchief, laid it on his bosom for an instant to soothe him to composure, and carried him into the hall to Honour. The girl cried out when she saw the cheek, and looked up at her master with inquiring eyes. But his were averted.

"An accident," he quietly said. "Wash it with a little warm water."

He returned to the room, closing the door on himself and his wife. He did not reproach her by so much as a word: he did not speak to her: he went to the window and stood there in silence, looking out, his back turned to her, and his forehead pressed against one of the panes.

She began to utter reproaches now, sobbing violently; fond reproaches, that all his affection was lavished upon Benja, leaving none for her child. He replied coldly, without turning round, that his affection was as lively for one child as for the other; he was not conscious of any difference, and hoped he never should be: but an infant of five months old who cried at his approach, could not yet be made the companion to him that Benja was.

"Oh, George, forgive me!" she sobbed, coming close to him, and laying her hand on him caressingly. "I love—I love you; and I could not bear it. He *is* our child, you know; yours and mine; and it seemed as if he was nothing to you beside Benja. Won't you forgive me?"

He could not resist the pleading words; he could not throw back the soft hand that was stealing itself into his. "I forgive it; if you think forgiveness lies with me, Charlotte," he answered, turning round at last, but speaking sadly and quietly.

"You have not kissed me," she whispered, the tears chasing each other down her cheeks.

He bent to kiss her at once : just in the same cold, quiet manner in which he had spoken ; as if his mind were withdrawn from the present. She felt it bitterly ; she blamed her "quick feelings" aloud ; and when her tears were dried, she ran up to the nursery in a sudden impulse, seized Benja, and sat down with him upon Honour's rocking-chair.

There she fondled him to her ; she pushed his hair from his brow ; she laid his hot cheek, clear again under the influence of the warm water, against her own.

"Benja love mamma still ? " she murmured softly in his ear. "Mamma did not mean to hurt him."

And the noble little fellow broke into a loving smile in her face, by way of answer, and kissed her many times with his rosy lips.

"Be very gentle with his poor cheek, Honour," she said, as she put him down and left the room. "It is only a little bruised, I see."

"Then it *was* an accident, as master said," decided the wondering Honour. "I declare if I did not think at the time she had done it herself ! "

Mr. Carleton St. John had not stirred from his place at the window. He stood there still, looking out, but seeing nothing. The entrance of his wife into the room did not arouse him.

" I have been to make my peace with him, George," she said, almost as inaudibly as she had spoken above. "Dear little Benja !—We are better friends than ever, and he has been giving me a hundred kisses of forgiveness. Oh, George, my husband, I am so sorry ! Indeed, indeed, I will strive to subdue my fits of passion. I will not strike him again."

But George Carleton St. John stood as one who understands not. He did not hear : his thoughts were in the past. The injunction—nay, the prayer—of his dying wife was present to him ; the very look on her sweet face as she spoke it ; the faint tones of her loving voice, soon to be silent for ever.

"When the months and the years go by, and you think of another wife, oh, choose one that will be a *mother* to my child. Be not allured by beauty, be not tempted by wealth, be not ensnared by specious deceit ; but take one who will be to him the loving mother that I would have been."

Bitterly, bitterly, the prayer came back to him. How had he fulfilled it ? He glanced round at the wife he had chosen, and could have groaned aloud in the anguish of his remorseful heart.

CHAPTER VI.

THE ALNWICK SUPERSTITION.

THE time went on at Alnwick Hall just as it goes on everywhere, and the two boys grew with it.   It was autumn weather.
Benja was a sturdy gentleman of nearly four, strong and independent; George, a delicate little fellow of nearly two, with
fair curls and a bright rose-tint in his cheeks.

Mr. Carleton St. John spent more time in London than was
absolutely demanded by his parliamentary duties, frequently
remaining there when the House was not sitting; and during
his sojournings at the Hall, it seemed that he never wanted an
excuse for being away from home.   Shooting, fishing, coursing,
hunting, riding about the land with his steward, superintending
improvements; presiding on the small magisterial bench of
Alnwick; going over to the county-town for more important
meetings;   staying a day or two with bachelor neighbours—
with one plea or another, the master of Alnwick Hall was
nearly always out.   What his wife thought of these frequent
absences cannot be told.   A dark cloud often sat upon her
brow, but things went on smoothly between them, so far as the
servants knew.   It was whispered that George St. John had
not found in Charlotte Norris the angel he had anticipated:
how many men *have* secured angels in marrying for beauty?

It was autumn weather, I say—September; and Mr. St. John
was at home.   He had thought of taking a walking-tour in Belgium during the month of October; but an illness that attacked
Mrs. St. John caused him to be summoned to Alnwick.

A serious if not dangerous illness, and brought on by some
unseemly and violent fit of temper.   Mr. St. John was growing
accustomed to hearing of these violent fits of temper now.
Four or five he had heard of during their married life, but the
one described in the last chapter was all he had himself witnessed.   Some temporary hurt to her child, through the carelessness of a servant, had this time caused it; and the immediate
result to herself was disastrous.   Mr. St. John found Mrs.
Darling at the Hall, and Mr. Pym was in frequent attendance;
but she was already beginning to improve.

Mr. St. John sat on a bench on the grassy slope before the windows, idly revelling in the calm beauty of the September day. The trees were glowing with the warm tints of autumn; and the blue sky, flecked here and there with delicate white clouds, seemed to rise to a wondrous and beautiful height. The two children, attended by their nurses, were gambolling in the park with the favourite dog, Brave: their shouts and Brave's deep bark reaching the ears of Mr. St. John.

He was plunged in thought, as he sat—rather lazy thought. The children before him, the sick wife upstairs, and the not very comfortable state of affairs altogether, furnishing its chief themes. It had carried him back to his second marriage. Caught by the beauty of Charlotte Norris, he had rushed into the union headlong, giving himself no time for proper deliberation; no time, in fact, to become well acquainted with her. "Marry in haste, and repent at leisure," he murmured to himself; and just then he became aware of the proximity of Mrs. Darling. She was coming across the park, having walked to her own house that morning, and back again. She was a great walker, enjoying it thoroughly: and she came up with a merry smile on her bright and still pretty face, as she nodded to her son-in-law.

"How idle you look, Mr. Carleton!" she exclaimed, as he made room for her beside him. She generally called him by that name.

"I have felt idle lately, I think. Did you find all well at home?"

"Quite well. Mary Anne has the mumps; but she is subject to them. I told her to lie in bed and rub hartshorn on her face. Is Charlotte up?"

"I don't know. I have been sitting here these two hours."

"Mr. Pym said she might get up to-day for a short time, provided she lay on the sofa. How those little ones are enjoying themselves."

She pointed to the park. Mr. St. John was also looking at the children, to all appearance. His right elbow rested on the arm of the bench; his hand supported his chin, and his eyes gazed out straight before him. In reality he neither saw nor heard; he was buried just then in the inward life of thought.

"What causes these illnesses of Charlotte?" he suddenly asked, without altering his position. "This is the second time."

If ever there was a startled look on a woman's face, it was on Mrs. Darling's then. "She is delicate, I think," was the answer given, after a pause.

"I think not; not naturally so," dissented Mr. St. John, with emphasis. "I hear of fits of temper, Mrs. Darling, so violent as to suggest the idea of madness for the time being," he resumed. "That was the source of this illness, I understand. The result was only a natural consequence."

"Who told you that?" eagerly asked Mrs. Darling. "Mr. Pym?"

"No; Mr. Pym has never spoken a word to me on the subject in his life. I mentioned it to him on the occasion of the other illness, ten months ago; but he would not understand me—turned it off in an unmistakably decisive manner."

Mrs. Darling bit her lips. That she was in some great and annoying perplexity, none could doubt who saw her countenance; but she kept it turned from Mr. Carleton.

"I have witnessed one of these scenes of violence myself," he resumed. "I declare that I never was so alarmed in my life. I thought Charlotte had suddenly become mad."

Mrs. Darling's lips grew white. But the revelation—that he had witnessed this—did not come upon her by surprise: for Prance had told her of it at the time.

"If I mention this to you now, Mrs. Darling, it is not done in the light of a complaint. I married your daughter, and I must abide——" he paused here, as if he would have altered or softened the phrase, but went on with it immediately—"by the bargain. She is my wife; the mistress of my house; and I have no wish that it should be otherwise: but my object in speaking to you is, to inquire whether you can suggest any means by which these violent attacks of temper can be prevented."

Still there was no answer. Mrs. Darling looked cold, white, frightened; and she turned her head further away than before.

"You have had a life's experience with her; you must know a great deal more of this failing than I," resumed Mr. St. John. "Has she been subject to it all her life?"

"Yes," said Mrs. Darling, speaking at last. "But not often. I speak the truth in all sincerity, when I say that until she married I cannot remember that she had been so put out more than three or four times. It is an unhappy failing; I acknowledge it to be so; but it is over in a minute, Mr. Carleton."

"But think of what it is for the minute! She might—she might kill some one in one of them. I am sure she had no control whatever over herself the day I saw her."

Mrs. Darling looked distressed, and spoke in pleading tones of excuse. "She is always so sorry for it afterwards, Mr. Carleton; she is repentant as a child. You are very sweet-tempered yourself, and perhaps cannot make allowance for those who are otherwise," she added, turning to him with a smile. "If you only knew how many thousands of violent tempers there are in the world! Charlotte's is only one amongst the number."

"That is not the question," he hastily replied. "I have said I am not complaining of the fact, and I am vexed at having to speak to you at all; I only wish to know whether they can be · in any way prevented."

"I don't know of any. It is very stupid of Charlotte; very. One might have thought her last illness would be a warning to her; and now this one again! She will never have another child to live, if this is to go on."

"It is not only the injury she does herself; there's the fear of her doing injury to others. She might, I say, strike a fatal blow; she is mad in these—— "

"No, no; not that," interrupted Mrs. Darling. "Pray do not say so, Mr. St. John. She is not mad."

"I am sorry to pain you. I mean, of course, that while the paroxysm is upon her, she is no more capable of self-control than a woman absolutely mad would be. If there were any means, any line of conduct we could adopt, likely to act as a preventive, it should be tried. I thought it possible you might have learnt how to check it in the past years."

"I never knew yet that there was any effectual remedy for violent temper. A clergyman will tell you it may be controlled by prayer; a surgeon, by the help of drugs; but I suppose neither is certain always to answer. I had a servant once, a very good and valuable servant too, who would fly into the most frightful passion once or twice a year, and break all the crockery."

Mrs. Darling spoke with a laugh, as if she would make light of the whole. It jarred on the feelings of Mr. St. John, and he knit his brow.

"Then there's nothing at all that you know of to be suggested, Mrs. Darling?"

St. Martin's Eve.   4

"I really do not. But I think they will wear out of themselves: as Charlotte grows older, she must grow wiser. I will take an opportunity of speaking to her. And she is so sweet-tempered in a general way, Mr. Carleton, though a little haughty, perhaps, that these few lapses may surely be pardoned."

Mr. St. John made no answering remark. He rose and stretched himself, and was moving away. Mrs. Darling detained him with a question.

"How did you learn that this illness was so brought on? Did Honour tell you?"

"No! I was not aware that Honour knew of it."

"Neither am I aware that she does. I mentioned Honour, because I should suppose her to be more of a confidential servant to you than are the rest, and might acquaint you with what takes place here in your absence."

Mr. St. John brought his clear truthful eyes to bear steadfastly on those looking at him. He was open, honourable, unsuspicious as the day; but he could not help wondering whether the words concealed any double meaning.

"I have no confidential servant, Mrs. Darling. If I had, I should not allow him, or her, to repeat tales to me of the home of which my wife is mistress. When Honour speaks to me, it is of Benja; and all the world might hear, patience permitting, for I believe she takes him to be a cherub without wings. The one to tell me of it was Charlotte."

"*Charlotte!*"

The echo fell upon empty air. Mr. St. John had turned off in the direction of the children.

"Is it this that has been worrying you in London?" asked Mrs. Darling, following him.

"Worrying me in London? Nothing has been worrying me in London."

"Has it not? You were looking so ill when you got down here: thin, and worn, and changed. I said nothing, for fear of alarming Charlotte."

"I have not felt well for some little time. But it is really my health that is in fault, Mrs. Darling; not worry."

"You were worn out with the long session: those late hours do fag a man. This country air will restore you."

"I hope so," he replied in a dreamy tone, and his eyes had a far-off dreamy look in them. "It would not be well just yet for yon little fellow to be the master of Alnwick."

Mrs. Darling thought nothing of the remark: perhaps George St. John thought as little. It was an indisputable fact that he was looking thin, ill, not so strong as he used to look: but many men, wearied with the late hours, the wear and tear of a London season, look so every autumn, and grow robust again by spring.

The fact was, he began to suspect that his health was failing. And when a man, neither a coddler nor a hypochondriac, suspects this, rely upon it, it is time he looked into the cause. Mr. St. John was careless of himself, as men mostly are; a year ago he would have laughed outright at the idea of going to a doctor. But the feeling of intense weariness, of almost utter want of strength, which had come upon him in London, coupled with a rapid wasting away, and all without any cause, had forced him to wonder what was the matter. He had made an engagement for a walking-tour, and then doubted whether his strength would be equal to it. That somewhat aroused him; not to alarm, more to a curiosity as to what could be wrong; and close upon that, came the summons to Alnwick.

For a day or two after his return, he felt refreshed, stronger, better in all ways. But the momentary renovation faded again, and by the time he had been a week at Alnwick he felt weaker than he had felt at all. The day previous to this conversation with Mrs. Darling, he spoke to Mr. Pym, telling that gentleman that he thought he wanted tonics.

"Tonics!" repeated Mr. Pym. "What's the matter with you?"

"Nothing that I know of. There it is. I haven't an ailment in the world, and yet I feel so weak and get so thin. It seems a sort of wasting away."

A recollection, sharp as a needle, and causing a great deal more pain, darted into Mr. Pym's mind as he looked at him. Other of the St. Johns of Alnwick had wasted away without apparent cause; wasted to death.

"We'll soon set you right again," said he, a shade more quickness in his speech than usual. "You shall have some tonics."

The tonics came; and Mr. St. John took them. He tried other means; cold bathing, driving out, living almost in the open air; but he did not grow stronger.

"Didn't my father waste away like this?" he suddenly said to Mr. Pym, one day.

"Oh, pooh, no!" quite angrily replied the surgeon. "Your father had a peck of troubles upon him—and I'm sure you can't remember anything about him, for you were only five years old when he died."

George St. John laughed. "You need not fear frightening me, Pym. I think he did waste away; but that's no reason, you know, why I should do so."

He said nothing to his wife of this feeling of indisposition, or that he was consulting Mr. Pym. This was from no particular wish of suppressing it; more, that he really did not think it sufficiently important to speak about. But it came to her knowledge incidentally.

She grew strong again, and was sitting on the slopes one afternoon with her embroidery, quiet, gentle, smiling, as if not a cloud of anger had ever distorted her fair features, when she saw Mr. Pym approach and enter the house. It suddenly occurred to her that she had so seen him once or twice lately, and had wondered, in a passing way, what he wanted. Certainly his visits were not to her now.

"What can it be that he comes for?" she said aloud, pausing in her work, and gazing at the door through which Mr. Pym had disappeared.

If the question was not addressed to air, it must have been meant for Benja, that young gentleman being the only person within sight and hearing. He was sitting astride on the arm of the bench at Mrs. St. John's elbow, absorbed in a new picture-book that Honour had bought him, and teasing Mrs. St. John's patience out with his demands that she should admire its marvels.

"Mr. Pym comes for papa," said quick Benja.

"For papa!" she repeated. "Nonsense, Benja! Papa's not ill. He's looking very thin, but I am sure he's not ill."

"Mr. Pym comes for him, and he sends him physic," persisted Benja. "For I was in the room yesterday, mamma, and heard them talking."

Mrs. St. John thought this rather singular. Presently she saw Mr. Pym and her husband come out and go strolling down the avenue together. The latter soon turned back.

"Benja, go and tell papa that I want him."

Mr. St. John caught up Benja when the boy met him, kissed him, fondly put him down again, and the two came on together; Benja leaping and holding his papa's hand. Mrs. St. John was watching with compressed lips. Even still she could not bear to see the love of her husband for Benja. It was very foolish of her, very wrong, and she knew herself that it was so : but, strive against it as she would, as she *did*, the feeling kept its mastery over her.

"George, what is the matter with you?" she asked, as her husband sat down beside her, and Benja ran off with his pictures. "Why does Mr. Pym come?"

"I think he comes partly because he likes the walk," was the answer, given with a smile. "I asked him for some tonics during the time he was attending you, and he constituted me a patient directly. It's the way with doctors."

"Don't you feel well?"

"I don't feel strong. It's nothing, I suppose. You need not look alarmed, Charlotte."

Mrs. St. John was looking more surprised than alarmed. She wondered her husband had concealed it, she said, half reproachfully.

"My dear, there was no concealment in the case. I felt languid, and spoke to Pym : that was all. It was not worth mentioning."

"You have no complaint, George?"

"None whatever, that I know of."

"And are in no pain?"

"None."

"Then it can't be anything serious," she said, reassured.

"Of course it can't. Unless any one chooses to look at it ominously. I accuse Pym of doing so, and he retorts by wanting to know if I think him superstitious. There's an old belief abroad, you must know, Charlotte, that the St. Johns of Alnwick never live to see their thirty-third birthday."

She looked up at him. He was speaking half jestingly, half seriously; with a smile, but not a gay one, on his lips.

"But that's not true, George?"

"As true as most of such sayings are, invented by old women over their tea-cups. It need not alarm either of us, Charlotte."

"But I mean, it is not true that such a belief is abroad?"

"Oh, *that's* true enough. Ask Pym. A great many of us have died just about that age; there's no denying it; and I presume that this has given rise to the popular fancy."

"What have they died of?"

"Some of one thing, some of another. A large proportion of the whole have fallen in battle. My great-grandfather died early, leaving seven little sons. Three of them were taken in childhood; the other four lived to see thirty, but not one of them saw thirty-three. I imagine that the premature death of so large a number of sons must have chiefly given rise to the superstition. Any way, there's no denying the fact that the St. Johns of Alnwick have not been long-lived."

"And the St. Johns of Castle Wafer?"

"It does not apply to them. Why, Isaac St. John is now all but fifty. It is owing to this mortality that Alnwick has been so often held by a minor. The Hall came to me when I was five years old."

"But George"—and she spoke hesitatingly and wistfully—"you *don't* think there's anything in it?"

"Of course I don't. Should I be telling you this gossip if I did?"

She thought not, either. She glanced at his fresh complexion, so bright and clear; at the rose-red on his cheeks, speaking, apparently, of health; and her mind grew easy, and she laughed with him.

"George! you are now thirty-three!"

"No. I shall be thirty-three next May, if I live until then."

"If you live till then," she echoed. "Does that imply a doubt of it in your own mind?"

"Not at all. I dare say I am in no more danger of dying than others—than Mr. Pym—than old Dr. Graves—than any man you like to think of. In one sense we are all in danger of it, danger continually; and, Charlotte, when any circumstance brings this fact to our minds—for we forget it too much—I think it should serve to make us very regardful of each other, more cautious to avoid inflicting pain on those we love."

His words and tone conveyed a pointed meaning. She raised her eyes inquiringly.

"Subdue those fits of temper for my sake, Charlotte," he whispered, letting his hand fall on hers. "You don't know how they pain me. I might recall to you their unseemliness, I might urge the sad example they give the children; but I would rather ask it by your love for me. A little effort of will; a little patient self-control, and you would subdue them."

"I will, George, I will," she answered, with earnest, willing acquiescence. And there was a look that told of resolution in her strange and dreamy eyes, as they seemed to gaze before her into a far-off vision of the future.

And all in a moment a thought rose up within her—a conviction, if you will—that this fancy, belief, superstition—call it what you please—of the premature deaths of the masters of Alnwick, must have been the secret and still unexplained cause of her mother's opposition to the match.

CHAPTER VII.

A SHADOW OF THE FUTURE.

OCTOBER came in, and was passing. George St. John sat at his desk, reading over a letter he had just penned, preparatory to folding it. It may facilitate matters if we read it also.

"MY DEAR MR. ST. JOHN,

"'It behoves all sane men to make a will.' Do you recognize the sentence? It was from your own lips I heard it spoken, years ago, when I was a little chap in tunics, and somehow it has never left my memory. Then, you will say, why have you, George St. John, lived to your present age and never made one? And in truth I can only plead carelessness as the excuse. I am about to remedy the omission. Not that there would be much trouble with my affairs were I to die without leaving a will, as Benja takes nearly all I possess; and there's my wife's marriage-settlement—you know how poor it is—to claim the remainder. On that score, therefore, the obligation is not a very onerous one; and perhaps that fact may have induced the carelessness I admit. But there is another phase of the question that has latterly forced itself on my attention—the necessity for providing proper guardians for my children in the event of my death.

"Will you, Isaac St. John, good and true man that you are, be this guardian? I say, 'this guardian;' for though another will be associated with you for form's sake, I shall wish you to be the acting one. The other of whom I have thought is General Carleton, my late wife's uncle; and the General, being a bilious old Indian, will not like to have any active trouble thrust upon him. I hope, however, the charge would not entail trouble upon you, any more than upon him; as my present wife will be constituted the children's personal guardian. Let me have an answer from you at your convenience, but do not refuse my request.

"Give my kind regards to Mrs. St. John. Is Fred with you? What about Lady Anne?

"Believe me,

"Ever your sincere friend and cousin,

"GEORGE CARLETON ST. JOHN."

The letter was folded, sealed, and addressed to Isaac St. John, Esquire, of Castle Wafer. George St. John laid it aside with others for the post, and then turned to a mass of papers, which he began to sort and look into. Indeed, he seemed latterly to have taken quite a mania for arranging his affairs and putting them in order: and his steward said privately to a friend, that Mr. St. John was growing as methodical as he had formerly been careless.

Whilst he was thus engaged, his wife came in, Georgy in her arms, whom she was making believe to scold. The two-year-old boy, indulged, wilful, rather passionate, did just as he liked, and he had now chosen to pull his mamma's hair down. He was a loving, charming little fellow; and whatever there was of wilfulness in his conduct, was the fault of his mother's great indulgence.

"Look at this dreadful little boy, papa!" she exclaimed, standing before her husband, her luxuriant hair, dark and shining as a gipsy's, flowing on to her light muslin dress. "See what he has done to poor mamma. Don't you think we must sell him to the old cobbler at Alnwick?"

Mr. St. John looked up from his crowded desk, speaking half crossly. The interruption annoyed him.

"How can you let him pull you about so, Charlotte? George, you want a whipping."

She sat down, clasping the boy to her heart in an access of love. "Whipping for Georgy!" she fondly murmured in the child's ear. "No, no: Georgy pull mamma's hair down if he likes." But Honour could have told a tale to prove that she was not always so tolerant. Benja had once pulled her hair down in play—it was just after she came to the Hall—and she had left the marks of her fingers on his face for it. It is true she seemed sorry afterwards, and soothed him when he cried: but she did it.

Letting George sit on her knee, she did up her hair as well as she could. George laughed and chattered, and tried to pull it down again; altogether there was a great noise. Mr. St. John spoke.

"I wish you'd take him away, Charlotte: I am very busy."

"Busy! But I came to talk to you, George," she answered.

"What about?"

"Something that I want to do—something that I have been thinking of. Here, Georgy, amuse yourself with these, and be quiet," she said, taking up a small plate containing a bunch of grapes, which happened to be on the table, and giving it to the restless, romping child. "Eat them whilst I talk to papa."

"Won't another time do, Charlotte?"

"I shall not keep you a minute. Next week November will come in. And the 10th will be—do you remember what the 10th will be?"

"Benja's birthday," said Mr. St. John, speaking without thought, his attention wholly given to the papers before him.

You should have seen the change in her face—it wore an evil look just then.

"And George's also!"

The tone jarred on Mr. St. John's ear, and he raised his eyes quickly.

"George's also, of course. What of it, Charlotte?"

The angry emotion had raised a storm within her, and her breath was laboured. But she strove for self-control, and pressed her hand to her heart to still it.

"You can think of Benja, you cannot think of Georgy! It is ever so."

"Nay, you are mistaken," said Mr. St. John, warmly. "I think as much of one as I do of the other: I *love* one as much as I do the other. If I answered you shortly, it is because I am busy."

Mrs. St. John was silent for a few moments, apparently playing with the child's pretty curls. When she spoke, all temper appeared to have been subdued, and she was cordial again.

"I want to keep their birthday, George."

"With all my heart."

"But to keep it grandly, I mean: something that will be remembered. We will have an outdoor *fête*——"

"An outdoor *fête!*" was the surprised and involuntary interruption.

"Yes; why not? Similar to the one you gave three years ago. Ah, George! don't you remember it, and what you asked me then? We have never had one since."

"But that was in September; this will be November—too late for that sort of thing."

"Not too late if this fine weather lasts. It is lovely yet."

"The chances are that it will not last."

"It may. At any rate, George, if it does not, we must entertain the crowd indoors instead of out. But I have set my heart on keeping this day."

"Very well: I have not the least objection."

"And now, George, shall we invite——"

"If you will kindly leave me alone for half-an-hour, Charlotte, I shall have done what I am about, and will talk it over with you as much as you please," he interrupted. "I expect the steward in every minute, and am not ready for him."

"We'll go then, Georgy, and leave papa alone. Make haste."

The "make haste" applied to eating the grapes, which Master Georgy was already accomplishing with tolerable speed. Mrs. St. John, her arm round him, held the plate on his little knees; the other hand was still wandering amidst his hair. A charming picture! The child's generally bright complexion looked very bright to-day; the fair skin white as snow, the cheeks a lovely rose colour. It might have been taken for paint; and the thought seemed to strike Mrs. St. John.

"If he could only sell that," she said to her husband, as she pointed to the bloom; "how many women there are who would give a fortune for it!"

"I would rather see him like Benja, though," was the prompt and prosaic answer. "That rose-red has been found a fatal sign before now in the St. Johns of Alnwick."

"You have it yourself," said Mrs. St. John.

"Something like it, I believe."

"Then, how can you say it is fatal? You—you—don't mean anything, surely, George?"

George St. John laughed out merrily; a reassuring laugh.

"Not as to him, at least, Charlotte. He is a healthy little fellow—as I hope and believe."

Georgy made an end of the grapes, and, by way of *finale*, tossed the plate up. Mrs. St. John caught it, so there was no damage done. Putting him down, he ran up to his papa, eager to see whether there was anything else on the table, either to eat or to play with. His mamma took his hand, and was rewarded with a cry and a stamp.

"You have been writing to Isaac St. John?" she exclaimed, her eyes falling on the letter that lay there. "Do you correspond with him?"

"Not often."

"Why have you been writing to him now?"

"Only to ask him a question."

"Oh!" she concluded, taking Georgy up by force, who resisted with all his might. "I thought you might have been writing to invite him here, and he would be such a trouble."

"He wouldn't come, if I did."

"Is he so very unsightly, George?"

"No: not unsightly at all."

"And the other one—Frederick? Is he so very beautiful?"

George St. John burst into another laugh.

"Beautiful! What a term to apply to a man! But I suppose he is what you women would call so. He *is* good-looking: better-looking, I think, than any one I ever saw. There, that's enough, Charlotte. Put off anything else you have to ask me until by-and-by."

This *fête*, as projected by Alnwick's mistress, was carried out. It need not have been mentioned at all, but for a misfortune that befel Benja while it was being held. The weather, though growing gradually colder, still retained its fineness; and when the day rose, the 10th of November, it proved to be bright and pleasant.

Crowds flocked to Alnwick. As it had been on the 10th of November, during Mr. St. John's widowhood, the *fête* or *fêtes*, so it was now—a gathering to be remembered in the county. The invitations had gone out far and wide; visitors were staying in the house, as many as it would hold; day-guests came from all parts, near and distant. It was one of those marked days that never fade from the memory.

But the guests, as it drew towards the close of the afternoon, might have searched for their host in vain, had they happened to want him. Mr. St. John was then in his own sitting-room (the one where you last saw him), leaning back in an easy-chair, and looking tired to death. A little thing fatigued him now : for there could be no mistake that the weakness he complained of was growing upon him. He lay back in the chair in that perfectly still attitude indicative of great weariness ; listlessly conscious of the noise outside, the music, the laughter, the gay and joyous sounds ; and amidst them might be caught distinctly the shouts and cries of the two boys, Benja and George, who were busiest of the busy that festal day.

Presently George St. John stretched out his hand, and took a letter from his desk—the answer from Isaac St. John. It had arrived only that morning, and Mr. St. John, engaged with his guests at breakfast, had only glanced at its contents. He opened it now again.

> *"Castle Wafer, November 9th.*
>
> "MY DEAR GEORGE,
>
> "You will think I have taken a great deal of time in replying to you, but I wished to give the question mature consideration, and could only snatch brief moments between my sufferings, which are just now very great.
>
> "I accept the charge. Partly because you were always a favourite of mine (as I believe you know), and I don't like to refuse you ; partly because I assume that I shall never (speaking in accordance with probability and human foresight) be called upon to exercise my office : for I hope and trust you have no reason to expect this. I had fully made up my mind never to accept another guardianship : not that I had reason to suppose one was likely to be offered me : the bringing up Frederick has been a great responsibility for one situated as I am.
>
> "However, as you say in this case there would be no personal guardianship required, I dare say I could manage the money matters, and therefore consent to accept it. Hoping at the same time, and assuming, that I shall never be called upon to fulfil it.
>
> "Why don't you come and see me? I am very lonely : Frederick is only here by fits and starts, once in a summer's day, and gone again ; and Mrs. St. John writes me word that she is prevented coming down this autumn. You can go about at will, and why not come? So much can scarcely be said of me. I should like to make the acquaintance of your wife and

of my future charges, who, I hope, never will be my charges. You ask about Anne : nothing is decided ; and Frederick holds back mysteriously.

"Ever truly yours, dear George,

"ISAAC ST. JOHN."

George St. John folded the letter again, and sat with it on his knee. He was beginning to think—with that unmistakable conviction that amounts to a prevision—that his cousin *would* be called upon to accept the charge. Perhaps at no very distant period. Pym was getting cross and snappish : a sure and certain sign to one who knew him as well as George St. John did, that he thought him ill : had he been improving, the surgeon would have been gay as a lark. But it needed not Pym or any one else to confirm the fact of his increasing illness : the signs were within himself.

He was glad that Mr. St. John had accepted the charge : though he had felt almost sure that he would do so, for Isaac St. John lived only to do good to others. A man, as personal joint guardian to his children, could not be proposed ; if they were left, as it was only right they should be left, under the guardianship of his wife. There had been moments in this last month or two when, remembering those violent fits of passion, a doubt of her perfect fitness for the office would intrude itself upon him ; but he felt that he could not ignore her claims ; there was not sufficient pretext for separating the mother from the child.

As he sat, revolving these and many thoughts in his mind, he became conscious that the sounds outside had changed their character. The gay laughter was turning into a murmur of alarm, the joyous voices to hushed cries. He held his breath to listen, and in that moment a wild burst of terror rent the air. With one bound, as it almost seemed, Mr. St. John was out and amongst them.

The crowd was gathering round the lake, and his heart flew to his children. But he caught sight of his wife standing against a tree, holding George to her side against the folds of her beautiful dress. That she was agitated with some great emotion, there could be no doubt : her breath was laboured, her face white as death.

"What is the matter? What has happened?" cried Mr. St. John, halting for a moment his fleet footsteps.

"They say—that—Benja's—drowned," she answered, hesitating between every word.

He did not wait to hear the conclusion: he bounded on to the brink of the lake, throwing off his coat as he ran, ready to plunge in after his beloved child. But one had been before him: and the first object Mr. Carleton saw as the crowd parted for him, was the dog Brave, swimming to shore with Benja.

"Good dog! Brave! Brave! Come on, then, Brave! Good old dog! Save your playfellow! Save the heir of Alnwick!"

All safe. Only on the bank did the good dog loose the clothes from between his firm teeth, and release Benja. Mr. St. John, more emotion on his face than had been seen there since the death of that child's mother, caught the boy with one hand and caressed Brave with the other.

His wife had not stirred. She stood there, calm, still, as one stunned. Was she frightened? those who had leisure to glance at her asked it. Had her love for her step-son, her dread at losing him, transformed her into a statue?

It was not that she was so much frightened; it was not that she loved Benja. Perhaps she was as yet unconscious of what feelings the moment had served to arouse; partially unconscious that the thought which had blanched her face with emotion and wildly stirred the pulses of her beating heart, was one fraught with danger: if Benja were drowned, her child would be the heir.

Voices were calling out that the boy was dead, and Mrs. St. John lifted her face, a sort of haggard, yearning look upon it. But Mr. Carleton, the boy pressed in his warm arms, knew that he was only insensible. He was hastening to the house, Honour, half frightened to death, at his side, and eager sympathizers following in his wake, when he bethought him of his wife.

"Honour, just run and tell your mistress that he'll be all right soon. She's there; under the elm-trees."

"Is he dead?" she asked ere Honour could speak, as the girl went up.

"Oh no, madam, he's not dead, thank Heaven! My master has sent me to tell you that he is all right."

Mrs. St. John did not appear to understand. It seemed to Honour—and the girl was a quick observer—as if her mistress had been so fully persuaded he was dead that her senses were at first sealed to the contrary impression, and could not admit it.

"Not dead?" she repeated, mechanically.

"He is not dead," said Honour. "He is in no danger of dying now."

For one single moment—for one moment only—a wild sort of glare, of angry disappointment, shot from the eyes of Mrs. St. John. Honour drew back scared, shocked: it had betrayed to the attendant more than she ought to know.

But do not set down Charlotte St. John as a wicked woman. She was not wicked yet. The feeling—whatever its precise nature—had arisen unbidden : she could not help it ; and when she became conscious of it, she shuddered at it just as much as Honour could· have done. But she did not detect its danger.

The party dispersed. And Mrs. St. John, in a soft muslin wrapper, was watching by the cradle of Benja, who was in a sweet sleep now. She had kissed him and cried over him when they first met ; and George St. John's heart throbbed with pleasure at these tokens of her affection for the child. Benja had slipped into the lake himself, and for two or three minutes was not observed ; otherwise there had been no danger.

The danger, however, was over now, and Mr. Pym had gone home, loudly promising Benja a hatful of physic as a punishment for his carelessness. Mrs. St. John and the household went to rest at midnight, leaving Honour sitting up with the boy. There was not the least necessity for her sitting up, but she would not hear of his not being watched till morning. The child, in fact, was her idol.

Presently Mr. St. John came in, and Honour started and rose. She had been half asleep in her chair, and she had thought her master had gone to bed.

He lay with his little face, unusually flushed, on the pillow, his silken hair rather wild, and one arm outside the clothes ; a charming picture, as most children are when asleep. Mr. St. John bent over the boy on the other side the crib, apparently listening to his breathing ; but Honour thought her master was praying, for his eyes were closed, and she saw his lips moving.

"We should not have liked to lose him, Honour," he observed with a smile, when he looked up.

"To lose him! Oh, sir! I would rather have died myself."

"It might have been a care less for me to leave, though!"
he resumed in an abstracted tone. "His mother gone, and
I gone: the world may be a cold one for Benja."

"But you are not—you are not fearing for yourself, sir!"
exclaimed Honour, quite forgetting, in the shock the words
gave her, that it was no business of hers to answer the thoughts
of her master.

"I don't know, Honour. I have fancied of late that I may
not be here very long."

"Heaven grant you may be mistaken, sir!" was the impulsive aspiration of the girl : "for this child's sake!"

Her master looked at her, struck by the tone of terror, as
much as by the words. "Why for his sake? Should anything
happen to me, Honour, you must all take the greater care of
him. Your mistress; you; all of you."

An impulse came over Honour to speak out somewhat
of her thoughts; one of those strange impulses that bear the
will with them as a torrent not to be controlled.

"Sir, for the love of mercy—and may God forgive me for
saying it, and may you forgive me!—if you fear that you will
be taken from us, *don't* leave this child in the power of Mrs.
St. John!"

"Honour!"

"I know; I know, sir; I am forgetting myself; I am saying
what I have no right to say; but the child is dearer to me than
any living thing, and I hope you'll overlook my presumption
for his sake. Leave him in the power of anybody else in the
world, but don't leave him to Mrs. St. John."

"Mrs. St. John is fond of him."

"No, sir, she is the contrary. She tries to like him, but she
can't. And if you were gone, there'd no longer be a motive—
as I believe—for her seeming to do so. I think—I think"—
and Honour lowered her voice beseechingly—"that she might
become cruel to him in time."

Bold words. George St. John did not check them, as
perhaps he ought to have done; rather, he seemed to take
them to him and ponder over their meaning.

"To any one else in the world, sir!" she resumed, the tears
forcing themselves down her cheeks in her earnestness. "To
any of your own family—to Mrs. Darling—to whom you
will; but do not, do not leave him in the power of his step-
mother!"

What instinct caused Honour Tritton thus to speak? And what made Mr. St. John quit the room without a word of reproof, as if he silently bowed to it?

CHAPTER VIII.

WASTING AWAY.

BUT though Honour's words certainly aroused Mr. St. John to a sense of precaution, they did not cause him to act upon it. A doubt lay almost in his mind as to whether his wife did, or *could*, like Benja: it was based upon her unmistakably jealous disposition, and on the blow she had once given Benja when she was as a mad woman : but with her daily conduct before him, her love displayed as much for Benja as for her own child, he could only believe that the boy was safe in her care. Certainly the words of Honour recalled those unpleasant doubts forcibly before him ; but he suffered the impression to wear away again. We all know how time, even if you count it only by days or hours, softens the aspect of things; and before November was out, the master of Alnwick had made his will, leaving both the children under the personal guardianship of his wife.

And the winter went on, and George St. John grew weaker and weaker. Not very perceptibly so to the eyes about him; the decline was too gentle for that. In February, instead of going up to London when Parliament met, he resigned his seat, and then people grew sensible of the change in him, and wondered what was wrong with Mr. Carleton St. John. Mr. Pym came up constantly, and was more and more testy at every visit. He sent drugs ; he brought other doctors with him ; he met a great physician from the metropolis ; but the more he did, the worse seemed to be the effect upon his patient.

"You'd better give me up for a bad job, Pym, and leave off worrying yourself," Mr. St. John said to him one day as they were strolling down the park together—for Mr. St. John liked to go out with the doctor when he had paid his visits. "I do you no credit."

"It's because you *won't* do it," gruffly retorted the surgeon. "I order you to a warm climate, and you won't go."

"No; I won't. I am best here. Send me away to those hot places, and I should only die the sooner. Pym, dear old fellow"—and Mr. St John put his hand into the surgeon's— "you are feeling this for me more than I feel it for myself. I have settled my business affairs; I have settled—I humbly hope —other affairs of greater moment; and I can wait my summons tranquilly."

"Have you made your will?" asked Mr. Pym, after a pause, which seemed to be chiefly occupied in clearing his throat.

"No end of weeks ago. The chief thing I had to settle was the guardianship of the children. Of Benja, I may say. George would have naturally fallen to his mother without a will."

"And you have left him—Benja——?"

"To my wife, just as I have the other. Mr. St. John, of Castle Wafer, and General Carleton, are the trustees. I thought of my wife's half-brother, Captain Darling, as one of them; but his regiment will probably be ordered abroad, and he may be away for years."

They walked on a few steps further in silence, to the spot that Mr. St John called his turning-place, for it was there he generally quitted the surgeon. As they were shaking hands, Mr. Pym retained his patient's fingers in his, and spoke.

"Will you forgive an old man for his advice? He is double your age, and has had twenty times the experience. For acquiring good practical lessons of life, commend me to a doctor."

"I'll take it," said Mr. St. John, "in anything except quitting Alnwick."

"Don't leave Benja under your wife's charge."

"Why not?" came the question, after a pause of surprise.

"I have my reasons. For one thing, she is not very strong, and the charge of the two children, with you gone, might be found a heavy task."

"I think that's nonsense, Pym," quietly replied Mr. St. John. "She has plenty of servants, and at a proper age Benja will go to school. George also. You must have some other reason."

"True. But I am not sure that you would like me to mention it."

"Mention what you will, Pym. Say anything."

" Has it occurred to you that it is within the range of possibility your wife may marry again?"

" My widow may. Yes."

" Then, should this prove the case, and she formed new ties about her, Benja might find himself neglected. George is her own child, secure in her love, whatever betide; Benja is different. Have you provided in any way for the contingency I have mentioned?"

" No. I have left my wife personal and resident guardian at Alnwick until Benja shall be twenty-one. At that period she must leave it, or only remain there as Benja's guest. It is right, I believe, that it should be so. And I have a precedent in my father's will."

" But his widow was your own mother."

Mr. St. John made no immediate reply. The distinction had probably not occurred to him.

" Take my advice, George St. John," said the surgeon impressively; " do not leave Benja under the charge of your wife. I would rather not discuss with you the why and the wherefore; but rely upon it some other plan will be better both for the boy and for Mrs. St. John."

He went away as he spoke, and George St. John turned slowly back to the Hall. The conversation recalled to his mind with vivid force the almost-forgotten words of Honour; and an uncomfortable feeling of indecision crept into it.

Still he did not see any feasible way of altering the arrangements he had made. When he died, Alnwick Hall would be Benja's, and must be the boy's chief home during his minority; he could not turn his wife out of it, and he could not place any one else in it as Benja's personal guardian. He had no means of providing a suitable residence for his widow if she left the Hall : in fact, it was only as the heir's guardian that he could at all adequately provide for her. Neither, it must be confessed, did Mr. St. John himself see any great necessity for separating them : but he was a man amenable to counsel, open to advice, and the opinion of two friends (surely both may be called so!) so attached to him as Mr. Pym and Honour, bore weight with him. It had not been George St. John had he ignored it.

" May God help me to do right!" he murmured, as he entered the house.

He dwelt much upon it during the remainder of the day;

he lay awake part of the night : and only when he came to a decision did he get to sleep.   Early the next morning he rang for his servant; and at eight o'clock the pony-carriage conveyed him to the railway station at Alnwick to take the train. As the market people looked at him, passing them betimes in the fresh February morning, at the bright colour in his face, the wavy brown hair stirred by the gentle breeze, they said to themselves, how well Mr. Carleton St. John was looking, though thin.

He was going over to Castle Wafer.   An hour and a-quarter's journey brought him to a certain town ; there he waited twenty minutes, and took another train.   Rather more than another hour and a-quarter of very quick travelling, for this last was an express, conveyed him to Lexington, and thence he took a fly to Castle Wafer.

It was one of the most charming houses ever seen, nestling in lovely grounds, amidst rising trees of many species.   A modern house, built by its present owner, Isaac St. John, who possessed a rare taste for the beautiful, and had made it exquisite.   That house was his hobby in life; his care was his half-brother, Frederick St. John.   The estate of Castle Wafer was the entailed inheritance of these St. Johns ; and Frederick was heir presumptive : the positive heir, said the world; for it was beyond the range of probability that its present owner would ever marry.

They were second-cousins to the St. Johns of Alnwick, and were next in succession.   Of great wealth themselves, far more so than was George St. John, and of more note in the world, they were yet below him in succession to what might be called the original family property.   That was not Alnwick. An old baronet of eighty-one, Sir Thomas St. John, held it ; he was childless, and therefore it would come at his death to George St. John, and to George St. John's sons after him. Had he, George St. John, also been childless, the whole, including the title, including Alnwick, would lapse to Isaac St. John.

George St. John had nearly a two-mile drive.   He noted the familiar points on the road and in the fine landscape, as they stood out in the clear but not very bright February day.   The sprinkling of cottages near Castle Wafer ; the solitary public-house, called the Barley Mow, with its swinging sign-board ; and the old-fashioned red-brick house, Lexington Rectory, which the wiseacres of other days had built nearly two miles from its church and Lexington proper. It stood close to the grounds of Castle Wafer; was the only house of any social standing very near to it; and as George St. John glanced at its windows as he passed, he remembered that its present possessor had received his title to orders from a church in the neighbourhood of Alnwick, of which his father was patron; but he had been a very, very little boy at the time. The house looked empty now; its windows were nearly all closed: and he supposed its incumbent, Dr. Beauclerc, Rector of Lexington and Dean of Westerbury, was away at his deanery.

"Mr. St. John is at home?" he asked, as the woman came out to throw back the lodge gates.

"Oh yes, sir." And indeed George St. John had little need to ask, for Mr. St. John rarely, very rarely, was away from Castle Wafer.

A few minutes' turning and winding, and then the front of the house burst upon George St. John's view, and he was close upon it. The sun broke out at the moment, and he thought he had never before seen any place so beautiful; he always did think so, whenever he thus came upon Castle Wafer. The glistening white front, long rather than high, with its elaboration of ornament; the green terraces, covered with their parterres of flowers, already in bloom, and stretching beyond to the less open grounds; the low French windows, open to the breeze—never did any dwelling impart so cheerful, so attractive a look as did Castle Wafer. To a stranger, having no idea of the sort of house he was going to see, perhaps surprise would be the first feeling; for the place was as unlike a castle as any place could be. Isaac St. John said laughingly sometimes that he ought to change its appellation. There might have been a castle on the lands in the old feudal ages, but no trace remained of it: and the house, which had been pulled down to give place to this fairy edifice, had looked like a companion to the Rectory—red, gaunt, and gloomy.

As the hall-door was thrown open, and the bright colours fell on its mosaic pavement from the stained-glass windows, gladdening the eye of George St. John, a tall, portly man, rather solemn and very respectable, not to say gentlemanly, was crossing it, and turned his head to see who the visitor might be. Mr. St. John at once stepped past the footman and greeted him. It was Mr. Brumm, Castle Wafer's chief and most respected servant; the many years' personal attendant, and in some respects a confidential one, of its master. George St. John held out his hand, as affable men will do by these valued servants, after years of absence.

"How are you, Brumm? I see I have taken you by surprise."

"You have indeed, sir," said Mr. Brumm, in the slow manner natural to him. "Not more so, I am sure, sir, than you will take my master. It was only this morning that he was mentioning your name."

"How is he now?"

"Better, sir, than he has been. But he has suffered much of late."

Mr. Brumm was leading the way into an inner hall, one light and beautiful as the first, with the same soft colours thrown from its several windows. Opening a door here, he looked in and spoke.

"A visitor, sir—Mr. Carleton St. John."

By a bright fire in this light and charming room—and if you object to the reiteration of the term, I can only plead in excuse that everything was light and charming at Castle Wafer—with its few fine paintings, its glittering mirrors, its luxuriant chairs and sofas, its scattered books, and its fine harmonium, sat a deformed gentleman. Not any hideous phase of deformity that repels the eye, but simply with a hump upon his back : a small hump, the result of an accident in infancy. He had a pale, wan face, with the sharp chin usually accompanying these cases ; a face that insensibly attracted you by its look of suffering, and the thoughtful earnestness of its bright, clear, well-opened hazel eyes. Of nearly middle height, that hump was the only unsightly point about him ; but he was a man of suffering ; and he lived chiefly alone, he and his pain. His hair was dark, silken, rather scanty ; but not a thread of silver could be seen in it, though he was close on his fiftieth year.

Laying down the book he was reading, Isaac St. John rose at the mention of the name ; and stepped forward in the quiet, undemonstrative way characteristic of him, a glad smile lighting up his face.

"George! how pleased I am to see you! So you have thought of me at last?"

"I was half ashamed to come, Mr. St. John, remembering that it is five years since I came before. But I have met Mrs. St. John repeatedly in London, and sometimes Frederick; so that I have, as it were, seen you at second-hand. I have not been well, too."

Suitable, perhaps, to the difference in their ages, it might be observed that while the elder man called the younger "George," he himself was addressed as "Mr. St. John." But Mr. St. John had been almost grown up when George was a baby, and could remember having nursed him.

"You do not look well, George," he said, scanning the almost transparent face before him. "And—are you taller? You look so."

"That's because I'm thinner. See !"—opening his coat— "I'm nothing but a skeleton."

"What is wrong?"

"I can't tell you. I grew thinner and thinner and weaker and weaker, and that's about all I know. I may pick up as spring comes on, and get right again; but—it may be the other way." .

Isaac St. John did not answer. An unpleasant reminiscence of how this young man's father had wasted away eight-and-twenty years ago kept him silent.

"What will you take, George? Have you come to stay with me?"

"I have come to stay with you two hours : I must be home again by nightfall if I can. And I won't take anything until my business with you is over; for I confess it is my own selfish affairs that have brought me here. Let me speak to you first."

"As you will. I am ready."

"Ever ready, ever willing to help us all!" returned George St. John, warm gratitude in his tone. "It is about the guardianship that I wish to speak. I thank you for accepting it."

Isaac smiled. "I did not see that I could do otherwise for you."

"Say for my children. Well, listen to me. I have left my wife personal guardian to my children. She will reside at the Hall until Benja is of age, and they with her, subject of course to their school and college intervals. This is absolute with regard to the younger, but in regard to the elder I wish it to be dependent upon your discretion."

" Upon my discretion ? "

George St. John had his hands upon his knees, leaning for-forward in his great earnestness; he did not appear to notice the interruption.

" I wish you (when I shall be gone, and the boys have only their mother) to take means of ascertaining from time to time that Benja is *happy* under his step-mother's care, and that she is doing her part by him in kindness. Should you find occasion to doubt this, or to think from any other cause that he would be better elsewhere, remove him from her, and place him with any one you may consider suitable. I dare not say take him yourself : children are noisy, and your health is imperfect ; but place him where you can be sure that he will be well done by. Will you undertake this, Mr. St. John ? "

" Why do you ask this ? " was the reply of Isaac St. John. " Is it a new thought—a sudden thought ? "

" It is a new thought, imparted to me chiefly through a conversation I had yesterday with Pym, our surgeon and old friend. He does not think it well that Benja should be left under the absolute control of Mrs. St. John, as he is not her own child. He said, for one thing, that she might marry again, and Benja would be as it were isolated amidst new ties ; but when I pressed him for other reasons—for I am sure he had others—he would not give them ; preferred not to discuss it, he said. He was—I could see that—for having the boy entirely away from her, but that is not to be thought of. I reflected a good deal on what he said, and have come to the conclusion that it may be as well there should be some clause inserted in the will that shall take absolute power from her, and hence I come to you."

" Your wife is kind to the boy ? " asked Mr. St. John. " Pardon me the question, George."

" Very much so. When George was born, she showed some jealousy of the oldest boy, but all that has passed away. Benja was nearly drowned last November, and she was quite hysterical afterwards, crying and sobbing over him like a child. The nurse, a most faithful woman, thinks, I know, with Pym, but that's nothing."

" You wish me, in the event of the children being left father-less, to ascertain whether the elder is well done by at the Hall, and is happy there. If not, I am to remove him ? This is what you ask, as I understand it ? "

"Precisely so. Should you, in your judgment, deem that Benja would be better elsewhere, take him away. I shall endow you with full power."

"But how am I to ascertain that?'

"In any way you please. Use any means that may suggest themselves. Go over and see for yourself, or send some suitable substitute, or question Honour——"

"Who is Honour?"

"Benja's nurse. She took to him when my poor Caroline died. My present wife does not seem strong; at least she has had one or two serious illnesses lately; and Pym says the care of the two boys is more than I ought to put upon her. Perhaps it would be."

"Why not at once leave Benja under another guardianship?"

"I should not like to do so. The world would regard it as a slight, a tacit want of confidence in my wife: and besides, in that case I should be divided as to whether to leave the Hall as a present residence to her or to Benja. I—mark me, Mr. St. John—I place full reliance upon my wife; I believe she will do her duty by Benja, and make him happy; and in that case there is no harm done. I am only providing for a contingency."

"I see. Well, I accept the charge, George, though it might be well that you should entrust it to a more active man."

"No, no; you and you only."

They continued talking together for the brief space George St. John had allotted for his stay. Little more was said on the one subject, for George quitted it somewhat abruptly, and they had other topics in common; family matters, news on either side, as is the case when relatives meet after a prolonged separation. At the appointed time he was driven back to Lexington in Mr. St. John's carriage, took the return train, and reached Alnwick about six in the evening.

His wife had sent the close carriage for him, fearing the night air. George St. John directed the coachman to drive round by Mr. Drake, the lawyer's; and when that gentleman came out to him he asked him to step up to the Hall on the morrow, on a little matter of business relative to an alteration in his recently-made will.

But Mr. St. John of Castle Wafer, pondering on these matters after his relative's departure, remained puzzled, and could by no means arrive at a satisfactory conclusion as to whether there was danger that Mrs. Carleton St. John might be cruel to Benja, after the fashion of the vindictive uncle of the "Babes in the Wood," or whether it was feared that she would kill him with kindness.

CHAPTER IX.

· CHANGES AT ALNWICK.

On a charming summer day in that favourite room whose windows overlooked the broad lands of Alnwick, sat Mrs. Carleton St. John in widow's weeds. Opposite to her, in mourning also, her travelling shawl unpinned and slipping from her slim, falling shoulders, her bonnet dusty, was Mrs. Darling, not five minutes arrived.

Changes had come to Alnwick, as these signs betrayed. Its master, so much loved and respected during life, was no more. In the month of May the deceitful, as poets have it, the crisis came for George Carleton St. John, and the Hall passed to another owner—the little boy too young to be conscious of his full loss, and whose chief idea connected with it was the black attire with which officious attendants hastened to invest him.

Death at the last was sudden, and Mrs. St. John was alone when it came. Her mother, Mrs. Darling, had gone abroad, and beyond a very brief note, just telling her of the event, Mrs. Darling received no direct news from her. She wrote letter after letter, for it was not convenient to return home immediately; but all the replies—when she received any—came from Prance. And Prance, who was in a degree in the confidence of Mrs. Darling, ventured to intimate that her mistress was " sulking," and much annoyed by the will.

The last item of intelligence stirred all the curiosity possessed by Mrs. Darling. It also troubled her. She was aware that George St. John had little actual property to bequeath to his wife—and George St. John's own private opinion had been that Mrs. Darling's opposition to his marriage with her daughter arose from that sole fact—but there were ways and means of remedying this ; and now Mrs. Darling supposed they had not been taken. As soon as she was able, after June came in, she made arrangements for returning to England, and hastened down to Alnwick Hall.

But for the escutcheon on the outer walls, and the badge of widowhood worn by her daughter, Mrs. Darling might have thought things were as they had been—that no change had occurred. The windows were open, the sun was shining, the park was green and flourishing: even Charlotte was not changed. And Mrs. Darling scanned her with a critical eye.

" My dear, you are looking better than I hoped for."

" I am pretty well, mamma. I wish Prance would come in with Georgy ! " she continued fretfully. " I want you to see him, he is so grown ! "

" Dear little fellow ! I was so sorry that I could not come over at the time, Charlotte, but—— "

" It did not matter," interrupted Mrs. St. John, speaking quickly. "Indeed I think I was best alone. You know, mamma "—turning her deep eyes full upon her mother—" I was always given to being independent. How is Rose ? "

" Oh, dear ! " returned Mrs. Darling, with a groan, as if recalled to some very annoying subject. " Don't talk of Rose."

A half smile crossed the young widow's lips. " Has she been doing anything very dreadful ? "

" No : but she is so rebellious."

" Rebellious ! "

" At being kept at school. Mary Anne and Margaret fully expected she would break bounds and conceal herself on board the boat. We had sighted Folkestone before they felt any sort of assurance that she was not there."

" Did Mary Anne and Margaret come over with you ? "

" Yes ; I left them in London. Frank is expected."

" I think Frank might come down to see me ! " said Mrs. St. John, haughtily.

" My dear, I am sure he will. But he cannot always get leave when he would."

There was a pause. Charlotte, cool, haughty, reserved, as she had ever been, even to her mother, turned to the window again, looking out for her little son. Mrs. Darling was burning to ask various particulars of things she wanted to know, but did not just now see her opportunity. She rose from her chair.

"I think I will go, Charlotte, and take off my travelling things. I am as dusty as I can be."

"Do so, mamma. Your old room. Prance will not be long."

Prance was entering the house even then: she had brought Georgy in the back way. There was a boisterous meeting; Mrs. St. John coming out to join in it. Georgy chattered, and shook his fair curls from his pink cheeks, and was altogether lovely. Mrs. Darling did not wonder at the faint cry of pain— that intense love, whose expression amounts to pain—with which his mother caught him to her heart.

"Where is Benja?" asked Mrs. Darling of Prance.

Oh, Master St. John would be coming in sometime, Prance supposed. Honour had begun with her insolence, as usual, so they parted company. And Mrs. Darling, as if she would ignore the words, made her way hastily towards the staircase, Prance following in attendance.

Mrs. Darling scarcely gave the woman time to close the chamber-door before she began to question her eagerly. Remember that Prance was, so far as Mrs. Darling was concerned, a confidential servant, and she imparted all she knew. Mrs. St. John was to remain at the Hall as Master St. John's guardian, with four thousand a-year.

"I heard the will read," said Prance. "Old Drake the lawyer came to us after they returned from the funeral, and said we were wanted in the large drawing-room. Mrs. St. John was there in her new mourning and her widow's cap; and she looked very cross and haughty as we filed in. The gentlemen who had gone to the funeral were there, and Dr. Graves, and Mr. Pym. I had the little one, and Honour came in with Master St. John——"

"Why do you call him Master St. John?—he was always called Master Benja," interrupted Mrs. Darling.

"He has been called so since that same time, ma'am," was the woman's answer. "A gruff old gentleman who was one of the mourners, upright and stiff as a backboard and yellow as gold—it was General Carleton, I believe—heard one of us call the boy Master Benja, and he spoke up very severely, saying he was not Master Benja, but Master St. John, and must be nothing else to us until he should be Sir Benjamin. The servants were quite taken to, and have called him Master St. John ever since."

"Well, go on."

"We found we had been called in to hear the will read. I did not understand it altogether; but I am quite certain that Mrs. St. John is to reside at the Hall and to be paid four thousand a-year as the heir's guardian. There was something I was unable to catch, through Master Georgy's being troublesome at the moment, about the four thousand being reduced to two if Master St. John went away. And, on the other hand, it is to be increased by two, whenever he comes into the title and the other estates. Which will make six thousand a-year."

"Then what did you mean, Prance, by sending me word that your mistress was annoyed at the terms of the will? Four thousand a-year now, and six in prospective! She cannot find fault with that. It is munificent."

"You may depend upon it, ma'am, that she is so," was the unhesitating reply of Prance. "She is very much annoyed at it, and she has shown it in her manner. It is some clause in the will that vexes her. That precious Honour——"

"Stay, Prance," interrupted Mrs. Darling. "How often have I warned you not to encourage this ill-feeling against Honour!"

"It's Honour's fault," promptly answered Prance.

"It is the fault of both of you," returned Mrs. Darling; "of the one as much as the other. It is a strange thing you cannot be at peace together! You will arouse jealousy between the two children next!"

"It never comes to open quarrelling between us," rejoined Prance. "But she's uncommonly aggravating."

"Be quiet, Prance! I desire once for all that there may be more pleasantness between you. It is a scandal that the two upper maids of the Hall should be ever at variance, and it's a thoroughly bad example for the children; and it's—you *know* it's not well for your mistress. Mrs. St. John requires peace, not——"

Prance uttered an exclamation: it caused Mrs. Darling, who was looking into a bandbox at the time, to turn sharply. Mrs. St. John was standing there, behind the bed-curtains—to the startled lady's intense dismay. How much had she heard?

"Charlotte, my dear, I did not know you were there. I was just giving Prance a lecture upon this ill-feeling that seems always to be going on between her and Honour. Have you come to stay with me, child, whilst I unpack?" added Mrs.

Darling, seeing that her daughter was seating herself comfortably in an easy-chair. "Then, Prance, I think you may go now."

But while she so spoke, Mrs. Darling was tormenting herself, as much as one of her easy disposition can do so, as to whether she *had* caught a word of her conversation with Prance —that part of it relating to money. There had been some noise in the room from the opening of drawers and moving of boxes, which must have prevented their hearing her come in. "I'll speak of it," thought Mrs. Darling. "It's better to take the bull by the horns and make the best of it, when one does get into these dilemmas."

She stole a glance at her daughter, while busily intent to all appearance in straightening the trimmings of a bonnet she had just taken out of a bandbox. Mrs. St. John looked cold and stern. *Had* she heard anything?

"Charlotte, my dear, I am so very anxious about you : as to how things are left, and all that. I dropped a remark to poor Prance, but she seems to think it is all right; that you are left well-off and remain here. These simple servants can't know much, of course. I am glad your husband made a just and proper will."

"He made an infamous will," cried the young widow, her cheeks flaming.

The words completely took Mrs. Darling aback, and she forgot to enlarge on the opinion she had just expressed of poor, simple Prance's imperfect knowledge. "An infamous will, Charlotte!" she exclaimed, "when you have the Hall and four thousand a-year."

"It *is* infamous. I am left dependent upon the heir."

"The heir! Do you mean Benja?"

"There's no other heir but he. Why did George leave me dependent upon him?"

"I don't quite understand you, my dear. In what way are you dependent upon Benja?"

"The four thousand a-year is paid to me as his guardian only,—as his guardian and Georgy's. I only remain at the Hall as Benja's guardian. It's all on sufferance."

"But, my dear, your husband had it not in his power to leave you comfortably off in any other manner. All the settlement he could make on you at your marriage—I really don't think it will amount to more than six hundred a-year—he did make,

This, of course, is yours in addition; and it will be your child's after you."

"Think of the contrast," was the rejoinder; and Mrs. St. John's bosom heaved ominously, as if the wrong were almost too great to bear. "The one with his thousands upon thousands, his title, his state, everything that's high and mighty; the other, with his few poor hundreds and his obscurity."

"But, my dear Charlotte, there was no help for this. Benja was born to it, and Mr. Carleton could no more alter it than you could."

"It is not the less unjust."

"Unjust is not the right word. The law of entail may not be an equitable law, but Englishmen live under it, and must obey it. You should not blame your husband for this."

"I do not blame him for it."

"You blame his will, which is the same thing."

Mrs. St. John was leaning back, the broad lappets of her cap thrown from her face; her elbows rested on the arms of the chair, and she pressed the tips of her fingers nervously together. The slight storm had passed outwardly, and all her habitual coldness of manner had returned to her.

"Why did he add that codicil to it?"

"Was there a codicil? What was it? But I don't know what the will itself was, Charlotte."

"He had left the children under my exclusive guardianship. They were to reside at the Hall here with me, subject to their absences for education, and he willed that a sum of four thousand a-year should be paid to me."

"Well?" said Mrs. Darling, for she had stopped.

"That was in the will. But the codicil altered this, and Benja's residence with me is subject to the pleasure of Mr. Isaac St. John. He has it in his power to remove Benja from me if he sees fitting; and if Benja is so removed, two thousand of the four are to be withdrawn, and my allowance reduced thereby one half. Why did George do this? Why did he do it secretly, and never say a word to me about it?"

"I'm sure I don't know," said Mrs. Darling, who was revolving the news in her mind. "Benja to be removed from you at the pleasure of Isaac St. John? But is he not a helpless invalid?"

"Physically he may be next door to it, but he is all powerful as to Benja. This codicil was dated the day subsequent to a visit George paid Castle Wafer at the close of winter, a long time after the will was made. Isaac St. John must have put him up to it that day. I will pay him out, if I live."

"Well, I can't tell why he should have done it," cried Mrs. Darling, who felt altogether puzzled. "*He* does not want the two thousand a-year; he is rich and an invalid. Did you question him of his motives, Charlotte? I should have done so."

"Question whom?—Isaac St. John? I have never seen him."

"Did he not come to the funeral?"

"No; he was too ill, they said. His brother came—handsome Fred. Mamma, I *hate* Isaac St. John."

"Hush, my dear. It is more than likely that he will never interfere with you. I have always heard him spoken of as one of the most just and honourable men breathing."

"I don't like it to have been done. I don't like the world to know that George could put so great a slight upon me. It is known everywhere. The servants know it. He desired that they should be present while the will was read. Did you ever hear of such a thing?"

"Your husband desired it?"

"He did; at least, Mr. Drake says so. When they were about to read the will, and I had come down into the drawing-room before them all, Mr. Drake said to me, 'I am going to call in the servants, with your permission; Mr. Carleton St. John desired me to do so.' I objected, but it was of no use; Mr. Drake appeared not to hear me; and I could not make a fuss at a moment like that. But now, mamma, don't you see the drift of all this?"

"N—o," said Mrs. Darling, gathering no idea of Charlotte's meaning.

"I do," said Charlotte, the keen look sometimes seen in them gleaming from her unfathomable eyes. "That will was read out to the servants on purpose that they might know they have it in their power to carry tales to Isaac St. John. I hate him! I hate him! But for him, I am sure my husband would have entrusted me absolutely with Benja. Who is so fitting to bring him up as I?"

"And I think you will bring him up, Charlotte. I don't understand all this that you are telling me; but I feel little doubt Isaac St. John will be all that is courteous and kind.

Whilst you do your part by Benja, there can be no plea for removing him. You *will* do it?"

"I shall do it, certainly;" and Mrs. St John fully meant what she said; "I shall make no distinction between the boys. If Benja needs correcting, I shall correct him. If Georgy needs correcting, I shall correct *him*. The thing's easy enough, and simple enough; and there was not the least need for interfering with me. What I dislike most, is George's having kept it from me."

"I dare say he did not think to mention it to you," said Mrs. Darling, soothingly; and it was notable that she was in the habit of smoothing things to her daughter always, as though she were afraid of her. "And you are quite right, my dear, not to make any difference between the children; your husband did not."

"Not outwardly, or in a general way. In his heart, though, he loved the one and not the other; and I love the other and not the one. Oh, Georgy! Georgy! if you were only the heir!"

"That's an unprofitable thought, Charlotte. Don't indulge it. Benja was the first-born."

"How can I help indulging it? Georgy is *my* first-born, and it seems as a wrong done him—done to us both."

"My dear, where's the use of this? You married George Carleton St John with your eyes open, in defiance of me. It is too late to repent now."

"I don't repent. I would marry him again to-morrow, though he had two heirs instead of one. But I can't help—I can't help——"

"What can't you help?"

"Never mind. The position is unalterable, and it is useless to dwell upon it. Mamma, I shall never speak of this again. If you want any other particulars of the will, you can get them from old Drake. Tell me now all about Rose and her rebellion. I have often thought I should like her to live here when she leaves school."

Why, Mrs. Darling could not have told; but she felt the greatest relief when Charlotte thus quitted the subject. It was next to impossible that any child could have been born with a disposition so jealous as had Charlotte Norris; and Mrs. Darling had been pleased, but for curtailing her income, that Benja should be removed from her. She had no fear that

Charlotte would be unkind to him; systematically unkind she believed Charlotte would not be to any one; but, so long as the boy was with her, he must and would keep alive the jealousy she felt on Georgy's account. Two thousand a-year, however, in Mrs. Darling's estimation, was—two thousand a-year.

Willingly she turned to the topic named by Charlotte—her youngest, her troublesome, but most lovable daughter. And it is quite time, my reader, that you made her acquaintance also. To do which it will be necessary to cross the water.

CHAPTER X.

MISS ROSE DARLING.

You all know that crowded seaport town on the other side the water—Belport-on-the-Sea; and are therefore aware that its educational establishments, good, bad, and indifferent, are numerous. But I must ask you not to confound the one you are about to enter, Madame de Nino's, with any of those others, no matter what their merits may be. The small, select, and most costly establishment of Madame de Nino was of the very highest standing; it was intended solely for the reception of gentlemen's daughters—was really confined to them; and no pupil could be admitted to it without an undeniable introduction. It was perhaps the only French school to which anxious parents could confide a daughter free from doubt on the score of her associations: whatever her fellow-pupils might be in mind and manners, they were sure to be of gentle birth.

On that very same day that took Mrs. Darling down to Alnwick Hall on the visit to her widowed daughter, Madame de Nino's pupils were gathered in the large schoolroom. Class was over for the day, and the girls were tired enough. They hated Fridays. There was no dancing, no drawing, no walking; nothing but hard unbroken learning, writing, and practising.

Look at this class of elder girls, their ages varying from sixteen to twenty, sitting on a bench at the first-class table. Those in the middle sit very back, their spines crooked into a bow, those beyond them on either side sit rather forward, and the two end girls are turned, each sideways, an elbow on the desk;

so that they form a semicircle. They are gossiping away in English, which is against the rules; but the teachers are also fatigued with the long and hot day, and do not pay attention. The studying for prizes had begun, and during that period the work was greatly augmented, both of pupils and teachers.

Look well at the three middle girls. We shall have little to do with the others, but a great deal with them. And they are noticeable besides, for two of them are beautiful, but so unlike in their beauty. The one is a very Hebe, with laughing blue eyes, brilliant complexion, and a shower of golden curls; and she is Mrs. Darling's youngest daughter, Rose. The other is Adeline de Castella, a name and face fit for a romance in history. She is graceful, charming, with dark-brown eyes and hair, and more exquisite features than were ever carved in marble. The third is Mary Carr, quiet and ladylike, whose good sense served to keep the wildness of Miss Rose Darling somewhat in check. For Rose was one of the wildest girls that had ever kept alive Madame de Nino's staid and most respectable school; wild, wilful, clever, careless; and vain as a peacock.

Had Rose been of a more sedate disposition, less given to random ways, Mrs. Darling might not have kept her at school so long, for Rose was eighteen. She was dreadfully rebellious over it, and perhaps the judiciousness of the measure, as a restriction, may be questioned. Mrs. Darling, by way of soothing the pill, allowed Rose to visit much; and when the girls came to this age Madame de Nino acquiesced in the parents' wishes, but Rose went out more than any previous pupil had ever been known to do. She had many friends sojourning in the town, and was courted on her own account, being excessively liked by every one.

Always in scrapes of one sort or another, or getting out of them, was she: and she had her own way in the school, and *would* have it.

One of Miss Rose Darling's propensities was to be continually falling in love. Almost every time she went out, she would favour the envious girls, on her return, with a description of some fresh cavalier who had laid siege to her heart; for half her pleasure in the thing lay in these boasts to her companions. The last idea of the kind had prevailed longer than usual. A gentleman, whom she had only seen at church or in their walks, was the new gallant. Rose did not know his name, but he was very handsome, and she raved of him. The school called him her *fiancé;* not in the least to Rose's displeasure. On this evening, as you look at them, Rose is in a state of semi-explosion, because one of the other girls, Miss Caroline Davis, who had been fetched out that evening by her friends, was now telling Rose that she had seen this gentleman as she was being conducted back to Madame de Nino's.

"That comes of my being kept at school. Mamma ought to be punished. You be quiet, Mary Carr! I shall talk against my mother if I like. Where did you see him, Carry Davis?"

"In the Grand' Rue. He was strolling up it. My aunt bowed to him."

"I know he was watching for me! These horrid Friday evenings! I wish the school could take scarlet fever, or something of that sort, and then perhaps Madame might send us out every day! Your aunt must know him. Davis, if she bowed: didn't you ask his name?"

"No, I forgot to ask it."

"What an idiot you are! If I don't learn it in a day or two I shall go mad. He——"

"Hush!" whispered Caroline Davis. "See how those French are listening! They'll go and tell Mademoiselle that we are speaking English. There's a new pupil come in to-night," she added aloud, in the best French she could call up.

"Not a pupil," dissented Adeline de Castella. "She used to be a pupil, but is coming now on a sort of visit to Madame, during her mother's absence in England. They have been travelling lately in Italy."

"Who is she?" asked Rose. "What's her name?"

"Eleanor Seymour. Her mother is the Honourable Mrs. Seymour; she was the daughter of Lord Loftus," continued Adeline, who spoke English perfectly, and understood our grades of rank as well as we do. "Eleanor Seymour is one of the nicest girls I know; but I suppose she will not be Eleanor Seymour very long, for she is engaged to Mr. Marlborough."

"Who's Mr. Marlborough?" asked Rose again.

"I don't know him," said Adeline. "He is very rich, I believe; he is staying at Belport."

"Le souper, mesdemoiselles," called out Mademoiselle Henriette, the head-teacher.

As Adeline de Castella said, Eleanor's mother was the

Honourable Mrs. Seymour and the daughter of Lord Loftus.
Being this, Mrs. Seymour held her head higher, and was
allowed to do it, than any one else in the Anglo-French
watering-place, and prided herself on her "blood." It sometimes happens that where this "blood" predominates, other
requisites are in scarcity; and it was so with Mrs. Seymour.
She was so poor that she hardly knew how to live: her
aristocratic relatives helped her out, and they had paid Eleanor's
heavy school bills, and so she got along somehow. Her
husband, Captain Seymour, dead this many a year ago, had
been of even higher connections than herself; also poor.
Lord Loftus had never forgiven his daughter for marrying the
portionless young officer; and to be even with her, erased her
name from his will. She was a tall, faded lady now, with a
hooked nose and supercilious grey eyes.

When Eleanor left school—as accomplished a young lady
as ever Madame de Nino's far-famed establishment turned out
—she went on a visit to her aristocratic relatives on both sides,
and then travelled to Italy and other places with her mother.
This spring they had returned, having been away two years,
and settled down in the old place. The tattlers said (and if
you want tattle in perfection, go to any of these idle continental
watering-places) that Eleanor would never get the opportunity
of changing away the name of Seymour: men of rank would
not be very likely to seek one situated as she was, and Mrs.
Seymour would never allow Eleanor to marry any other. The
battle was soon to come.

There came into Belport one day, on his road to Paris, a
good-looking young fellow named George Marlborough. Mrs.
Seymour was introduced to him at the house of a friend, and
though she bowed (figuratively) to his personal attractions, she
turned up her haughty nose afterwards when alone with Eleanor,
and spoke of him contemptuously. One of the rich commoners
of England, indeed! she slightingly said; she hated commoners, especially these rich ones, for they were apt to forget
the broad gulf that lay between them and the aristocracy.
The old Marlborough, Mr. George's father, had begun life as
a clerk or a servant—she could not tell which, neither did it
matter—and had plodded on, until he was the proprietor of an
extensive trade, and of great wealth. Iron works, or coal
works; or it might be cotton works; something down in the
North, she believed; and this George, the eldest son, had been

brought up to be an iron man too—if it was iron. She desired Eleanor to be very distant with him, if they met again : he had seemed inclined to talk to her.

Now poor Eleanor Seymour found this difficult to obey. Mr. George Marlborough remained in the town instead of going on to Paris, and was continually meeting Eleanor. She, poor girl, had not inherited her mother's exclusive notions ; labour as Mrs. Seymour would, she had never been able to beat them into her ; and Eleanor grew to like these meetings just as much as Mr. Marlborough did. It was the old tale—they fell in love with each other.

Mrs. Seymour, when the news was broken to her, lifted her haughty eyelids on George Marlborough, and expressed a belief that the world was coming to an end. It might not have been disclosed to her quite so soon, but. that she was about to depart for England on a lengthened visit to an elder sister, from whom she cherished expectations, during which absence Eleanor was to be the guest of Madame de Nino. Mr. Marlborough, who had never once been admitted within Mrs. Seymour's house, took the opportunity of asking for an interview one evening that he had walked from the pier in attendance on them, by Eleanor's side. With a slight gesture of surprise, a movement of her drooping eyelids, the lady led the way to the drawing-room, and Eleanor escaped upstairs.

She sat in her own room, listening. About ten minutes elapsed—it seemed to Eleanor as many hours—and then the drawing-room bell was rung. Not loud and fast, as though her mother were in anger, but quietly. The next moment she heard Mr. Marlborough's step, as he was shown out of the house. Was he rejected? Eleanor thought so.

The bell rang sharply now, and a summons came for Eleanor. She trembled from head to foot as she went down.

"Eleanor!" began her mother, in her sternest tone, "you knew of this application to me?"

Eleanor could not deny it. She burst into frightened, agitated tears.

"The disgrace of having encouraged the addresses of an iron man! It *is* iron: he made no scruple of avowing it. Indeed, you may well cry! Look at his people—all iron too : do you think they are fit to mate with ours? His father was nothing but a working man, and has made himself what he is by actual labour, and the son didn't blush when he said it to me! Besides

—I hope I may be forgiven for plotting and planning for you—
but I have always hoped that you would become the wife of
John Seymour."

"*His* wife," sobbed Eleanor. "Oh, mamma, John Seymour's
nobody."

"Nobody!" echoed the indignant lady. "Lord John Seymour nobody!"

"But I don't like him, mother."

"Ugh!" growled Mrs. Seymour. "Listen. I have not
accepted the proposals of this Mr. Marlborough; but I have
not rejected them. I must say he seems liberal enough and
rich enough; proposing I don't know what in the way of
settlements: but these low-born people are often lavish. So
now, if you have made up your mind to abandon your rank
and your order, and every good that makes life valuable, and
to enter a family who don't possess as much as a crest, you
must do so. Mr. Marlborough obligingly assured me your
happiness was centred in him."

Ah, what mattered the contempt of the tone, while that
sweet feeling of joy diffused itself through Eleanor's heart?

"No reply now," continued Mrs. Seymour, sternly. "The
decision lies with you; but I will not have you speak in haste.
Take the night to reflect on the advantages you enjoy in your
unblemished descent; reflect well before you take any step to
sully it. To-morrow you can announce your answer."

You need not ask what Eleanor's answer was. And so, when
she entered on her visit at Madame de Nino's, she was an
engaged girl; and the engagement was already known to the
world.

Miss Seymour requested that she might be treated entirely
as a pupil. She asked even to join the classes, laughingly
saying to Madame de Nino that it would rub up what she had
forgotten. She took her place in the schoolroom accordingly.
Rose Darling saw a pale girl, with dark hair and a sweet
countenance; and Rose criticized her mercilessly, as she did
every one. Another of the schoolgirls, named Emma Mowbray, a surly, envious girl, whom no one liked, made ill-natured
remarks on Eleanor. Miss Seymour certainly presented a
contrast to some of them, with her beautifully arranged hair,
her flowing muslin dress, and her delicate hands. Schoolgirls, as a whole, are careless of their appearance *in* school;
and, as a rule, they have red hands. Madame de Nino's pupils

were no exception. Rose was vain, and therefore always well-dressed; Adeline de Castella was always well-dressed; but Emma Mowbray and others were not. Emma's hands, too, were red and coarse, and more so than even those of the careless schoolgirls. Adeline's were naturally beautiful; and Rose took so much care of hers, wearing gloves in bed in winter, with some mysterious pomade inside.

Rose made little acquaintance with Eleanor that day. She, Rose, went out to tea in the afternoon, and came back very cross: for she had not once set eyes on her *fiancé*. The story was told to Eleanor Seymour; who sympathized with her of course, having a lover of her own.

The next day was Sunday. The French girls were conducted at ten o'clock to mass; the English would leave the house as usual for church a quarter before eleven. Rose was dressed and waiting long before; her impatience on Sunday mornings was great. Rose was in mourning, and a source of secret chagrin that fact was, for she liked gay clothes better than sombre ones.

"And so would you be worrying if you had some one waiting for you at the church as I have," retorted Rose, in answer to a remark on her restless impatience, which had been proffered to Miss Seymour by Emma Mowbray.

"Waiting for you?" returned Eleanor, looking at Rose, but not understanding.

"She means her lover, Miss Seymour," said Emma Mowbray.

"Yes, I do; and I don't care if I avow it," cried Rose, her face glowing. "I know he loves me. He never takes his eyes off me in church, and every glance speaks of love."

"He looks up at the other schools as much as he looks at ours," said Emma Mowbray, who could rarely speak without a sneer. "Besides, he only returns the glances you give him: love or no love, he would be a sorry gallant not to do that."

"Last Thursday," cried Rose, unmindful of the reproof, "he smiled and took off his hat to me as the school passed him in the street."

"But little Annette Duval said she saw you nod to him first!" said Charlotte Singleton, the archdeacon's daughter.

"Annette Duval's a miserable little story-teller. I'll box her ears when she comes in from mass. The fact is, Miss Seymour," added Rose, turning to the stranger who had come amidst them, "the girls here are all jealous of me, and Emma

Mowbray doubly jealous. He is one of the divinest fellows that ever walked upon the earth. You should see his eyes and his auburn hair."

" With a tinge of red in it," put in Emma Mowbray.

" Well, you must point him out to me," said Eleanor, and then hastened to change the conversation, for she had an instinctive dread of any sort of quarrelling, and disliked ill-nature. Emma Mowbray had not favourably impressed her: Rose had, in spite of her vanity and her random avowals. " You are in mourning, Miss Darling ? "

" Yes, for my eldest sister's husband, Mr. Carleton St. John. But I have a new white bonnet, you see, though he has not been dead many weeks : and I don't care whether mamma finds it out or not. I told the milliner she need not specify in the bill whether the bonnet was white or black. Oh dear ! where *is* Mademoiselle Clarisse ? "

Mademoiselle Clarisse, the teacher who took them to church (and who took also a book hidden under her own arm to read surreptitiously during the sermon, not a word of which dis-course could her French ears understand) came at last. As the school took its seats in the gallery of the church, the few who were in Rose's secret looked down with interest, for the gentleman in question was then coming up the middle aisle, accompanied by a lady and a little girl.

" There he is ! " whispered Rose to Eleanor, next to whom she sat, and her voice was as one glow of exultation, and her cheeks flushed crimson. " Going into the pew below. There : he is handing in the little girl. Do you see ? "

" Yes," replied Eleanor. " What of him ? "

" It is he. He whom the girls tease me about, my *fiancé*, as they call him, I trust my future husband. That he loves me, I am positive."

Eleanor answered nothing. Her face was as red as Rose's just then ; but Rose was too much occupied with something else to notice it. The gentleman—who was really a handsome young man—was looking up at the gallery, and a bright smile of recognition, meant for one of them, shone on his face. Rose naturally took it to herself.

" Did you see that ? *did* you see that ? " she whispered right and left. " Emma Mowbray, who took first notice now ? "

The service began. At its conclusion Rose pushed uncere-moniously out of the pew, and the rest followed her, in spite

of precedent, for the schools waited until last; and in spite of
Mademoiselle Clarisse. But, on the previous Sunday, Rose
had been too late to see him: he had left the church. On
this, as the event proved, she was too early, for he had not
come out; and Mademoiselle Clarisse, who was in a terrible
humour with them for their rudeness, marched them home at
a quick pace.

"If ever truth and faith were in man, I know they are in
him!" raved Rose, when they got home, and were in the
dressing-room. "He'll make the best husband in the world."

"You have not got him yet," cried Emma Mowbray.

"Bah! Did you see the look and smile he gave me? Did
you see it, Miss Seymour?—and I don't suppose you are pre-
judiced against me as these others are. There was true love
in that smile, if ever I saw love. That ugly Mademoiselle
Clarisse, to have dragged us on so! I wish she had been
taken with apoplexy on the steps! He—— Where's Miss
Seymour gone to?" broke off Rose, for Eleanor had quitted
the dressing-room without taking off her things.

"I heard her say she was invited to dine at Mrs. Marlborough's," answered Mary Carr.

"I say! there's the dinner-bell. Make haste, all of you!
I wonder they don't ring it before we get home!"

That afternoon Madame de Nino conducted the girls to
church herself. A truly good Catholic, as she was, she was no
bigot, and now and then sat in the English church. The
young ladies did not thank her. They were obliged to be on
church-behaviour then: there could be no inattention with
her; no staring about, however divine might be the male part
of the congregation; no rushing out early or stopping late,
according to their own pleasure. Rose's lover was not there,
and Rose fidgeted on her seat; but just as the service began,
the lady and little girl they had noticed in the morning came
up the aisle, and he followed by the side of Eleanor Seymour.
The girls did not dare to bend forward to look at Rose,
Madame being there. The tip of her pretty nose, all that
could be seen of her, was very pale.

"The forward creature! the deceitful good-for-nothing!"
broke from Rose Darling's lips when they got home. "You
girls have called me bold, but look at that brazen Eleanor
Seymour! She never saw him until this morning: I pointed
him out to her in church for the first time; and she must go

and make acquaintance with him in this barefaced manner!
As sure as she lives, I'll expose her to Madame de Nino! A
girl like that would contaminate the school! If our friends
knew we were exposed to her companionship, they'd remove——"

Rose's passionate words were cut short by the entrance of
Madame herself, who came in to give some instructions to the
teachers, for she was going out for the evening. Rose, too
angry to weigh her words or their possible consequences, went
up to Madame, and said something in a fast, confused tone.
Madame de Nino, a portly, dark-eyed, kind woman, concluded
her directions, and then turned to Rose, who was a favoured
pupil.

"What do you say, Mademoiselle Rose? Did I see the
gentleman who was at church with Miss Seymour? Yes; a
very prepossessing young man. I spoke with him to-day when
they came for her."

A moment's puzzled wonder, and then a frightful thought
took hold of Rose.

"Do you know him, Madame?" she gasped. "Who is he?"

"Young Mr. Marlborough. Mademoiselle Eleanor is betrothed to him."

Madame left the room. And the girls sat breathless with
astonishment, scarcely daring to steal a glance at Rose Darling's
white and stony features.

The weeks went on to the sultry days of August, and most
of the girls were studying away might and main for the prizes.
A day-pupil had temporarily entered the school, Anna Marlborough, the youngest of the Marlborough family, and the
only one who had come abroad with her mother. It was not
Madame de Nino's habit to admit day-pupils, but she had
made an exception in favour of this child, who was to be in
the town but a few weeks.

Will it be credited that Rose Darling was still pursuing her
preposterous flirtation with George Marlborough, in the face
of the discovery that he was engaged to Eleanor Seymour?
But there was something to be urged in her favour, though you
are no doubt surprised to hear me say it. Had a jury been
trying Rose, they might have returned a verdict, "Guilty, with
extenuating circumstances." Rose seemed bewitched. There
is no doubt that a real, an ardent passion for George Marlborough had arisen in her heart, filling its every crevice; and

she regarded Eleanor (she could not help it) with a fierce, jealous rivalry. But the girl, with all her random folly, was no fool; and but for certain events that arose, might have remained as quiescent as she could, until her ill-starred love died out.

It did not, and could not, contribute to any good resolutions she might have had strength and sense to form, to find herself on intimate terms with Mr. Marlborough, a frequent visitor to his house. *That* mistake was, in the first instance, Eleanor Seymour's. Eleanor had been commissioned by Mrs. Marlborough to invite three or four of the young ladies to accompany her there to dinner; something was said in the school about her not *daring* to ask Rose; and Eleanor invited Rose forthwith. Rose went. It had been more prudent had she stayed at home: but Rose was not one of the prudent sort: and the temptation was irresistible. Mrs. Marlborough was charmed with her, and so was George. Whether the gentleman detected Rose's feelings for himself, and was flattered, or whether he had no objection to a flirtation with a pretty girl, although engaged to another, certain it was he paid Rose considerable attention, and laughed and joked with her much.

Joked with her. It was all done on his part in the spirit of joking, as Eleanor Seymour might have seen; but joking sometimes leads to something more. Messages from one to the other, begun in folly, often passed; and Anna Marlborough, a giddy girl of twelve, was the go-between. Just upon this, Rose's brother, Captain Darling, came to Belport; he soon struck up a friendship with Mr. Marlborough, and here was another link in Rose's chain. She would meet the two young men in the street, and leave the ranks, in defiance of rules, ostensibly to shake hands with Frank, really to talk nonsense with Mr. Marlborough. Even Eleanor Seymour, when out with the school, would conform to its rules and only bow and smile as he passed. Not so Rose. The girls would have gone the length of the street, two sometimes, before she caught them up, panting and flushed and looking radiant, and boasting of what George had said to her. It was of no use the teachers remonstrating and forbidding; do it she would, and do it she did.

This was what may be called the open, harmless stage of the affair. But it was to go on to another.

There was a large party given one night at a Scotch laird's,

Sir Sandy Maxwell, and Miss Seymour and Rose were invited.
You may be aware, perhaps, that it is the custom in French
schools, generally speaking, for the pupils to visit or not,
according to the directions left by the parents. This had been
accorded to Rose by Mrs. Darling; and Eleanor Seymour was
not as a schoolgirl—therefore Madame de Nino, though openly
expressing her disapprobation of these large parties while young
ladies were pursuing their studies, did not refuse. Emma Mowbray offered a bet to the school that Mr. Marlborough would
dance more dances with Rose than with Eleanor; and so eager
were the girls to hear the result, that those in the large *dortoir*
kept awake until they came home. It had struck one o'clock,
and Madame was up in arms; she had only given them to
half-past eleven, and they had kept the coach waiting all that
time, while Madame's own maid, old Félicité, was inside it. After
all, there was nothing to hear, for Mr. Marlborough had not
made his appearance at the party.

Class was not over the next morning until very late; it always
was late just before giving the prizes. It was the third Thursday in August, the *sorts* day, and three of the girls were going
with Eleanor to dine at Mrs. Marlborough's: Rose, Mary Carr,
and Adeline de Castella. The invitations were left to Miss
Seymour, and she always fixed on Rose, in a sort of bravado,
but she never once chose Emma Mowbray; and this gave that
young lady considerable offence, as was known to the school.
They were to partake of the usual dinner at school by way of
luncheon, the Marlboroughs not dining until six. While the
cloth was being laid, the girls dispersed about, some in the
courtyard, some in the garden, all in the shade, for it was very
sultry. There was certainly something more than common the
matter with Rose: she appeared half-crazy with joy.

"It is because she's going out," remarked Mary Carr to
Eleanor.

"Is it, though!" put in Emma Mowbray; "that's only a
little item in the cause. She has just had a love-letter from
Mr. Marlborough."

Eleanor Seymour's cheek changed.

"Don't talk absurdities," said Mary Carr to the Mowbray
girl.

"Absurdities!" she retorted, moving away. "If I can, I'll
convince you."

A minute or two, and she came back with a letter in her

hand—an open letter, addressed in George Marlborough's hand to Rose—and handed it to Mary Carr.

"Am I to read it?" asked the latter.

"If you choose. It is *pro bono publico*, Rose says." And Miss Carr read the letter aloud.

"MY DEAREST,

"You must have been surprised not to see me at Sir Sandy's. I was dressing to come, when a message arrived for me from the Hôtel du Nord; poor Priestley had met with a sad accident to his hand from the bursting of a gun. I have been sitting up with him until now, four o'clock a.m., but I write this to you before I sleep, for you have a right now to my every thought, to know every movement. You dine here to-day, my fair *fiancée* also; but I wish you were coming alone.

"Ever yours only,
"GEORGE MARLBOROUGH."

Was there any mistake in the letter? Mary Carr had often heard of such. *Could* it have been written to Rose? Alas, yes! it was all too plain. The writing was George Marlborough's; the address, "Miss Rose Darling, En Ville," was his; and the seal, "G. M.," was his also. Mary rose, and stood before Eleanor, shielding her from observation, as she beckoned to Anna Marlborough : while Emma Mowbray looked defiant, and asked whether they would believe her next time.

The child was dancing about the courtyard. She was young, and the school made her a sort of plaything : she came dancing up to Miss Carr.

"Now, Anna, I have something to ask you; and if you equivocate by so much as a word, I will acquaint Madame de Nino that there's a letter-carrier in the school; you would be expelled that same hour. Did you bring a note here from your brother this morning?"

"Yes, I did," stammered Anna. "Don't tell of me, please."

"I'll not tell, if you speak the truth. To whom did you bring it?"

"To Miss Darling."

"Did he send it to *her?* What did he say when he gave it to you?"

"He told me to give it into her own hands when nobody

was by, and to give his love with it," answered Anna. "Oh, pray don't tell of me, Miss Carr! It's nothing much more than usual; he often sends his love by me to Miss Darling."

"Was *this* the letter you brought?" holding out the one she still retained in her hand.

"Yes, it was that. I'll never do it again," continued Anna, growing frightened, and bursting into tears.

Which caused Miss Mowbray to rate her for a "little fool;" and Anna ran away, glad to be released. Close upon that, up dashed Rose in agitation, having discovered the loss of her note. The note had *not* been declared by Rose to be *pro bono publico*, and Emma Mowbray had dishonourably abstracted it from her apron pocket. Rose got possession of it again, but she was in a great passion with Emma Mowbray: in fact, with them all.

And poor Eleanor Seymour! She was white as marble when Mary turned to her. Sitting there, on the old wooden bench, so outwardly calm and still, she had heard the whole. Clasping Mary Carr's hands with a painful pressure, she burst into an uncontrollable fit of weeping, and glided in at the porch-door to gain the staircase. "Make any excuse for me at the dinner-table, Mary," she whispered.

Need you be told that that letter was really written to Eleanor? The words "fair *fiancée*" in it alone related to Rose, and Mr. Marlborough had penned them in laughing allusion to the joke in the school. The plot was Emma Mowbray's, a little bit of revenge on Eleanor and Rose, both of whom she envied and disliked. She had made Anna her tool. The child, at her prompting, wrote a letter to Rose, and got her brother to direct and seal it; and Emma Mowbray opened the two envelopes cleverly by means of passing a penknife under the seals, and substituted the one note for the other. Thus Eleanor's letter was conveyed to Rose; the other Emma Mowbray burnt; and she promised a whole *charrette* full of good things to Anna to keep her counsel. Being a mischief-loving little damsel, Miss Anna did so; though she was nearly frightened out of it by Miss Carr.

This may sound very shallow, very weak, but I assure you the circumstances took place just as they are described. Had George Marlborough only put Eleanor's *name* in the note, the trick could not have been played. But he did not do so. And neither Rose nor Eleanor suspected for a moment that there

was anything about the note not genuine; or that it had not
been written to Rose.

They went to dinner at Mrs. Marlborough's—Eleanor with
her beating heart of resentment and her outraged love, Rose
radiant with happiness and beauty. The evening did not mend
matters, but rather added very much to the broil. May the
word be forgiven?—I was thinking of the French one. Eleanor,
cold, haughty, contemptuous, was almost insulting to Mr.
Marlborough; and Rose, it is to be feared, let him see, that
evening, where her best love was given. He took more than
one opportunity of asking Eleanor how he had offended her,
but he could get no answer. If she had only given him a clue
to it, how much trouble and misery would have been saved!
but the very *asking* on his part seemed to Eleanor only adding
insult to injury. You see they were all at cross-purposes, and
just for the want of a little word of explanation.

From that hour there was no peace, no mutual understanding
between Eleanor and Mr. Marlborough. He repeatedly sought
an explanation of the sudden change in her behaviour, sometimes by letter, sometimes in words. She never would give an
answer to either. She returned his letters in blank envelopes,
or tore them to pieces before the messenger's eyes; she refused
to see him if he called; she haughtily held aloof from him when
they met. Mrs. Marlborough saw that something was wrong,
but as neither of them made her their confidant, she did not
interfere, and she supposed it to be only a lovers' quarrel. She
had not known Eleanor long, having come to Belport only the
week before that Sunday Rose first saw her at church. Rose
alone seemed in a state of happiness, of ecstatic delight; and
Anna now carried no end of notes and messages to and fro,
and kept it secret from the school. Rose had committed one
great folly—she had written to Mr. Marlborough after the
receipt of that first letter. But then, it must be always
remembered that no suspicion had yet crossed her mind that
it was not *written to her* and meant for her. Rose fully
believed—let it be her excuse—that Mr. Marlborough had
transferred his affections from Eleanor to herself: the school
believed it. Whether she really hoped she should succeed in
supplanting Eleanor in the offer of marriage, in becoming
afterwards his wife, cannot be told. The girls thought she did,
and they were sharp observers. At any rate, Rose now deemed
the field as legitimately open to her, as it was to Eleanor.

The day for awarding the prizes was a great day. The girls were attired in white, with blue sashes and blue neck-ribbons; and the hairdresser arrived very early in the morning to get done in time. A large company arrived by invitation; and just before the hour for going in, some of the girls saw Rose in the garden talking to a gentleman. Madéleine de Gassicourt, usually so short-sighted, espied her out.

"It must be her brodare wid her," cried Madéleine, who was not in the secret. "She will derange her hair before we do go in."

Emma Mowbray peered through the trees. It was no "brodare," but Mr. Marlborough. He was bending down to Rose; she appeared to be crying, and he held her hand in his as he talked to her earnestly. Emma Mowbray glanced round at Eleanor, who was at the window, and saw it all. She was very pale and still, her lips compressed.

But Rose's stolen interview could have lasted only a few fleeting minutes. The hands of the clock were then pointing towards two, and as the hour struck she was amongst them, and they were being marshalled for the entrance to the prize-room. It was a pleasing sight when they went in, making their reverences to the assembled visitors. Two pretty young English girls walked first—sisters; and certainly the two prettiest of the elders walked last; Rose Darling and Adeline de Castella; both beautiful, but so unlike in their beauty. Adeline gained nine prizes; Rose only two. But Rose had been studying for another sort of prize.

The holidays succeeded—dull and quiet. Of the elder girls, Adeline, Rose, and Mary Carr alone remained, and there was, of course, Miss Seymour. Mrs. Marlborough was leaving the town; George was not. Eleanor, who seemed to be visibly declining, would not go out anywhere, so she did not meet him; but Rose, always out, met him constantly.

One afternoon, when Eleanor was growing paler day by day, a bit of folded paper was brought to her in the schoolroom. She opened it, and saw a few words in pencil—

"I am now waiting in the salon. You have been denied to me as usual; yet, Eleanor, let me entreat you to grant me, for this once, an interview. I leave by the boat for London to-night, but if I can see you now, my voyage may not be necessary. By the love we once bore each other, I beseech you, Eleanor, come.—G. M."

Eleanor read it, tore the paper deliberately in two, and handed the pieces to Clotilde. "Give that to the gentleman," she haughtily said. "There is no other answer."

Rose·followed the maid from the room. "Clotilde," she whispered, "who is in the salon?"

"The handsome monsieur that was going to marry himself, as people said, with Mademoiselle Seymour," was the servant's rejoinder.

"Give me the answer," said Rose, taking the torn pieces from her hand. "I want to send a message to Madame, his mother, and will deliver this. I say, Clotilde, don't tell Madame that he's here."

The unsuspicious servant went about her business; and Miss Rose tripped to the salon, and stayed as long as she dared.

That same evening Eleanor Seymour was giving Mary Carr a description of Rome; they were seated in a corner of the small class-room; and Adeline de Castella corrected her when she was wrong, for *she* knew Rome well. Mademoiselle Joséphine (Mam'selle Fifine, the school called her in general), the only teacher remaining, was at her table in front of the window, writing letters. When it grew too dark to see, she closed her desk, turned round, and suddenly, as if surprised not to see her with the others, asked where Rose was.

The young ladies did not know. Rose had been upstairs in the bedroom since the afternoon. She came down for collation, and went up again directly.

Mam'selle Fifine began to scold; she was the crossest of all the teachers, except Mam'selle Clarisse. It was not likely Miss Rose was stopping upstairs in the dark; she must have got a light, which, as Mesdemoiselles knew well, was contrary to rules. And she told Miss Carr to go and desire her to come down.

Mary Carr rose with a yawn; they had been sitting there long, and she felt cramped. "Who will go with me?" she asked.

Both the young ladies responded, and all three stumbled up the dark staircase together. They found no light in the bedrooms, and could see nothing of Rose. Thinking it possible she might have fallen asleep on one of the beds, Adeline ran down and got a candle from one of the servants.

There was no Rose; but on her bed lay a sealed note, addressed to Miss Carr:—

"DEAR MARY,

"I know you have been against me for some time. Miss Seymour and I were rivals—equals on a fair ground; you would have helped *her* on, though it left me to a broken heart. I believe it has been a neck-and-neck race between us, but I have won. I hope mamma will reconcile herself to the step I am taking; I always longed to make a runaway marriage, it is so romantic; and if Frank flies out about it, I shan't care, for I shan't hear him. When next you see me I shall be

"ROSE MARLBOROUGH."

"Look to Miss Seymour!" broke from the quivering lips of Adeline de Castella. And it was timely spoken, for Eleanor was fainting. Scarcely had she revived, when Mam'selle Fifine came up, angry at the delay.

The note they did not dare to show; but were obliged to confess to the absence of Rose, saying, *tout bonnement*, as Adeline called it, that they could not find her.

Rose not to be found! Madame de Nino was dining out, and Mam'selle Fifine was terrified out of her sober senses. In the midst of the hubbub that ensued, Julie, the head fille-de-chambre, put her head in at the door, and said, "The Honourable Mrs. Seymour."

At a time of less commotion they would have burst out laughing. Julie had been nurse in a nobleman's family in England; she had there become familiar with British titles, and was as fond of using them as she was of using her English. One day Ethel Daw's mother came to see her; a very fine lady, all flounces, and feathers, and gold chains. It was Julie's luck to show her to the salon; and she came to the schoolroom afterwards, flung open the door, and called out, "Mrs. Daw, Esquire." Julie did not hear the last of that. The girls called her ever after Squire Daw.

"The Honourable Mrs. Seymour."

With a sharp cry Eleanor started up, and flew into her mother's arms, sobbing convulsively.

"Oh, mamma, take me home! take me home!"

Mrs. Seymour was thunderstruck, not only at Eleanor's cry of pain, but at the change in her appearance. She had just returned from London. Mary Carr disclosed a little of the truth. She thought it best; and, indeed, was unable to evade the keen questioning of Mrs. Seymour. But Rose's note, with the information it contained, was buried in silence still. Mrs. Seymour took her daughter home at once; and there Eleanor told the whole—that Rose had really gone away with Mr. Marlborough. Mrs. Seymour folded her aristocratic hands, and distinctly desired that no further allusion to it should ever pass her daughter's lips, as it would not her own. It was a retribution on them, she said, for having trusted an "iron man."

Meanwhile, Adeline de Castella and Mary Carr kept their own counsel through sheer obligation: as they had not declared all they knew at once, they dared not declare it now. And Madame de Nino verily believed Rose had been spirited away to the skies.

It was three days afterwards. Mrs. Seymour sat in her drawing-room, the green Venetian shutters partially closed, and the blinds down, for Eleanor lay on the sofa quite prostrated. Mrs. Seymour was in a state of as much indignation as was consistent with her high birth and her proclaimed assertion that they were "well rid of him;" for, in spite of the "iron" drawback, she had grown to hug to her heart the prospect of this most desirable establishment for Eleanor.

Suddenly the door opened, and the iron man himself walked in. Eleanor struggled up from the sofa, and Mrs. Seymour rose in hauteur, all the blood of the Loftuses flashing from her light grey eyes. Then ensued a contest; each side struggling for the mastership; Mrs. Seymour refusing to hold commune with him, and Mr. Marlborough insisting upon being heard.

He had gone to England three days ago in search of her, he said; he then found she had left for France, and he had followed her. His object was to request that she would lay her commands on Eleanor to afford him an explanation. Eleanor had been his promised wife; and without offence on his part, without any known cause, her behaviour had suddenly changed to him. In vain he had sought an explanation of her; she would afford him none; and his only resource was to appeal to Mrs. Seymour. If Eleanor refused to fulfil her engagement with him, he could not insist upon it; but he must insist upon knowing the reason for the change: to that he had a right.

"You had better leave the room quietly, sir," said Mrs. Seymour in frigid tones. "It will not be pleasant to you if I call my servants."

"I will not leave it without an explanation," he replied. "Mrs. Seymour, you cannot refuse it; if Eleanor will not give it me in courtesy, I repeat that I must demand it as a right. Eleanor's conduct at the time seemed to imply that there was some cause of complaint against me. What was it? I declare to you solemnly that I was unconscious of it; that I was innocent of offence against her."

His words and manner were painfully earnest and truthful, and Mrs. Seymour hesitated.

"Has there been any mistake, Eleanor?" she hesitated, appealing to her daughter.

"Oh, let me know what it is," he implored, before Eleanor could speak. "Whatever it may be—mistake—cause—reality —let me know it."

"Well, sir," cried Mrs. Seymour, making a sudden resolution, "I will first ask you what you have done with that unfortunate young lady, whom you took away from her sheltering roof and her duties, three days ago?"

"I took no young lady away," replied Mr. Marlborough.

"What have you done with Miss Darling?"

"Not anything."

"You did not induce her to elope with you? You did not take her to London?"

"Indeed, no. I saw Miss Darling on the port the evening I went away, and left her there. She was with her brother. But this is no explanation, Mrs. Seymour. Eleanor," he added, walking up, and standing before her, "I once again appeal to you. What was the cause of your first and sudden coldness?"

"Speak out, Eleanor," said her mother. "I know almost as little as Mr. Marlborough, but I now think the matter should be cleared up, that we may come at the truth. There must be a strange mystery somewhere."

Eleanor pressed her thin hands upon her side in agitation. She could only speak in a whisper, in uneven sentences: and she told of the love-letter written to Rose the day following the dance at Sir Sandy Maxwell's.

"It was written to you, Eleanor," said Mr. Marlborough.

"I read that note," she answered, gasping for breath. "It was written to Rose."

"It was written to you, Eleanor. I have never written a loving note, as that was, to Rose Darling in my life; on my sacred word of honour."

"You have written several notes to Rose!"

"True; since; but never loving ones: they might all have been posted up on the schoolroom walls, and even Madame de Nino herself could not have found fault with them. If this note was given to Rose, Anna must have changed the envelopes. I remember directing one for her to Miss Darling that morning. Eleanor," he gravely said, "I fear you have been running your head against a chimera."

"Rose loves you," she whispered, her heart and voice alike softening.

"No; nonsense!"—but for all his denial there was a glow of consciousness on Mr. Marlborough's countenance. "Eleanor, I honestly believe that you have been listening to the folly talked by those schoolgirls, and taken it for gospel. Rose Darling is very pretty, and likes to be admired; and if I have been thrown a good deal with her, who threw me? You, Eleanor, by your coldness and avoidance of me. I don't deny that I have talked lightly and gaily with Rose, never seriously; I don't deny that——" I have kissed her, he was going to add in his candour, but thought it might be as well to leave that out before Mrs. Seymour. "But my love and my allegiance have never swerved from *you*, Eleanor."

She burst into happy tears. Mrs. Seymour cut them short sternly.

"Eleanor, this note that you talk of, left by Miss Darling on her bed the other night, must have been meant as a hoax upon you and the two credulous young ladies, your companions. I did think it a most strange thing that a young lady of position should be guilty of anything so vulgar as an elopement. Not but that it was excessively bad to make it the subject even of a jest."

"I suppose it must have been," sobbed Eleanor. "And it seemed so earnest!"

Mr. Marlborough could have disclosed *how* earnest, had he chosen. In that interview in the salon with Rose, when he told her he was going away, he learnt how much she loved him. In the anguish of parting, Rose dropped words that sufficiently enlightened him—if he had not been enlightened before. He passed it all off as a jest; he said something to the effect that he had better take her with him to Gretna, all in jest, in simple folly: and he spoke in this light manner for Rose's sake: he would not suffer her to think she had betrayed her secret. What, then, was his astonishment when, in coming out of the permit office at night on the port, preparatory to stepping on board the boat, to see Rose! *She had taken his words seriously.* What he would have done to save the boat in his dilemma—for he must inevitably have lost it while he escorted Rose back to Madame de Nino's—he did not know; but at that moment who should come up but Captain Darling. He gave the young lady into her brother's charge, with a half-word of explanation; and he never supposed but that Rose had been safely lodged at school within the hour. But Mr. Marlborough was a man who could keep his counsel on these particulars, even to Eleanor, and he did keep it.

"Let this be a warning to your wedded life, Eleanor," observed Mrs. Seymour. "Never have any concealments from your husband. Had you frankly spoken to Mr. Marlborough of that first misdirected letter, which seems to have been the primary cause of all the mischief, the affair would have been cleared up at once."

"It's enough to make a man swear he will never use another envelope," exclaimed Mr. Marlborough, with his old happy smile of love. "But you need not have doubted me, Eleanor."

Meanwhile, where *was* Rose? Madame de Nino, in the eleventh stage of desperation and perplexity, sent ten times a day to Captain Darling's lodgings; but he had disappeared also. Mam'selle Fifine, who of course came in for the blame, alternately sobbed and scolded aloud; and Adeline and Mary Carr felt sick with the weight of the secret they were keeping. This state of things, stormy within doors as the weather was without, lasted for three days, and then Rose returned, escorted by her brother.

But what a shocking plight she was in! Drenched with rain and sea-water; clothes soaked and clinging round her; quite prostrated with three days' sea-sickness; lying half-dead all that time in a rolling fishing-smack, the wind blowing great guns and she nearly dead with fright; nothing to eat and drink on board but salt herrings and sour beer, even supposing she could have eaten at all!—no wonder Rose forgot her good manners and told her brother he was a brute for taking her. Rose had happened to put on her best things, too: a white chip bonnet and pearl-grey damask dress. You should have seen them when she came in!

So it was quite a mistake, Miss Carr and Adeline found, a

trick, no doubt, played them purposely by Rose, and there had been no elopement at all, or thought of one : nothing but a three-days' cruise round the coast with her brother, in the fishing-smack of some honest, rough, hard-working sailors ! Captain Darling made a thousand apologies to Madame de Nino when he brought her home—the object that Rose presented upon his handing her out of the coach !—and laid it all to the fault of that treacherous wind ; which had kept them at sea three days, when he had only contemplated treating her to a little excursion of an hour for the good of her health.

Madame was appeased at length. But Mam'selle Fifine is sore upon the point to this day. As she justly observed, there must have been something out of the common amiss with that particular fishing-boat. Granted the rough wind ; but other boats made the port fast enough, so why not that one? Rose could or would give no explanation, and was as sullen as a bear for a whole month.

And ere that month had well run its course, news came down from Paris of the marriage of George Marlborough and Miss Seymour.

CHAPTER XI.

GEORGINA BEAUCLERC'S LOVE.

WE must go to Castle Wafer. Isaac St. John has his writing-table drawn to the open window this mellow September day, and sits at it. But he is not writing now. He leans back in his padded chair, and the lines of thought—of care—lie on his otherwise serene face. Care for Isaac St. John the recluse? Verily, yes ; even for him. If we could live lives of utter isolation from our species, we might escape it ; otherwise, never.

Looking at him now, his back buried in the soft chair, his face, so pleasant to the eye, turned rather upwards, and his thin white hands resting listlessly, one on the elbow of the chair, one down on his knee, a stranger would have failed to detect anything amiss with the person of Isaac St. John, or that it was not like other men's. For the first forty years of Isaac St. John's existence, his days had been as one long, ever-present mortification; that disfiguring hump and his sensitiveness doing battle together. Why it should be so, I know not, but it is an indisputable fact, that where any defect of person exists, any deformity—two of the qualities pertaining to our nature exist in the mind in a supereminent degree, sensitiveness and vanity, perhaps for the good of the soul, certainly to the marring of its peace. It has been so since the world began; it will be so to its ending. Isaac St. John was no exception. There never can be an exception; for this seems to be a law of nature. Remember the club-foot of Byron, and what it did for him. This shrinking sensitiveness, far more than his health, had converted Mr. St. John into a hermit. It was terrible to him to go forth unto the gaze of his fellow-men, for—he carried his deformity with him. Now that he was advancing in years, growing onwards to be an old man, the feeling was wearing off; the keen edge of the razor which had cut all ways was becoming somewhat blunt: but it must ever remain with him in a greater or lesser degree.

He was not thinking of it now. It was when he was in the presence of others, or when making up his mind to go into their presence, that the defect was so painfully present to him. As he sat there, his brow knit with its lines, two things were troubling him: the one was a real, tangible care, the other was only a perplexity.

His own mother had lived to bring him up; and how she had cherished and loved her unfortunate son, the only heir to the broad lands of the St. Johns, that son's heart ached even now to think of. At the time she died, he wished he could die also; his happiest thoughts now were spent in her remembrance; his most comforting moments those when he lost himself in the anticipation of the meeting that awaited them hereafter. He was a grown-up man, getting old it almost seemed to his lonely heart, when the little half-brother was born, the only issue of his father's second marriage. How Isaac St. John took to this little baby, loved it, fondled it, played with it, he might have been half ashamed to tell in words. The boy had been his; as his own; since the death of their father, he had been his sole care; and now that boy, grown to manhood, was going the way of the world and bringing trouble into his home. No very great and irremediable trouble yet: but enough to pain and worry the sensitive heart that so loved him.

As if to compensate for the malformation of the one brother, the other was gifted with almost surpassing beauty. The good looks of Frederick St. John had become a proverb in the gay world. But these favoured sons of men are beset by temptations in an unusual degree, and perhaps they may not be much the better for the beauty in the long-run. Had Frederick St. John been less high-principled by nature; or been less carefully and *prayerfully* trained by his brother Isaac, things might have been a great deal worse with him than they were. He had not parted with honour, but he *had* parted with money; a handsome patrimony which he had succeeded to when he became of age, was mortgaged thick and threefold, and Mr. Frederick was deep in debt and embarrassment.

Mr. St. John glanced towards some letters lying on his table. The letters had brought the trouble to him. It would seem as if Frederick's affairs had in some way come to a sudden crisis, for these letters, three of them, had all arrived in the course of the past week. They were ugly letters from ugly creditors asking *him* to pay them; and until their reception Mr. St. John had not possessed any knowledge of the state of affairs. He had believed Frederick to be in the habit of getting rid of a great deal more money than he had need to do; but he had not glanced at debt, or embarrassment. It had so completely upset him—a little thing did that in his delicate health—that for a day and a night he was incapable of action; he could only nurse his pain. Then he sent answers to the parties, saying that the matters should be examined into; and he wrote to Frederick, who was in London, to come to him without delay. He was waiting for him; the senses of his ears were opened now, listening for his footsteps: he was growing anxious and weary, for Frederick might have responded to the call on the past day.

That was the trouble. The other care mentioned, the perplexity, regarded his little cousin at Alnwick. He had promised George Carleton St. John (as you may remember) to take means of ascertaining whether Benja was well done by, happy, and cared for by his step-mother; but now that it came to action, Isaac St. John did not quite see how he was to set about it. Something he must do; for the promise lay on his conscience: and he was, of all men, the most conscientious. Mr. Carleton St. John had died in May; it was now September; and Isaac knew little or nothing of the affairs at

Alnwick. He had corresponded a little with Mrs. Carleton
St. John in the intervals of his own illness—for he had been
seriously ill twice this summer; at the time of the death, and
for some time after it, and again in July—and he had addressed
two letters to Benja, simple letters fit for a child, and desired
that that young gentleman would answer him by deputy. Somebody had scrawled these answers, probably the nurse, or guided
Benja's fingers to do it. "He was very well, and Brave was
very well, and he thanked his gardian, Mr. Saint John, for
writeing to him, and he hopped he was very well, and he sent
his love." This did not tell Mr. St. John much: and the involuntary thought crossed him that had Benja been her own
child Mrs. St. John might herself have helped him with the
answers.

He had therefore been making up his mind to go over to
Alnwick, much as he disliked to show himself amidst strangers.
But for this news concerning Frederick which had so troubled
him, and the expected arrival of his brother, he would have
been already away; but now he had put it off for a day or two.
This was Tuesday; and he thought, if all went well, and
Frederick came to-day, he should go on Thursday. It was
not the loss of the money that brought care to Isaac St. John;
his coffers were deep; but the great fear that this young man,
dear to him as ever son could be to father, might be falling
into evil.

He was aroused from thought by the entrance of his attendant, Mr. Brumm. The master of Castle Wafer looked up
wistfully: he had thought it might be another entering.

"Will you have luncheon brought in here to-day, sir, or take
it with Mrs. St. John and Lady Anne?"

"Oh, I don't know"—and the sweet voice bore its sound of
weariness. "I will take it with them to-day, I think, Brumm:
they say I neglect them. Is it one o'clock?"

"Hard upon it, sir."

Mr. St. John rose. Ah, how changed from the delicate-faced
man whose defects of form had been hidden! The hump was
all too conspicuous now.

Passing out of the room, he crossed the inner hall, so beautiful with its soft rose-coloured hues, its tesselated pavement, and
opened a door on the other side, where luncheon was laid.
Two ladies entered almost at the same moment. The one was
a tall, fine, still elegant woman, not much older than Mr. St.

John himself, though she stood to him in the relation of step-mother; the other was an orphan daughter of the highest branch of the St. John family, the Lady Anne: a nice-looking girl of two or three and twenty, with dark-brown eyes and a pointed chin. Castle Wafer belonged exclusively to Isaac St. John; but his step-mother frequently resided at it. The utmost good-feeling and courtesy existed between them; and Frederick, her only son, and his half-brother, was the link that drew them together. Mrs. St. John never stayed there in the character of visitor: Isaac would not allow it: but as its undisputed mistress. At these times, however, he lived a good deal in his own rooms. She had been there about a month now, and had brought with her this young cousin, Lady Anne. It had been a cherished project in the St. John family, that Lady Anne St. John should become the wife of Frederick. All wished it. The relatives on both sides wished it: they were several degrees removed from each other in relationship, she was an heiress, he would inherit Castle Wafer: altogether it was very suitable. But the parties themselves—were they anxious for the tie? Ah, less was known about that.

Mrs. St. John gave an exclamation of pleasure, for the sight of her step-son amidst them was somewhat rare. He shook hands with her, and then Anne St. John came merrily up to be kissed. She was very fond of Isaac, and he of her. Nearly the only friend he had had in life, as these men of rare minds count friendship, had been the earl, Anne's father.

"Mrs. St. John," he said, as they were at table, Brumm alone being in the room in attendance on his master, for sometimes the merest trifle of exertion, even the lifting of a plate, the filling of a glass, was a trouble to Isaac, "will you believe that I am contemplating a journey?"

"A journey! You, Isaac!" exclaimed Lady Anne. "Is it a drive round the farm in your low carriage?"

"It is a longer journey than that. It will take me five or six hours' hard posting, with good roads and four good horses."

"Oh, Isaac! How can you continue to travel post when you can take the railway?"

"I do not like the railway," said Isaac, quietly.

"Well, I hope you will find relays. I thought all the old posting horses were dead and buried."

"I have not found any difficulty yet, Anne. Brumm sends on to secure them."

"But where are you going, Isaac?" asked Mrs. St. John.

"To Alnwick. I think I ought to go," continued Isaac, speaking in his grave, earnest, thoughtful manner. "Poor George left his boy partly in my charge, as you know; but what with ill-health, and my propensity to shut myself up, which gets harder to break through every year, I have allowed too long a time to elapse without seeing him. It has begun to lie upon my conscience: and whenever a thing does that, I can't rest until I take steps to remedy it."

"The little boy is in his own home with his mother," observed Mrs. St. John. "He is sure to be all right."

"I do not fear that he is not. I should be very much surprised to find that he is not. But that probable fact does not remove from me the responsibility of ascertaining it. I think I shall go on Thursday, and return on Friday."

"How dull we shall be without you," said Lady Anne.

Mr. St. John smiled, and raised his soft dark eyes to hers. The fingers of one thin hand had been wandering amidst the crumbs of his bread, putting them into circles or squares: a habit of his when he talked at table, though perhaps an unconscious one. He did not eat much, and had generally finished long before others.

"I hope, Anne, you and Mrs. St. John will have some one here by Thursday, who will be a more effectual remedy for dulness than I could be at my best. Mrs. St. John, I am expecting Frederick."

"Oh!" The mother's heart leaped within her; the bright flush of expectancy rose to her cheek; a fair and soft cheek still, for all her fifty years. "When?"

"I hope he will be here to-day. I think he may even have come by this morning's train. I wish to see him on a little matter of business, and have written to him to come down. Are you glad, Anne?"

"I am more glad than I can tell you," was the warm, eager answer. "I wish he could be here always."

Ah, Isaac St. John, why that inward glow of satisfaction at the words? Are you so little skilled in the signs of *love* as not to read them more correctly? Don't you know that if there were any love, of the sort you have been hoping, in that fair girl's heart, she would go by the rules of contrary, and protest that it was a matter of perfect indifference to her whether Mr. Frederick came or not? There is no blush on her cheek;

there is no faltering in her tone : why should you deceive yourself?

The surmise was correct : Frederick St. John had come down by the morning's express train. You may see him as he walks out of the station at Lexington : it is that tall, slender, aristocratic man, with dark hair, pale refined features, and eyes of the deepest blue. The people at the station touch their hats to him and smile a greeting, and he smiles and nods at them in return, kindly, genially, as if he really thanked them for their welcome. There was neither heartlessness nor hypocrisy in Frederick St. John : he was a true gentleman at heart.

"Would you like a fly, sir? I don't see any carriage come down for you."

"No, thank you, Williams. I prefer walking such a day as this. Is Mr. St. John well, do you happen to know?"

"As well as usual, I think, sir," was the man's reply, who drove his own fly. "He walked through the fields to church on Sunday. The ladies came in the basket-carriage."

"What a fine harvest you have had!"

"Beautiful, sir. Couldn't be better. My little stock of corn never was finer."

"By the way, Williams. I had a portmanteau somewhere in the train : the guard put it out, I suppose. You can bring it up if you like."

"Thank you, sir."

Frederick St. John walked on. Striking into a path on the left, he continued his way through the fields, and came in due course to the back of the Rectory. From thence the way was through the cultivated grounds, the lovely gardens of Castle Wafer : the whole way being not much more than a mile and a half. By the highway it was a good deal longer.

Seated under a projecting rock, a sketch-book and pencils lying beside her, was one of the fairest girls ever seen. She was reading. Going out to sketch, that mellow day, she had yielded to idleness (as she often did), and was passing the time in reading, instead of working. She was the Dean of Westerbury's niece, Sarah Beauclerc : and the dean was wont to tell her that she should not take a book with her when she went out to sketch. It might come to the same thing, so far as working went, she would answer in her independence : if she did not read, she might only sit and dream. But the dean was not at the Rectory just now : only his wife, daughter, and niece. This young lady's home had been with them since the death of her mother, the Lady Sarah Beauclerc: her father was in India.

The soft bloom mantled in Sarah Beauclerc's cheeks when she saw who had turned the corner and was upon her. His appearance took her by surprise: neither she nor any one else had known that he was coming. She put down her book and was about to rise: but he laid his hand upon her and sat down on the bench beside her. He kept her hand in his; he saw the blushes on her cheeks; and that her eyes fell beneath the gaze of his own.

But the liking between them was not destined to go on to love: though indeed on her part, and perhaps also on his, the feeling had been very like love once. In her behaviour to him she had been a finished coquette: *he* set it down to caprice, to a want of real affection for him; in reality it grew out of her love. She believed that, come what would, he was to marry Lady Anne St. John; she believed that he accepted the destiny, though he might not be unwilling to amuse himself before he entered on it: and, one moment she had been gentle, tender, yielding, in obedience to her secret love; the next she would be cold, repelling, the very essence of scorn. This had partially worked his cure; but in a meeting like the present, coming suddenly upon her in all her beauty, the old feelings would rise again in his heart. Ah! how different might things have been in this life for one other woman, had Sarah Beauclerc only known the real state of affairs between him and Lady Anne!

But she still retained enough of the past feeling to be confused—confused in manner as in mind. She put questions as to his unexpected appearance, not hearing one syllable of the answers; and Frederick St. John detected the secret joy, and his voice grew more low and tender as he bent over her, and a smile, than which earth could possess nothing sweeter, sat on his lips. Perhaps even now, had he remained at Castle Wafer —but of what use speculating upon what might have been?

"I think you are glad to see me, Sarah."

One flash of answering avowal, and then the lovely consciousness on the face faded, the light of love died out of it; it grew hard, satirical, half angry. That she should so have betrayed herself! She raised her head, and looked out straight before her from the depths of her cold light-blue eyes.

"We are glad to see any one in this lonely desert, where
the only gentleman of degree is Mr. St. John. Not but that
I would rather see him than many others. Did you leave
London this morning?"

Frederick St. John dropped the hand and rose.

"I shall never understand you, Sarah. Yes, I left it this
morning. Where's Georgina? She will be glad to welcome
me, if you are not."

"There's one will be glad to welcome you at Castle Wafer,"
she rejoined, laughing now, but the laugh sounded cold and
cheerless. "Lady Anne has been wishing for you for some
time."

"Yes, I think she has. I must go on now. I shall see you
again, no doubt, by-and-by."

He hastened on his way, utterly unconscious that a pair of
eyes, more lovely than those he had been gazing on, behind
the grove of trees, had been unintentional witnesses to the
interview. Georgina Beauclerc had been strolling about when
she saw his approach through the trees. She was the dean's
daughter—a lithe, active girl of middle height with a pleasing,
piquant, rather saucy face, these wide-open grey-blue eyes,
light-brown hair, and a healthy blood mantling under the sun-
burnt skin of the dimpled cheeks—a daring, wild, independent
young lady, but one all truth and ingenuousness; and that is
saying a very great deal in these days of most detestable arti-
ficialty. Georgina had no end of faults, but Dr. Beauclerc
knew her heart, and he would not have exchanged his daughter
for any girl in the world.

She, Georgina Beauclerc, had looked on from between the
trees, all her veins throbbing, her pulses beating. A stronger,
a purer, a more enduring love never made glad the heart of
woman, than this one that filled Georgina Beauclerc's for
Frederick St. John. To hear his step was rapture; to touch
his hand was as a ray of that unforgiven fire "filched for us
from heaven;" to see him thus unexpectedly was as if the
whole earth had become suddenly flooded with a brilliant,
rose-coloured light. But, even as she watched that other
meeting with her cousin, the sharp pain—often enough felt
there before—seized her heart, the loving light faded from her
face, and her lips paled with anguish. Of keen, discerning
faculties, *she* had seen all along that it was not from Lady
Anne danger was to be feared, but from Sarah herself. A

faint, low cry, as of a bird in pain, escaped her as she watched the meeting, and drank in its signs.

Did anything in the world ever run so crookedly as *this* course of love? Every one—uncles, aunts, guardians—wanted Frederick St. John to wed Lady Anne. Frederick did not want to marry her at all; did not intend to marry her; and she, on her part, hoped to marry some one else. But that was a secret not yet to be breathed to the world; Frederick alone shared it; and if things came to a crisis he intended to take on himself the whole onus of declining the match, and so spare Anne. They understood each other perfectly; and that is more than can be said for any other two actors in our story. Nothing so very crooked there, you will say; but look a little further. Georgina loved Frederick St. John with her whole heart; and he never gave a thought to her. He must have known of her love; there had been things to reveal it to him—trifles in the past; but he passed her by, and felt all too inclined to give his love to her cousin. She, Sarah, could have made him her heart's resting-place, ah! how willingly! but her head was filled ever with Lady Anne, and she met his incipient love with scorn. It was curing him, as I have told you; but if the whole truth could have been laid bare, the lives of some of them would have been widely different.

Georgina was obliged to come forth from her hiding-place, for his path lay through the shrubbery, and he must have seen her. Her colour went and came fitfully as she held out her hand; her bosom heaved beneath the thin summer dress, a flowing robe of muslin, adorned with blue ribbons. Her large straw hat was hanging from her arm; and she began to talk freely and wildly—anything to cover her agitation. Their intercourse was familiar as that of brother and sister, for they had been intimate from childhood.

"Well, Georgie! In the wars as usual, I see, amidst the brambles."

He pointed to her robe, and she caught it up; a long bramble was trailing to it.

"It is your fault, sir. Hearing a strange voice, I came through the thorns to see who might be the intruder. What a strange, flighty way you have got into! Coming down by fits and starts, when no one expects you! We heard you were off to Finland, or some other of those agreeable spots. You'll frighten Castle Wafer into fits."

"Wrong, young lady. Castle Wafer sent for me."

"That's one of your stories," politely returned Georgina. "I was at Castle Wafer after breakfast this morning, and Mrs. St. John was regretting that you did not come down this autumn; some one else also, I think, though she did not say it."

He looked down at her as she spoke. There were times when he thought she divined the truth as regarded himself and Lady Anne St. John.

"*I* wonder," she continued, "that you have kept away so long."

"How is the dean?"

"He is not here—only mamma. Tell me; what has brought you down?"

"I have told you. I was sent for."

"By——"

"Isaac. You are as curious as ever, Georgina. But now, can you tell me *why* I am sent for; for that is a puzzle to me. I fear——"

He stopped suddenly. Miss Beauclerc raised her eyes to his face. There was a shade of uneasiness in his tones, as if he were ill at ease.

"I know nothing about it," she answered, earnestly. "I did not even know you were sent for. I would tell you if I did know."

He nodded an acknowledgment, courteously enough, but very abstractedly, as if he thought little of Georgina or of anything she could tell him, and walked on alone, never once looking back. She leaned her forehead against a tree, and gazed after him; her wild love shining forth from her yearning blue eyes; her whole heart longing to call after him ere he should be quite beyond view, and the day's sunshine have gone out in darkness: "Oh, stay with me, my love! stay with me!"

He went on to the house, straight into the presence of Isaac, who was then in his own room, and learnt why he had been summoned. That his embarrassments would, of necessity, become known to his brother some time, he had entertained no shadow of doubt; but he was one of those high-bred, honourable men who look upon debt as little less than crime; and now that the moment had come, it brought him terrible mortification.

"I have no excuse to offer," he said. "But do not think

worse of me than you can help. Not one shilling of it has gone
in dishonour."

That he spoke the truth Isaac knew, and his heart went out
to him—him whom he had ever loved as a son.

"I will set you straight, only be more cautious in future," he
said, never speaking, in his generosity, one word of reproach.
"And, Frederick, this had better be kept from your mother. It
would pain her, and perhaps alarm Anne. Don't you think it
is time you married? There's nothing to wait for. I'm sure—
I fancy at least—that Anne is ready."

And Frederick St. John, bound by a promise to Lady Anne,
did not speak out openly, as he might have done, but evaded
the question.

On the following Thursday, in the long, low room at the
Rectory, its windows opening to the lawn, sat Sarah Beauclerc,
practising a piece of difficult music. She and her cousin were
contrasts. The one, cold, calm, calculating, did things by rule;
the other did all by impulse, and could not be cold if she tried.
Sarah was the least in the world artificial; Georgina was too
natural.

Mrs. Beauclerc, thin and discontented-looking as of yore, the
red tip of her nose growing redder year by year, sat at the
French window of the room, talking to Georgina. Georgina, in
a clear pink muslin dress, with open lace sleeves on her pretty
wrists, stood just outside the window. She was partly listening
to her mother,—as much as she ever did listen to Mrs. Beauclerc's grumblings,—partly humming to herself the piece that
Sarah was playing, as her eyes wandered wistfully, far far out in
the distance, seeking one who did not come.

"What are you looking at?" Mrs. Beauclerc suddenly asked
in sharp tones. "You never pay attention to me, Georgina."

"I thought—I thought——" and though the answer was given
with hesitation, she spoke the straightforward truth—"I thought
I saw Frederick St. John. Some one was there, but he has
turned away again, whoever it was. What do you want to say,
mamma?"

"Mrs. St. John and Anne partly promised to come in and
dine with us, *sans cérémonie*, this evening. I want you to go
and ask them whether they are really coming."

She stepped gaily over the threshold into the room, all her
inertness gone. The short secluded walk through the private

grounds would be charming enough on that warm autumn day;
but had it been one of stones and brambles, Georgina had
deemed it Eden, with the prospect of *his* presence at the end
of it.   She halted for a moment to ask a question; to ask it
indifferently, as if it were of no moment to her, and she tossed
her handkerchief carelessly about as she spoke it."

"Is Frederick to come with them?"

"Dear me, Georgina!   *Is* he to come!   He can come if he
likes."

Absorbed in her music, Sarah Beauclerc had heard nothing
of this.   Georgina came in again with her bonnet on.   "Sarah,
I am going up to Castle Wafer.   Will you come?"

The light of assent shone all too eagerly for a moment in
Sarah's eyes; but she recollected her resolution—to *forget*—and
declined.

"Not this morning."

"Very well," said Georgina.   "Don't say I didn't ask you.
You said so once before, if you remember, Sarah, and a great
passion you were in."

Sarah Beauclerc's lip curled.   "I don't think I was ever in a
passion in my life.   It is only the uncontrolled, the ill-regulated,
who so forget themselves."

"I would rather go into a good hearty passion and get it over,
than be cold as an icicle.   What a passion I once put Fred St.
John into!" added Georgina, half losing herself in the remembrance.   "*He* can be passionate, if you like!"

"I don't believe it."

"*Dis*-believe it, then," equably returned Georgina.   "I have
seen him in more rages than one.   It's not a thing to forget, I
can tell you.   He is sweet-tempered in ordinary life; ay, very;
but on rare occasions he can be roused.   Ask Mrs. St. John;
ask Anne."

She stepped out from the window, nodding to Mrs. Beauclerc,
who was now at a distance bending over her favourite flower-
bed, and pursued her walk.

Suddenly a butterfly crossed her path; she was then getting
near to Castle Wafer.   It was one of those beautiful insects, its
wings purple and gold; and Georgina, no better than a butterfly herself and variable as one, began to give chase to it.   In
turning suddenly the corner of a hedge of variegated evergreens,
she came upon a stranger.

Springing back as one startled, her heart beat a shade quicker,

Not that there was anything particularly to startle her, except that he was unknown, and that he stood in a stealthy attitude. He wore a rather remarkable hat, inasmuch as its crown was higher than those of ordinary hats and went tapering off in sugar-loaf fashion; his clothes were shabby-genteel. Altogether he put Georgina in mind of the portrait of Mephistopheles, as represented on the cover of one of her pieces of music.

He had been bending forward, peering through the trees at Castle Wafer; the position he held commanded full view of the front of the house. But he appeared equally startled with Miss Beauclerc, at being interrupted, glided away, and was lost to view.

"What a strange-looking man!" exclaimed Georgina. "And what was he doing there? Perhaps wanting to take a photograph of Castle Wafer! *That* tall hat must have been the one I saw from our house."

She emerged from the sheltered path, crossed the lawn, stepped over the terrace, and into the drawing-room. The families were too intimate to stand on any sort of ceremony with each other, and as frequently entered each other's houses in this manner as by the more formal doorway. The room was empty, but almost immediately Frederick St. John came into it.

His eye fell upon her for a moment only, and she caught the half-wistful, half-eager glance that went roaming round in search of another.

"Are you alone?" he asked, as he shook hands with her.

"Sarah is not with me," was the petulant answer. It was utterly impossible to Georgina Beauclerc not to betray her moods: and none but herself knew how cruel was the pain ever rankling in her heart. "But I did not come to pay a visit to you," she went on pointedly. "Where's Mr. St. John?"

"He has gone out, and will not be back until to-morrow."

She had only asked the question in that listless fashion that requires no answer. The answer, however, aroused her surprise. Isaac St. John gone out until to-morrow!

"He left this morning for Alnwick," said Frederick. "He has gone to see his little ward, Benja St. John. A long journey, for he is posting. Did you want him, Georgina?"

"No; I came to see Mrs. St. John. Mamma supposes she and Anne remember their engagement to come in this afternoon and remain to dinner. Will you come also?"

"Is it a dinner-party?

"A dinner-party here! Don't expect that. You may find nothing but mutton," she added, with a laugh. "It's ourselves only. Will you come?"

"I think not, Georgie. Perhaps, though: I'll see between now and dinner-time."

He stepped out without further word or look. Ah, it needed not his coldness of manner to convince Georgina Beauclerc how utterly indifferent she was to him! Lady Anne came in, and she began laughing and talking as though there were not such a thing as misplaced love in the world. In a few minutes Georgina left again, bearing Mrs. St. John's message of acceptance of the invitation. As she was walking leisurely along she caught sight of Frederick in the distance. He was standing still, apparently examining something in his hand. Georgina's quick thought wondered whether it was the beautiful butterfly of purple and gold. Suddenly, in this same moment, as she looked, she saw the strange man go rather swiftly up to him and touch him on the shoulder.

She saw Frederick St. John wheel round; she saw him fling the man's arm off with a haughty gesture. And after a few minutes' parleying, during which the man showed him a paper —minutes of hesitation as it seemed, for Mr. St. John looked about him as a man uncertain of his course—they finally walked away together. Georgina went home wondering.

Mrs. St. John and Lady Anne came in about four o'clock, bringing their work with them. Lady Anne was making a collection of ferns, and she began doing something to a dried leaf with water and a sponge. Mrs. St. John and Mrs. Beauclerc were each knitting a soft woollen counterpane of divers colours, and began comparing progress.

"Where's Frederick?" asked Mrs. Beauclerc. "Is he not coming?"

"I don't know where he is," cried Mrs. St. John, in quick tones and looking up, as though the question recalled something to her recollection. "We have seen nothing of him since the morning, and just now I received a pencilled note from him, saying he might not be in until to-night, or perhaps not at all, if he found his business detained him very late."

"Has he gone to Lexington?"

"We don't know where he has gone. But it is very strange he should go out for any length of time, without mentioning it

to me. The note was not dated, and the servants said a strange
boy brought it. So very thoughtless of Frederick, to go out
in this flighty manner! Anne was dreaming of him this
afternoon."

"Dreaming of him!" repeated Mrs. Beauclerc.

Lady Anne laughed. "Mrs. St. John insisted at the time
that I was dreaming," she said. "We drove out in the pony-
carriage after luncheon, and on passing the Barley Mow, I
could have declared that I saw Frederick at one of the upper
windows. But when we drew closer he had turned into a
strange man in a tall hat. I suppose I must have been
thinking of him, and so fancied it: or else the sun, which was
full in my face, caused the mistake. Georgina, what is the
matter?"

It was time to ask. Georgina Beauclerc was standing as
one transfixed. She was as clever a girl at putting two and
two together as could well be found; and the whole mystery
seemed to suddenly clear itself. Very rapidly she drew
her conclusions: Frederick St. John had been arrested for
debt, and the man was keeping him prisoner at the Barley
Mow!

A mist gathered before her sight: her heart sank within her.
Georgina had long known that he was in some temporary
embarrassment; it came to her knowledge through an incautious word of his own; and she had cherished the
knowledge as a secret link between them. But she had not
suspected *this*, and it came upon her with a crushing fear.

She burst into laughter, for the question of Lady Anne recalled her to herself, making some evasive excuse. She would
have died rather than betray him.

"I know," she said. "He has gone over to Lexington to
avoid dining with so many women. You could not expect him
to stay for us, Mrs. St. John."

"Very true, my dear; the same thought had occurred to
me," was the satisfied answer. "But I don't see why he should
hint at not coming home to sleep."

"There may be a thousand things to detain him," said
Georgina, throwing back her pretty head, as if to cool the
fever crimsoning her cheeks. "And who knows but he may
have gone on to Sir John Ingram's? I made him so mad one
day last year, teasing him about that gawky Jane Ingram!
Mamma nearly boxed my ears for it."

Watching her opportunity, Georgina stole away, snatched her hat and a garden mantle from the peg in the hall, and went out. Where was she going, this wild girl? Need you ask? In her impulsive, free, careless fashion, she was hastening to the Barley Mow, to see Frederick St. John.

It sounds very bad, no doubt to the reader's ears. The name of the "Barley Mow" itself would be enough to alarm modest people, without the gentleman. But in this quiet little spot, the Barley Mow was as sedate and respectable a house to enter as any private one; and Georgina had many a time gone into it with Dr. Beauclerc to sit ten minutes with one of its daughters, who had been an invalid for years.

She went flying onwards, and gained the door in a few minutes. The landlord, a respectable, simple old yeoman, in a yellow waistcoat and top-boots, who was a farmer as well as an innkeeper, met her at the entrance.

"Mary ain't quite so well, miss," he began, more hastily than he was in the habit of speaking. "She's lying down. I'm afeared I can't ask you to go up this afternoon."

"I have not come to see her," returned Georgina, ignoring ceremony. "Is Mr. Frederick St. John here?"

The man seemed taken back. He might not admit it; he could not conscientiously deny it; and he only stared by way of answer.

"I know he is here," said Georgina. "You need not hesitate."

"Well, miss, he is here, and that's the truth. But I mightn't say it."

"I want to see him," she continued, walking into the family parlour, then vacant. "Ask him to come to me."

It appeared that he could not come without his attendant in the curious hat, for when Mr. St. John, who came down immediately, entered the room, that gentleman's hat and head appeared over his shoulder. Very haughtily Mr. St. John waved him off, and closed the door to shut him out.

"Georgina, what brings you here?"

"How did it happen?" she asked eagerly. "Are you really arrested?"

"Really and truly," he said, speaking in a tone of hauteur that perhaps veiled a feeling of bitter mortification. "The marvel does not lie in that, but in how you came to know of it."

" I guessed it," said Georgina.

" *Guessed* it ! "

She quietly told him the whole from the beginning: her meeting with the man in the morning, the news Mrs. St. John brought about the note, the fancied view of Lady Anne.

" The truth seemed to come over me in a moment," she concluded. " I knew you were arrested; I was sure it was nothing else. And I ran all the way here to ask if I can do anything for you. I saw by the note that you dare not tell Mrs. St. John."

" Dare is not quite the word, Georgina. If I can spare her I will do so, for I know it would grieve her cruelly. The affair would not have been the trouble of a quarter-of-an-hour, but for Isaac's being away. Things always do happen by contraries."

" You think he would—he would—what could he have done?" she asked, her anxious face and its earnest eyes turned up to him.

" He would have paid the claim and set me free. As it is, nothing can be done until he comes home to-morrow."

" How much is the claim?"

Frederick St. John drew in his lips. " It is amidst the hundreds. Nay, how scared you look! It was a clever trick, their sending the fellow down here after me."

" Who is he?" asked Georgina, lowering her voice, with an instinctive conviction that the individual in question was rather near the outside of the door.

" He's nobody," was the reply. " But, nevertheless, he is master of me just now, by virtue of the law. He considers himself a model of consideration and benevolence, and will expect me to acknowledge it substantially : otherwise he would have taken me off pretty quickly."

" Where to?"

" To—it is an ugly word, Georgina—prison."

" Oh ! But you will stop that, won't you?"

" Isaac will. The annoying part of the business is, that he should be away just this day of all days. It is rather singular, too, considering that he is at home from year's end to year's end. There's no help for it, however, and here I must stop until he does return, hiding myself like a mouse, lest I should be seen, and the news carried to my mother."

" Can't I help you?—can't I do anything for you?"

"Thank you always, Georgina. You are a good little girl, after all. No, nothing."

She pouted her pretty lips.

"Except keep the secret. And go home again as soon as possible. What would your mamma say if she knew you had come?" he asked.

"Scold me for a week. Will Mr. St. John be home early to-morrow?"

"I wish I knew. Any time, I suppose, from midday up to night. We must set some one to watch for him. He is posting, and therefore goes and comes the upper road, not passing here. I dare not send a note to Castle Wafer to await his arrival, for my mother, seeing my handwriting, would inevitably open it; neither can I entrust the matter to any of the servants to inform their master: they might make a mystery of it, and so bring it in that way to the ears of my mother. Besides, to tell the truth, I don't care that the servants should know of it. Brumm alone would be safe, and he is with his master."

"Entrust it to me," said Georgina, eagerly. "Let me manage it for you. I will take care to tell Mr. St. John the moment of his arrival. If I can't see him, I'll tell Brumm."

Mr. St. John paused a minute. The proposal certainly sólved a difficulty.

"But I don't like you to do this, Georgina," he said, following out his thoughts.

"I *will* do it," she answered, the colour mantling to her cheeks. "You can't prevent me now."

He smiled at her eagerness; he saw how pleasant it was to her to serve him. She laid her hand on the door to depart.

"Be it so, Georgina. I shall call you henceforth my friend in need."

She opened the door quickly. On the opposite side of the narrow passage, his back propped against the wall, a cautious sentinel, stood the man. Mr. St. John saw him, closed his lips on what he was about to say, and motioned her into the room again.

"You will not speak of this misfortune, Georgina, at your own house? Is it known there?" he continued, a sudden fear betraying itself in his voice. "Does Sarah know of it?"

"And if she did," retorted Georgina, the old pain seizing upon her heart again, "she does not know of it from me."

Throwing back the door, she went straight out of the house, running all the way home lest she should be missed, her brain busy with the one thought.

"Sarah, Sarah! It is all he cares for in life!"

CHAPTER XII.

THE FAIR AT ALNWICK.

IN the long, straggling street, which chiefly comprised the village of Alnwick, there was a break in the houses on the left-hand side. This was filled up by the common, or waste land ; it belonged to the lord of the manor, and no one might build upon it. It was a wide, untidy piece of ground, branching off into far-away corners and dells, which did very well for harbouring trampers and gipsies. Once a year, for three days in September, this common was delivered over to all the bustle and confusion of a fair. Shows and booths, containing (if you could believe them) the wonders of the world, living and dead ; caravans ; drinking-tents ; stalls for fruit, gingerbread, and penny trumpets ; and here shoals of pleasure-seekers reigned in triumph during those three days. Sober shopkeepers, driven half wild with opposition drums and horns, talked a great deal about "getting the nuisance done away with ;" but the populace generally believed that no man living could put the threat into execution, except the lord of the manor : and *he* could only do it by refusing the use of the ground. However that may have been, the ground had not been refused yet, and the populace was triumphant.

It was a bright September day, and the fair was in full glory ; as far as was consistent with the comparative quiet and respectability of the first day. Things on that day were ordered with a due regard to decorum : the music was kept within bounds, the bawling showmen were subdued and persuasive, the ladies' dresses and dancing were gentility itself. For on this first day the better families around would send their children to the fair (some had been known to go to it themselves), and ladies'-maids and butlers congregated there in great force. The second and third days were given over to what these domestics called the riff-raff.

The fair was in its full radiance on this fine September day. Drums were beating, fifes were playing, pantaloons were shouting, ladies were dancing, and rival showmen in scarlet and gold tunics were shouting out their seductive attractions, when two respectable-looking maid-servants, each in charge of a little boy, might have been observed in the street, about to enter the enchanted regions. The children were attired in black velvet, trimmed with crape, and their straw hats had black ribbon round them. The younger, a lovely child with a bright complexion and a mass of fair curls, looked nearly three years old; the other was nearly five; not a pretty child, but his countenance one of noble intelligence. An insignificant little fellow enough in years and stature, this elder one; no one to look at: and yet a great many people touched their hats to him, child though he was, and that very fair was being held upon his own land; for he was lord of the manor, and inheritor of Alnwick.

Benja and George had been wild to set off to it. Indeed, for a week beforehand, from the raising of the first plank for the booths, it could hardly be said that either servants or children for miles round were in their sedate senses. Prance, however, was an exception. Prance seemed to have no affinity with fairs; and she had drawn in her thin lips in withering contempt at Honour's open longing for it. There was no more cordiality between the two servants than there used to be, and a sharp quarrel would occur now and again, in which Honour, as far as words went, had the best of it. Honour was free-spoken; there was no denying it. This fair had caused a desperate quarrel that same morning. Honour said everything she could to enhance its glories to the children; Prance contradicted every word, and protested it was not a fit place to take them to.

Mrs. Carleton St. John favoured Honour in the matter, told Prance she would not deprive the children of the shows for anything, and finally ordered her to be quiet. George took his nurse's part, and said Honour was a "nasty beast." Benja retaliated that Prance was, and George struck him. Mrs. Carleton St. John for once reproved George, and kissed and soothed Benja. It was a curious thing, not noticed at the time, but recalled by Honour in the future, that this little graciousness on the part of her mistress, this displayed affection for Benja, should have occurred on the day afterwards characterized by the unexpected visit of Mr. Isaac St. John. "As if it had been on purpose !" Honour was wont to repeat to herself with a groan. However, all this partisanship for herself and Benja only put her into a good humour at the time; she could not see the future; and when they started, after an early dinner, Honour was in a state of great delight, satisfied with everything and every one.

Excepting, perhaps, with Prance. Prance showed no signs whatever of her discomfiture, but followed to the fair with George, impassive and silent as ever. As they were entering the bustle, and the little legs already began to dance to the drums, and the charmed eyes caught the first glimpse of the spangles and all the other enchantments, a dusty travelling carriage-and-four came bowling down the street, and stopped at the Bell Inn, which was situated opposite to the common. Such travelling equipages had become sufficiently rare to be almost a curiosity in the county, and both the maids turned to stare, utterly unsuspicious that it contained one who, as guardian, had all power over the heir of Alnwick.

The first show they entered (on the principle of keeping the best to the last) was a very sober sort of affair, and purporting to be "An Emporium of Foreign Curiosities." The admission was threepence, the trumpet was loud, and the showman was magnificent both in person and persuasion.

"I shall go into this," said Honour. "I should think *you* needn't be afraid of what you'd see inside," she added to Prance in tones, it must be confessed, of aggravation. "There's no dancing here."

Prance's only answer was to draw down the corners of her thin lips and walk off with George to a leviathan booth whose company were executing a complicated quadrille before it. Honour paid her threepence, disputed with the money-taker about admitting Benja for three-halfpence, that functionary protesting that there was no half-price for gentlemen's children, and went into the show.

Like many other shows, its interior did not realize the outward promise. There was a crocodile in stone, and a few more dead wonders, which Honour turned up her nose at, saying something about demanding back her money: but Benja's attention had become riveted by the pretty model of a church rising from the midst of green moss. It was white, and its coloured windows were ingeniously shown up by means

of a light placed within it. It really was a pretty and conspicuous article in the dark booth, and Benja could not be
moved from it. How little did Honour think that that sight
was to exercise so terrible an influence on the unconscious
child !

"Come along," she said, rather impatiently. "I could make
you as good a one any day, Benja."

"How could you make it?" promptly asked Benja.

"With white paper and thin strips of wood for the frame.
Master Benja, then ! we shall have Prance going home and
telling your mamma that we lost her on purpose. She's as
deceitful as yonder crocodile."

"Couldn't you buy it for me, Honour?" returned Benja,
not stirring a peg.

"Of course I couldn't," answered Honour. "What a little
simpleton you must be, to ask it ! The things here are not for
sale ; the folks get their living by showing them. And a fine
set of worthless rubbish it is ! Once for all, are you coming,
Master St. John?"

"Will you promise to make me one?" persisted Benja.

"Yes, I will. There !"

"When?"

"As soon as I can get the things together. Now come."

Benja reluctantly moved away ; but his head and eyes were
turned for the last glance, up to the moment when Honour
pulled him through the low green-baize opening.

Meanwhile Mrs. Carleton St. John was sitting alone. She
was of remarkably quiet habits by inclination, a great stay-at-
home, rarely seeking society or amusement abroad ; and the
still recent death of her husband tended to keep the Hall
pretty free from idle visitors. One sole passion seemed to
absorb her whole life, to the exclusion of every other ; it filled
every crevice of her heart, it regulated her movements, it buried
even her natural grief for her husband—and this was love for
her child. The word love most inadequately expresses the
feeling : it was a passion, threatening to consume every healthy
impulse. She was quite aware of it : indeed, her conscience
did not allow her to be otherwise.

One thought was ever present to her ; it may be said that it
had never left her mind since the day her husband died : that
Benja was chief of Alnwick Hall, with all its wealth and
dignity ; that she, Charlotte St. John, so arrogant by nature,

was there only on sufferance, a home accorded to her as his personal guardian ; and that George was as nobody. They were as a sharp thorn, these reflections, ever piercing her. They ate into her ill-regulated heart and rankled there. And they went on to another thought, an unwholesome thought, which would have been a wicked thought but that it was not there of her own will : a thought that carried danger in its train. In the first waking of early morning, in the fevered dreams of midnight solitude, in the glare and bustle of noon-day, it was ever thrusting itself forward—if Benja were to die, her child would be the inheritor.

Was she aware of its danger? No. And yet she was fond of tracing it back to its original source—the accident to Benja. When the boy was taken out of the water, drowned as was supposed, and as some one called out, the wild beating of Mrs. St. John's bosom—*not with sorrow*—called into life the thought that had certainly never existed there before, or else had lain dormant.

Her increasing dislike of Benja should have acted as a warning to her. It was generated by the false view she took of the existing state of things : that Benja was a sort of ogre, whose sole mission on earth was to stand in the light of her child and deprive him of what might have been his birthright. She strove against this dislike—it might be better to call it hatred, for it had grown into that—and she had to exercise a constant check upon herself in her behaviour towards him. None but she knew what it cost her to treat Benja with a semblance of love, or to make no very apparent difference between the children. She did strive against it—let us do her justice !—not from any suspicion of danger, but from her own sense of equity. That very morning, in taking Benja's part and kissing him, she had acted from an impulse of good principle, an endeavour to do right. But no sooner were the children out of her sight, than the old bad feelings got the better of her, and she sat indulging all sorts of foolish dreams and visions of what she would do were Alnwick George's instead of Benja's. Will you believe that she had fallen into the habit of repeating their Christian names to herself, with the prospective title before them ? " Sir Benjamin St. John," " Sir George St. John ; " and she thought the one (you need not ask which of the two) sounded a thousand times more charming than the other.

Though very conscious of all this, she yet detected no danger in it. The night of her husband's death, she made a resolve to do her duty by her little step-son; and when the codicil to the will was read, giving Mr. St. John of Castle Wafer the power to remove him from her, she resented it bitterly as a mark of want of confidence in her shown by her husband. No woman could have been more willing in intention to do right by a step-son than Charlotte St. John. If only her strength of will did not fail her, she might succeed. One result of the desire to carry out her resolve, was retaining Honour in her service. She very much disliked the girl, for her strong attachment to Benja in contradistinction to George, and her always taking his part against that rather capricious younger gentleman; but she would not discharge her. To this desire to do her duty, rather than because her husband in dying had expressed a wish that Honour should be retained about Benja, the girl owed the fact that she was still in her place. Honour alone of the servants, save and except perhaps Prance, had detected all along the second Mrs. St. John's dislike to her little charge. She was aware, as surely as though she had seen it recorded, that her mistress regarded George as he who ought to be the heir, Benja as a usurper; and it aroused within her a feeling of indignation, which sometimes peeped out in her manner. Not sufficiently so for Mrs. St. John openly to find fault with; and she only thought the girl quick in temper. And now I think I have said as much as I can say about the state of mind of Mrs. Carleton St. John. She deliberately intended to do right: but passion and prejudice are strong; unusually strong were they in her; and her mind was undisciplined and ill-regulated.

As she sat there to-day, the approach of a vehicle in the avenue attracted her attention. She soon saw that it was a fly from the Bell Inn, and all her motherly fears were at once up in arms, lest any accident had happened to Georgy, and he was being brought home, or she fetched to him. But it seemed to contain only one gentleman; and he a stranger; a delicate-looking man, who sat low in the fly.

Not for a long time had she been so surprised as when the card was brought to her, and she found that her visitor was Mr. St. John of Castle Wafer. Had he come to remove Benja? The thought awoke a momentary affection for the child in her heart, and called up a resentful flush to her cheeks. But resentment faded away as Isaac came in, and held out his hand to her in his open courtesy. She saw she had nothing underhand to fear from him.

What was perhaps more agreeable to her, as it is to all vain women—and Charlotte St. John was one of them—was the look of honest admiration that shone out of Isaac's face and manner. She presented a picture deeply interesting—in her young widowhood, in her beauty, in her manner so quiet and subdued. She burst into tears as they talked of her husband, of Benja; and she told Mr. St. John that if he removed Benja from her it would break her heart.

It was only a figure of speech. And it is very probable that the fact of two thousand a-year of her income being in peril, may have swayed her to earnestness more than any other feeling. Mr. St. John took it all for loving earnestness, and assured her he thought no cause would ever be likely to arise for his removing Benja. In point of fact, Isaac St. John was most warmly impressed in her favour; it was almost as if she had fascinated him.

"Will you answer me a question?" asked Mrs. St. John. "I cannot get it solved by any one else. Why did my husband leave this power in your hands? Did he doubt me?"

"I do not know why he left it," was the answer of Mr. St. John: "unless he thought that you might be too kind to the boy—might indulge him to his detriment. I remember, too, his saying that you were not very strong, and the charge of the two children might be a tax upon you."

She did not answer. She began to speak of more general things, and Isaac St. John sat talking with her for some time. She expressed her regret that Benja should happen to be at the fair, and laughed when Mr. St. John spoke of the noise that had assailed his ears from the drums. She pressed him to take up his quarters at the Hall until the morrow, but this he declined; he was only an invalid at best, he said. He had engaged rooms at the Bell for himself and his servant, and he invited Benja to come and breakfast with him on the following morning. Mrs. St. John readily assented to the invitation.

"You will allow his nurse to attend him," he said to her, as he rose to leave. "I should like to see and converse with the attendant of my little ward, and offer her a gratuity as an earnest of my favour."

As readily as the other request was this acceded to, and

Mr. St. John departed, taking final leave of his cousin's widow—for he intended to leave Alnwick soon after breakfast the following morning.

The fly had conveyed him almost through the park on his return to the Bell, when he saw two women-servants, in charge of two children. Rightly guessing who they were, he stopped the fly, opened the door, and talked to them from his seat.

A noble boy, his ward, with an open, intelligent countenance; a pretty little toy-boy the other, with his bright face, his fair curls, and his indulged petulance peeping out even then. The children were at home with him at once, showing him the fairings they carried—one a child's kaleidoscope, the other a drum. Benja told him some unintelligible story of a "church" Honour was going to make for him; Georgy sounded the rataplan on his drum. He inquired of Honour whether she was the nurse mentioned to him by her late master, who had been with the child from his birth. Upon her saying she was, he told her she was to be at the Bell with Master St. John the next morning at nine o'clock; he handed a sovereign to Prance; he won the boys' hearts by a promise of a whole cargo of fairings to be sent up that evening; and then he drove on. Not one of them had noticed his hump; but they thought what a little low gentleman he was in stature.

Benja had taken home a fairing for his mamma—a blue-and-white smelling-bottle, flat as a half-crown, with a narrow neck in which was a little cork as stopper. It had cost threepence, and he kissed her as he gave it to her. George's fairing to his mamma had been a Banbury cake, but he had unfortunately eaten it on his way home. Whether the contrast touched her, or that with Mr. St. John in the vicinity she did not choose to be otherwise than loving, certain it was that she kissed Benja heartily in return, praised his present as she put it into her waistband, and told Georgy he was a selfish little fellow. How gratified Honour was, and how, in manner, she crowed over Prance, Prance would not condescend to observe. Mrs. St. John was all graciousness, bade Honour make Master Benja very nice indeed for the following morning, and said the pony-carriage should take them down.

The appointment was kept. Benja was treated to jam and other good things as he sat at breakfast with Mr. St. John—Brumm and Honour waiting on them. Afterwards, when the cloth was removed, Mr. Brumm had orders to take Master St.

John to the fair and show him the elephant, or anything else Mr. Brumm might deem expedient; and Honour was requested to take a seat while Mr. St. John talked to her.

He really saw no means of ascertaining whether Benja was well done by at the Hall, excepting this—the putting a direct question to the nurse. After what he had seen of the Hall's mistress the previous day, he would as soon suspect himself of being ill treated, as any child over whom she had control. Still it was as well to make sure upon the point.

Honour answered his questions as straightforwardly as she could. But, it should be remarked, that in her present mood of graciousness towards her mistress (or it should perhaps rather be said of that lady's graciousness to her), she spoke more favourably of Mrs. St. John than she would have done at almost any previous time. She was not indulgent to Master Benja; but on the other hand she was not generally unkind to him, was the substance of her answer.

This rather surprised Mr. St. John. "I should have thought her in danger of being too kind," he said.

Honour shook her head. "Mrs. St. John is too kind by a great deal to her own child, sir; she indulges him dreadfully; but there's no fear that she will ever do that by Master Benja."

"I suppose you do not mean to say that Mrs. St. John is unkind to him?" returned Mr. St. John, rather at a loss how to frame his words with a due regard to what was due to the dignity of that lady, when speaking of her to her servant.

"Well, no, sir, I can't say that she is unkind. She treats the two very much alike, only that she is always kissing and clasping the little one, and has him so much more with her. She boxed Master Benja's ears the other day and made him cry. For no fault, either, that I could find out."

Mr. St. John smiled. "A little wholesome correction is good for boys, you know."

"I'm not saying that it isn't, sir. Altogether, things have gone on much more comfortably since my master's death than I used to fancy they would. There's not much to complain of."

"On the whole, then, you cannot see cause for any interference on my part? You see no reason why Master St. John should not remain at the Hall under his step-mother's charge?"

"No, sir; I cannot say that I do. And of course I am always with him, and can take care of him there as well as

I could anywhere else. I shall never let harm come nigh him from any one."

It was conclusive, and Mr. St John intimated that the conference was over.

"You see, I speak to you as the confidential attendant of the child," he said. "You were named to me by your late master as one in whom every confidence might be placed. Do me the favour to regard what I have said as between ourselves, in the interest of this little orphan. And always remember, that in case of any emergency arising, where any—any counsel, or advice, or interference on my part should be desirable, a letter will find me at Castle Wafer. I shall come over from time to time—not often, for my health does not permit it; and I shall hope to have a letter frequently from the little boy."

He pressed a very handsome present into her hand as he concluded, saying it was in recompense of her trouble and attention to the child. Honour's eyes filled with tears as she took it; it needed not money to enhance her jealous love for Benja.

And the boy came back with Mr. Brumm in a state of ecstatic delight, for he had seen the elephant and everything else. He was despatched to the Hall with Honour, bearing compliments to its mistress, and a cargo of good things for himself and Georgy. And Mr. St. John set off on his homeward journey to Castle Wafer.

CHAPTER XIII.

ONLY AS BROTHER AND SISTER.

THE September afternoon was passing into the twilight of evening ere the master of Castle Wafer drew near his home. Miss Georgina Beauclerc was almost at her wits' end. Determined to carry out her promise of informing him of the mishap that had befallen his brother, she yet saw no means of doing it without its coming to the observance of Mrs. St. John, but by speaking to him in the moment that intervened between his stepping from his carriage and entering the house. For this purpose had she been hovering about almost ever since midday, keeping out of range of the windows, and ready to walk quietly forward as any ordinary visitor, as soon as the carriage came in sight.   But the carriage did not come; and Georgina, conscious that the Rectory dinner-hour was approaching, knew not really what to do.

Just as she was ready to take some desperate step, had she only known what, she heard the sound of wheels, and the dusty carriage with its four horses drew quickly up.   Georgina was not less quick.   But ere she had well gained the entrance, ere the carriage door was opened, who should come out of the house, but Mrs. St. John, her hands raised, her voice lifted in consternation.

It was a very unusual proceeding, and Georgina halted : she would. not approach Isaac then.   Devoutly wishing Mrs. St. John over in Asia, Georgina listened, and caught sufficient of what passed to hear that Castle Wafer was in alarm about Frederick.   He had not been seen or heard of since the preceding day.   It turned out afterwards that he had written a second note to Mrs. St. John, which the messenger, sent with it, had never delivered.   Georgina could not approach ; and while she looked, Mr. St. John and his step-mother disappeared within doors together.

Excitement was rendering Georgina ill.   Have you realized what *an arrest* such as this must be to a young lady, shielded from the ways of the world ? a threatened prison for one all too dear ?   As she stood there, crouching behind the dwarf shrubs on the lawn, not very conspicuous in the evening light, Mr. Brumm came to the carriage, opened the door to take something from the seat, and she darted up to him.

"Brumm," she said, emotion lending a catching sound to her voice, "I want to see Mr. St. John.   I must see him, and without delay.   If I go round by the other door and get into his sitting-room, will you contrive to send him to me ?   I dare say he is in the drawing-room with Mrs. St. John."

For a minute or two Brumm only stared.   He looked upon the dean's daughter, if the truth must be told, as a rather flighty damsel ; and he did not believe she could want anything with Mr. St. John.   That is to say, nothing of importance.

"My master is excessively fatigued, Miss Beauclerc," he said at length.   "I fear he will not be able to see any one to-night."

"Don't be an idiot, Brumm," peremptorily retorted the young lady.   "I tell you I *must* see him : the matter is almost one of life or death. You get him to me in some way; but take care you do it without arousing suspicion in Mrs. St. John."

She stole round the house as she spoke, on her way to Mr. St. John's own sitting-room—the pleasant room you have sometimes seen him in. Brumm, in doubt still, yet seeing no remedy but to obey, collected the things from the carriage, handed them to a footman, and then went to the drawing-room.

His master was not seated, but standing. By this Brumm knew that he did not intend to remain in the room. Mrs. St. John was telling him of what she called Fred's mysterious conduct, and showed him the note received on the previous day. She spoke complainingly, and avowed her belief that her roving son had taken French leave to go back to London.

At any rate, there was nothing Mr. St. John could do in the matter; and in point of fact his fatigue was such he could not in any case have done much. Excessive bodily fatigue takes from the power of the mind; and he did not seem to attach much importance to what Mrs. St. John was saying. He went out of the room, carrying the note with him; and there he was arrested by Brumm.

"Will you be so kind, sir, as step into your sitting-room for an instant?"

"I am going upstairs, Brumm. I have not felt so tired for years."

"But—I beg your pardon, sir," resumed Brumm, speaking in the covert tone he had before used, and which a little surprised his master—"you—you are wanted there. If you will step this way, sir, I will explain."

Mr. St. John quitted the proximity of the drawing-room, which was evidently what Brumm wished. "Miss Beauclerc was waiting to speak to him," he whispered as he crossed the hall. "She said she wanted a word with him in private."

"Miss Beauclerc!" Wondering very much, not perhaps at her wishing to speak to him, there was nothing extraordinary in that, but at the air of secrecy that Brumm seemed to invest the affair with, Mr. St. John went to his sitting-room. Georgina was pacing it somewhat like a caged bird, hardly able to suppress her impatience.

"I have been waiting outside for you since twelve o'clock!" she exclaimed, ignoring all ceremonious greeting. "I thought you would never come!"

" Do you want me ? " asked Mr. St. John.

" Do I want you ! I never wanted any one so much in my life. Has Mrs. St. John been telling you that Frederick has disappeared ? "

" Yes. She thinks he has gone to London."

" What nonsense ! " ejaculated Georgina, pushing back her bonnet from her flaming cheeks. " As if he would go off to London in that manner ! I have come to tell you about him, Mr. St. John. He had no one to trust, and so he trusted me. He could not send a letter to await you, lest Mrs. St. John should open it. He is at the Barley Mow all this time ; a prisoner."

" A what ! " exclaimed Mr. St. John.

" He was arrested yesterday morning. I saw it done, but I did not understand it then. It's a horrible man in a great high hat, and he has got him at the Barley Mow, until you release him."

Isaac St. John sank into a seat, in his pain—his consternation. Living always completely out of the world, never having been brought into contact with its rubs and crosses, a thing of this nature was calculated to shock him in scarcely a less degree than it had shocked the young girl before him, who stood there looking at him with her large grey-blue eyes.

" Arrested ! " he murmured. " Frederick ! "

" You will go and release him, won't you ? " said Georgina, anxiously. " It is a great deal of money ; he told me it was some hundreds ; but you will pay it for him ? "

" Yes, I will pay it," replied Mr. St. John, speaking as one lost in thought. " How came he to tell *you* about it, Georgina ? "

" Oh, I went and saw him there. I guessed what had happened ; there's no time to tell you how ; and I went. I promised to keep his counsel. He is in a fever lest Mrs. St. John should get to know it."

" And you will keep it, my dear ! " cried Mr. St. John, seizing her hand and speaking in imploring accents. " It is a cruel disgrace for a St. John."

" Trust me ; trust me ever," was the girl's earnest answer, as she said a word of farewell and stole away.

Little more than an hour later, Frederick St. John was sitting in that same room with his brother—a free man. He was disclosing to him the *whole* of his embarrassments ; which he had not done previously. Not disclosing them altogether willingly, but of necessity; for Mr. St. John's questionings were searching. The more Frederick told, the more amazed grew Isaac St. John; it may be said the more utterly astounded and angry. He had never himself been exposed to the temptations that beset a young man of position on entering the world, and he judged them in by no means a tolerant spirit.

"Frederick, I could not have believed that any human being, gifted with reasoning faculties, had been guilty of such extravagance!"

"The money seems to have melted. *I* had no idea it was diminishing so fast."

"It has been recklessness, not simple extravagance."

Frederick St. John was seated at the table opposite his brother, one elbow leaning on it, the hand of the other playing with the seal attached to his watch-chain. The attitude, the voice, the bearing altogether, seemed to display a carelessness; and it vexed Mr. St. John.

"How has the money gone? Is it of any use my asking?"

"It would be of no use if I could tell you," was the reply. "I declare, on my honour, that I do not know. As I say, the money seems to have melted. I was extravagant; I acknowledge that; I spent it thoughtlessly, heedlessly; and when once the downward path in money-spending is entered upon, a man finds himself going along with a run, and can't pull up."

"Can't?" reproachfully echoed Mr. St. John.

"Well, Isaac, it is more difficult than you could imagine. I have found it so. And the worst is, you glide on so easily that you don't see its danger; otherwise one might sit down halfway and count the cost. I wish you would not look so grieved."

"It is not the wilful waste of money that is grieving me," returned Isaac; "it is the—the thought that *you* should have suffered yourself to fall into these evil ways."

Frederick St. John raised his earnest dark-blue eyes to his brother. "Believe me, Isaac, a man can get out of money without running into absolute evil. I can with truth say that it has been my case. A very great portion of mine has gone in what you and my mother have been wont to call my hobby: buying pictures and running about after them. Wherever there was a gallery of paintings to be seen, I went after it, though it might be at the opposite end of Europe. I bought largely,

thoughtlessly; never considering how I was to pay.   I assisted
a great many struggling artists, both English and foreign, and
set them on their legs.   I always travelled—and you know how
very much I have travelled—as if I were a wealthy man; and
that is costly.   But of evil, in your acceptation of the word,
those vices that constitute it, I have not been guilty.   Of
extravagance, even, I have not been so guilty as you may
think."

Mr. St. John lifted his eyebrows.   "Not guilty of extravagance?"

"Isaac, I said not so guilty as you may deem me; not so
guilty as appears on the surface.   I fell into that dangerous
practice of drawing bills.   When I bought pictures and could
not pay for them, I would give a bill for the amount.   When
the bill was due, if I could not meet it, I borrowed money upon
another, and so patched up the deficiency in that way.   It is
that that has ruined me.   If I owed a hundred pounds I had
to pay two for it, sometimes three.   Let a man once enter
upon this system, and he won't be long above water."

"Did you never think of the ending?"

"Yes, often.   But I could not pull up.   There it is!   Fairly
enter on the downhill path, and there's no getting back again.
I can redeem myself in time, Isaac.   If I choose to give up all
sources of expense, and live upon a shilling a day, as the saying
runs, things will right themselves."

"How long do you think you would be doing it?"

"Four or five years, I suppose."

"Just so.   The best years of your life.   I should not like to
see it, Frederick."

"It might do me good."

"It would scarcely be a position for the heir of Castle
Wafer."

"Isaac, believe me, I have never presumed upon that idea;
have never acted upon it.   There have not been wanting
insidious advisers urging me to forestall my possible right to its
revenues, but I never listened to them.   Though I squandered
my own property, I have not trenched on yours."

"Quite right," said Mr. St. John.   "If anything in the
world could make me wish to deprive you of that heirship, it
would be the finding that you had presumed upon it for unjustifiable purposes.   Though you are as much the heir-apparent
to Castle Wafer, Frederick, as though you were my son,

instead of younger brother, and I have assured you of this before, it is well that the world should remember that the doubt exists."

"I wish to remember it also, Isaac. It would be simple folly on my part not to do so. So long as you live, your intentions may change."

"Well now, listen to me. This matter has shocked me very greatly, but I see that it might have been worse; and if it has purchased for you that experience without which I conclude you worldly young men cannot settle down, I shall not think the cost too dear. You must begin again upon a fresh footing. A totally different one. I will help you upon two conditions."

"What are they?"

"The first is, that you give me your word of honour never to put your name to another bill."

"I will give it with all my heart. It is only these embarrassments that have caused me to draw bills, and I had already made a firm resolution never to touch another, if once clear. I hate bills."

"Very well then, so far. The other condition is, that you marry."

For a minute Frederick St. John was silent. The avowal seemed to cause him no surprise. He did not look up, only paused in thought. It may be that he had anticipated it.

"I fear I must demur to that, Isaac."

"Hear me farther. It has always been my intention to resign to you Castle Wafer on your marriage. If I have made the abode beautiful, Frederick, I have only done it for you. I shall go to that little place of mine in the North, and when I come to Castle Wafer, it will be as your guest. Do not interrupt me. No right to deprive me of it? Nonsense! I dare say I should be here six months in the year. Let me go on. Your own property I will free at once from its encumbrances; and I should make over a liberal income to you besides; one fitting for the occupant of Castle Wafer. The settlements on your wife also shall be liberal. Is there anything more that you would desire?"

"I do not desire half this," was the warm reply. "You have ever been too generous to me, Isaac. But"—and Frederick St. John laughed gaily—"before I can say that I will marry, it is necessary to fix upon a wife."

"That, I hope, has been done long ago, Frederick."

"Not by me," he answered, speaking very quietly. "It has not of course escaped my observation that you and my mother have had your wishes turned towards Anne : but—I—I—have not encouraged this."

"It has been the universal wish of the St. John family that you and Anne should marry."

"I dare say it has. But the fact is, Isaac, I and Anne do not care for each other. As well perhaps avow it, now it has come to a point. Hitherto I have only evaded the question."

"Could you wish for a better wife than Anne?"

"I could not find a better in real worth. But we marry for love, not for worth : at least, worth goes for little when there is no love. My inclinations do not lie towards Anne."

Mr. St. John's face looked deathly pale as he leaned forward. The fatigue of the day was making itself acutely felt : and at these times crosses tell upon the heart.

"Do you know that her father wished it?" he said in low tones. "He mentioned it to me more than once when he was dying—how glad he should be if he thought you would marry Anne. You were but a boy then; but you were a favourite with the earl."

"Fathers' wishes go for little in such matters," was the unwelcome reply.

"Let me ask you a question, Frederick. Have you formed any other attachment?"

"No. At least"—and he laughed again—"I am not sure but I had a fancy of the sort once. I believe it has passed."

"Is there anything between you and Georgina Beauclerc?" asked Isaac. "Any love?"

"Not on—" my side, had all but escaped him in his impulsiveness. But he was in time to alter the phrase. "Not anything." •

"Then it is not she who is keeping you from Anne?"

"Neither she nor any one else. I decline Anne of my own free will. But indeed, Isaac, one great and essential objection is, that I do not care to marry at present."

"Why don't you?"

"I am unable to give you any particular reason, except that I don't. And I really do not know who would have me."

"Anne would have you."

A peculiar smile hovered for a moment on his lips. It was followed by words that bitterly offended Mr. St. John.

"I shall not ask her."

Bit by bit the dissension grew. One word led to another, and a grievous quarrel ensued. It was the first that had ever taken place between the brothers. Hasty words were spoken on both sides : things that leave a sting upon the mind : and when, an hour later, Frederick dashed out of the room, it was because he could not control his passion within it.

Lady Anne was the first he encountered. The sounds had penetrated outside, and she was in a paroxysm of alarm and uneasiness. "Oh, Frederick, what has been the matter? Is it anything about me?"

Even then he was generous. Putting the cause upon himself, rather than on her, and disclosing what at a calmer moment he would not have done. "I was arrested, Anne, and Isaac and I have been quarrelling over it. Where's my mother?"

"Waiting dinner all this time. We thought you were never coming. They are coming in for the evening from the Rectory, and will be here before we have dined."

He was turning away in search of his mother, when Lady Anne caught him by the arm, speaking in a whisper :

"Nothing came out about Captain Saville?"

"Not a word. Be easy. Have I not told you you might trust me?"

Seeking the presence of his mother, he startled her by saying he was at once going up to London, by a night train. In vain Mrs. St. John strove to combat his resolution, to ascertain particulars of the stormy interview just passed. Even as she was pressing for it, he kissed her, and was gone; asking Brumm to see that his things were sent after him.

Swinging away from the door in his independence, he commenced his walk to the station at Lexington, with a step firm and fleet, as became an angry man. For a very short way his road lay through the covered walk, and here, as he was going along in his haste, he encountered Mrs. Beauclerc, her niece and daughter.

"Were you coming to escort us?" asked Georgina, her words ready as usual.

"I am hastening to Lexington," he said. "I am going back to London by the first train that passes."

"What for?"

He made no reply. He turned to Mrs. Beauclerc, asking if he could do anything for her in town.

"Nothing, thank you," she answered, "unless you should see the dean. He was to be in London about this time, I believe. If you do see him, tell him that the sooner he joins us the better it may be for Miss Georgina. *I* can do nothing with her; she's placing herself beyond my control. Would you believe that she was out some hours to-day, never coming in until dark, and she will not tell me what was keeping her or who she was with!"

Frederick St. John hardly heard the complaint. He turned to Sarah, who had walked on, as if impatient at the encounter.

"Will you not say God speed to me? I may not be here again for a long, long time."

She did not put out her hand. She simply wished him good evening. Just this same freezing conduct had she observed to him in the one or two interviews that had taken place since his arrival. Who knows but it was the turning-point in their destiny? But for this repellent manner, made unnecessarily so, and which had told so disagreeably on him, he might in this contest with his brother have said: "Not Anne my wife; change her for another, and I will not say you nay." That it would have been listened to by Isaac St. John, there was little doubt.

"I never saw mamma in such a passion," whispered the giddy girl to him when the others went on. "I had kept dinner waiting, you see, and nothing exasperates her like that. Then she wanted to know where I had been: 'Out with the gipsies,' I answered. I couldn't tell the truth, you know. She was so mad!"

"And where had you been?"

"Where had I been! That's good! In this very grove; here; watching for the carriage of Mr. St. John. I came into it at half-past twelve, and never got out of it until between six and seven!"

"You are a good and true girl, Georgina, though you are random," he said, taking her hand and speaking in a softer tone than she generally heard from him. "How shall I repay you for what you have done for me?"

"Oh, it's not much," she said, her large grey eyes raised to his, discernible in the clear night. He might have thought he saw a moisture in them, but for her light tone, her careless laugh. "It's not much, I say. Tell me why you are going to London?"

"Because I have had a dispute with Isaac. Fare you well, Georgina; take care of yourself, child. Thank you ever for what you have done for me."

The eyes had tears in them now, unmistakably; and her hand rested in his with a lingering pressure. Mr. St. John stooped in his heedlessness and left a kiss upon her lips.

"There's no harm in it that I know of, Georgina. We have ever been as brother and sister."

Her cheeks crimsoned, her pulses beating, her whole frame thrilling with a rapture hitherto unknown, she stood motionless as he disappeared round the turning of the walk. But ere she had realized the emotion to her own soul, it gave place to sober fact, untinged with sentiment. The delusive mist cleared away from her eyes, and she saw things as they *were*, not as they might have been.

"As brother and sister!" she murmured in her pain. "Only as brother and sister!"

CHAPTER XIV.

ST. MARTIN'S EVE.

IT was the 10th of November, St. Martin's Eve, the birthday of the young chief of Alnwick, and of his little brother George; the first birthday, as you will remember, since the death of Mr. Carleton St. John, and of the boy's inheritance. Benja was five, George three, that day.

The day was one of ovation for Benja. With early morning a serenade of music had been heard underneath the windows, proceeding from some of the tenantry; the servants came in with their respectful congratulations; and sundry visitors drove up after breakfast to pay the same. A present had arrived for Benja in the morning from General Carleton—a handsome gold watch, which must have cost twenty or thirty guineas. The General had never married, and knew far less about children than he did about Hottentots, so no doubt thought a gold watch was a suitable present for a young gentleman of five. Benja was highly pleased with the costly toy, and of course wished to appropriate it forthwith; so Honour attached some black watered-ribbon to it, which she put round his neck, and let

him display the watch and key from his belt. It was a key
and seal in one; Master Benja's crest and initials were engraved on it, and it was attached to the watch by a short gold
chain.

Matters were not progressing favourably between Prance and
Honour. And if you think, my readers, that the squabbles of
two maid-servants are, or ought to be, too insignificant to be
thus frequently alluded to, I can only say that the fact bears
so much upon the tragic event soon to be related, that the
allusion could not be avoided. About a fortnight before this,
Honour had had a day's holiday to go and see some relatives;
she had wished to take Benja with her, but Mrs. St. John
would not allow it, and he was left under the charge of Prance.
In the course of the afternoon, Mrs. St. John drove over to
Alnwick Cottage, taking George. They remained there to
dinner, and during this absence of hers Prance and Benja came
to an issue. When Honour returned to the Hall—and she
reached it before Mrs. St. John did—she found that Benja had
not only been whipped with more severity than was seemly, but
that he had been locked up alone in an isolated room, where
his cries could not be heard. She found him exhausted with
weeping, marks raised on his back—altogether in a sad state.
Whether, as Prance affirmed, Master Benja had been unbear-
ably insolent to her; whether, as Honour said and believed,
she must maliciously have taken the opportunity to pay off old
scores of dislike to him, was not satisfactorily settled. Probably
the real fact might lie between the two. But you may judge
what sort of an explosion came from Honour. Prance shut
herself up in her chamber, and would vouchsafe no answer to
it; the servants took part with Honour, for Prance had never
yet found favour with them. Mrs. St. John returned home in
the midst of the commotion. Honour carried Benja and the
complaint to her; but she seemed to treat it with indifference,
and did not reprove Prance, as far as the household could
learn. Honour had been in a state of indignation from that
day to this, and her animosity to Prance was bitter. "She'd
kill the boy if she could," was a remark of hers that went
openly through the house.

Mrs. St. John sat in her drawing-room, waiting for the boys.
She had promised to dine with them that day at two, and cut
the birthday-pudding, foregoing her usual late dinner. Being a
rather strict disciplinarian as to the children taking their meals

regularly, she preferred to change her own hour for once, not theirs. The boys were being attired, and she sat waiting for them, her outward demeanour calm as usual, her mind a very chaos of rebellious tumult.

The marks of honour shown to Benja that day had not been extended to George. They were paid to the boy as *the heir*, not simply as Benja St. John. People had kissed Georgy, and wished him many happy returns, but there it ended. There had been no court paid to him, no music, no set congratulations ; *they* had been rendered to the chief of Alnwick. And Mrs. St. John was resenting this ; ah, how bitterly ! It was the first time the wide contrast between the position of the boys had been brought palpably before her, and but for the very greatest control, she had burst into a frenzy.

" I can't bear it ; I can't bear it," she exclaimed to herself, clasping her hands in pain. " Why should my boy be displaced for that other—despised—passed over as nothing ! My darling ! my life ! my all ! If he had only been born first ; if he had only been born first !"

She unclasped her hands, and bent her head down on them, striving to subdue her emotion ; striving, indeed, to put away the unhealthy train of thought. None knew better than herself how utterly futile it was to indulge it, how much happier it would be for her if she could drive it away to some far-off Lethe, whence it would never rise again. There is not the least doubt that this poor young woman, who had been born into the world with unwholesome passions, and had not had them checked in childhood, was really trying to do a good part by her step-son ; and she believed she was doing it. She relied entirely on her own strength : she had not learnt yet where to look for any other. The daily struggle was getting rather formidable. It was directed to two points : on the one hand, she strove partially to hide her most passionate love for her own child ; on the other, she tried to overcome her jealous dislike of Benja. But there were times, as to-day, when this jealousy raged within her, seeming to scorch her breast to madness.

The children came in, radiant with good humour and happiness : Benja with his face of intelligence, Georgy with his shower of fair curls and pretty ways. Mrs. St. John lifted her pale face and kissed them both : she *was* striving, in her own feeble way, against her evil spirit. They wore new black velvet birthday-dresses, with narrow crimped cambric frills round the neck, and on the left sleeve of each dress was a knot of crape, badge of their mourning. From Benja's belt was conspicuously displayed the new watch; and Benja did not tire of rattling the chain. Even that little trifle, the present of the watch, was made a subject of resentment by Mrs. St. John. Benja had two watches now. In the last days of his father's illness he had taken his watch off and given it to Benja. "When he shall be twelve years old, Charlotte, let him take it into use," he said to his wife. Yes; Benja had two watches; Georgy none.

Georgy began, in his noisy fashion, to climb on his mother's knee, and Mrs. St. John threw back the white crape lappets of her cap as she clasped the boy to her. Georgy, however, did not favour clasping as a rule, and he struggled out of it now.

"What's that?" cried he, snatching at a note that lay on the table at his mother's elbow.

"That's a note from grandmamma, Georgy; she cannot come to us to-day."

"Oh, I am so sorry," cried Benja, who was exceedingly fond of Mrs. Darling, always kind and good-humoured to the children. "Why can't she come, mamma?"

"She's not well," answered Mrs. St. John, languidly, but in a tone that seemed to indicate she did not care much about the matter, one way or the other. Mrs. Darling had been invited to spend the birthday with them; but in the note just received from her by Mrs. St. John, she intimated that she was very unwell indeed. A rare excuse for Mrs. Darling to put forward, who was always in the possession of rude health.

"Mamma, me want a watch."

"You shall have one, my son."

"When?" continued Georgy.

"As soon as I can get out to buy you one."

"One that goes, like Benja's?" demanded Master Georgy.

"It shall be the best gold watch that I can buy for money," answered Mrs. St. John, allowing the passionate emotion that the subject called up to become momentarily apparent.

An opportune interruption intervened: the butler came in and announced dinner. Mrs. St. John, feeling a relief, she could not tell from what, went quickly to the dining-room, Georgy held in her hand, Benja following.

It was a sumptuous repast. The housekeeper had put forth

her strength to do honour to the birthdays; but, had you asked her *why* she had so exerted herself, she might have said it was the heir she had thought of, more than the little one. Inviting as the entertainment was, however, there was one of the three who did little justice to it, and that was Mrs. St. John. She could not eat: but, as if the fire of her restless spirit had imparted itself to her body, she drank frequently, as one parched with thirst. Sherry and champagne were the wines used with dinner. She was kind and attentive to the boys, helping both to whatever dishes they chose, and to as much as they chose. Prance, who was in attendance upon Master George, seeing that his birthday-dress did not come to grief, forgot her good manners by telling him that he "ate enough for a little pig:" of which Mrs. St. John took no manner of notice, but continued to heap his plate according to his fancy. Honour was not present, Master Benja being considered old enough now to be waited on by the men-servants.

Dinner came to an end, the servants and Prance withdrew, and the children were left to take dessert with their mamma. Mrs. St. John was drinking port wine then and cracking walnuts, of which fruit she was very fond. By-and-by, when the boys grew tired of sitting, they slid off their chairs, and began to look out for some amusement. Had Mrs. St. John been wise, she would have rung the nursery-bell then, and sent them to the nursery, where they might play at leisure; but she was absorbed with her walnuts and port wine, and did nothing of the sort. After capering about for a short time, George went up to Benja.

"Let me have the watch on now," he began

"No," said Benja, "you'll break it."

"Me shan't break it," lisped Georgy.

"I'm afraid," returned Benja, rather undecidedly. "Honour said you would."

"Mamma, Benja won't let me have his watch!"

"Don't ask him, my darling," said Mrs. St. John, her mother's heart more resentful at the refusal than Georgy's was, for the conversation had penetrated to her senses. "I will buy you a better one than that."

"But me want that now," retorted resolutely Master George, who had a will of his own. "Me won't break it, Benja."

Benja possessed one of the kindest hearts beating. He looked at his watch, thinking he should not like it to be broken, and then he looked at Georgy, who stood turning up his pretty face, eagerly protesting he would take care of it. In another moment, Benja had hung the watch round the younger one's neck.

Gratification enough for the time. Georgy paraded up and down the room, the watch hanging before him on his velvet tunic, as if the walls were alive with eyes, and he was challenging their admiration. Presently he stood still, took off the watch, and began to open it.

"Don't do that," interposed Benja, who had been watching all the time. "You'll spoil it. Give it back to me."

"No," said Master George, very positively.

"Give it back to me, I tell you, Georgy."

"Give him back his watch, Georgy, my dearest," interrupted Mrs. St. John. "Let him keep it to himself if he is so selfish."

Benja, child though he was, felt a sense of injustice. But the reproach told, and he made no further remonstrance. There was ever a certain timidity in his heart when in the presence of Mrs. St. John. So George thought he could go as far as he pleased with impunity, and his next movement was to take firm hold of the short gold chain and swing the watch round and round after the manner of a rattle.

"Oh, mamma, mamma!" cried Benja, in an agony, running up to Mrs. St. John and laying his hands upon her knee, to attract her attention, "do not let him spoil my watch. See what he is doing with it!"

Mrs. St. John's usual self-control deserted her. That self-control, I mean, which enabled her to treat Benja and George with equal justice. Whether the morning's doings, the ovations to Benja, were really exciting her more than she could bear, or whether—but let that pass for the present. However it might be, she tacitly refused to interfere, and pushed Benja from her with a gesture of dislike. The boy, finding he could get no redress where it ought to have been afforded, ran back to Georgy and seized him just as he was flying to his mother for protection. The naughty, spoiled child, finding he might no longer retain possession of the watch, dashed it into a far corner, and they heard its glass crash on the floor, beyond the turkey carpet.

Benja was by nature a sweet-tempered child: he had also been kept under by Mrs. St. John; but this was more than he could bear. He burst into a loud fit of weeping, and struck out at Georgy with all his might and main. Georgy roared, screamed, kicked, and tried to bite.

As a tigress flies to protect its young, up rose Mrs. St. John, her voice loud, her eyes wearing that strangely wild look at times observable there. A passion, mad and fierce as that you once saw her in, in the presence of her husband, overpowered her now. As she had hurled Benja to the ground that ever-to-be-remembered day, so she would have hurled him this; but the boy was older and stronger now, and he struggled against it. Better that he had yielded! It might in a degree have appeased the mad woman who was upon him: and his strength was as nothing compared with hers. His little head was struck against the table, his costly new birthday-dress was torn. He screamed with pain, Georgy screamed with terror, and Honour, who happened to be near the door at the time, came rushing in.

"Good Heavens!" she exclaimed, "what is it? What has he done?"

"Me took his watch," sobbed little Georgy, in a fit of remorseful generosity. "Me not want mamma to hit him like that."

"How can you for shame treat him in such a manner, ma'am?" cried Honour, indignantly, as her own passion rose; and she spoke to her mistress as she had never dared to speak before. "Poor orphan child! Nobody to protect him! How can you reconcile it to the memory of my dead master?"

Mrs. Carleton St. John stood glaring at the girl, her hand pointed imperiously, her voice low now with command. It was as if some soothing oil had been thrown on the wounds of passion.

"To-morrow morning you quit my service, Honour Tritton? I never tolerate insolence, and I find that you have been here too long. Take that boy out of my sight."

Somehow in the fray, they had all hemmed themselves into a corner, and the broken glass was cracking under Mrs. St. John's feet. Honour picked up the watch with a jerk which bespoke the temper she was in, clasped the sobbing boy tenderly in her arms, and went upstairs with him, meeting Prance at the dining-room door, as she was gliding in.

"It's a burning shame!" broke forth Honour, sitting down by the nursery fire and dashing the coals about with the poker,

while she held Benja to her with the other hand—"it's a burning shame that he should be so treated! If she does turn me
away, I'll go every step of the way to Castle Wafer and tell all
I know to your guardian, Benja. If I don't do it, may Heaven
never prosper me!"

Poor little ill-treated child! He lay there in her lap, smarting
with the pain, his trembling heart beating.

"Let the worst come to the worst, my precious lamb, it can
only be for a few years," began Honour again. "I know it said
in my master's will that you were to be sent early to Eton."

"What's Eton?" sobbed Benja.

"Something very good," rejoined Honour, who had no definite
ideas on the subject herself. "And when you are of age, my
darling, all Alnwick will be yours, and she and Master Georgy
must turn out of it."

"Where will they go?" asked Benja.

"I don't know where, and it don't matter where," continued
the woman in her injudicious partisanship. "You will be master
at Alnwick, and nobody can live here then unless you choose to
let them."

"Who is master now?" questioned Benja.

"You are, my pretty boy, and have been ever since your papa
died; only she lives in it and gives orders because you are not
old enough. Master's wits must have gone a wool-gathering,"
added the exasperated Honour in soliloquy, "when he left her
with any power over the child at all."

Honour was right in the main.

Benja remained on her lap, his sobs gradually subsiding. He
lay thinking of many things, such as occur to children, his ideas
running from one topic to another. Presently he spoke.

"Honour, when is my church to be finished?"

"Suppose I finish it this afternoon," cried Honour, starting
up. "There's scarcely anything left of it to do, and if I am
turned away it may never get done at all."

Opening a closet-door, she took from it what seemed to be
the model of a very pretty country church, with its spire, begun
in pursuance of her promise to Benja after the visit to the
"Emporium of Foreign Curiosities." Like many another thing
entered upon in haste, this coveted treasure had not yet been
completed. The fact was, Honour found more trouble over it
than she had anticipated, and Benja, in the protracted waiting,
forgot his eagerness. All that was left to be done now was the

pasting on of the coloured windows. They were cut out of thin rose paper; the walls of the structure being of thicker paper and white, and the framework of thin wood.

Honour collected her materials, and soon accomplished her task, though she had not been sparing of her windows. Benja forgot his troubles in watching her. She had taken off his velvet dress, with many a lamentation over the rent, and put on him a brown-holland tunic, handsomely trimmed with black silk braid. Over that she tied a white pinafore, lest he should make too free acquaintance with the paste.

At dusk all was completed, and this famous church lighted up by means of the bit of candle inside. Benja clapped his hands with delight. It was a novel, ingenious, picturesque sight, especially to a child. The fire had burned low and there was no other light in the room, so that the church was shown off to perfection, and was a really striking and conspicuous object. Suddenly the flame inside began to whiffle.

"It's the draught from that door," observed Honour. "Shut it, Benja; shut it gently."

She spoke of the door which opened into Mrs. St. John's dressing-room. It is possible that you may remember there was formerly no door there; but Mrs. St. John had caused one to be made at the birth of George, that she might pass into the nursery at will, without going into the corridor. Now that George was beyond babyhood, this door was generally kept bolted, the bolt being on Mrs. St. John's side, not any on that of the nursery; but it was sometimes, as now, left open.

Honour turned her head to the door as she spoke, and saw the little boy place his hands upon the panel to push it to, after the manner of children, and it closed gently. Benja came to the table again to feast his eyes. The flame was steady now.

"There ought to be moss all round here," observed Honour, pointing to the board on which the church rested. "But it's too late to put it on to-night: and, for the matter of that, I have no moss. If I stop, we will ask the gardener to get some."

Benja did not care for the moss. To his admiring eyes nothing could improve its present aspect. He gazed at it on the drawers, he danced before it on the table, he carried it to and fro in the room, obeying Honour's injunctions to keep it upright and steady. In this manner some time passed, and they allowed the fire to go out.

"Bother take the fire!" ejaculated Honour. "And I have neither wood nor matches up here."

She had her hand upon the bell, when it suddenly occurred to her that she would go down for the things herself. No one living liked a gossip better than she, and the scene in the dining-room was burning her tongue. Placing the church on the table, and strictly charging Benja not to touch it while she was away, Honour went out by the ordinary door, and descended the back-stairs. To *this* door, and I would have you note the difference, the fastening was inside. It was not a bolt, but a common button, placed high up beyond reach of the children.

Never had Honour relished a gossip more than the one she now entered on with the servants. Every little detail of the dining-room affray, so far as she had been a witness to it, was related by her to the servants, who did not spare their comments or their sympathy. Honour was quite unable to tear herself away, until by the striking of the clock she found she must have been there nearly half-an-hour. Hardly believing her ears, she caught up a bundle of faggots and a box of matches, popped them into her apron, together with a pair of snuffers and an extinguisher, and ran up the stairs. Turning the handle of the door to enter hastily, she was surprised to find that she could not open it.

"Master Benja, why have you fastened the door?" she called out. "Come and undo it."

There was no reply.

"He must have got upon a chair and turned the button," soliloquized Honour. But at that moment she became conscious of a smell of burning, as of wool. Letting the things she carried fall with a crash, she flew along the passage and turned into her mistress's dressing-room, that she might obtain entrance that way. That door was also fastened, but on the outer side. It was no unusual occurrence—in fact, it was usually kept bolted, as was just now observed, and Honour at the moment thought nothing of it. Slipping back the bolt, she went in.

Oh! what did Honour see! Where was the young heir of Alnwick? A dark mass smouldering on the floor at the far end of the room, the carpet smouldering, no trace whatever remaining of the pretty and dangerous toy she had made, no trace of *him*, save that shapeless heap from which the spirit had flown!

With awful cries, with wild shrieks of terrified alarm, Honour flew through the dressing-room, and down the grand staircase, her cries arousing the household, arousing Mrs. St. John.

CHAPTER XV.

CONFLICTING STATEMENTS.

How the night subsequently went on, few at the Hall could tell. For some time it was one scene of horror and confusion. One of the grooms, unbidden, saddled a horse and went galloping for Mr. Pym; and in an almost incredibly short space of time, the surgeon was there. But what could he do? That one precious little spirit had gone, never to be recalled by leech of this world. Another, however, wanted the attentions of Mr. Pym,—and that was little George. The child, aroused by the cries of Honour from a sleep he had fallen into in the dining-room, had escaped upstairs into the nursery. A rush of terror overtook him, baby though he was, at what he saw there, and at being told it was Benja, and he fell into a succession of fits of sickness and shivering.

It must be assumed—it was so assumed in the house—that this burning was the result of accident; the result, it may also be said, of Honour Tritton's carelessness. She had gone down secure in the belief that the boy would obey her mandate and not touch the church. Oh, how could she have been so foolish! To look at a new toy and not touch it, to gaze at its attractions from a distance and not examine them, is philosophy beyond a child. Perhaps the little boy—for he was an obedient boy naturally—tried for some minutes to exercise his patience; but no doubt could be entertained that he at length took the church in his hands again. In how short a time the accident occurred, and how it occurred, was as yet unknown—it may be said, it was hidden in mystery.

The position of those in the house during this time appeared to be as follows. The servants were all downstairs, with the exception of Prance; and Honour, as you have heard, was with them. Mrs. St. John and George were shut up in the dining-room, the latter asleep, the former, as she said, nearly if not quite asleep also. Where Prance was at the time did not as yet appear, neither had any question been raised in regard to it.

But in the midst of the dreadful horror which had taken possession of the unhappy Honour, two points thrust themselves prominently forward in her brain. The one was, How did the child get fastened in the room? the other was, that she had seen Prance hiding in a recess of the passage as she ran along it. This was not so much a *remembrance* as a *conviction;* and it seemed to Honour as if she had not noticed, or had very superficially noticed, Prance's being there at the time, but the fact had flashed into her mind afterwards. On the opposite side of the passage, about midway between the nursery-door and the dressing-room door, the recess was situated—a small arched recess. Poor Mr. Carleton St. John in his life-time had wondered laughingly whether the architect had put it there for ornament or for use.

The first person Mr. Pym sought on his arrival, after he had taken a hopeless look at that sight in the nursery, where the floor was now half-inundated by the water employed to put the fire out, was Mrs. St. John. She was in the dining-room, and he found her almost unnaturally calm and collected; some people are so in these moments of calamity. The only sign of emotion was her death-like pallor. She gave him the account of what had occurred, so far, she observed, as she knew it; candidly confessing to the fracas that had taken place in the room after dinner. Benja had set upon George unmercifully, and in return she had corrected Benja: boxed his ears, and, she really believed, had shaken him. It was very rare indeed that she was so hasty with either of the children; and she would give the whole world not to have touched him, now that he was gone. After Honour took him away to the nursery, she had remained in the dining-room, not quitting it until disturbed by the shrieks of Honour. Prance came in once or twice to ask if she should take George, but she did not let him go. The boy went to sleep in his papa's large chair, and she sat down by him and took his legs upon her lap. She was nearly asleep herself when the cries began, and she had felt startled almost to death. The whole fault, she feared, lay with Honour. The woman had confessed the facts in the first moment of terror: she had left Benja alone with some dangerous paper toy lighted up with a candle, while she went downstairs and

stayed gossiping with the servants.   The poor little fellow must
have set himself on fire.

"But did no one hear his cries?" asked Mr. Pym, who had
not previously interrupted the narrative.

Mrs. St. John supposed not.   All she knew was, that they
had not penetrated to the dining-room.   The surgeon listened.
He knew the walls on that side the house were massive, and
if the child was shut up in the nursery—as it appeared he had
been—it was hardly likely that he would be heard, unless any
one had happened to be upstairs.   The dining-room was in the
other wing of the house, its doors were double ; and the kitchens
were beyond the dining-room.

"The odd thing to me is, that he did not run out of the
room," cried Mr. Pym.   "A strong lad of five years old would
hardly stop in a room to be burnt, for the want of escaping out
of it.   The first thing most of us attempt in a similar calamity
is to run from the room : often a fatal step.   But he does not
seem to have attempted it."

Mrs. St. John shook her head.   She did not know any of
the details : they must of course be left to supposition.   Honour
deserved hanging for having left the child alone with a lighted
toy.

It was at this juncture that Mr. Pym's attention was called
to George.   The child was very sick ; had been sick at intervals
since the fright.   After attending to him ; Mr. Pym went in
search of Honour.   He found her alone, in a lamentable state
of distress, in the bedroom that had been hers and the unhappy child's.

And now it must be mentioned that Honour had been
arriving at a sudden and very dreadful doubt.   As the mists
cleared away from her brain and she was able to reflect more
calmly upon the probabilities of the accident, she began to
think whether it had not been wilfully caused.   And the doubt
was assuming the aspect of certainty in her mind, when Mr.
Pym came in.

For some minutes she could not speak ; she could only cry
and sob, and cover her face with her apron in very shame and
remorse.   Mr. Pym did not reproach her in her distress : he
rather set himself, when she had gathered calmness, to learn
what he could of the particulars.   Honour freely confessed all.
She told of the affair in the dining-room, giving a different
colouring to it from that her mistress had done, and causing

Mr. Pym's grey eyebrows to scowl themselves into ugliness. She told how she had afterwards finished the church for him, describing what it was, and where the idea had been taken from. She said she had left it with him lighted, had gone down for wood, and stayed talking the best part of half-an-hour. Not a thing did she conceal; not a point that could tell against herself did she gloss over.

"He was always an obedient boy," she wailed, "and I did not think he would touch it when I bade him not. And I never thought I had been down so long, till I heard the clock strike!"

"It is strange you did not hear his cries!"

"The kitchens are too far off."

"And it is very strange that the boy did not run out of the room: unless smoke overpowered him from the first. I cannot make out why he did not. It is a bad plan in general, but in this instance it might have saved his life by bringing help to him."

Honour made no immediate remark. She had been sitting in a low chair, swaying her body backwards and forwards in her distress. Suddenly she looked up at the surgeon and spoke in a low tone.

"I want to know who fastened the doors."

"What do you mean?" asked Mr. Pym, after a pause of surprise.

"I don't think he was burnt by accident, sir," she continued, glancing at the walls as if afraid of being overheard, and speaking in the faintest possible whisper. "I think it was done on purpose."

"Good Heavens, woman!" exclaimed the astonished surgeon, really wondering whether the trouble was turning her brain.

"There are things connected with it that I can't understand," she continued. "They did not strike me particularly at the moment, but they do now that I can think of them. He *couldn't* get out of the room; he was fastened in."

That she was not suffering from mental aberration at present, was apparent enough to the surgeon; the girl was as sane as he was. Honour thought he was never going to leave off staring at her.

"When I left him upstairs, I left both doors open; that is, unfastened," she went on. "When I got back again, both were fastened; the one on the inside, the other on the out. *I want to know who did it.*"

It might have been a fancy of Honour's, but she thought the doctor changed countenance. "Are you sure of this?" he asked.

"As sure as I am that I am living and my darling child is dead."

Mr. Pym's eyebrows contracted themselves yet more. "Just describe to me consecutively what occurred, will you?" he said. "How did you know that the doors were fastened?"

"Because I couldn't get in," said Honour, thinking it rather a simple question. "When I got back with my little bundle of faggots, I found the door was buttoned inside. I thought the child had got upon the chair and done it; but, short as the moment was that I had for thought, it struck me as being strange, for I had never known him to do such a thing before. As I called to him to unfasten it, I fancied there was a smell of burning, and I ran round through my mistress's dressing-room and turned the handle of the door to open it, and found that door was also fastened, bolted on the outside. The smell was very strong then, and in my frenzy I forgot the strangeness of the circumstance, for the door is in general kept bolted——"

"Then why should you be surprised at finding it bolted then?" interrupted Mr. Pym.

"Because it was not bolted when I went down," returned Honour. "It was open while I was finishing the church, and I told the child to shut it, as the draught caused the flame inside the paper walls to whiffle about. He pushed the door to with his dear little hands, and I watched him. That's how I know it was unfastened then, sir."

"In your flurry afterwards, when you attempted to enter, you perhaps only fancied it was fastened," suggested Mr. Pym.

"No, sir. When I tried to open it and could not, I found the bolt was pushed into the grove to its full extent. The end came beyond the grove, and I pushed it back with my fingers."

Mr. Pym rose impulsively, as if he would look at the door for himself; but halted suddenly and sat down again.

"That could not have been done without hands," proceeded Honour. "And why was it done?"

The surgeon made no attempt to answer the question. He

seemed very greatly put out, as if the revelation had alarmed or unnerved him, scarcely noticing Honour.

"Mrs. St. John says she heard nothing," he presently observed to himself, as one in abstraction. "Honour, he continued in straightforward tones to the girl, "I think you must be mistaken. There appears to have been no one upstairs who would have bolted it. Mrs. St. John tells me she did not quit the dining-room : the servants say they never came up at all during the afternoon."

"One of them was up," rejoined Honour in the same low voice, and the same roving gaze round the walls, "and that was Prance. I saw her myself; I can't be mistaken. Does *she* say she was not upstairs, sir ?"

"She has said nothing to me one way or the other," replied Mr. Pym. "I heard it said generally that the servants had not been upstairs."

"Prance was ; and if she says she was not, she tells a lie. She was hidden in the recess outside, opposite the doors."

"Hidden in the recess. When ?"

"After I dropped the things from my apron, and was running round to the dressing-room, I saw Prance standing inside the recess ; she was squeezing herself against the wall, sir, as if afraid I should see her."

"Did you speak to her ?"

"No, sir ; and you may feel surprised at what I am going to say, but it's the truth. I was so flurried at the time, what with finding the first door fastened and with the smell of burning, that I did not seem then to be conscious of seeing her. I suppose my eyes took in the impression without conveying it to my mind. But afterwards it all came into my mind, and I remembered it, and how she was standing. It was just as if she had fastened the doors, and then put herself there to listen to the child's dying cries."

"Hush," authoritatively reproved Mr. Pym. "You are not yourself, girl, or you would not say it."

"I don't think I am," candidly acknowledged Honour, bursting into tears. "My brain feels as if it were on the turn to madness. Prance has been cross and hard and cruel to the child always, and I'm naturally excited against her."

"But she would not shut the doors upon him if he were burning," retorted the surgeon, some anger in his tone. "You should be careful what you say."

"I wish I could be put out of my misery!" sobbed Honour. "I wish they'd hang me for my carelessness in leaving him alone with a lighted toy! I did do that; and I hope I shall be punished for it. I shall never know another happy moment. Thus far the fault is mine. But I did not fasten the doors upon him, so that he could not escape for his life: and I am perfectly certain that in any fright, or calamity, or danger, the child's first impulse would have been to fly down the back-stairs to me."

She threw her apron over her head, sobbing and crying, and swaying her body backwards and forwards on the chair as before, in the intensity of her emotion. The surgeon sat still a few moments, endeavouring to recall his scattered senses, and then rose and touched her shoulder to command attention. She let fall her apron.

"This thing that you affirm must be investigated, look you, Honour. For—for—for the sake of all, it must be sifted to the bottom. No one in their right minds," he emphatically added, "would shut the doors upon a burning child; and that appears to be the theory you have adopted, so far as I can gather it. Have you stated these facts to your mistress?"

"I have not seen her since," answered Honour. "Except at the first moment, when I ran down in my terror."

"And she came out of the dining-room then?"

"She did, sir. The little child—he is the heir now—ran out after her."

"Honour," said the surgeon, gravely and earnestly, "I do not fancy the bent of your thought just now is a wholesome one. You had better put it from you. I want you to come with me and tell your mistress about the doors being fastened."

He went out of the room, Honour following. In the passage outside, suspiciously near to the door, was Prance. She made a feint of being in a hurry, and was whisking down the back-stairs.

"Here, Prance, I want you," said the surgeon. "I was about to ask you to come to me."

The woman turned at once, quite readily, as it appeared, and quite unruffled. She stood calm, cool, quiet, before Mr. Pym, in her neat black gown and silk apron, the black ribbon strings of her close cap tied underneath her chin. Not a shade of change was observable on her impassive face, not the faintest hue of emotion lighted her pale, sharp features.

"This is a very dreadful thing, Prance," he began.

"It is, indeed, sir," she answered in her measured tones, which, if they had not any demonstrative feeling in them, had certainly no irreverence.

"How did the doors get fastened on the unfortunate boy?"

Prance paused for about the hundredth part of a minute. "I was not aware they were fastened, sir." And the answer appeared to be really genuine.

"Honour says they were. Upon returning from the kitchen, and attempting to enter by this door"—pointing to the one still closed on the miserable scene—"she found she could not enter. The inside button had been turned during her absence below. Did you go into the nursery yourself and fasten it? No one else, I believe, is in the habit of frequenting the nursery but you and Honour."

"I did not go, sir. I did not go into the nursery at all during the afternoon. Master George was downstairs with his mamma, and I had nothing to take me into it. If the button was turned in the manner described, I should think Master Benja must have got upon a chair and done it himself."

Still the same impassive face; and still, it must be acknowledged, the same air of truth.

"That may be," remarked Mr. Pynn. "The same thought had occurred to me. But there's another point not so easily got over. Honour says that the other door was also fastened, the one leading into the dressing-room—was bolted on the outside."

"I'm sure I don't know, sir," replied Prance; and this time there was a shade of uncertainty, of hesitation, in her voice; not, however, very perceptible to ordinary ears. "That door generally is kept bolted," she added more freely, raising her eyes to the doctor's. "My mistress took to keep it so, because Master George was always running in while she was dressing."

"But——"

"Be quiet, Honour," said Mr. Pym, cutting short the interruption. "You are in the habit of attending on your mistress, I believe, Prance, and therefore are sometimes in her dressing-room," he continued. "Do you remember whether that door was open to-day?"

"No, sir, I don't," said Prance, after a minute's consideration.. "I dressed my mistress this morning for the early dinner, and put the room straight afterwards, but I do not remember whether the door was open or shut. I should think it was shut."

" It was wide open this afternoon," burst forth Honour, unable to keep quiet any longer, and believing Prance could remember if she chose. " The poor dear child shut it with his own hands while I was finishing his church."

" Is it possible?" responded Prance, her perfect coolness of demeanour, her propriety of tone, presenting a contrast to the excitement of the miserable Honour. " I cannot remember how it was when I was dressing my mistress, and I had nothing to do in the room after that."

" And did not go into it?" pursued the surgeon.

" And did not go into it," repeated Prance.

" Then you know nothing at all as to how the doors could have got fastened?" proceeded Mr. Pym.

" No, sir, I do not. I could take an oath, if need be, that I did not know the doors were bolted until you spoke to me now," added the woman, the least possible sound of emotion, arising as it seemed from earnestness, at length perceptible in her tones. " I assure you, sir, I had no idea of it until this moment. I—I should scarcely think it could have been so."

There was an ominous glare in Honour's eye at the expressed doubt. Mr. Pym did not want a passage-at-arms between the two then, and raised his hand to command silence.

" Did you hear the child's cries, Prance?" he asked. " It is incredible to suppose that he did not cry; and yet no one seems to have heard him."

" You mean when he was on fire, sir?"

" Of course I mean when he was on fire."

" I never heard them, sir. A child could not burn to death without making cries, and desperate cries, but I did not hear them," she continued, more in soliloquy than to the surgeon. " It is an unfortunate thing that no one was within earshot."

Honour looked keenly at her from her swollen eyes. Mr. Pym spoke carelessly.

" By the way, you were in the recess, Prance, just about the time. Did you neither see nor hear anything then?"

" In the recess, sir?" rejoined Prance, turning her impassive face full on Mr. Pym in apparently the utmost astonishment. But not her eyes. " I was in no recess, sir."

" Yes you were. In that recess; there," pointing to it. " Honour passed you when you were in it."

"It is quite a mistake, sir. What should I do in the recess? If Honour says she saw me there, her sight must have deceived her."

"How do you account for your time at the period of the occurrence?" inquired Mr. Pym. "What part of the house were you in?"

"I suppose I must have been in the dining-room, sir," she answered readily. "I was in there until just before the alarm was given, and then I had come up to my bedroom." ,

"Let's see. That is the room on the other side Mrs. St. John's bedroom?"

"Yes, sir; formerly my master's dressing-room. After his death, Mrs. St. John placed me and Master George in it. She felt lonely with no one sleeping near her."

"And that's where you were when you heard the alarm?"

"I was in there with the door shut when I heard Honour come screaming along the passage, running towards the grand staircase. I had not been in my room above a couple of minutes at the most. I had come straight up from the dining-room."

"And you did not go into the recess?"

"Certainly not, sir. What object could I have in doing so? I'd rather keep out of the place."

Mr. Pym looked at Honour. His expression said plainly that he thought she must have been mistaken.

"What had you done with yourself all the afternoon?" he demanded of Prance.

"I was about in one place or another," she answered. "Part of the time I was in the onion-room. I went there for a handful of a particular herb I wanted, and stayed to pick the leaves from the stalks. And I was twice in the dining-parlour with my mistress, and stayed there pretty long each time."

"Talking to her?"

"No, sir, scarcely a word passed. My mistress rarely does talk much, to me or to any of us, and she seemed a good deal put out with the scene there was after dinner with Master Benja. Master George was put out, too, in his little way, and I stayed in the room soothing him. My mistress gave me a glass of wine then, and bade me drink the children's health. I went in later a second time, and stayed longer than the first, but I was waiting for Master George to awake that I might bring him up to the nursery, for it was getting the children's tea-time."

"But you did not bring him?"

"No, sir, he did not awake, and I got tired of waiting. I came straight upstairs, and went into my room, and I had not been there two minutes when Honour's cries broke out. I had not had time to strike a match and light any candle, and when I ran out of the room to see what was the matter, I had the match-box in my hand."

This seemed to be as comprehensive an account as Prance could give; and Mr. Pym himself saw no reason to doubt her. Honour did. She had done nothing but doubt the woman ever since she came to the house. Honour believed her to be two-faced, thoroughly sly and artful; "a very cat in deceit." But in a calmer moment even Honour might not have brought herself to think that she would deliberately set fire to an innocent child, or close the doors on him that he might burn to death.

Again Mr. Pym went into the presence of Mrs. St. John, the two servants with him. She looked more ghastly than before, and she was sitting with Georgy on her lap, the child sick and trembling still. Mr. Pym mentioned to her what Honour said about the doors being fastened, asking if she could remember whether the one leading from her dressing-room was open in the morning. She answered at once—and she spoke with the calmest and coldest self-possession, which seemed as a very contrast to her ghastly face—that she could not say with any certainty whether the dressing-room door was open that day or not. She remembered quite well that she had unbolted it that same morning while she was getting up, upon hearing the children's voices in the nursery. She had gone in to kiss them and wish them happiness on their birthday. Whether she had rebolted the door afterwards or not, she could not say. She generally rebolted it when she had been that way into the nursery, but it was possible she had not done so this morning. "I wish you would not ask these questions," she concluded, momentarily raising her eyes to Mr. Pym, for she had spoken with her face bent down, almost hidden.

"But I must ask them," said the surgeon.

"It frightens George so," she added. "See how he is shivering."

And in truth the child was shivering; shivering and trembling as one in an ague. Almost as his mother spoke, he raised himself with a cry, and was violently sick: and all Mr. Pym's attention had to be given to him.

CHAPTER XVI.

INVESTIGATION.

THE inquest was held the day following the death. A somewhat hurried arrangement; but in these small local places the convenience of the coroner has to be studied. It happened that the county coroner was coming to Alnwick that day to hold an inquest on a poor old man who had been accidentally killed; and the Alnwick parish officials, represented chiefly by the beadle, decided that the second inquest should take place as soon as the first was over.

It did so. The first was held at the workhouse, and was over and done with in half-an-hour; the second was held at a public-house nearer the Hall: the Carleton Arms. The same jury sworn for the other inquest, attended for this one; and the witnesses were hurriedly collected without any formal process of summons-serving.

It was universally believed that the ill-fated little child had taken the lighted church, in defiance of the nurse's injunction and had then fastened the door to prevent her surprising him in his disobedience. Honour's conviction alone protested against this; in silence, not openly; she was weary of arguing against the stream. That he had taken the church in his hands, she feared was too probable, but not that he had fastened the door to conceal his disobedience. A more open, honourable nature than his, child never possessed: he was always the first to tell candidly of a fault; and she thought he would rather have thrown wide the door that Honour might see him at his disobedience, than close it against her. This, however, was not the popular view of the case: *that* was, that the child had taken the dangerous toy in his hand, had slipped the button, not to be caught, and then by some means set himself on fire; the remote distance at which all the inmates of the Hall happened to be, just then, preventing them from hearing his cries.

The fastening of the dressing-room door, which was spoken of by Honour, who was the principal witness, gave rise to some discussion. Nothing could be clearer or more positive than her sworn testimony that the dressing-room door was not fastened when she went downstairs, and that it was fastened when she came up—bolted on the outer side. The puzzle was, who had fastened it? No person whatever had been in the rooms, so far as could be learned. Witnesses were examined on this point, but nothing was elicited that could throw any light on the affair. It was Honour's word against facts— facts so far as they seemed to be known. The housemaid, whose duty it was to attend to Mrs. St. John's rooms, proved that she had not been into them since the morning. From the time of putting them to rights after breakfast, she was not in the habit of again entering them until about seven o'clock in the evening, after Mrs. St. John had dressed for dinner; neither did she on this unfortunate day. The other servants said they had not been upstairs at all: some wine had been given to them, and they were making themselves comfortable below. Honour was with them, talking, but not Prance. Prance was not downstairs, so far as the servants knew, after she left the housekeeper's room at the conclusion of dinner. Prance herself was called as a witness, and accounted for her time. Had gone into the dining-room whilst her mistress was at dessert with Master George, she said, Honour having then taken Master St. John upstairs. Had stayed there some little time. Her mistress had given her a glass of wine. She (witness) said that she had already taken a glass downstairs, but her mistress answered that she could no doubt take another. She did so, drinking to the two young gentlemen's health. After that, went upstairs to her room; stayed there some time, doing a bit of work for herself, and putting up Master George's morning things, which she had not had time to see to after dressing him to dine with his mamma. Yes, she said in answer to a question from the coroner, this room was very near the dressing-room; Mrs. St. John's bedroom only dividing them; but could swear most positively that she did not go into the dressing-room. She entered no room whatever except this, her own.

A juryman interrupted with a question. Where was deceased at this time?

With Honour in the nursery, the witness answered. It was

then that the paper toy, spoken to, was being finished and lighted up—as the Hall had learnt subsequently. Afterwards, witness continued, pursuing her evidence, she had gone downstairs into the onion-room, as it was called, a place where herbs were kept; had stayed there some time, getting an herb she wanted, and plucking its leaves from the stalks. Then—

Another juryman interrupted, a worthy grocer and oilman, with whom the Hall dealt. What might witness have wanted with the herb?

The witness replied, with exemplary patience and the impressive manner that always characterized her, that she occasionally took a decoction of this herb medicinally. The cook was in the habit of preparing it for her, but when it was left entirely to that functionary, as much stalk as leaf was put in, and the decoction suffered in consequence; therefore she liked to pluck it herself.

Very good, the juryman answered. She could go on with her evidence.

After preparing the proper quantity of herb, had taken it to the scullery and laid it on what was called the cook's shelf. Did not see any of the servants except the under-housemaid, who was lighting up the lower passages, but heard their voices in conversation. Could not tell whether the under-housemaid saw her; thought not. Went then into the dining-room, to ask if she should not take Master George, as it was getting the hour for the nursery tea. Did not take Master George. He was asleep in the large chair. Waited some time, hoping he would wake; but he did not. At last got tired of waiting, and left the dining-room, Master George still asleep, with his feet on his mamma's lap. Went straight upstairs then, and was about to get a light in her own room, when she heard alarming cries from Honour. Could only see the outline of her form as she flew along the corridor to the grand staircase. The upper part of the house had not been lighted up, only the lower, and a very faint reflection came upstairs. The cries were alarming, full of terror. Witness was frightened, and it was not a little thing that frightened her. Ran down after Honour, and saw Mrs. St. John come out of the dining-room, frightened also at the cries. For the next few minutes could not give a precise account of what happened. The chief thing she remembered was running back with others to the nursery. Poor little Master George also went. He stole up unnoticed in the confusion, and saw what was left of his brother burning, or, rather, smouldering. That was all she knew.

Mrs. St. John was not called as a witness. Having been shut up—as was understood—the whole of the time in the dining-room with little George, her evidence could not be of importance, and the jury had respect to her feelings and did not call her. It was announced to the jury that she freely acknowledged having gone from her dressing-room into the nursery in the morning, and that it was very possible she had omitted to fasten the door afterwards. That, however, was of no consequence : the door *had* been left open as Honour had proved : by whom did not matter.

All the evidence was taken, and a discussion ensued in regard to the point not cleared up, the fastening of this door. Half the jury, including Mr. Pym, inclined to the view that it had not been bolted at all, only shut; but that Honour's state of haste and agitation had prevented her getting the door open at the first moment, and caused her to fancy that it was fastened. The other half of the jury including the coroner, thought that when the unfortunate little child had pushed-to the door in obedience to Honour, the bolt had shot into the groove with the movement : and this appeared the more reasonable solution. In vain Honour protested that neither was correct : that the door *was* bolted, and that it *could not* have bolted itself when the child closed it; he shut it very gently, and she must have heard the movement had there been any. She might as well have talked to the wind : and to her excessive surprise Mr. Pym approached her with a stern whisper and a warning look.

"I wouldn't say any more about this, Honour."

Will it be believed that Mrs. Darling only heard of this calamity when the jury were sitting? Living some distance on the other side of Alnwick, news did not at all times penetrate quickly to her house. At any rate, *this* had not done so : reversing for once the popular saying that ill news travels fast. Mrs. St. John had omitted to send to her—perhaps it was excusable in the dreadful confusion—and it was a positive fact that the inquest was being held before the tidings were carried to Mrs. Darling.

She might not have heard it even then, but that she happened to send a servant into the village to execute a commission, and the maid brought back the news. As is usual in such cases, she ran open-mouthed with it to her mistress. Mrs. Darling, who had been feeling very poorly ever since the previous day, and was saying to herself that if no better on the following one she should send for Mr. Pym, was lying on the sofa, when the door abruptly opened, and the servant burst in with the news, her very haste rendering her incoherent. Mrs. Darling started from the sofa in terror, only half comprehending.

" *What* do you say has happened, Cole?"

"One of the little boys is killed," spoke up the servant eagerly. "Oh, ma'am, it's true! He was killed last night, and they are already holding the inquest on him. It was the heir, Master Benja."

Almost as one turned to stone, stood Mrs. Darling. If ever woman looked in awful fear, it was she. She could not speak at first: she only gazed at the maid-servant, her lips apart, her eyes wild.

"Killed! Master Benja!" she gasped.

"He was burnt to death," cried the woman, with sobs of emotion. "I don't know the rights of it, though the place is full of nothing else; some said one thing and some another. Any way, the fault was Honour's. She left him alone with a lighted candle, and he set himself on fire. There is a tale that somebody fastened the doors upon him to let him burn; but you know, ma'am, it can't be true. Not a bit of business is doing at Alnwick, and most of the shops have a shutter or two up. The inquest is on now, at the Carleton Arms."

With a prolonged shudder, Mrs. Darling seemed to come to herself. "How is it that I was not sent for?" she asked: and though the servant took the question to herself, and answered that she did not know, it was evident that it was not put to her.

All her indisposition forgotten, her bodily pain no longer felt in the greater mental pain, Mrs. Darling put on her cloak and bonnet and went out. The maid remonstrated that she was not fit to walk; wished her to at least wait until a fly could be sent for: she was as one who heard not. Striking into the field-path, by which means she avoided the gossiping village —and she was in no mood for it then, Mrs. Darling emerged from the fields almost close to Alnwick Hall, just below the Carleton Arms. Had there been any way to avoid passing the inn, Mrs. Darling had surely chosen it: but there was none. As she came within view of it, and saw the idlers congregated around it in small groups, a sick feeling of dread took possession of her, and she shuddered as she had done in her own drawing-room. Dread of what? Perhaps Mrs. Darling could not precisely have defined what: but she did think it would be a mercy had the earth opened and let her through to the opposite side of the globe, away from all trouble and care.

Not a word did she speak to any one, not a question ask. She drew her veil over her face, pulled her cloak more closely around her, and was hastening on, looking neither to the right nor to the left, when she nearly ran against Mr. Pym the surgeon, who had just strolled outside from the heat and bustle of the crowded inquest-room.

"Is it you, Mrs. Darling?"

"What *is* all this?" was the rejoinder of Mrs. Darling, throwing back her veil for a moment, and then seeming to recollect herself, and putting it down again. "Is Benja really dead?"

"Really dead!" echoed Mr. Pym. "He has been dead since yesterday evening. Had you not heard of it?"

"I never heard a word until half-an-hour ago. What was it? How was it done?"

"Honour left him alone in the nursery with some paper toy that had a candle in it. When she got back he was burnt to death."

Mr. Pym was speaking strangely, in a cold, hard sort of manner; and, instead of looking at Mrs. Darling, his eyes were directed straight over her head.

"Then it was an accident," said Mrs. Darling, after a pause.

"That will no doubt be the verdict of the jury."

The two stood in silence. Mr. Pym with his far-away gaze, Mrs. Darling stealing surreptitious glances at him through her veil. Presently she spoke, scarcely above a whisper.

"What tale is it that people have got hold of, about the child being locked in the room?"

"Ah," said Mr. Pym, "that's Honour's tale. She says that when she left the boy, to go downstairs, the nursery doors were unbolted; that when she returned, both were fastened. *Her* theory is, implied if not avowed, that the doors had been deliberately closed upon the burning child."

Mrs. Darling turned her face away. She was as little given as any one to betraying signs of emotion, but the eyes, for all they were not looking at her, saw that the face was turning livid.

"It can't be true," she whispered.

"As I tell Honour. Are you going to the Hall? Most of its inmates are here, at the inquest."

"Charlotte is not here!" exclaimed Mrs. Darling, turning to him in what looked like alarm.

"No. The jury dispense with her evidence."

"Is—is—little Benja here?"

Mr. Pym shook his head. "The coroner and jury went up to look at the remains, and adjourned here. It is a dreadful thing; *very* dreadful."

At the emphasized word, a sound, that was as much like a groan as anything, escaped Mrs. Darling's lips. The surgeon turned towards the inn door, she continued her way. Striking into the avenue amongst the fine old park trees, she threw back her veil where no eye was on her, gasping as it seemed for air, in the twilight of the coming night.

A servant answered her summons, and she walked straight through the hall to a small sitting-room, where the man said he believed his mistress was. She went in gently, not to disturb her: but Mrs. St. John was standing still in the midst of the room in an attitude of breathless expectation; of what looked like terrified expectation; and unless the darkness of the evening deceived her, Mrs. Darling had never seen her face so intensely pale, or with that haggard look upon it.

"Charlotte!"

"Is it you, mamma? I thought you were ill."

"I was ill; ill for me, who never ail anything. But this—this—— What's that?"

Mrs. Darling sprang aside. A heap of something covered over on the sofa had startled her. Surely her nerves were unstrung to-night!

"It's Georgy," answered Mrs. St. John. "He has been ill since yesterday. Hush! don't wake him."

She took off her cloak and untied her bonnet, and sat down by the fire near her daughter. Mrs. St. John did not speak.

"Charlotte, I have been dreadfully shocked. You should not have allowed me to hear of this by accident. How did it happen?"

"You must ask Honour that."

"Was no one with him? Could no one hear his cries?"

"It seems not."

"Will you not give me the details, Charlotte?"

"I only know them from hearsay."

"But you—were—in the house at the time?"

"I was in the dining-room."

Mrs. St. John was evidently not inclined to be communicative. She sat looking at the fire, and Mrs. Darling stole surreptitious glances at her face, as she had recently done at Mr. Pym's; not that the face was very discernible in the increasing gloom of the November evening.

"Do give me the particulars, Charlotte!"

"I can't, I tell you, mamma. I only know them myself from hearsay. I was shut up in the dining-room with Georgy, and knew nothing until startled by Honour's cries."

"You were shut up in the dining-room!"

"Just as you found me shut up in this room now. Georgy was asleep, and I had his feet on my lap. I wish you wouldn't ask me about it. It is not a pleasant thing to talk of. I am sorry now for having beaten him."

"You beat him?—Benja?"

"He was naughty after dinner. He had a new watch, and would not lend it to Georgy, and they got quarrelling. He beat Georgy, and I beat *him*. I am sorry for it now."

"But it was not then that he was burnt!" exclaimed Mrs. Darling, scarcely understanding.

"No. Honour took him away, and I stayed in the dining room with Georgy."

"Did the accident happen immediately?"

"Not for a long while. Two hours, perhaps, I don't know how long exactly. I had been to sleep. It was daylight when he went away, and it was dark when we heard the screams."

"And you, my poor child, had never moved from the dining-room!"

"Don't I say so, mamma!" came the answer, a shade of peevishness at being questioned in the otherwise impassive tone. "I had kept Georgy with me."

Mrs. Darling drew a long sigh: it seemed like a relief from some nightmare. "How came Honour to leave him with a lighted candle?" she exclaimed in anger.

"Mamma, I *wish* you would not ask me these things! I don't care to talk of them."

For some minutes there was silence, but Mrs. Darling was an impulsive woman, and it was almost impossible for her to think of any fresh point without breaking out with a question. She did so now; suddenly, abruptly.

"Is it true that the doors were fastened?"

"Who told you they were?" exclaimed Mrs. St. John.

"Mr. Pym. I saw him as I came up here."

"Mr. Pym told you the doors were fastened?" repeated Mrs. St. John, fixing her strange eyes upon her mother.

"Yes. At least—— What he said was, that Honour asserts they were fastened."

"Ay, *that's* true. But no one believes her. Mr. Pym does not believe her; he told her she must be careful what she said. Prance thinks Honour was so flurried at the time, that her recollection is not clear."

Again there was a pause. Mrs. St. John sat as before, gazing at the fire, her haggard face—yes, it certainly was unnaturally haggard—bent on her hand. Mrs. Darling seemed buried in perplexity, and her fingers unconsciously smoothed down her bonnet-strings. Georgy stirred in his sleep, and they both looked at the sofa; but he did not awake, and both were silent for a moment.

"Is the inquest over, do you know?" asked Mrs. St. John.

"It was not when I came past. Charlotte, have you written to Castle Wafer?"

"I have not written to any one. Surely there's time enough!"

"My dear, I did not mean to anger you. I—— What's this? They must be coming back from the inquest!"

The noise of many steps outside had called forth the interruption. Mrs. St. John rose from her seat and stood in the middle of the room, facing the door; waiting defiantly, as it seemed, to confront any who might enter. It was just the same position, the same look that had surprised Mrs. Darling when she arrived. The butler came in.

"The verdict is 'Accidental Death,'" he said. "Appended to which was a severe censure on Honour Tritton for leaving the child alone with so dangerous a toy. And ma'am," he emphatically added to his mistress, "she deserves it: and she seems to think so."

The mistress of Alnwick sat down again. Mrs. Darling caught up her cloak and went out of the room, her curiosity on the rack for the sad details withheld by her daughter.

Honour did seem to think she deserved the censure, as the butler had observed. Fully, fully had her repentant heart echoed the condemnation of the jury. A never-dying remorse had taken up its abode within her. Mrs. Darling came upon her on the staircase. The girl's face looked flushed, her eyes glistening; and there was a wildness in their expression that spoke of incipient fever, had any been at leisure to note the signs, or been capable of understanding them.

"Oh Honour! what an awful thing this is!" breathed Mrs. Darling.

"It's more than awful," answered Honour. "I suppose I shall get over it sometime, if I live: I don't know. Perhaps God will be pleased to take me."

She spoke almost with the unnatural calmness of her mistress. That alone would have told of something mentally wrong, or becoming so.

"Honour—indeed I don't wish to reproach you, for I'm sure your pain must be too great to need it; but I must speak—*how* could you leave the child alone with that lighted candle?"

"Will you see him?—what's left of him?" was the rejoinder. And without waiting for reply, Honour went into the nursery. Something was resting there on trestles with a sheet thrown over it. Whether it was a coffin, whether it was not, Mrs. Darling did not stay to inquire. She arrested Honour's hand.

"No," she said. "I don't know that I could bear the sight."

Honour dropped the corner of the sheet again. "Well," she said, "he is there; my darling treasure that was dearer to me than anything in life. They were beating him black and blue in the dining-room, and I brought him out, and I finished the paper toy to soothe and comfort his poor little sobbing heart, and I did leave him alone with it, the candle lighted inside it. If I ever forget my folly, or cease to mourn for it in repentance, I hope God will forget me. But, I am not the sole author of his death; Mrs. Darling, I am *not*. Those who came and fastened the doors upon him, and so let him burn, are more guilty of it than me."

"Hush, Honour! You were mistaken. The doors could not have been so fastened."

Honour laid her hand upon the sheet again, touching what was beneath it.

"Mrs. Darling, don't *you* be deceived. Some do not believe what I say, and some are wishing to hush the matter up. I swear that it was as I assert: I swear it by *this*, all that's left of him. They say Benja must have buttoned the one door himself; let it go so: I don't think he did, but let it go so:

but he could not have bolted the other on the outside. They are hushing the matter up; and I must do the same: I am only one against many."

"Who is hushing it up?" asked Mrs. Darling, from between her white lips.

"Mr. Pym, for one. I say nothing about others, I am only one amongst them. From this time I shall drop the matter, and speak of it no more: but I should like you to remember what I say, and to believe me. It is the truth. Heaven knows it is. The doors were fastened upon him, and he was left there —in a living tomb—to burn to death. When the facts come to light, as they will sometime, if there's justice in the world, we shall learn the truth. At present I don't pretend to understand it."

Mrs. Darling felt frightened at the girl's words, at her resolute manner (her impassiveness had now changed to passion), at her hectic cheeks and wild eyes—all the symptoms of threatening fever or insanity. She quitted the room, retaining a last glimpse of Honour's throwing herself beside the trestles in a burst of anguish, and sought Prance. Scarcely able to speak from an agitation which she vainly endeavoured to suppress, Mrs. Darling commanded Prance to furnish her with the particulars, to the minutest detail.

Prance obeyed without the slightest hesitation, her account differing in no wise from the one she had just given to the coroner and jury. Mrs. Darling questioned her as to the alleged fastening of the doors: Prance maintained that the one door, at any rate, had been fastened in Honour's fancy only. It was possible, nay probable, that the poor little boy had himself fastened the one; but as to the other, nothing but Honour's haste (as she, Prance, believed) had prevented her opening it. "The fact is," concluded Prance, "Honour was half paralyzed with fear at the time, through smelling the burning; and she has been as one mad ever since."

"And your mistress was shut up, I hear, in the dining-room all the time with little George."

"Oh yes," said Prance, "and the servants were shut up downstairs. Nobody could have gone near the room. If that door was fastened, why, the bolt must have slipped as well as the latch when the child closed it," added Prance. "The coroner and jury thought so."

Mrs. Darling sighed in very perplexity. She could not get

over Honour's positive and solemn assertion; but it seemed
equally impossible to believe any one had been near the door
to bolt it. This last suggestion, that the bolt had slipped, was
a welcome one, and Mrs. Darling would have given half her
remaining lifetime to have been able fully to believe in it.

There went forth another announcement in the local papers,
Mrs. Darling wording it.

"Died, on St. Martin's Eve, at Alnwick Hall, on his fifth
birthday, Benjamin Carleton St. John, eldest son and heir of
the late George Carleton St. John, Esquire."

CHAPTER XVII.

HONOUR'S RAVINGS.

IT needed not many days for Honour Tritton to be in a fever,
accompanied by delirium, the symptoms of which had been
plainly showing themselves. Mr. Pym pronounced it a malady
of the brain, brought on by grief, horror, and remorse. It would
prolong her stay at the Hall, for she could not be removed;
otherwise Mrs. St. John had given her notice to quit it as soon
as the funeral was over. Mrs. St. John had taken a shuddering
dislike to her. The word is used advisedly. Once or twice,
when she met Honour in the corridors, she was seized with a
fit of shuddering that affected her whole frame. Freely she
avowed that she could not bear the sight of the girl; but for
her, she said, Benja would be still living. But when the girl
was taken ill they could not turn her out; and Honour lay in
bed, in the room that had been hers and Benja's. The pretty
rosewood cot, shorn for ever of its occupant, was yet in the
corner. At first she was not dangerously ill; hot and feverish,
and a little excited at times; but not in danger. It was the
day before the funeral that she took to her bed.

Mrs. St. John seemed more affected by the death than was
apparent to ordinary observers. Not a shade of emotion had
been seen on her impassive face; not a tear, so far as any one
could trace, had been shed. But that she was grievously
affected by it, those about her saw plainly. A species of nervousness—if the word may be applied to one so outwardly

calm—seemed to have taken possession of her. She was ever brooding on the dreadful event; she was afraid to go about the house alone after dark; not all the cordage of a seventy-gun ship would have dragged her into the dressing-room, for it was next to the nursery where Benja was lying. She chiefly sat nursing George, who was ill still—remaining for an hour or two intensely calm and quiet, then starting up and pacing the room violently, as if unable to bear her own reflections—her grief for Benja. "My dear, be still, be calm," Mrs. Darling remonstrated one afternoon as she paced the room with wild steps. "All the sorrow in the world cannot bring him back: in a little time, if you can only realize it, you will gather comfort from the fact that he is better off." "Mamma, I would *hang* Honour Tritton if I could!" was the only answer.

What Mrs. St. John would have done without her mother at this time, it is impossible to tell; though perhaps, had necessity imposed it on her, she might have been aroused to exert herself. Mrs. Darling, forgetting her own ailments, and she was feeling really ill, took everything upon herself, and *had* to do it. It was she who wrote letters to apprise friends of the calamity; it was she who made arrangements for the funeral: Charlotte would take neither act nor part in it. Mrs. Darling did what she could to amuse her daughter, and divert her mind from the fatal night. She talked to her of family interests, she read letters to her from her daughter Margaret, who was in Berkshire; she enlarged upon the letters from her son Frank. There had been some trouble or escapade, or something unpleasant with Rose, during his visit to Belport in the autumn, she said, but she could not get to the bottom of it, and perhaps never should: she expected it all arose from Rose's rebellion at being kept at school. These, and similar topics, did Mrs. Darling pursue; but her daughter was as one who heard not. It might, in fact, be questioned whether she did hear; and if she answered it was only mechanically.

The day of the funeral arrived, and friends and relatives came from far and near to follow to his last resting-place the ill-fated little heir of Alnwick. As it had been in the days when George St. John died, so it was again. Mr. St. John of Castle Wafer was too ill to attend, but Frederick St. John came down from London in his place. Captain Darling also came. Neither of them stayed beyond the day, and they agreed to travel back to town together. Indeed, none of the guests were asked to remain : the Hall was not in a mood for welcoming visitors just now.

Mrs. Darling took the opportunity of asking her son what the hinted escapade of Rose's might have been ; but he only laughed it off, and did not explain. *He* had corrected her for it, he said, and he didn't think she would attempt a second.

So the child was laid in the vault with his father and his poor young mother, whose life he had cost; and the train of mourners and attendants returned to the Hall, and then dispersed, none of them, Captain Darling excepted, having seen Alnwick's mistress. Something had been said about little Georgy—now the heir—going to the funeral; but it was decided that he was too young. And besides, he was not well.

There was estrangement still between Isaac St. John and his brother; but the aspect of affairs had changed, and Isaac, on his part, would have been all too willing to be reconciled. Lady Anne St. John was on the point of marriage with Captain Saville, who had unexpectedly come into a large inheritance. Anne confessed all to Isaac. How there had been a secret understanding between her and Captain Saville, and Frederick was keeping league with them, and to screen Anne, taking on himself the blame of refusing to marry her. Isaac St. John would then have been reconciled to his brother. He did not make any decisive move towards it, but he allowed his wishes to become known to Frederick through Mrs. St. John. Mr. Frederick, however, had a spice of obstinacy in his composition, and chose to hold on his own way. He had recently come into some money through an aunt, and this he was applying to liquidating his own debts, living meanwhile quietly in London, and spending all his time at his favourite art—painting.

The day of the funeral came to an end. Everything had passed off quietly, without undue bustle and agitation, which might perhaps have been expected under the circumstances of the case. Little George had burst into wailing sobs when the mourning carriages came back to the Hall, saying he wanted Benja. They told him Benja was gone to heaven to be happy for ever, and to play upon a golden harp. But the child still cried bitterly. Captain Darling carried him out on the slopes, and in due time brought him back soothed ; having entered upon some magnificent promises touching a live pony, when

the young gentleman should have grown as tall as Benja
was.

On the following morning Mrs. St. John was to leave the
Hall for a time. It was her own proposition, but Mrs.
Darling seconded it. At first she was only going to the
cottage, her mother's residence; later she would take Georgy
to some watering-place, and return to the Hall for
Christmas.

You cannot keep gossiping tongues still. Since the inquest,
a great deal of discussion had taken place as to the disputed
question of the dressing-room door. In the Hall, and out of
it for miles, it formed the theme of conversation, and speculation was rife as to the real truth. Once establish the fact of
the door's having been *previously* bolted, and there was an end
to all mystery. Honour's unwavering assertion that it *was*
bolted when she arrived, made weight gradually and silently;
the almost as indisputable fact that no one had been near to
bolt it received full credence; and the solution gradually
arrived at was, that when the little boy had closed the door,
the bolt had slipped. It appeared to be the only feasible
explanation. The more it was talked of and dwelt upon, the
more certain did it appear, and by the day of the funeral it was
received as an undoubted fact. Mr. Pym so received it; Mrs.
Darling spoke of it as a discovery, not a supposition. Even
Honour, weak, ill, and miserable, was brought to acknowledge
that such might have been the case.

"What a mercy that it's cleared up!" cried Mrs. Darling to
her daughter. "It was so very unpleasant to have any mystery
connected with it: the event was unhappy enough in itself,
without that. We can so far dismiss the unpleasantness from
our minds now, Charlotte."

Mrs. Darling intended to return to the cottage with her
daughter. She was busy in her room after breakfast on the
morning of departure, putting together the few things which
had been sent over for her use from home, when one of the
housemaids happened to mention that Honour was worse, and
"saying queer things."

"What queer things?" asked Mrs. Darling, in the midst of
folding a crape collar.

"Oh, ma'am, about the accident; about the bolting of the
door, that there has been so much talk over——"

"The door bolted itself when Honour caused it to be closed;

it has been conclusively decided so," sharply interrupted Mrs. Darling.

"I know it has, ma'am," replied the maid. "But Honour is off her head, and does not know what she is saying. She has been raving about her mistress, fancying she's at the bedside, and asking her whether *she* did not bolt the doors on Master Benja when he was burning, or whether she set him on fire? It's dreadful to hear her, poor thing."

If ever a sudden change was seen in a woman, you might have seen it then in Mrs. Darling. Her ruddy, good-humoured countenance assumed the hue it had worn when shunning Mr. Pym's look that night before the Carleton Arms—though for the matter of that, he had equally shunned hers.

"I'll go to her," she said, presently. "Poor creature, she must be quite mad! I'll go and see what can be done for her. Perhaps a strait-waistcoat will be necessary."

Accordingly Mrs. Darling made her way along the corridor. Crouching against the nursery-door, as she turned the corner, was what at first looked like a huge black balloon. It proved to be the petticoats of her daughter, who appeared to be listening to something in the nursery.

"Charlotte!"

Mrs. St. John lifted her scared face: a white face, not so much of terror as of some great anguish, with wild eyes gazing from it. Softly rising, she spoke in a whisper.

"I can hear his cries—*his*. I heard them last night, all night long."

Mrs. Darling's heart leaped, as the saying runs, into her mouth. Was *she* going mad—was every one going mad?

"Listen! There it is again!"

"Charlotte, my dear child, you cannot be well this morning. These troubles have unhinged you. When you——"

Mrs. Darling suddenly stopped, and began to feel a little "unhinged" herself. There certainly was a sound within the room; a repetition of faint whining or moaning.

"I knew they could never take him out of it!" whispered Mrs. St. John. "Hark! But his cries were louder then."

Mrs. Darling looked at her. Could she be succumbing to superstitious fears? Mrs. Darling hardly thought it possible, being herself so very practical a woman, in contradistinction to an imaginative one. She no more believed in ghosts than she

did in the spirits recently become fashionable : and she opened
the nursery-door very gingerly and peeped in.

It was the dog Brave. Poor Brave must have found his way
into the room on the previous day, on the removal of the coffin,
and had been shut in ever since. Not barking, not making any
noise to attract attention, simply sitting there under the trestles,
whining and crying. There had been some trouble with Brave
since the death : he would find his way into the corridor, and
there howl and moan.

"See, Charlotte !" said Mrs. Darling, in reassuring tones.
"Poor dumb creature !"

Deeming it well that her daughter *should* see, as the most
effectual antidote to any such fears as those alluded to above,
she gently took her arm to pull her forward. Charlotte drew
back in sudden fear.

"I *can't* look !" she gasped. "You dare not force me ! Is he
walking about with the lighted church ?"

"Oh, Charlotte, do, do just glance in ! You are not yourself, I see "—and poor Mrs. Darling looked as terrified as her,
as *she* was looking at the door. "It is only poor Brave ; he
must have been shut in here."

She threw the door open, went in, and drove out the dog.
Mrs. St. John stood against the wall as it passed her, carefully
avoiding all sight of the chamber. Her mood changed to
anger when she saw Brave.

"I gave orders that he should not be allowed to enter the
house—that he should be kept chained up in the stables—sent
away—sold—anything. How dare they disobey me !"

Mrs. Darling put her daughter's arm within her own and led
her to her own chamber. "I will see that the dog does not
annoy you again, Charlotte. Lie on the sofa and keep yourself quiet : we shall be ready to go in half-an-hour."

Closing the door on Charlotte, she proceeded to Honour's
chamber at the end of the passage. The girl was in bed, lying
in all the restlessness of delirium. Her head was turning from
side to side, her face was flushed, her speech rambled. Mrs.
Darling involuntarily asked herself whether the whinings of the
dog through the night in the adjoining chamber, which must
have penetrated to Honour's ears, had contributed to this
increase of the malady.

No less than three maid-servants were posted round the bed,
staring, listening, whispering. The sound of Mrs. Darling's

entrance seemed to attract the attention of the patient, who
looked momentarily towards her; but the ominously-bright
eyes evidently saw nothing: they turned to the opposite wall,
gazing, as it were, beyond it.   The words that escaped from
her lips—not consecutively as they are about to be written, but
by fits and snatches—startled Mrs. Darling as few things had
ever startled her in all her life before.   They were equivalent
to accusing her mistress of the *murder* of her step-son.

"He was the heir, you see, sir," she said, addressing some
imaginary personage; "he was keeping her own flesh and blood
out of the inheritance.   I saw all along that it was more than
she could bear.   Don't you remember the scene that day when
you came home from London, and we took the two children to
meet you in the park?   You took up Benja and carried him in,
but the little one cried and we left him.   Don't you remember
it, sir?—she struck Benja to the ground and bruised him.   *You*
said it was an accident, but I knew better.   Oh, sir, why did
you leave him under her charge?   Wasn't it as well to make
your will one way as the other?"

She was evidently in the past, and he whom she was addressing in imagination, was her dead master.

"It was so easy to accomplish!" went on Honour, her head
turning faster than ever, but her eyes fixed as before.   "It was
only the running up the stairs from the dining-room, where she
was shut in, and setting fire to him, and bolting the doors on
his screams, and running back again.   Oh, why did you leave
him to her?   Didn't you remember that he was keeping out
Georgy?   She says she never left the dining-room, but don't
you believe her.   She *did*, and I can speak to it."

Mrs. Darling, who had been slowly gathering her presence
of mind, and could not do it all at once, turned her ashy countenance on the gaping servants.   Perhaps she hardly knew
what to say, or how to treat the ravings.

"It is a very bad case of brain fever," she said, striving to
speak with unconcern.   "Her mind is quite gone, poor thing,"
—as indeed it was.   "I had a governess once who suffered
under an attack of the same.   She persisted that I had killed
my youngest daughter, Miss Rose Darling, and all the time the
child was alive and well at her elbow.   The two cases seem
precisely similar.   Go down, will you?   I think the room
ought to be kept quiet: and send one of the men instantly to
hasten Mr. Pym."

They filed out of the room in obedience, and Mrs. Darling sat down to remain, thinking, poor woman, that her lines were hard just now. She sat there until the doctor entered.

"Ah, ha," said he, "so the brain's touched in earnest. I thought it would be so."

"She is quite deranged, Mr. Pym; she has been saying the strangest things."

"What things?"

Mrs. Darling turned the question off. "All sorts of nonsense," she said, coughing. "Mr. Pym, I think I shall stop here and nurse her myself. She is too ill to be left to servants."

"And let Mrs. St. John go alone?"

"I think I must. Prance will be with her, and she will have her child. Perhaps in a few hours Honour may be better."

Mr. Pym had drawn nearer to the bed. Honour was wandering again; was repeating again the same "nonsense," as Mrs. Darling had called it. Alas! she must go on repeating it until some turn to the malady came. The excited brain had its task to perform, and could only go over it, over it, over it, until better moments should dawn. The surgeon listened and heard as much as Mrs. Darling had heard.

"Yes," said he, "it may be as well that you should nurse her. Servants are such gossips."

"Three of them were in, listening, just now. Mr. Pym, how is it that these false notions take possession of an invalid's brain?" asked Mrs. Darling.

Mr. Pym paused before he replied. "How is it that dreams take possession of it?" he returned. "The girl has had an awful shock, and the brain is suffering. The imagination is apt to be erratic at these times, indulging in absurd and fantastic fancies."

"Very absurd and fantastic in this case!" pronounced Mrs. Darling. "Well, I shall stay with her. It must be either myself or Prance."

"Prance won't do," said the surgeon. "She and Honour hate each other like poison."

The plan was carried out. Mrs. St. John, her child, and Prance departed for the cottage; Mrs. Darling remained at the Hall in attendance on Honour; and Mr. Pym did hardly anything but dodge in and out of it all day, walking to and from Alnwick at the pace of a steam-engine. Honour was dangerously ill.

In the dusk of evening, when the house was quiet, and Mrs. Darling sat by the bedside, her brain almost as busy as the one she was there to guard, the thought arose to her that she would put at rest (as far as it could be put to rest) a question that troubled her. In closing the nursery-door quietly—as it had been represented the unfortunate child did close it—would the bolt slip into its groove? Was it possible that it could do so? Mrs. Darling had pondered the doubt that day more than she would have cared to tell. Rising from her chair, she was about to cross the room when some one came in.

"Who's that?" sharply called out Mrs. Darling, somewhat startled.

It was only one of the under-maids, bringing in some beef-tea in a cup. "How quietly you must have come up!" exclaimed Mrs. Darling.

"I have list shoes on, ma'am," replied the girl.

She put down the cup and advanced on tiptoe to take a glance at Honour. The fever still continued, the brain was still at work; but just now the head was quiet.

"She seems a trifle better!" cried the girl.

"I fear not in mind," answered Mrs. Darling. "Her last fancy seems to be that *she* set fire to the child, and then ran away and left him."

"Poor creature! Well, so in a manner she did, ma'am, for it was through her want of caution that it happened."

The girl gazed a few minutes and went down. Mrs. Darling —by the way, was that last assertion of hers a true one or a flight of fancy?—listened to the receding footsteps. She thought she heard them come back again, those or others, but silence supervened, and she concluded she was mistaken.

Now or never! She did want to try that door, and the opportunity seemed favourable : for she would not for the whole world, no, nor for ten worlds, suffer it to be known that any doubt could enter her mind, or any one's mind, upon the point. Quitting Honour's room, she stepped to the nursery-door, and there—paused.

What feeling came over Mrs. Darling at the moment she could never afterwards tell. Had she been of a superstitious nature it might have been accounted for ; but she was not. Some feeling or impulse, however, did cause her to walk away from the door without entering, and go on to the dressing-room, intending to see if she could try the experiment from that side.

As she quitted it she could have declared she heard a chair move within, only that she knew she must be mistaken.

She went with soft tread across the dressing-room carpet in the twilight of the evening. The door stood half open; to her surprise; for since the fatal night it had been kept rigidly shut. She was about to pull it to, when it was closed from the other side, pretty smartly. In her consternation she opened it at once, and—stood face to face with Surgeon Pym. He had been trying the experiment on his own score.

Their eyes met; and it was curious to note the difference in the demeanour of the two as they stood gazing at each other. Mrs. Darling, agitated, nervous, almost terrified; the surgeon, collected, keen, perfectly self-possessed. She tried to frame an excuse.

"I was going to look into the nursery, to see whether the servants have set it to rights to-day. I fancy they have not."

"And I," said the surgeon, "was seeing whether the bolt would slip if a person merely shut the door. I find it won't."

Honour Tritton's ravings, the effect of a diseased brain, ceased with her recovery; and there remained with her no recollection whatever of having uttered them, for Mr. Pym tested her on the point. With her restoration to reason, Mrs. Darling was less confined, and she divided her time between the Hall and the Cottage, but did not yet finally quit the former. Mrs. Darling resolved to speak to her, and the opportunity came. One evening when she was alone in the drawing-room, Honour knocked at the door and came in. The girl looked the wreck of her former self; thin, pale, shadowy, her black gown seemed much too large for her, and the dark circles under her eyes were excessively conspicuous on her naturally light skin.

"Could I speak to you for a few minutes, ma'am?" she asked.

"Yes," said Mrs. Darling, a feeling of nervousness arising within her at the request. "You had better sit down, Honour; you are weak still."

Honour obeyed. She had come to speak of her own departure; to thank Mrs. Darling for her care of her, and to say that the sooner she was away now, the better. She thought of going on the following day, or the day after, if Mrs. Darling would allow it.

Mrs. Darling heaved a sigh of relief, perhaps she could hardly tell why or wherefore. " I did not think you were strong enough to go anywhere yet. But as you please. Are you aware, Honour, what cruel things you said of your mistress ? " she resumed, in low tones.

Honour looked up in genuine surprise. *"I* said cruel things, ma'am ! What did I say ? "

" I hardly like to tell you what you said," replied Mrs. Darling. " You accused her over and over again of having set fire to the child and left him to burn to death. Were you to say such words in your right senses, you might be in danger of transportation for speaking them."

Honour burst into tears. She had no recollection whatever of her fault, and humbly begged pardon for it.

" Of course we do not look upon you as responsible for what you said," continued Mrs. Darling; " the ravings of a diseased mind go for nothing. But they are not the less unpleasant to hear, and your mistress feels enough grief from this matter without its being unnecessarily added to. You, of all persons, should be careful not to add to her sorrow. It was only this very day, when we were speaking of Benja, that she fervently exclaimed, if her whole fortune could bring him back to life, it should be given. There are moments "—Mrs. Darling dropped her voice as though she were speaking to herself, rather than to Honour—" when I have fancied she would sacrifice even Geórge's life, could that bring his brother back again. Believe me, she regrets him as much as you can do."

Subdued, weak, humble, Honour could only give vent to excuses and penitent tears. She had never really suspected her mistress, she said, and, indeed, she had never suspected any one of her own good will ; it was her wicked thoughts that would rise up in spite of her. Not her mistress, however; if she had indulged these thoughts, it was of Prance. It was desperately wicked, she knew, but the boy's death seemed to take her reason from her. She hoped Prance would not come to hear of it ; and for herself, she would never, never harbour such fancies again.

So Honour left Alnwick Hall. She had to go first of all to Castle Wafer, Mr. St. John having sent for her. The fact was, the occurrence had made a most startling and unhappy impression on the master of Castle Wafer. The account he had received of it was a very partial one, and he naturally wished for correct details. When the summons came, Honour had flung up her hands in a sort of terror. How should she dare to meet Mr. Isaac St. John, and proclaim to him personally her wicked carelessness? Mrs. Darling also had seemed much put out: but there was no help for it, and she cautioned Honour.

"Take care," she gravely said, "that not a hint of those wicked and foolish suspicions is dropped to Mr. St. John."

In anything but an enviable frame of mind, did Honour enter on the interview with Mr. St. John at Castle Wafer. He sat on the sofa in his own sitting-room, his back propped up with soft pillows, and Honour, whom he invited to a seat, sat in her new mourning, and wept before him. The first timidity over, she confessed the whole; made, as it were, a clean breast of it, and told how her own thoughtlessness, in leaving the child alone with the lighted toy, had been the cause of the calamity. Mr. St. John was painfully interested in the little coincidence she mentioned—that the first idea of the toy, the lighted church, had been gathered at the fair that was being held the very day he came to Alnwick. It was at this point that Honour burst into tears, which she was quite unable to control.

However Mr. St. John might have been disposed to condemn the carelessness, he could only feel compassion for the sufferer. She should never know another truly happy moment, she sobbed, should never cease to reproach herself as long as life should last. She gave herself the whole blame; she said not a word of the old doubts; and when Mr. St. John questioned her as to the fastening of the doors, she declared that she could not tell herself how they had become fastened, but mentioned the conclusion come to by the household and the coroner. *They* decided that the little boy had himself fastened the one; and for the other, some thought it had never been fastened at all; only she, Honour, had fancied it in her flurry; others thought it must have bolted itself when the little boy shut it, and she could only suppose that it did so bolt. She spoke of the great sorrow of her mistress, as testified to by Mrs. Darling, and told how she had left the Hall because she could not yet bear the sight of it: and not a whisper did she breathe of the unseemly scene which had occurred on that memorable afternoon. In short, it seemed that Honour was striving to make amends for the harsh and unjustifiable words she had used of her mistress in her delirium.

Mr. St. John inquired whether she was going back to the Hall. "Never, never!" she answered; she should take service as far away from it as possible, where folks would not point at her as having caused the death of an innocent child. Not as a nurse—who would be likely to trust her in that capacity now?—but as a house or laundry maid. A moment's deliberation with himself, and then Mr. St. John offered her a service in his own household. One of the housemaids was about to leave to be married; if Honour would like the situation the housekeeper should engage her.

Again burst forth the tears. Not suppressed sobs this time, but soft tears of gratitude. For there was a tone of compassion in Mr. St. John's voice that found its way to the heart of the unhappy woman; *none* had addressed such to her since that miserable day, the Eve of St. Martin; and she could have been his slave in all reverence for life. Thankfully did she accept the offered situation; and it was decided with the housekeeper afterwards that she should enter upon it in a month's time, when both health and spirits might be somewhat renewed.

Before the first week of that month had elapsed, Mr. St. John made an effort, and went over to Alnwick. In his courteous sympathy he deemed that a visit was due to Mrs. Carleton St. John; the more especially that he had not been able to make it at the time, or to attend the funeral. There were also certain little matters of business to be mentioned to her, now that George was the heir, to whom he was also guardian; but without any of the additional power vested in him, as it had been in regard to Benja.

He went this time by rail. Brumm said so much of the additional length of the journey by road in his master's present weak state, that Mr. St. John yielded for once, and a compartment was engaged, where he would be alone, with Brumm to attend upon him. On arriving at Alnwick, they found Mrs. Carleton St. John was still at her mother's cottage; and to the cottage Isaac went.

Had he arrived only a day later, he would not have seen her whom he came to see. Mrs. Carleton St. John was on the wing. She was starting for Scarborough that very evening, as Mrs. Darling sharply expressed it, as if the travelling by night did not meet her approbation; but she had allowed Charlotte to have her own way as a child, she whispered to Mr. St. John, and Charlotte chose to have it still.

What struck Mr. St. John more than anything else in this visit, was the exceeding *stillness* that seemed to pervade Mrs. Carleton St. John. She sat in utter quietness, her hands clasped on her knee, her black dress falling around her slender form in soft folds, the white crape lappets of her cap thrown behind. The expression of her bent face was still, almost to apathy; her manner, and voice were subdued. So young and pretty did she look in her grief, that Mr. St. John's heart went out to her in compassion. He saw a slight shiver pass through her frame when she first spoke of Benja: she *grieved* for him, she murmured; and she told the tale of how she had struck him that fatal afternoon—oh, if she could only recall that! it weighed so heavily upon her. Oh, if she could—if she could— and Mr. St. John saw the fervour with which the wish was aspirated, the drawn lines about the pretty but haggard mouth, the hands lifted for once and clasped to pain—if she could only recall him back to life!

She wanted change, she said; she was going to Scarborough. George did not seem to grow strong again, and she thought it might do him good; he was fractious and ailing, and perpetually crying for Benja. Mamma was angry at her travelling by night, but no one but herself knew how long and tedious her nights were; she seemed to be always seeing Benja. When she went to sleep she dreamt he was alive again, and to awake up from that to the reality was more cruel than all.

Isaac St. John, as he sat and listened to the plaintive voice, pitied her beyond everything. There had not been wanting people, even within his small sphere of daily life, to comment on the gratification it must be to Mrs. Carleton St. John (apart from the loss of the child and its peculiar horror) to see her own son the inheritor. Isaac St. John resentfully wished they could see her and hear her now. He acquiesced in the expediency of change, both for herself and the child, and warmly urged her to exchange Scarborough for Castle Wafer. His step-mother, Mrs. St. John, was there, and they would make her so much more comfortable than she could be at any watering-place. But he urged in vain. She thanked him for his kindness, saying she would prefer to go to Scarborough now, but would keep his invitation for a future opportunity.

To the business matters she declined to listen. If it was at all necessary that he should discuss them, let it be with her mamma; or perhaps with Mr. Drake the lawyer. Mr. Drake knew all about everything, she supposed; and he would attend on Mr. St. John if requested.

So, after a two hours' sojourn at the cottage, Isaac St. John quitted it; and the following day he returned to Castle Wafer. He had not mentioned that Honour was about to enter on service at Castle Wafer. Upon Honour's name occurring in conversation in connection with the accident on St. Martin's Eve, Mrs. Carleton St. John had shown symptoms of excitement : she wished Honour had died, she said, before she had wrought such ill : and Isaac, perhaps feeling rather ashamed to confess that his household was going to shelter her, let the subject drop.

Mrs. St. John and the child started for Scarborough, Prance and three or four other servants in attendance upon her. Not Mrs. Darling. The younger lady had civilly but firmly declined her mother's companionship. She would rather be alone, she said, and Mrs. Darling yielded—as she had done all through Charlotte's life.

But it appeared that Scarborough did not please her. She had been in it little more than a week, when Mrs. Darling heard that she had gone to some place in Westmoreland. From thence, after another short sojourn, she made her way to Dover. It was getting close to Christmas then, and Mrs. Darling, feeling an uneasiness she could not well define, hastened to her, under the pretext of accompanying her home. She found Charlotte anything but benefited by her travellings, if looks might be trusted, for she was more thin, more wan, more haggard than before ; and George was ill still.

Whether George St. John had eaten too much at that memorable birthday dinner, or whether the shock and horror of seeing Benja, as he had seen him, was telling upon his system, certain it was the child had declined from that night. Mr. Pym had treated him for indigestion, and he seemed a little better for a few days, but the improvement did not continue. Never again was he the merry boy he had been : fractious, irritable, and mourning incessantly for Benja ; his spirits failed, his appetite would not return. *He* had not derived benefit from the change of scene any more than his mother, and that, Mrs. Darling on her arrival saw.

"What can be the matter with him ? " was the first question Mrs. St. John addressed to her mother, and the anxiety visible in the wild eyes alarmed Mrs. Darling.

"Charlotte, calm yourself, my dear; indeed there is no cause for uneasiness. I think you have moved him about too much; children want repose at times as well as we do. The quiet of the Hall and Mr. Pym's care will soon bring him round. We will go back at once."

"I am not going back to the Hall," said Charlotte.

"Not going back!" repeated Mrs. Darling.

"Not at present."

"My dear Charlotte, you must go back. How is the Hall to get on at Christmas without you?"

"Must?" significantly returned Charlotte. "I am my own mistress; accountable to none."

"Of course, my love; of course. But, Charlotte"—and Mrs. Darling seemed unduly anxious—"it is right that you should spend Christmas there. Georgy is the heir now."

"He is the possessor," said Charlotte, calmly. "He is the possessor of Alnwick, he will be the inheritor of more; he will be Sir George Carleton St. John—as his father would have been had he but lived."

"Yes," said Mrs. Darling, stealing a side glance at her daughter, who was resting her cheek upon her slender fingers, her gaze fixed upwards.

"But, mamma, I wish now it were Benja; I wish Georgy was as he used to be. I think a complete change of scene may do him good," she added after a pause, "and I shall take him abroad : immediately : for perhaps a year."

Mrs. Darling stood aghast. "But, what's to become of the Hall? what's to be done with it?"

"Anything," was the indifferent reply. "It is mine to do what I choose with—that is, it's Georgy's—and who is to question me? Live in it yourself, if you like; let it; leave servants in it; I don't care. Georgy is my only care now, mamma, and I shall take him abroad to get him strong."

Yes, Alnwick Hall and its broad acres were George's now, but they did not seem to have brought pleasure in their train. Was it that the almost invariable law of nature was obtaining in this case, and the apples, *coveted*, proved bitter ashes in possession? Charlotte St. John looked back to the days and nights of warfare with existing things, to the rebellion of her own spirit at her child's secondary position, to the vain, ardent longing that he should be the heir and supplant Benja. Well, she had her wish. But where was the pleasure she had looked forward to as in a vision, where the triumph? It had not come; it seemed to have vanished utterly and outwardly, even as had poor Benja. What was, what could be, the cause for this?

She crossed over at once to the Continent, hoping there to find relief for the new ailments of Georgy as for her own worn spirits; and Mrs. Darling went back to her cottage in dudgeon, and then took wing to her mother's to spend Christmas. And servants alone reigned at Alnwick Hall.

CHAPTER XVIII.

ADELINE DE CASTELLA.

CHRISTMAS came for other lands, just as surely as it did for England; and the young ladies of Madame de Nino's finishing establishment at Belport were gathered round the schoolroom stove on that festal morning. Rose Darling taking the best place as usual; and also, as usual, swaying all minds to her own imperious will. Rose was in a vile humour; believing herself to be the worst-used mortal in the world. She had fully reckoned on going home for Christmas—or at least into Berkshire; and Mrs. Darling's excuses about the uncertainty of her own movements only angered her the more.

"Don't bother here about your privileges and advantages!" she wrathfully exclaimed, elbowing the girls away from her, and tossing back her shower of golden curls. "What do the French know about keeping Christmas? France is a hundred years behind England in civilization, just as the French girls are behind us."

"Well done, Rose!" cried Adeline de Castella.

"Adeline excepted, of course," went on Rose, addressing no one in particular. "Why, the French don't know as much as the use of the mistletoe!—and our friends send us here to be trained and educated! No Christmas! no holidays—except a month in autumn, which you are not expected to take! It is a pernicious country; an unnatural state of things; and the British government ought to interfere and forbid the schools to receive English girls."

"But don't the French keep Christmas?" asked a new girl, and a very stupid one, Grace Lucas.

"Bah!" ejaculated Rose. "As if they kept anything except the Jour de l'An!"

"The what?" timidly asked Grace Lucas.

"Qu'elle est bête!" cried Rose in her careless manner.

"Have some consideration, Rose," spoke Adeline in French.

"Why, she has heard it fifty times!" retorted Rose in English.

"Every one is not so apt as you."

"Apt at what?" asked Rose fiercely, a glowing colour rising to her face. Since the episode connected with Mr. Marlborough, Rose's conscience was prone to conjure up hidden sarcasm in every sentence addressed to her.

"I meant at picking up French," laughed Adeline. "What else should I mean?"

"Oh, thank you," chafed Rose. "I understand."

"Don't be cross, Rose. Have I not elected to spend my Christmas here, with you all? You show me no gratitude."

"*You* can afford to laugh—and to make a merit of stopping here," retorted Rose. "When in seven days from this you leave for good!"

"If Rose could only change places with you!" interrupted Mary Carr.

"Speak for yourself, if you please, Mary Carr," was Rose's fiery answer: "who wants to change places with her? But, Adeline, I do envy you the balls and gaiety between now and Carême."

The Castella family must not be classed with the ordinary run of people frequenting Belport. Monsieur de Castella—in his own family chiefly called Signor de Castella—was descended from a noble Spanish family on the paternal side; his mother had been a proud and well-born Italian. His usual place of residence was Paris. But some years previous to this present time, symptoms of delicacy became apparent in Adeline; the medical men strongly recommended the seaside, and she was brought to Belport. It appeared to agree with her so well, so establish her health and strength, that Monsieur de Castella took on lease one of the handsomest and largest houses in the town. Sometimes he had to make long absences in Paris, in Spain, and in Italy; Madame de Castella always accompanied him, and Adeline would then be left at Madame de Nino's. This winter would probably be their last in Belport; the summer was to be spent at the French château of Madame de Castella's mother, an English lady by birth; and after that they intended to resume their residence in Paris. They were very wealthy, highly connected and considered, and Adeline was their only child. There had been an elder girl, Maria, but she died: and this made Adeline all the more precious to them. As you read on, you will know her better—and love her.

She was now about to be introduced to the world. New Year's Day was her birthday, when she would be eighteen; and I dare say you are aware that it is about the greatest fête the French keep, always excepting All Saints' Day. Madame de Castella had issued cards for an assembly in the evening, and Adeline was to be introduced. The schoolgirls called it Adeline's inauguration ball.

Amidst other hidden secrets, sedulously guarded from the teachers, Madame de Nino's pupils were in possession of a pack of what they called fortune-telling cards. They were not playing cards, but thin, small, transparent squares, made from the leaf of the sensitive-plant. On each square was a carefully painted flower, purporting to be an emblem. Rose, happy love; cross-of-Jerusalem, sorrow; snowdrop, purity; bachelor's-button, vanity; hyacinth, death; and so on. Three or four of these squares were placed on the palm of the hand, the flowers downwards, so that one square could not be distinguished from another. They would in most cases curl slightly and leap from the hand; but should any one adhere to it, it was deemed a proof of affinity with the owner, a foreshadowing of her fate to come. For instance: if it were the cross-of-Jerusalem that remained, the holder was pronounced to be destined to sorrow; if the bachelor's-button, the girl's life was to be passed in vanity. It was at the best but a silly pastime, meet only for those silly girls; but there are of those schoolgirls who, to this hour, would confess to a superstitious belief in them, unexplainable alike to themselves and to any known law of reason. Else why, they would ask, should one particular leaf have clung always to Adeline de Castella, and been so singularly exemplified in her destiny? That it did cling to her is a fact: otherwise, I should never have thought of noticing any pastime so puerile.

The first time these cards were tried, the girls were in their room, supposed to be in bed. Mam'selle Fifine had gone down with the light, and Rose had lighted one of her large wax tapers, which she kept locked up from prying eyes. Adeline had both her hands stretched out, three squares on each. Five of the squares rolled off quickly, more quickly than usual; the sixth slightly fluttered, and then settled down, quiet and passive on her palm. Janet Duff took it up at length, but dropped it again as one startled.

"Oh! it is bad!" she said, in a whisper.

Mary Carr turned the square. It was a French marigold.

"'French marigold: unhappy love; its end possible death,'" read Janet Duff from the explanations. "It is about the worst in the pack."

Some of the girls shivered—that dortoir was always cold. Adeline laughed merrily. "It is only nonsense," she said: and she spoke as she thought.

And the singular part was, that Adeline de Castella had tried those cards since, a dozen times at least; and this ill-omened French marigold had always clung to her whenever it was of those placed on her hand. The hyacinth had been dreaded so much from the first, that Janet Duff took it out of the pack. And the French marigold, so far as was seen, never rested on any other hand than Adeline de Castella's.

"It is certainly singular," mused Adeline, when she tried her fate at the cards for the last time before leaving school, and the French marigold clung to her as usual.

New Year's Day came in: and with its evening a clash of many carriages, impatient horses, and quarrelsome coachmen filled the streets, for the gay world of Belport was flocking to the house of Signor de Castella.

It was a brilliant scene, those reception-rooms, brilliant with their blaze of light and their exotics. Adeline de Castella stood by her mother. The guests had known and thought of her but as a plainly attired, simple schoolgirl, and were not prepared to recognize her as she stood before them in her costly attire and wondrous beauty. Her robes of white lace, flowing and elegant, sparkled with emeralds; single chains of emeralds encircled her neck, her arms, and confined in their place the waves of her silken hair; lustrous emeralds, heirlooms of the ancient family of de Castella. Her features, pure and regular as if chiselled from marble, were glowing with the crimson flush of excitement, rendering more conspicuous her excessive loveliness.

"Oh, Adeline," whispered Mary Carr, when she could steal a few words with her, "how beautiful you are!"

"What! have you turned flatterer too!"

"Flattery—to *you!* How mistaken they were to-night, when they supposed Rose would outshine all! If they could only see you now!"

Miss Carr brought her words and her breath to a standstill, for, coming in at the door were Mr. and Mrs. Marlborough.

"Yes," said Adeline, answering her exclamation of astonishment; "mamma met them to-day, just as they arrived from Paris, and made them promise to look in to-night. They are on their road to England. Lord John Seymour is with them."

"What will Rose say?" ejaculated Mary Carr.

Mr. and Mrs. Marlborough, Adeline, and others were standing together when Rose came up. Rose was not aware in whose presence she was, till she stood face to face with George Marlborough. A random remark she had been about to make to Adeline died upon her lips, and her face turned white. Eleanor was crimson; and there might have been an awkward pause, but for the readiness of Mr. Marlborough.

• "How do you do, Miss Darling?" he said, with a pleasant smile. "Nearly frozen up with this winter cold? It has been very severe in Paris."

Rose recalled her scattered senses, and began to talk with him at random: but she barely exchanged courtesies with Eleanor.

"Ellen," whispered Mr. Marlborough to his wife, later in the evening, "may I dance a quadrille with her?"

"How silly!—to ask me that! I think it is the best thing you can do." But there was a shy, conscious blush on Mrs. Marlborough's cheek, as she answered. Her husband saw it, and went off laughing, and the next minute Rose was dancing with him.

"Which of my presents do you admire most?" asked Adeline of Mary Carr, directing her attention to an extensive display of articles ranged together in the card-room: all offerings to her that day from friends and relatives, according to French custom on New Year's Day.

"What a lovely little clock in miniature!" exclaimed Rose looking over Mary's shoulder.

"It is a real clock," said Adeline, "it plays the chimes at the hours, and those are real diamonds. My grandmamma always said she should give me something worth keeping on my eighteenth birthday, and she sent me this.   I am so sorry she was not well enough to come to us for to-night !   Stay, I will touch the spring."

As Adeline raised her right hand hastily, anxious that Rose and Mary Carr should hear the melodious chimes of this ingenious ornament, the chains of her emerald bracelet caught in the button of a gentleman's coat, who made one of the group pressing round her.   With a slight jerk she disentangled the chain, but it brought away with it a flower he had held in his hand.   *It was a French marigold !*

The brilliant hue deepened upon Adeline's cheek as she looked at the flower.   She turned and held it out to the owner.

He was a stranger, a young and most distinguished-looking man, possessing in no common degree that air of true nobility which can neither be concealed nor assumed.   His countenance was one of rare beauty, and his eyes were bent with a pleasant earnest expression of admiration upon Adeline.   *You* have met him before, reader, but Adeline had not.

She addressed an apology to him, as she restored the flower, speaking intuitively in English : it required not an introduction to know that that tall, high-bred man was no Frenchman.   He was answering a few words of gallantry, as he received it—that the fair hand it had been in invested the flower with an extrinsic interest—when M. de Castella came into the circle, an aged man by his side.

" Adeline," he said to his daughter, " have you forgotten your old friend, the Baron de la Chasse ? "

With an exclamation of pleasure, Adeline held out her hand. She had been so much with the English, that she had fully acquired their habit of hand-shaking.   The old baron did not seem to understand her, but he took her hand and placed it within his arm.   They moved away, and there was a general breaking up of the group.

" Lottie Singleton," began Rose, " do you know who that handsome man is ? "

" Handsome ! " returned Miss Singleton.   " Everybody's handsome with you.   I call him old and ugly."

" I don't mean the French baron.   That distinguished-looking Englishman with the marigold."

" He !   I know nothing of him.   He came in with the Maxwells.   I saw Sir Sandy introduce him to Madame de Castella."

"Where could he have found that French marigold at this season of the year?" wondered Rose.

"Oh, Miss Maxwell has all sorts of odd flowers in that box of hers, four feet square, which she calls her conservatory," returned the archdeacon's daughter. "He must have found it there."

"Lord John," cried Rose, summarily arresting Lord John Seymour, who was passing, and whom she had never seen but once in her life, and that months before, "who is that handsome man I saw you talking with just now?"

"It is my cousin's husband, Miss Darling," lisped Lord John, who had an impediment in his speech. "Young Marlborough."

"I don't speak of *him*," cried Rose, impatiently, an association dyeing her cheeks. "A tall, pale man, features very refined."

"You must mean St. John."

"Who?" repeated Rose.

"Frederick St. John. Brother to St. John of Castle Wafer."

Rose Darling drew a deep breath in her utter astonishment. "And so that's Frederick St. John! I have heard of him and his beauty."

"He *is* handsome," assented Lord John, "and he's more pleasing than handsome. Fred St. John's one of the best fellows going. We were together at Christchurch."

"Is he staying at Belport?"

"Only passing through, he tells me. He has been dining at the Maxwells' and they brought him here this evening."

"I wish you'd introduce him to me."

("Well done, Rose," thought Mary Carr, who was near.)

"With pleasure," replied Lord John : and he offered his arm to Rose.

"No," said Rose, in her changeable, capricious, but most attractive manner, withdrawing her own as soon as she had taken it, "I think I'll go up to him myself. We are relatives, you know."

"Indeed!" said Lord John.

"Connections, at any rate," concluded Rose.

She chose a moment when Mr. St. John was alone, and approached him. Beginning the self-introduction by holding out her hand. Mr. St. John looked surprised.

"You don't know me," said Rose. "Lord John Seymour

offered to introduce you to me, but I said it was not needed between relatives. I have heard a great deal of Frederick St. John: we are cousins in a degree, you know. I am Rose Darling."

The name did not recall any association to Mr. St. John. He stood smiling on the bright girl before him, with her sunny blue eyes and her mass of golden hair.

"You forget, I see, and I must be more explanatory. My half-sister, Charlotte Norris, married Mr. Carleton St. John. Mamma saw you recently at Alnwick Hall. My brother Frank was there."

His answer was to take both Rose's hands into his, as an apology for his stupidity, and assure her that he was proud and pleased to find such a cousin. Rose remained talking to him.

"What a dreadful thing it was, that little boy's death!" she exclaimed. "I had heard of him often; little Benja St. John! And to be burnt to death!—oh, it was terrible! Who was in fault?"

"The nurse. She left him alone with a paper toy that had a lighted candle within it, and by some means he set himself on fire. It was at his funeral that I met Captain Darling."

"So much about the accident, mamma has told me in her letters; but particulars she has given none," said Rose. "It is too shocking a thing to write about, she says. Poor little fellow! I wish he had been saved. What do you think of Charlotte?"

"Of Mrs. Carleton St. John? I never saw her. She did not appear the day of the funeral. The child's sad death has had a great effect upon her, I hear; both on her health and spirits. She has left the Hall for a time, and is travelling."

"*I* know that," returned Rose with emphasis, in which there was a world of resentment. "Charlotte has been whirling about from place to place like a troubled spirit. It has kept mamma in a most unsettled state, and prevented her having me over for Christmas. I was so mad when I found I was not to go home! Such a shame, you know, keeping me at school! I shall be nineteen next birthday. We have had to give way to Charlotte all our lives."

Mr. St. John smiled on the pretty, pouting, rebellious face. "I fear your sister has been grievously shocked by the death," he said. "Change of scene may be absolutely requisite for her."

"Well then, all I can say is, that it is most unusual, for it is not in Charlotte's nature to be much affected by any earthly thing. She is apathetic to a degree. Of course, she could not help being shocked and grieved at the death; but I *don't* understand its making this lasting impression on her and affecting her health, as mamma says it does. And now that her son is the heir—you are thinking me hard and cruel to say such things, Mr. St. John," broke off Rose, "but you don't know Charlotte as I do. I am certain that the succession of her own child, George, has been to her a long day-dream, not the less cherished from its apparent impossibility."

"I think you don't regard your sister with any great degree of affection, Miss Darling," Mr. St. John ventured to say, smiling on her still.

"I don't, and that's the truth," candidly avowed Rose. "If you only knew how mamma has made us bend to Charlotte and her imperious will all our lives, you wouldn't wonder at me. I was the only one who rebelled; I *would not;* and to tell you a secret, I believe that's why mamma sent me to school."

The strains of music warned Mr. St. John that he must listen to no more; and, as Rose was herself led away, she saw him dancing with Adeline. He was with her a great deal during the rest of the evening.

"The play has begun, Adeline," whispered Rose when she and Mary Carr were leaving.

"What play?"

"You are already taken with this new stranger: I can see it in your countenance: and he with you. What think you of the episode of the French marigold? Rely upon it, that man, Frederick St. John, will exercise some powerful influence over your future life."

"Oh Rose, Rose!" remonstrated Adeline, her lips parting with merriment, "we are not all so susceptible to 'influence' as you."

"We must all fall under it once in our lives," rejoined Rose, unheeding the reproof. "Don't forget my counsel to you hereafter, Adeline. Beware of this stranger: the French marigold is an emblem of unhappy love."

Adeline de Castella laughed: a slighting, careless, triumphant laugh of disbelief: laughed aloud in her pride and power, as she quitted Rose Darling's side, on her way to play her brilliant part in the crowd around her. It was spring-time with her then.

There was a singular fascination attaching to her, this child of many lands. It is no fable to call her such. England, France, Spain, Italy; it was singular that she should be, through her grandparents, a descendant of all. But her nature was essentially English. Her rare beauty of form and feature is seldom found united with brilliancy of complexion, as it was in her, save in the patrician daughters of our own land: and the retiring, modest sweetness of her manners, their graceful self-possession, were English to the core. A stranger could have taken her to belong to no other country, and her perfect knowledge of the language, the absence of all foreign accent, would contribute to the delusion. She had been familiar with it from her infancy: Madame de Castella, speaking it herself as a native, took care of that. She had placed English nurses about her children; and subsequently an English governess, a lady of good birth and breeding but fallen fortunes, had taken charge of them until Maria de Castella's death. It was from this lady that Adeline especially learnt to appreciate and love the English character; insensibly to herself, her own was formed after the model. In short, Adeline de Castella, in spite of her name and her mixed birth, was an English girl.

A month or two rolled away. Adeline de Castella paid an occasional visit to her old schoolfellows at Madame de Nino's; but her time was taken up with a continuous scene of gaiety and visiting. Balls, theatres, *soirées*—never was she in bed before two or three o'clock in the morning, and sometimes it was later than that. Madame de Castella, still a young woman in every sense of the word, lived but for the world. The school-girls noticed that Adeline wore a pale, wearied look, and one afternoon that she came in, she coughed frightfully.

"That's like a consumptive cough!" exclaimed Rose, with her usual want of consideration.

"I have coughed a great deal lately," observed Adeline; "and coming in from the cold air to the atmosphere of your stifling stove, has brought it on now."

No one, however, thought anything serious of the cough, or the weariness. But that time was to come.

It was Ash-Wednesday: and Mary Carr was invited to spend the day at Signor de Castella's. Madame de Castella had given a fancy-dress ball the previous Monday night, *Lundi gras.*

Rose and Mary had been invited to it, but Madame de Nino refused the invitation for them, point-blank, which nearly drove Rose wild with exasperation. After church, one of the servants attended Miss Carr to Madame de Castella's—for I suppose you know that in France a young unmarried lady never goes out alone.

The house seemed to be in some extraordinary commotion. Servants ran hither and thither with a look of consternation on their faces, and Madame de Castella, when Mary reached her presence, was walking about in her dressing-gown, sobbing hysterically, her breakfast cold and untouched at her side, and her maid, Susanne, standing by her.

"What is the matter?" cried Mary, in terror.

"Oh, it is dreadful!" ejaculated Susanne, by way of answer. "Unhappy Mademoiselle Adeline!"

"She is dying!" sobbed Madame de Castella. "My darling child! my only child! She is dying, and I am the cause. Heaven forgive me!"

"Oh, Susanne!" exclaimed Miss Carr, turning to the maid, "what is it all?"

Susanne and Madame explained between them, both weeping, the latter violently.

They were engaged, on the previous night, *Mardi gras*, to "assist" at the crowning ball of the Carnival; but when it became time to dress, Adeline felt so ill and weary that she gave up the task in despair. Madame de Castella urged her to exert herself and shake the illness off, but the Signor interfered, and said Adeline had better go to bed. And to bed she went, at nine o'clock. Madame departed at ten for the ball, but came home before twelve, anxious about Adeline. She went into the latter's bedroom, and found her coughing violently, with every appearance of serious illness upon her. Adeline could say nothing, except that she had coughed like that for many nights. Terror-stricken, the unhappy lady alarmed the household, and the medical attendant was sent for. He came at once, aroused out of his slumbers.

He thought consumption had set its seal upon Adeline. The seeds of it were, no doubt, inherent in her constitution, though hitherto unsuspected, and the gay scenes she had indulged in, that winter, had brought them forth: the exposures to the night air, to heat and cold, the thin dresses, the fatigue, and the broken rest. He did not say she would not be restored to health; but he wished for a consultation.

So, when the early hours gave place to day, the faculty were called together, both French and English. They said just what the family doctor had said, and no more.

"I suppose I may not ask to see Adeline," said Mary Carr, when she had learnt these particulars.

"Not for the world," interposed the lady's-maid. "Perfect quiet is ordered. Mademoiselle has now a blister on her chest, and a sick-nurse is with her."

But, just then, Louise, Adeline's maid, came into the room, with her young lady's love to Miss Carr, and an inquiry why she was so long going up to see her.

"There!" sobbed Madame de Castella, "they have told her you are here. Just go to her for five minutes. I rely upon you not to stay longer."

Mary Carr followed Louise into Adeline's room, and went on tiptoe to her bedside. The tears came into her eyes when she saw her lying there, so pale and wan.

"So their fears have infected you, Mary!" was her salutation, as she looked up from the pillow, and smiled. "Is it not a ridiculous piece of business altogether? As if no one ever had a cough before! Do you know we had half-a-dozen doctors here to-day?"

"Susanne said there had been a consultation."

"Yes, I could scarcely help laughing. I told them all it was very ridiculous: that beyond the cough, which is nothing, and a little fatigue from the pain in my side, I was no more ill than they were. Dr. Dorré said it was his opinion also, and that I should outlive them all yet."

"I hope and trust you will, Adeline! Is that the nurse?"

"A sick-nurse they have sent in. She is English, and accustomed to the disease. Her name's Brayford. You know consumption is common enough in your island."

Mary Carr thought then—thinks still—that it was a grievous error, their suffering Adeline to know the nature of the disease they dreaded. It was Madame de Castella who betrayed it, in her grief and excitement.

"There is so much more fuss being made than is necessary," resumed Adeline. "They have put a blister on my chest, and I am to lie in bed, and live upon slops. I dislike slops."

"Is your appetite good?" asked Mary.

"I have not any appetite," was Adeline's reply. "But in illness we fancy many things, and Louise would have brought me up anything I asked for. There's no chance of it, with this nurse here. She seems tiresomely particular, and determined to obey orders to the letter. I asked her, just before you came in, for some wine-and-water, I almost prayed for it, I was so painfully thirsty. I could have coveted that three-sous beer some of the English girls at school are so fond of."

"Did she let you have it?"

"No. She told me she would not give me a drop of wine if I paid her for it in gold. I cried about it, I was so disappointed and thirsty. What with the flurry and excitement there has been all the morning, and,—papa and mamma's anxiety, my spirits were low, and I actually cried. But she would not give it me. She brought me some toast-and-water, and said she was going to make me something nice, better than wine. There she is, coddling at it over the fire—very nice I dare say it *is* /"

Mrs. Brayford came forward, and whispered Miss Carr to take her leave. Talking was bad for Mademoiselle de Castella.

"Farewell, dearest Adeline! I shall soon come to see you again. I know I shall find you better."

She was half-way across the room when Adeline called to her. The nurse, who was again leaning over her saucepan, looked up, a remonstrance in her eye if not on her tongue, but Miss Carr returned.

"Mary," she whispered, " go in to mamma, assure her, *convince* her, that I am not so ill as she fears : that it is her love for me which has magnified the danger."

"Oh, it's nothing," cried Rose Darling, slightingly, when Miss Carr carried the tale of Adeline's illness back to school. "She will soon be well."

"Or die," said Mary Carr.

"Die ! You are as absurd as the French doctors, Mary. As if people died of a little night visiting ! I wish they would let *me* run the risk !"

"If you had seen the house to-day, and Madame de Castella—— "

"I am glad I did not," interrupted Rose ; "such scenes are not to my taste. And nothing at all to judge by. The French are always in extremes—ecstasies or despair. So much the better for them. They feel the less."

"That is a harsh remark, if intended to apply to Madame de

Castella," observed Miss Carr. "More intense grief I never care to witness."

"No doubt. As intense as it is in her nature to feel; and shown as the French always do show it, in ravings and hysterics. But I can tell you one thing, Mary Carr, that the only grief to be feared, that which eats into the heart, and tells upon it, is borne in silence!"

What a remark from Rose Darling!

Adeline de Castella grew gradually better; apparently quite well. But the cold winds and frosts of winter continued that year very late, even to the end of April, and for all that period she was kept a close prisoner to the house. The medical men recommended that she should spend the following winter in a warmer climate. It was therefore decided that the summer should be passed at the Château de Beaufoy, as had been previously agreed upon, and, with the autumn, they would go south.

A new rumour reached the schoolgirls—that Adeline was about to be married. It was brought to them by Madéleine de Gassicourt, and her friends were intimate with the Castellas.

That was a singular year, so far as weather went. Frost and snow, drizzling rain, bleak and biting winds, alternated with each other to the beginning of May: there had been no spring; but, with that month, May, there came in summer. It was hotter than it often is in July. And this hot weather lasted for several months.

It was the second day of this premature summer, and the usual Thursday holiday at Madame de Nino's. The girls were in the inner court, Rose in a furious state of indignation, and ready to quarrel with every one, because she had not been fetched out, when the roll of carriage-wheels was heard, and they peeped through a slit in the great wooden door so as to get a glimpse of the gate of the outer courtyard.

Springing down the steps of the carriage, came Adeline de Castella, followed by her mother. A shout of delight arose, excited fingers pushed back the great lock, and a group burst into the outer courtyard. Adeline ran towards them, as delighted as they were. Madame de Castella, with an amused laugh and a pleasant word, passed on to the apartments of Madame de Nino, and Mademoiselle Henriette ordered forth Julie, and had the door double-locked.

Adeline looked infinitely beautiful: for though the face had little more colour in it than there is in Parian marble, the features retained all their exquisite contour, the flowing hair its silky waves, the dark-brown, lustrous eyes their sweet and sad expression. In the midst of Adeline de Castella's brilliant loveliness, there was, and always had been, a peculiar expression of sadness pervading her countenance. It never failed to strike on the notice of the beholder, investing such a face as hers with a singular interest, but it was more than usually observable since her illness. Was it that the unearthly part of her, the spirit, conscious of and mourning for what was in store for her, cast its shadow upon her features? The girls crowded round silently to look at Adeline's teeth, for one day, during the time she lay ill, Charlotte Singleton had said that the transparent teeth of Adeline de Castella were an indication of a consumptive tendency, and the girls could not agree amongst themselves whether they were so very transparent.

"So I have come to see you at last," began Adeline, as she sat down with her two friends, Rose and Mary, on the bench outside the schoolroom windows. "What hot weather has come in all at once!"

"Adeline, how long your illness has been! We heard you were going to Nice."

"Not until autumn. And I don't know whether it will be Nice."

"There's Julie!" cried Rose, springing up. "Julie, who's fetched?"

"Pas vous, mademoiselle," answered the servant, laughing at Rose's anxiety.

"Ah bah! Adeline, we have heard something else. Ah! you know what I mean. Is it true?"

"I believe it is," she answered, a faint blush upon her face, and a careless smile.

"Is he handsome?" continued Rose. Of course the first thought that would arise to *her*.

"I have never seen him."

"Oh, Adeline!" uttered Mary Carr, involuntarily, whilst Rose stared with unqualified amazement.

"Not yet. He comes from Paris this week to pay us a visit."

"Who is he?"

"The Baron de la Chasse. Do you recollect seeing, on my

ball night, an old gentleman who remained most of the evening by the side of papa?"

"Yes. Well?" answered Rose, impatiently.

"It seems he made overtures then to papa for my hand, though I did not know it, and——"

"It is a sin, an unholy thing, to sacrifice you to an old man!" interrupted Mary Carr, starting up in her sharp disappointment. "Why, his sands of life must be well-nigh run out!"

"A moment, Mary," rejoined Adeline, calmly laying her hand upon Miss Carr's arm: "who is hasty now? That old man's sands are run out. He died soon after he had played his part in that festal night, which he had come down from Paris purposely to join in. He and papa were old and very dear friends; closer friends it would not be possible to conceive, though there was a difference of twenty years in their ages. His nephew inherits his fortune and title, and it is for him they destine me."

"How old is he?" inquired Rose.

"I have not asked," said Adeline. "Mamma says he is good-looking. It appears that this scheme of uniting the families has been a project of years, though they never told me. Had my sister lived, the honour was to have fallen to her."

"I hope you will be happy," observed Miss Carr.

"Thank you, Mary. But you speak with hesitation."

"Not as to the *wish*. The hope might be more assured if you already knew, and loved, him who is to be your husband. It is a great hazard to promise to marry one whom we have never seen."

"It is the way these things are managed in France," said Adeline.

"And the cause that such doubtful felicity condescends to alight on a French *ménage*," broke forth Rose, who had been temporarily silent. "The wives make it out in their intrigues, though. It is a dangerous game, Adeline. Take care."

"I hope you do not consider it necessary to warn *me* against such danger," exclaimed Adeline, the crimson flying to her cheeks.

"No; for you have not a particle of the French nature about you," fearlessly returned Rose. "To you, strong in right principle, in refinement of feeling, it can bring only suffering—a yearning after what must never be."

"Englishwomen do not always marry where they love," mused Adeline.

"Seldom or never," answered Rose. "With them the passion is generally over. They go more into society, have opportunities of mixing freely, as girls, with the other sex, which you have not, and so the years pass, and by the time their marriage comes, the heart is at rest; its life has left it."

"Then their marriage, even by your own showing, seems to be much on a par with what mine will be."

"Their marriage is, Adeline, but their love is over, *yours has to come.* There lies the difficulty: and the danger."

"Where did you get all these wise ideas from?" inquired Adeline, much amused.

"I'm not an idiot," was Rose's answer. "And I am apt to speak freely when I feel disappointed. I thought you would be sure to marry an Englishman. You have often said so, and you admire the English so much more than you do the French. You remember that handsome Englishman, of French-marigold memory? I set it down in my mind that your destiny and his were to be linked together."

"You have set many things down in your mind, Rose, that never had place out of it," retorted Adeline, with a merry laugh. "I have not seen him since that night, and probably never shall see him again."

"Mademoiselle Rose Darling," exclaimed Clotilde, putting her head out at the schoolroom window.

"Oh the joy!" cried Rose, as she flew away. "I know it's the Singletons."

The Baron de la Chasse arrived from Paris, and was betrothed to Adeline de Castella. A small circle of friends were invited to meet him on the evening of the betrothment, and Adeline did not forget a promise she had made to invite Rose and Mary Carr.

A man of thirty years, of middle height, and compact, well-made figure; pleasing features, regular in their contour; auburn hair, curly and luxuriant by nature, but sheared off to bristles; yellow whiskers, likewise sheared, and a great fierce yellow moustache with curled corners. Somehow Rose, when Adeline said he was good-looking, had pictured to herself a tall, handsome man: she caught sight of the cropped hair and the moustache, and went through the introduction with her handkerchief to her mouth, splitting with laughter. Yet there was no mistaking the baron for anything but a gentleman and a high-bred man.

"Mary!" whispered Rose, when she found the opportunity, "what a sacrifice for Adeline!"

"How do you mean? Domestic happiness does not lie in looks. And if it did, the baron's are not so bad."

"But look at his sheared hair, and those frightful moustaches! Why does he not cut the ends off, and dye them brown?"

"Perhaps he is afraid of their turning green—if he has read 'Ten Thousand a Year.'"

"Oh, Adeline! Adeline! I wonder if she is really betrothed to him?"

"That's a superfluous wonder of yours, Rose," said Mary Carr. "The white wreath is on her head, and the betrothal ring on her finger."

"If a shaven goat—and that's what *he* is—put the ring upon mine, I should look out for some one else to take it off again," retorted Rose. "Dear Adeline!" she continued, as the latter advanced, "let me see your ring."

Adeline drew off her glove and her ring together.

"You should not have taken it from your finger," remarked Mary Carr. "We hold a superstition in Holland—some do—that a betrothal ring, once removed from the finger, will never be exchanged for a nuptial one."

"Sheer nonsense, like most other superstitions," said Adeline; and her perfect indifference of manner proved that no love had entered into *her* betrothal—as, indeed, how should it?

"What had you both to do?"

"Only sign some writings, and then he placed the ring on my finger. Nothing more."

"Except a sealing kiss," said Rose, saucily.

The colour stole over Adeline's face. Even her fair open brow, as it met the chaplet of white roses, became flushed.

"Who but you, Rose, would dream of these vulgar familiarities?" she remonstrated. "Amongst the French, they would be looked upon as the very essence of bad taste."

"*Taste!*" ejaculated Rose, contemptuously. "If you loved, you would know better. Wait until you do, Adeline, and then remember my words—and yours. It does not require much time for love to grow, if it will grow at all," she continued, in that half-abstracted manner which was now frequent with her—

as if she were communing with herself, rather than talking to another.

"Probably not," remarked Adeline, with indifference. "But even you, Rose, susceptible as you are known to be, will scarcely admit that a few hours are sufficient to call it forth."

"Nor a twelvemonth either, situated as you and he are," replied Rose, vehemently. "The very fact of being expected and required to love in any given quarter, must act as a sure preventive."

M. de la Chasse drew up, and entered into conversation with them. He appeared a sensible, agreeable man, at home in all the polite and literary topics of the day. In his manner towards Adeline, though never losing the ceremonious politeness of a Frenchman, there was a degree of gallantry (I don't know any better word : the French would say *empressement*) not unpleasing to witness, and, Rose thought, he had a large share of vanity. But where you would see one of his nation superior to him, you might see ninety-nine inferior.

"It may be a happy marriage after all, Rose," observed Miss Carr, when they were once more alone

"Possibly. If she can only induce him to let his hair grow, and to part with those yellow tails."

"Be serious if you can," reproved Mary Carr. "He seems to be in a fair way to love Adeline."

"He admires Adeline," dissented Rose; "is proud of her, and no doubt excessively gratified that so charming a girl should fall to his lot without any trouble on his part. But if you come to speak of love, it sets one wondering how much of *that* enters into the composition of a French husband."

No shadow, or doubt of the future, appeared that night to sit upon the spirit of Adeline de Castella. There was a radiant look in her countenance, rarely seen ; hiding, for the moment, that touching expression of sorrow and sadness, so natural to it. As the betrothed of a few hours, in a few months to be a wife, she was the worshipped idol of those around her, and this called forth what latent vanity there was in her heart, and she was happy. She could only think it a great thing to be an engaged girl. All do. Why should Adeline de Castella be an exception?

How little did she know, or think, or suspect, the true nature of the contract she had that day made in her blindness !—what it involved, what it was to bring forth for her !

The Château de Beaufoy, formerly belonging to the Chevalier de Beaufoy, was now the property and residence of his widow. She was of English birth, as you have heard. Of her two children, the younger was the wife of Signor de Castella; the other, Agnes de Beaufoy, a maiden lady, had never left her. The property was situated near to Odesque, a small town some leagues from Belport on the Paris line of railroad.

The Castellas departed for the château on their promised summer's visit. Mary Carr accompanied them at the pressing invitation of Adeline. But Madame de Nino would only grant her leave for a week.

Adeline de Castella had represented the château in glowing colours; which caused Mary Carr to be surprised, not to say disappointed, when she saw it. A long, straight, staring, whitish-grey building, all windows and chimneys, with a primly-laid-out garden stretched before it, flat and formal. Precise flower-beds, square, oval, round; round, square, oval; and long paths, straight and narrow; just as it is the pride of French château-gardens to be. The principal entrance to the house was gained by a high, broad flight of steps, on either side of which was a gigantic lion, grinning its fierce teeth at all visitors. And these lions, which were not alive, but carved out of stone, and the steps, were the only relief given to the bare, naked aspect of the edifice. Before the house were two fountains, the carriage approach running between them. Each was surrounded by eight smaller lions, with another giant of the same species spouting up water from its mouth.

Very ugly and devoid of taste it all looked to Mary Carr. But on the western side of the château improvements were visible. A stone terrace, or colonnade, wide, and supported by pillars, with a flight of steps at each end and in the middle, rose before its windows, and lovely pleasure-grounds extended out to the far distance. A verdant, undulating lawn; fragrant shrubs; retired walks, where the trees met overhead; sheltered banks, grateful to recline upon in the noonday sun; a winding shrubbery; a transparent lake: all of their kind charming. For all this, Beaufoy was indebted to the taste of its English mistress.

In the neighbourhood, within easy drives, were located other châteaux, forming a pleasant little society. The nearest house was only half-a-mile distant, and the reader is requested to take especial notice of it, since he will sometimes go there. It was not a château, not half large enough for one, and Beaufoy, with its English ideas, had christened it "The Lodge."

It was a compact little abode, belonging to the Count d'Estival, an intimate friend of the Beaufoy family. This M. d'Estival was gifted by nature with an extraordinary love for painting and the fine arts. He had built a room to the lodge expressly for the reception of pictures, had travelled much, and was continually adding to his collection. Whilst other people spent their money in society and display, he spent his (and he had plenty of it) in paintings. Mary Carr was a connection of his : her eldest brother, an English clergyman, now dead, had married his niece, Emma d'Estival. You have heard of these Carrs before, in a previous work : of their birth and residence in Holland ; of the singular romance attending the early history of their father and mother ; of the remarkable action at law in Westerbury, by which their rights were established. You will not hear more of them in this history, for I don't suppose you like *réchauffés* more than I do.

CHAPTER XIX.

TAKING A PORTRAIT.

MADAME DE BEAUFOY, née Maria Goldingham, was a genial old lady, stout and somewhat helpless. Her daughter Agnes, with her grey hair and her fifty years, looked nearly double the age of Madame de Castella—she was some ten years older. They were not in the least alike, these sisters : the elder was plain, large-featured, eyes and complexion alike pale ; Madame de Castella was a slight, small, delicate-featured woman, with rich brown eyes, and a bright rose-colour on her cheeks. To Mary Carr's surprise—for Adeline had never mentioned it—she saw that Miss de Beaufoy was lame. It was the result of an accident in infancy.

On the morning following their arrival at Beaufoy, Adeline asked her grandmother if she knew whether M. d'Estival was at the Lodge, and was answered in the negative. He had come down from Paris with visitors, it was said ; but had gone away again almost immediately, the old lady thought to Holland.

"So much the better," remarked Adeline, "we can go as

often as we like to his picture-gallery. You are fond of paintings, Mary; you will have a great treat, and you have a sort of right there. Suppose we go now?"

"Now?" said Madame de Castella. "It is so hot!"

"It will be hotter later in the day," said Adeline. "Do come with us, mamma."

Somewhat unwillingly, Madame de Castella called for her scarf and bonnet to accompany them, casting many dubious glances at the cloudless sky and blazing sun. They took their way through the shrubbery; it was the longest road, but the most shady. And whilst they are walking, let us take a look at this said painting-room.

It bore an indescribable appearance, partaking partly of the character and confusion of an artist's studio, partly of a gorgeous picture-gallery. The apartment was very long in proportion to its width, and was lighted by high windows, furnished with those green blinds, or shades, which enable artists to procure the particular light they may require. The room opened by means of glass doors upon a lovely pleasure-ground, but there were shutters and tapestry to draw before these doors at will, so that no light need enter by them. Opposite, at the other end of the room, a smaller door connected it with the house.

That same morning, about seven o'clock, there stood in this apartment a young man arranging French chalks, crayons, painting-brushes, and colours, which lay about in disorder, just as they had been last used. A tall, pointed easel stood a few feet from the wall, near it a stand with its colour-box and palettes. There were classical vases scattered about; plaster-casts from the best models; statues and busts of porphyry, and carving from the marbles of Lydia and Pentelicus. The sculptured head of a warrior; a group of gladiators; a Niobe, in its weeping sorrow, and the Apollo Belvedere; bas-reliefs, copied from the statue of the Discobolon, and other studies from the antique. There was beauty in all its aspects, but no deformity, no detached limbs or misshapen forms: as if the collector cared not to excite unpleasing thoughts. On the walls hung copies from, and *chefs-d'œuvre* of, the masters of many lands: Michael Angelo, Salvator Rosa, Rembrandt; groups by Raphael; beautiful angels of Guido; Carlo Dolce, Titian, all were represented there, with Leonardo da Vinci, the highly-gifted and unhappy. Of the Spanish school there were few specimens, Velasquez, Murillo, and one after Zurbarban; and less of the French, Nicholas Poussin, Le Brun, and Watteau; but there were several of the Flemish and Dutch masters, copies and originals, Van Dyck, Ruysdael, William Van de Welde, and the brothers Abraham and Isaac Ostade.

The gentleman finished his preparations, arranged his palettes, rolled the stand nearer, and sat down before his easel. But, ere he began his task, he glanced up at the window nearest him, and, rising, stood upon a chair, and pulled the green shade lower down to regulate the light. Then he began to work, now whistling a scrap of a popular melody, now humming a few bars, and then bursting out, in a voice of the deepest melody, with a full verse. He was copying a portrait by Velasquez, and had made considerable progress towards its completion. It was a lovely female head, supposed to be a representation of Mary Magdalen. But not even the head on which he was working; not all the portraits and sculptured busts around; not Girodet's "Endymion" by his side, betrayed more winning beauty than did the artist's own face and form.

The rare intellect of his open brow, the sweet smile on his delicate lips, the earnest glance from his deep-blue eyes, *these* could not be imitated by painter's brush or Parian marble. Yet, though his head was cast in the most shapely mould, not to be hidden by the waves of the dark, luxuriant hair, and the pale features, regular to a fault, were of almost womanish beauty, it was not all this, but the *expression* which so won upon a beholder. Lord John Seymour was right when he said the countenance was more prepossessing than handsome— for you have been prepared no doubt to hear that the painter was Frederick St. John—because in the singular fascination of the expression was forgotten the beauty of the features.

Mr. St. John worked assiduously for some hours, until it was hard upon mid-day. He then rose, stretched himself, walked across the room, drew aside the tapestry and shutters, and opened the glass doors.

This part of the room seemed to be consecrated to indolent enjoyment; all vestiges of work were towards the other end. An ottoman or two, some easy-chairs, and a sofa were here, on which the tired artist might repose, and admire the scene without—or the many scenes within. How beautiful was the repose of that outside prospect !—It was but a small plot of ground, yet that, of itself, seemed fit for Eden. A green level lawn, from which arose the spray of a fountain, with its jets of crystal and its mossy banks; clustering flowers of the sweetest scent on the lawn's edge; high, artificial hills of rock beyond, over which dripped a cascade, its murmurs soothing the ear; all very lovely. The whole, not an acre in extent, was surrounded by towering trees, through whose dancing leaves the sun could penetrate but in fitful gleams; fragrant linden-trees, which served to shut the spot out from the world.

Mr. St. John threw himself upon an ottoman and looked out. He had a book in his hand, but did not open it. He was too hungry to read, for he had only taken a cup of coffee and a crust of bread that morning at half-past six, and he fell into an idle reverie.

"Shall I be able to keep my resolution and bear on with this monotony?" he said, half aloud, as he watched unconsciously the flickering sunlight upon the lawn. "A few months of this inexpensive life, and I shall see my way out of embarrassment more clearly than I do now. I will *not* be indebted to Isaac for my deliverance—no, I won't; and if there were only some break in the life here—some relief—if d'Estival himself were only back——"

The door at the opposite end of the room opened, and a portly, pleasant-looking woman, who might be the mistress of the house in her plain morning costume, or its respectable housekeeper, looked in, and told Mr. St. John his breakfast was served.

"Thank you, Madame Baret," he said, not in the least sorry to hear it. And as he followed her from the room, in all the alacrity of hunger, he did not observe that his pocket-handkerchief fell to the ground.

It was about this time that the party from Beaufoy reached the Lodge, Madame de Castella grumbling dreadfully. She had borne the heat pretty patiently through the shaded shrubbery, but in the open ground, and in that brazen cornfield, which had not so much as a hedge, or a green blade of grass on which to rest the dazzled eye, it had been intensely felt. A shocking state her complexion would be in! She could feel incipient blisters on it already.

"Dear mamma, it is not so bad as that," laughed Adeline, "it is only a little red. Let us go in by the gate at once to the painting-room! Madame Baret will keep us talking for an hour, especially when she gets to know who Mary is."

"I am too hot to look at paintings," querulously returned

Madame de Castella. "You may go to the painting-room,
but I shall seek Madame Baret, and get a draught of milk. I
never was so hot in my life."

She went on to the house as she spoke. Adeline and Mary
passed through the little gate of the secluded garden, and sat
down in the painting-room.

Oh, how delightful it was there! how delightful! They had
come in from the broad glare, the sultry mid-day heat, to that
shady place; the eye, fatigued with the dazzling light, had
found a rest; the fields looked burnt up and brown, but here
the grass was fresh and green; the cool, sparkling waters of
the fountain were playing, and those lovely flower-beds emitted
the sweetest perfume. It was grateful as is the calm, silvery
moonlight after a day of blazing heat. Never had Mary Carr
seen a place that so forcibly spoke to her mind of rest and peace.

Adeline was the first to rise from her seat: something in
another part of the room attracted her attention.

"Mary! look at this! a painting on the easel! and in progress! Grandmamma said M. d'Estival was away!"

Miss Carr turned her head, and in that glance, the first she
had really bestowed on the apartment, thought its contents the
most heterogeneous mass she had ever beheld. Adeline continued to look at the easel.

"There are touches here of a master's hand. It must be
M. d'Estival. He paints beautifully. Many of these copies
are by him. Or can it be an artist he has here?"

"Adeline, you have dropped your handkerchief," said Miss
Carr, rising, and picking up one from the floor. She turned
to its four corners. In the first three there was no name; in
the last, not "A. L. de C.," as she expected, but, worked in
hair, and surmounted by a crest, "Frederick St. John."

A presentiment of the truth flashed across her brain. A
confused remembrance of a young man of noble presence,
a French marigold, and Rose Darling's superstitious fears that
he would exercise some blighting influence over *her* future life.
She called to Adeline with breathless interest, and the latter
came to her immediately, aroused by the tone.

"See this, Adeline!" pointing to the name. "It is neither
yours nor mine."

Adeline read it quite indifferently.

"*Don't* you remember—on your ball-night--he with the
French marigold?"

"Frederick St. John," said Adeline, carelessly, taking the handkerchief in her hand. "Yes, it is the same name. Probably the same person."

How calmly she spoke; how indifferently! An utter stranger, a name she had never heard, could not have excited in her less interest. There was no shadow on her spirit of what was to come.

At that moment the inner door opened, and Mr. St. John entered. Mary Carr started with surprise, for she had not observed that any door was there. Mr. St. John also stood, momentarily transfixed, wondering, no doubt, who they were, and how they got there, like the flies in amber. He at once apologized for having so unceremoniously entered the room, not being aware that it was occupied.

"The apology is due from us, Mr. St. John," interrupted Adeline. "You do not recollect me?" she continued, seeing his surprised look at the mention of his name.

Was it likely? He had seen her but once, months before, in her brilliant ball-dress; now she was in morning attire, her face shaded by a bonnet.

"It seems my fate to be in unlawful possession of your property," continued Adeline, holding out the handkerchief. "The first time we met, I deprived you of a flower, and now——"

"My dear Mademoiselle de Castella!" he interrupted, his features lighting up with pleasure as he took both her hands. "Pray pardon me. Do not think I had forgotten you. But indeed you were almost the last person I could have expected to meet here." True. That there was such a place as Beaufoy in the neighbourhood he knew, but not that the Castellas were in any way connected with it.

"Are you staying here?" asked Adeline.

"Yes." And he explained how it happened that he was so. He had met the Count d'Estival (whom he had known previously) in Paris this spring, and had accepted an invitation to accompany him home. Soon after their arrival the count had received a summons to Holland on family business, and he had made St. John promise to await his return.

"This young lady is a connection of M. d'Estival's," said Adeline. "You have heard of the Carrs of Holland—of Rotterdam?"

Mr. St. John smiled. "The Carrs of Holland are renowned

people in my county. Westerbury boasts of its famous trial still."

"And you know, then, that the Reverend Robert Carr married Emma d'Estival," continued Adeline. "This is Mary Carr, his only sister."

A saddened light came into Frederick St John's eyes as he took her hands in greeting. The reminiscences brought all too palpably to his mind one who had been very dear to him—the dead college boy.

Madame de Castella entered the room, and they all seemed at home with each other at once. Mr St. John went round the walls with them, pointing out the beauties and merits of the paintings, though the Castellas had seen them before.

"I perceive you are an artist," observed Madame de Castella, looking at the painting on the easel.

"I have only the talents of an amateur, greatly as I love the art, much as I have practised it. If I ever wish myself other than what I am, it is that I could be one of our great painters. How little is known in England of Velasquez' portraits!" he exclaimed, looking lovingly on the original he was copying.

"Or in France either," returned Madame de Castella. "Believe me, Mr. St. John, no one can appreciate the Spanish school of painting until they obtain a knowledge of the collections in Spain."

"You are quite right," he answered.

"Have you been in Spain?"

"I believe I have been everywhere, so far as Europe goes, where there is a gallery of paintings to be seen."

"And do you like the Spanish school?"

"Pretty well."

"Only that? I am sorry to hear you say so."

"Spanish painting has a character peculiar to itself," resumed Mr. St. John. "At least, I have always thought so. The artists were not free: they were compelled to bend to those laws that restricted their pencils to delineations of religious subjects. Had they been at liberty to exercise their genius unfettered, they would have left more valuable mementos behind them. Imagination is the very life and soul of painting; curb that, and you can expect but little."

"I suppose you are right," said Madame de Castella.

Madame Baret came in, and joined the party. She was related to the Count d'Estival. Some years before, her husband,

who was then a small proprietor, risked his money in a speculation, and was ruined. M. d'Estival stepped in, and offered
them an asylum with him. They accepted it, upon condition
that they should be permitted to be useful. Madame became
the active mistress and manager of the house, her husband the
superintendent of the land and farm. But though they did
make themselves useful, both indoors and out, somewhat after
the manner of upper servants, they were gentlepeople still, and
received due consideration and respect.

"Who is that painting by?" inquired Madame de Castella,
stopping before a group of portraits.

"It is a copy of one of Van Dyck's," said Mr. St. John.
"There hangs the original. But it is admirably executed."

"It is, indeed," replied Madame de Castella. "To my un-
practised eye, it looks equal to the original."

"Almost," assented Mr. St. John. "Except in the transpa-
rency of the skin, and there Van Dyck cannot be rivalled."

"Whose is that gorgeous landscape?"

"An original of Claude Lorraine's."

"To be sure. I might have told it by the colouring. And
that next, Mr. St. John?"

"One of Correggio's."

"I don't much admire it."

"It is cold, but faultless," was Mr. St. John's reply, "as Correggio's productions generally are."

"Do you paint portraits from life, Mr. St. John?"

"I have done so; and would again, if I found a subject to
my taste."

"What better study, for a fine old head, than your good
hostess, here?" rejoined Madame de Castella, lowering her
voice.

St. John laughed; a pleasant laugh. To Mary Carr's ear it
seemed to imply that he did not care to paint old women.
"Will you permit me to try my hand at yours?" he said to
Madame de Castella.

"No, indeed, thank you," she answered. "Mine has already
been taken three times, and I don't like the fatigue of sitting."

The silvery chimes of the antique clock on its pedestal told
three before they took their departure. Not half the time
appeared to have elapsed: could it be the charm of St. John's
conversation that caused it to fly so rapidly, or the merits of the
pictures? He escorted them across the fields to the gate of

their own shrubbery: and Madame de Castella invited him to visit them in the evening.

At dinner, the conversation fell upon Mr. St. John. Madame de Castella expressed herself delighted that so agreeable a man should be located near them, and laughed at her sister, Mademoiselle Agnes, for not having found him out before. He was a thorough gentleman, a high-bred man of the world, she said, and his society would help them to pass away the time pleasantly during M. de Castella's absence in Paris. Before they had done talking of him, St. John entered.

He was in slight mourning, his evening attire very plain and quiet, but he bore about him always a nameless elegance. Mary Carr looked at him with admiration—as did probably the rest; but for them she could not answer. There was a peculiar charm in his manner she had never seen in any other man's. Describe in what it lay, she could not; but it attracted to him all with whom he came in contact. His conversation was eloquent and animated, but his bearing calm and still. Before he left, he promised M. de Castella to dine with them the next evening.

In the morning, M. de Castella, Adeline, and Mary Carr, walked over to the lodge, where they stayed some hours. M. de Castella, unlike his wife, could never tire of looking at the paintings. The time seemed to fly. It is scarcely to be described how very much they had become at home with Mr. St. John—they were as familiar and dear friends.

Something was said in jest about his taking Adeline's likeness; but these jests grow into earnest now and then. Mary Carr could hardly tell how it came to be decided, but decided it was when he came up to dinner in the evening. Signor and Madame de Castella were delighted at the idea of possessing a portrait of her, and the old lady was so eager, she wanted it to be begun off-hand. Adeline, too, was nothing loth: it was gratifying to her innocent and pardonable vanity.

On the Friday morning—unlucky day!—Adeline sat to Mr. St. John for the first time. Her father and Miss Carr were with her. Afterwards he again went to dine at the château: the evening seemed dull now that did not bring them Mr. St. John. Truly the acquaintance was short enough to say this. On the following morning early, M. de Castella departed for Paris, and after breakfast Adeline and Mary Carr proceeded to the lodge with Madame de Castella. The sitting was long, and Madame de Castella could not conceal her weariness. To many, the opportunity of examining the paintings would have been pleasure sufficient, but not to her. In point of fact, she had no taste for the fine arts, and after Tuesday's cursory renewed view of them, the task proved irksome. She complained much, too, of the walk in the morning heat. The truth was—and it is as well to confess it—that during these periodical visits to the Château de Beaufoy, Madame de Castella lived in a chronic state of ennui. Young and good-looking still, fond of the world, the dulness of Beaufoy was a very penance to her. She went through it willingly as a duty: she loved her mother ; but she could not help the weariness affecting her spirits.

The sitting this first morning was long and weary : but for talking with Mr. St. John, she never could have sat through it. Their conversation turned upon Rome—a frequent theme. Mary Carr thought that were she to remain long with them she should become as well acquainted with the Eternal City as though she had visited it. St. John seemed wonderfully attached to it ; as were the Castellas. He had a portfolio of drawings of it, from his own pencil : some of them highly-finished coloured specimens ; others bare sketches, to be filled up from memory ; the lines of genius apparent in all. The portefeuille was often referred to : even Madame de Castella had been content to look over it for a full hour. It was a motley collection. A sketch of the lovely Alban hills ; the ruins of an aqueduct; a temple of Pæstum ; the beauties of Tivoli; the ruins of the Cæsars' palaces ; St. Peter's in its magnificence ; a view from the Appian Way ; a drawing of the Porta San Giovanni ; an imaginative sketch of a gorgeous palace of Rome in its zenith ; a drawing of one of its modern villas; a temple of Jupiter ; Sallust's garden ; and the tomb, still so perfect, of Cecilia Metella. There were fanciful moonlight views of the now almost uninhabited hills, Paltaino, Celio, and Aventino. There was one masterly, gloomy painting of a grove of pines and cypress trees, overlooking a heap of ruins. Lying side by side with it, was one of a life-like garden, with its marble fountains, its colonnades, its glimpses of tinted flowers, its blooming orange and lemon trees, its cascades and pillars, its wreathing vines, its polished statues, and its baths of Alexandrian marble ; and, over all, the bright blue of an Italian sky, and the glowing beams of an Italian sun.

"May I ask a favour of you?" said Madame de Castella, addressing Madame Baret when they were going away.

"As many as you like," returned the smiling dame, ever good-humoured.

"I cannot possibly endure these hot walks every day until the sittings are over. When I do not come myself, will you kindly bear my daughter company while she is here, and take charge of her? Louise can attend her in walking hither."

"With the greatest pleasure," returned Madame Baret. "I will take every care of her. But there is nothing here that can harm Mademoiselle."

"*I* will take care of her," interrupted St. John, in low, earnest tones to Madame de Castella. "No harm shall come near her. I will guard her from all: more anxiously than if she were my own sister."

Adeline partly caught the words, and blushed at their earnestness. It was impossible to doubt the young man's honourable feeling, or his wish to save her from all harm, real or imaginary. What *his* exact meaning was, Mary Carr did not know, but some of the others, it would appear, were think-ing of outward, visible danger. Madame Baret had been cautioning Adeline never to come through the field where the savage bull was let loose, though it did cut off a portion of the road; and Madame de Castella besought her not to sit with the two doors open, and always to keep her bonnet on for a few minutes after she came in, that she might become cool before removing it. Adeline laughed, and promised obedience to all.

Louise, the lady's-maid, commenced her attendance on the Monday. She did not appear to relish the walk more than did her mistress, and displayed an enormous crimson parapluie, which she held between her face and the sun. At the door of the painting-room, she handed the young ladies over to the charge of Mr. St. John, and then left them. Madame de Castella never understood but that Louise remained with her young mistress in the painting-room: does not understand the contrary to this day. She certainly intended her to do so, notwithstanding her request to Madame Baret. But Louise was a most inveterate gossip, and to sit silent and restrained before her superiors in the painting-room, gaping at its beauties, which she could not comprehend, when she might be exercis-ing her tongue with Madame Baret's housemaid and bonne,

Juliette, in her sewing-chamber, or with Madame Baret's stout maid-of-all-work in the kitchen, was philosophy beyond Mademoiselle Louise. Neither did Madame Baret always sit with Adeline. Her various occupations, as active mistress of the house, and especially of those two idle servants, frequently called her away. Nor did she give a thought to there being any necessity for her doing so. What harm, as she had observed, could come near Adeline?

"How long have you been here, Mr. St. John?" inquired Mary Carr, as, the sitting over—sooner than it need have been —they strolled into the garden.

"Nearly a month. Perhaps I may stay here until winter."

"In this dull place! Why?"

He laughed as he avowed the truth. That he had been extravagant—imprudent—and had outrun his income. In the world he should only get deeper into the mire, but there he was spending next to nothing. A little patience: it would all come right in time.

"What shrub do you call this, Adeline?" inquired Mary Carr, by way of changing the conversation, and vexed at her inquisitiveness.

"Candleberry myrtle, in English," replied Adeline. "We were staying at Rambouillet some years ago, and brought some suckers from the forest. It grows there in great abundance. Mamma gave some to M. d'Estival, and he planted them here."

Suddenly, Mr. St. John made a motion of silence, and, bending stealthily towards Adeline, half closed his hand, and swept it quickly over the side of her throat. A wasp had settled on her neck.

"There it goes," he said, dashing it into the water of the fountain. "You know," he continued, half playfully, half tenderly, gazing into her face, and interrupting her efforts at thanks, "that I have undertaken to shield you from harm. It shall be my earnest care to do so, now and ever."

A shade crossed Adeline's countenance. Did she *already* regret her marriage contract? or was she in danger of forgetting it altogether? There was nothing to remind her of it: even the engagement-ring was no longer on her finger. It was too large for her, and quite a source of trouble to keep on, so she had put it into her jewel-box: where it lay, uncared for.

" Mr. St. John ! the wasp has stung your hand !"

" Yes, he revenged himself by leaving his sting there. It is nothing. And, indeed, will serve as an excuse to Madame de Castella for my idleness to-day."

" You know I leave to-morrow," said Mary, turning to him. " Will you send me up a bouquet of these beautiful flowers to take to Rose Darling ?"

" You shall be obeyed, fair lady. How large will you have it ? The size of Louise's parapluie ?"

With the next morning came the bouquet, Mr. St. John himself being the bearer. His visit had a twofold purport, he observed : to bid adieu to Miss Carr, and to walk with Adeline down to the Lodge. He had been thinking it might be better, he said to Madame de Castella, that he should escort Adeline to and fro, until the return of M. de Castella. Mary Carr glanced at his countenance as he spoke : she saw that his words were honest; that there was no hidden meaning; that the protection of Adeline was then the sole motive which actuated him.

Ten o'clock struck as they were talking, and, with the last stroke, came round the carriage to convey Miss Carr to Odesque, where she was to take the train.

" May I whisper a caution to you ?" said Mary, pressing her lips to Adeline's, in parting.

" A caution ! Fifty, if you like."

" Do not fall in love with Frederick St. John."

" Mary !"

" From the position in which you stand—engaged to another —it might lead to endless misery."

" There is no danger of it," returned Adeline, breathlessly. " If there were, do you suppose papa and mamma would suffer me to be with him ? How could any such idea enter your head, Mary Carr? You are taking a leaf from Rose's book."

·   Papa and mamma ! Truth was in her accent, but how little she understood.

" I am willing to believe that there is no danger," was Miss Carr's reply. " *I hope you will be able so to speak when we next meet.* Do not feel angry with me, Adeline. I have but your interest at heart."

Mr. St. John conducted Miss Carr to the carriage, and, in shaking hands, he jestingly begged her to give his love to Rose: they had talked much of her. As he stood there on the stone steps, bareheaded, until Mary should drive away, her last look lingered on him; and again that uneasy doubt shot through her mind—how impossible that Adeline should live in continual companionship with such a man, and not learn to love him!

Miss Carr was received by Madame de Nino with a scolding and a threat of punishment. She had exceeded her time of absence by a day. But Mary laid the blame upon Madame de Castella, and handed in a note of apology from that lady. Madame was only half soothed; but she graciously remitted the punishment.

Mary drew Rose Darling aside. "Won't you admire these lovely flowers? They were sent for you."

Rose was sulky. She had been in a furious state of envy during Mary's visit, because she was not invited herself.

"Of all the human race, Rose, playing out their course upon this variable world of ours, who do you suppose is located just now within a stone's throw of the Château de Beaufoy?"

"I dare say it's nobody I know," said Rose, cross still.

"You know and admire him. A young and handsome man. He gathered these flowers for you—see how rare they are!—and he sent them with his love."

She looked up sharply; and her mind reverted to one who, perhaps, was seldom absent from it. But another moment sufficed to show how idle was the thought: and the current of ideas led her to another.

"Not Lord John Seymour?"

"No; what should bring him there? Frederick St. John."

"He! You are joking, Mary Carr."

"I am not. He is staying quite close to them. We saw a great deal of him. And—Rose!—he is taking Adeline's portrait!"

"Allez toujours," exclaimed Rose, using a familiar French expression. "I told you once before, Mary Carr, that that man, my pseudo-cousin, would exercise some extraordinary influence over Adeline de Castella's future life; and I now tell it you again."

CHAPTER XX.

LOVE'S FIRST DREAM.

HOURS, days, weeks, rolled on, after the departure of Miss Carr from the Château de Beaufoy, and no outward change had taken place in its occupants. But in the inward heart of one, how much !

The portrait progressed towards its completion, though not rapidly. It was a good likeness of Adeline, and admirably executed. St. John had exactly caught that sad expression which sometimes sat on her features, forming their chief interest : earth's sorrow mingling with the heavenly beauty of an angel. Had the portrait been preserved, people might have said afterwards they could read her history there.

St. John was also teaching Adeline drawing : or, rather, trying to improve her in it. One day Madame de Castella desired her to produce her school-drawings—and she had done none since she left. Accordingly, some chalk-heads and a few landscapes came forth. There was not much taste displayed in the heads, St. John observed ; more in the landscapes, in two of them especially—a glimpse of the Nile and some lotus lilies, its fountains surrounded by their date-trees ; and a charming scene in her own fair land. That there was great room for improvement, every one could but acknowledge, and Mr. St. John offered to give her some lessons. All of them— Madame de Castella, Aunt Agnes, and the old grandmother —were pleased at his offer. How could they be so blind? How could they be so thoughtless? St. John had acquired an extraordinary influence over them all. Madame de Castella was much attached to him ; she seemed to feel a sort of pride in him, as a fond mother will feel in the perfections of an only son. He frequently dined with them ; all his evenings were spent there as a matter of course. He had become necessary to their every-day life. When he was away, nothing went right ; when he was present, it was sunshine to all. And yet they forgot that there was another who might be equally awake to the charms his presence brought ; the only one to whom it could bring real danger. Perhaps the thought of danger to Adeline's heart never entered the head of Madame de Castella :

perhaps, if it ever did momentarily cross her, she deemed that Adeline, from her engagement, was safe.

Many an hour, when Madame de Castella innocently deemed that Adeline was sitting mumchance in the painting-room, Louise embroidering her own caps, at which she was a famous hand, by her side, and Mr. St. John working hard at the portrait, without a thought beside it, would two out of those three be idling their morning underneath the lime-trees, St. John reading to her, chiefly books of poetry, its theme often love. Then he would lay down the book, and talk to her, in that tender, persuasive voice so soothing to the ear but dangerous to the heart. Thus they would sit on for hours, her hand sometimes clasped in his, he the reader, she the listener, devouring together this sweet and subtle poetry, which has in it so much of fascination. Oh, the hazardous life for the heart's peace!—when both were in the heyday of youth, singularly attractive, and one, at least, had never loved. And yet it was neither stopped nor interfered with, nor was its danger suspected.

One day they were standing at the open doors of the painting-room. Mr St. John was speaking of Castle Wafer. He had before described its attractions, natural and imparted, to Adeline, had made sketches for her of some of its points, from memory. He was saying that when Castle Wafer was his own—and it would be some time—he should build a room similar to the one they were now in, for himself and his work, and lay out a plot of ground as the plot before them was laid out: it would serve as a momento of this period of their early acquaintance. "And in that room, Adeline," he continued, "we will spend a great portion of our time."

"We!" exclaimed Adeline.

The interruption awoke him to reality; for he had been as one buried in a dream, and was unconscious at the moment that he spoke aloud. Laughing as he made his apology, he bent his head towards her; but even then his voice took a dangerously sweet and persuasive tone.

He had spoken inadvertently. But, the truth was, he had latterly been so accustomed, in his inmost self, to associate Adeline with hereafter—his future plans, his future home, his future happiness—that he had unguardedly given utterance to his presumptuous thoughts: he would not so offend again.

She glanced timidly at him, earnest tears in her eyes, glowing blushes on her cheeks. In her heart she would have wished to tell him how far he had been from giving her offence.

Another time he was walking home with Adeline, Louise and her great crimson parapluie streaming, as usual, a good way behind them, when, in jumping from a stile, Adeline twisted her foot. The pain for the moment was intense : Mr. St. John saw it, by her countenance ; and he stole his arms round her and sheltered her head on his arm. All these signs must mean —something.

That time had come for Adeline which must come for us all —the blissful period of love's first dream. She did not at first understand the magic of the charm that was stealing over her, making all, within and without, a paradise. She had assured Miss Carr that there was no danger of her loving Mr. St. John, yet even then, though she suspected it not, the golden links of the net were fastening on her heart. And when she awoke to the real nature of these sweet sensations, it was too late to fly the danger—the power and the will to do so were alike over.

How many varied degrees of the passion called love there are, can never be ascertained, for one human being cannot experience the feelings of another. The love—so called—felt by the generality of mortals, every-day, practical men and women, is so essentially different from that which takes root in a highly passionate, imaginative temperament, refined and intellectual, that the two have no affinity one with the other. This last passion is known but to few, and apart from themselves, can be imagined by none. The world could not understand this love ; it is of a different nature from anything they can know ; they would laugh at, while they disbelieved in it. It has been asserted that this highly-wrought passion, the ecstatic bliss of which, while it lasts, no earthly language could express, never ends happily. I believe that it never does. The dream comes to an end, and the heart's life with it. Perhaps nearly a whole existence has yet to be dragged through, but all enjoyment in the world and the world's things is gone, and nothing can ever again awaken a pulse in the veins, a thrill in the worn and beaten heart. The smile may sit upon the lip, the jest may issue from it ; gay beaming glances may dart from the eye, and their hollowness is not suspected, nor the desolation that has long settled within. You who read this, may meet it in a spirit of dispute and ridicule : then it is because you cannot understand it. And be thankful that it is so—that to you the power, so fatally to love, has been spared.

It was a passion of this latter and rare description which had taken root in the bosom of Adeline de Castella. She could not have loved as the world loves, for she was one of those who live but in the inward life. There was a mine of sentiment and poetry within her, and it wanted but a touch like this to awaken it. Now, she lived in the present; before, she had lived in the future; hereafter, she would live in the past. She rose in the morning, and there was no wish beyond the day, the seeing Mr. St. John; she retired to rest at night, only to dream of him, and to awake to the bliss of another day. Nature had never looked to her as it looked now : the grass had been green, but not of this green; the fragrance of the flowers had been frag-rance, but they had not borne their present sweetness; the song of the birds, hitherto unmeaning, seemed now a carol of joyous praise to their Creator; there was music in the winds and in the fluttering breeze; there was rapture in the whole bright earth. Adeline was living in a dream, not of this world but of Paradise; it could be called nothing else; she was walk-ing on the wings of the morning, treading on the yielding flowers. It was well for her that it was not destined to last; it is well for us all : or we should never ask, or wish, for the heaven that is to come.

And what of Mr. St. John? Did he love her? Beyond all doubt he loved her, and would have made her his wife, and cherished her as such : but whether in the idolatry of a first and impassioned attachment, or whether in but the passing prefer-ence which some men will feel ten times for as many women, can hardly be known. It was not given to the world to pene-trate Mr. St. John's secret feelings; but events shall be faithfully related as they occurred.

And meanwhile, as if Fate determined fully to have her fling, news came from M. d'Estival, begging Mr. St. John to remain on at the Lodge. That gentleman was detained in Holland by the lingering illness of his brother; but he was happy, knowing that his cherished pictures were under the care of his friend.

And Mr. St. John did stay on, nothing loth, making the sun-shine of the château and the *life* of Adeline.

Existence was somewhat monotonous in itself at Beaufoy, as you may readily conceive, if you have had the honour of sojourning in any of these half-isolated French country houses: but there arrived an invitation one day at Beaufoy, for dinner at a neighbouring dwelling. Madame de Beaufoy had given up dinner-parties, but the others went. Adeline would have liked to decline, but she dared not.

She entered the carriage on the appointed evening, and sat in it listless and absorbed. Mr St. John was not going, and the hours not spent with him were to her now as dead and lost. Madame de Castella noticed her abstraction, and inquired if she were ill.

"I have only a headache," replied Adeline, who was too English not to have acquired the common excuse.

"Maria!" exclaimed Mademoiselle de Beaufoy, suddenly addressing her sister, "I declare, there's Mr. St. John! Where can he have been walking to in this heat?"

Adeline turned and saw him, a thrill of rapture rushing through her veins. They returned his greeting, and drove on.

Where can he be walking to? *She* surmised—that it was but to obtain a glimpse of her as their carriage passed. She was no longer pensive: a heightened colour shone in her cheek, a brilliancy in her eye: her spirits rose to exultation, and she went the rest of the way as one on fairy wings.

They sank again ere the evening was half over, the long, tame, spiritless evening. To others it might seem gay; but not to her: her heart was far away, and she only cared that it should end and the morrow be nearer. No singing, after his voice, brought music to her ear; the dancing was no longer the dancing of other days.

The next day was the birthday of Mademoiselle de Beaufoy; a fête always kept with much ceremony. A dinner was to be given in the evening, and M. de Castella was expected to arrive for it from Paris. In the course of the day a note was handed to Adeline, its handwriting bringing a wild flush of pleasure to her cheeks. It was from Mr. St. John, stating that he was called to Odesque to meet a friend, who would be passing through it on his way to Paris, and he did not know whether he could return for dinner. It was only a short note, worded as a brother might write to a sister; yet she hung enraptured over its few lines, and held it to her heart; she almost cried aloud in her excess of ecstasy; and stealthily, her cheeks a rosy red, and her face turned to the darkest corner of the room, she pressed to her lips its concluding words—"Frederick St. John."

The first letter from one we love!—what an epoch it is in life! It stands alone in memory; the ONE letter of existence; bearing no analogy to the stern real ones of later years.

The return of Signor de Castella, after an absence, had once been a joyous event to Adeline. Now, she looked forward to it with indifference. It was not that she loved her father less; but other feelings had grown tame in comparison with this new passion that absorbed her. The day wore on, however, and the Signor did not come.

The guests arrived, all save one, and dinner would be announced immediately. Adeline was waiting and hoping for Mr. St. John: but she waited in vain. How inexpressibly lovely she looked in her evening dress, with the rose-flush of excitement on her cheeks, some of those guests remember to this day. A strange, sick feeling of expectancy had taken possession of her; she scarcely knew what was passing. Questions were addressed to her, which she answered at random, scarcely hearing their purport. Was *another* evening to pass without seeing him?

A sudden opening of the door. The servant threw it wide upon its portals. Adeline caught one glimpse beyond it, and heard the man's words:

"Monsieur de Saint John." For those French servants always put in the "de" when speaking of *him*.

She turned, in her agitation, to one who sat next to her, and spoke rapid sentences to cover it. She did not look, but she felt he had advanced to Madame de Beaufoy, now to Madame de Castella, and now he was speaking a few whispered words of congratulation to Agnes. She hoped he would not come to her just then; her tremor was already too great for concealment. Oh, the rapture, the unspeakable rapture that thrilled through her whole soul at his presence! That a human being, one like ourselves, should bring such!

They were pairing off to the dining-room. St. John was talking with one of the lady guests, and Adeline saw him turn sharply round, as if he would have advanced to her. But a wealthy neighbouring proprietor, rejoicing in the long-sounding title of Monsieur le Comte Le Coq de Monty, took the white tips of Adeline's gloved fingers within his own.

But he sat next her. Whether by accident, or successful manoeuvring, or original design, he sat next her. More than once, in the course of the elaborate dinner, their hands—*their* hands!—met, under cover of the table-linen, and then the whole world around was to her as nothing.

Frederick St. John shone to advantage in society. Handsome without affectation, gay without levity, accomplished without display, he yet possessed, amidst all his solid conversational powers, that apt gallantry which wins its way, that readiness at light phrases which takes captive the ear. He had the great advantage also of speaking French almost as a native: only by a slight accent once in a way, could a Frenchman detect the foreigner. If he held those guests spell-bound that evening, in what sort of spell do you suppose he must have held Adeline! It was a man of subtle wisdom who first recorded that phrase of truth—Man's heart is lost through the eye, but woman's through the ear.

Mr. St. John remained after the guests had departed. When he said farewell, Madame de Castella, in talking, stepped out with him to the colonnade, and descended the steps. Her sister and Adeline followed. It was a lovely night. The transition from the hot rooms, with their many lights, to the cool pure atmosphere without was inexpressibly grateful, and they walked with him to the shrubbery and part of the way down it. Madame de Castella suddenly recollected Adeline. Her voice, as she spoke, had a tone of alarm in it.

"This change to cool air may not be well for you, Adeline. You have nothing on. Let us run back: who will be indoors first? Good night, Mr. St. John."

She turned with Agnes de Beaufoy, and the windings of the shrubbery soon hid them from view. Adeline would have followed, but a beloved arm had encircled her and held her back. Frederick St. John drew her towards him, and snatched the first sweet tremulous kiss of love. Maidenly reserve caused her to draw away from him, otherwise she could have wished that kiss to last for ever. "Oh, Frederick! if mamma——" was the only agitated rejoinder that came from her lips, and she sped away, her hand lingering, to the last, in his.

"Why, Adeline!" exclaimed her aunt, as she came up, "lame as I am, I can beat you at running."

She went up to her chamber. She stood at the window, looking out on the lovely scene, yet scarcely heeding it; her hands pressed upon her bosom to keep down its agitation and its excess of happiness. She glanced up at the starry heavens, and wondered if the bliss, promised there, could exceed this of earth. She seemed to be realizing some ecstatic fairy-dream of her childhood. How long she stood there, she knew not. Silently she paced her chamber, unable to rest. She recalled his whispered words: she recalled those fleeting moments which had been an era in her life: and when she at last sank into a wearied slumber, it was only to live the reality over again; to dream that that light touch of Mr. St. John's on her lips was present, not past.

The next morning Madame de Beaufoy was ill: she had an indigestion; a very favourite malady with the French. Madame de Castella was anxious, somewhat uneasy; for no letter had arrived from her husband to account for his non-appearance. She hoped it might come by the evening post. They had many visitors that day, and Adeline thought it would never end.

After dinner Madame de Beaufoy was well enough to sit up and play at cards in her dressing-room, her two daughters bearing her company. Adeline was downstairs alone, privately expecting Mr. St. John; now, standing before a mirror, hastily passing a finger over the braids of her luxuriant hair: now glancing, with conscious vanity, at the rich crimson which expectancy called to her cheeks; now, stealing to the colonnade, and looking and listening.

Suddenly the room-door opened, and Adeline stepped in from the colonnade, her heart beating wildly. But it was only her mother: who began to rummage amongst the silks and worsteds of an ivory basket. "Only her mother!" How full of ingratitude is the heart to those who have cherished us from infancy, when this all-potent passion for a stranger takes root in it!

"Adeline, your aunt has mislaid her green floss-silk. Will you look in my work-box?"

Adeline unlocked the box, found the silk, and handed it to her mother. Again the door opened, and this time her pulse did not quicken in vain. It was Mr. St. John.

"I am glad to see Madame de Beaufoy is better," he observed as he came in. "She nodded to me from her dressing-room."

"Oh yes, thank you. Ah, here's news at last!" exclaimed Madame de Castella, as the old Spanish servant, Silva, entered with a letter. And with a "pardon" to Mr. St. John, she broke the seal. She was very French sometimes.

"M. de Castella has been detained," she explained, skim-

ming the contents: " he will not be here for a week. The
truth is, Mr. St. John, he always finds Beaufoy painfully triste,
and makes excuses for remaining away from it. Adeline, here
is a message for you."

Adeline glanced up half frightened. These instincts are
rarely wrong.

"Your papa desires his love to you, and—— You are quite
a family friend now, Mr. St. John," broke off Madame de
Castella, " so I do not hesitate to speak before you. I dare say
the subject is as well known to you as it is to ourselves: you
are like a son of the house, a brother to Adeline."

Mr. St. John bowed.

"This is what your papa says, Adeline," continued Madame,
translating as she read: " ' Make my love to my dear Adeline;
tell her not to be vexed at my additional week's delay, for I
shall bring De la Chasse with me when I come.' You are no
doubt aware, I say, Mr. St. John, of the position the baron
holds in our family in regard to Adeline."

Another bow from Mr. St. John.

"And now I must ask you to excuse me for a few minutes,
while I take this silk to my mother," pursued Madame.
"When not well she is a little exacting. I will be down
almost immediately. Adeline, do your best to entertain Mr.
St. John."

He closed the door after Madame de Castella, and returned
to Adeline. She was leaning against the window-frame,
endeavouring to look all unconscious and at ease, but evidently
hardly able to support herself. Her face had turned pale; a
sort of startled despair had settled on it. The evil moment,
which throughout all this golden time she had never dared to
look in the face, was at hand now.

Mr. St. John wound his arm round her, and became himself
her support. He called her by the most endearing names, he
pressed the sweetest kisses on her lips: he besought her not
to give way to despondency: he assured her there was no
cause for it, for that never, never should she be any other's
wife than his.

He had been silent hitherto, so far as open avowal went;
but that was over now. He spoke cheeringly of his plans and
prospects; of winning the consent of Signor de Castella to their
union. He pictured their future home in the land of his birth
—the land which she had always loved. And Adeline, as she

listened to his soothing words, never a shade of doubt clouding them, grew reassured and calm. She almost felt, as she stood there by his side and looked into his honest earnest eyes, that no power on earth could avail to separate them, if he willed that it should not.

When Madame de Castella returned to the room, delightfully unconscious, words which no time could obliterate, at least in *one* heart, had been spoken. They had betrothed themselves, each to the other, until death should divide them. A less formal betrothal, it is true ; but oh, how much more genuine than that other in which Adeline de Castella had borne a part.

CHAPTER XXI.

A FADING CHILD.

THERE arrived one morning a missive at the house of Madame de Nino, addressed to that renowned preceptress herself. It was from Madame de Castella, and contained a pressing invitation for two of her pupils—you will be at no loss to divine which—to spend some weeks at Beaufoy.

Madame called the two young ladies up after morning class, told them of the invitation, and handed to each a little sealed note from Adeline, which had been enclosed in the letter. This much certainly must be said for Madame de Nino's establishment: bad as the soup and bouilli were, she never opened the girls' letters.

"Of course you cannot go," observed Madame. "It would be unreasonable to suppose it."

"Oh, Madame !" exclaimed Rose.

"You would lose all chance of the prizes, my children," cried Madame. "And this is your last term at school, remember."

"But we are too old, Madame, to care for school prizes."

"Well," said Madame, "of course the decision as to Mademoiselle Rose does not lie with me. Madame Darling being at present in the town, I yield my authority to hers. If *she* chooses to allow such an absence at the most busy portion of the year, of course it must be so ; but I can only say that it will be more unreasonable than anything I have met with in all my experience. In that case, Mademoiselle Mary——"

"In that case, pray, pray dear Madame, suffer me to accompany her," interrupted Mary Carr, in her pleading, soft, quiet tone. "My friends would like me to do so, I know. Beaufoy is close to M. d'Estival's."

"I think you are both in league against me," returned Madame. "You English demoiselles never do care properly for the prizes."

And she went away, saying no more then. Mary Carr wrote a little note to her brother Robert's widow, in England, once Emma d'Estival, asking her to intercede for her with Madame de Nino.

Mrs. Darling, as you have gathered from Madame's words, was at Belport. She had come to it only within a day or two, with her two daughters, Margaret and Mary Anne. Not to see Miss Rose; that was not the object of her visit; but hoping to meet her eldest daughter Charlotte.

All these past months, since she first quitted her native shores, had Mrs. Carleton St. John been travelling about the Continent. Travelling *about;* the word is put advisedly. Now hither, now thither; to-day in one place, to-morrow in another; ever restless, ever on the wing. France, Germany, Savoy, Switzerland: and now back on the coast of France again and intending to try Flanders and Belgium. It seemed that some power impelled her forward, forced change upon her; for no sooner had she settled down in one spot, saying she should remain in it, than she would suddenly start away for another. Her attendants wondered whether she were quite sane: but she appeared more as one labouring under the torture of a troubled spirit. It seemed like remorse. Remorse for what? Ah, none could tell. That first foolish supposition of Honour's was surely not a correct one—that the young heir, who stood in her own son's light, had owed his death to her hands! Nonsense! It was not likely. But, if so, why, how fearful a retribution had overtaken her! She must know now that she had perilled her soul for worse than nought; for the halls of Alnwick and their rich lands were passing rapidly away from her into the hands of strangers; passing away with her child's life.

It was a singularly strange thing—and people talk of it yet—but George St. John never recovered that memorable birthday night. The puzzle was—*what* had harmed him? Had he taken too much?—a fit of over-eating, of indigestion if you will, is soon cured in a child. Had he suffered a shock from fright?—*that* was not likely to bring on the bodily ailment, the weakness, under which he now laboured. His mother had asked, asked with feverish lips and eager eyes, what could be the matter with him. No one could answer her then; he would soon get well, they supposed. She knew—it must be that she knew—all too surely now. George St. John was in a decline—the same disease that had killed his father.

In writing to her mother in England, with whom she communicated from time to time, Mrs. St. John had mentioned that she intended to take Belport on her way into Flanders from Normandy, where she now was. She should endeavour to get an experienced English sick-nurse in that Anglo-French town, to travel with them and attend on George, and she should of course see Rose. Mrs. Darling read the letter, and determined she should also see some one else—herself. Charlotte had been dexterously evading her all these months—as it seemed to the anxious heart of Mrs. Darling. All her overtures to join her had been declined; all her plans to reach some place where her daughter spoke of staying were frustrated, because before she could start for it, news came, generally from Prance (who was a private correspondent), that Mrs. Carleton St. John was on the wing again and had left it. But in the very hour that she read of this projected journey to Belport, Mrs. Darling packed up her things in haste, and started. Mrs. St. John had not arrived when she got there; and Mrs. Darling allowed Rose to think the visit was paid for her especial benefit. This was from no wish to deceive; Mrs. Darling was of too open a nature for that; but she had an invincible dislike to speak of the affairs of Charlotte. .

Rose did not exhibit any particular gratitude. She was in a state of chronic resentment at being kept so long at school; and she was shy at first with her mother, not knowing how much Frank might have communicated to her of the previous autumn's trip in the fishing-boat. As to those two staid ladies, her sisters, Rose made no secret of the contempt in which she held them. Rose was in perpetual hot water with both: they were severe upon what they were pleased to term her wildness; and Rose quietly shrugged her shoulders, French fashion, in return, and called them "old maids" in their hearing.

Rose carried Madame de Castella's invitation to her mother, and at once received her sanction for the visit. Mrs. Darling, unless interest led her the other way, was a most indulgent mother—just such a one as Rose herself would make in time. She mentioned that Frederick St. John of Castle Wafer was located close to the château, with some of Mary Carr's friends.

"Is he rich?" asked Rose.

"Rich!" echoed Mrs. Darling. "Frederick St. John! He is rich in debts, Rose. Frederick St. John came into a great deal of money when he was twenty-one, but it is all gone; mortgaged, or something. Frank told me about it. He went the pace, I conclude, as other young men do, and there's no doubt that he gave away a great deal: he is large-hearted. But what had helped to ruin him is his love for what he calls 'high art,' his passion for pictures. He is half mad upon the point, I should say: and what with buying up pictures of the old masters, and lavishing money upon the painters of modern ones, and dancing all over the world after galleries that nobody in their senses would ride a mile to see, Frederick St. John and his means parted company. It is impossible to help liking him, though, with all his imprudence. I knew he was out of England—to the reputed sorrow of Sarah Beauclerc."

Rose pricked up her ears. "Sarah Beauclerc! One of those Gorgon girls in Eaton Place?"

"No, no; quite the other branch of the family. The daughter of General and Lady Sarah Beauclerc. Since Lady Sarah's death she has resided with the Dean of Westerbury."

"I think I saw her once," mused Rose, speaking slowly. "One of the loveliest girls living."

"Frederick St. John seemed to think so, I believe. But your sister Margaret can tell you more about it than I can: she used to meet them last year in town. Captain Budd said there was nothing in it; it was only a case of flirtation; but Frank thought he was jealous; and wanted to make up to Miss Beauclerc himself. By the way, Rose, he has come into his title and is no longer Captain Budd. He is still in the regiment, though: it was said that his uncle, old Lord Raynor, wished it."

"Mamma," interrupted Rose, "if anything should happen to little George St. John, if he should die—would not Frederick St. John be the heir to Alnwick Hall? And his brother of Castle Wafer its possessor?"

Mrs. Darling started; she glanced over her shoulder, as though fearing the walls had ears. "Hush, Rose! Better not

think of such things. Were you so to speak before Charlotte,
I don't know what the consequences might be. No one must
breathe a hint that the child's life is in danger—that there's so
much as a chance of his dying."

"If he be as ill as you give me to understand—and I suppose you have your information from Prance," added Rose, in
a spirit of hardihood, for that subject also was interdicted—
"Charlotte can't avoid seeing his state herself. She possesses
just as much keen sense as you do, mamma, I can tell you that."

"It is not a question of *sense*. Love blinds fond eyes to the
very worst, Rose."

Rose threw back her golden curls. "Why does Charlotte
go about in this manner? One would think she had St. Vitus's
dance. George might stand a better chance of recovery if she
would let him be at rest."

"Rose, you are not to reflect on Charlotte, or on anything
she chooses to do," sharply reproved Mrs. Darling. "If she
considers constant change necessary for the child, she is right
in giving it him. I hope we shall find him better than we
anticipate."

Rose shrugged her shoulders—the retort for the reproof.
"I'm sure *I* hope we shall find him well, poor little fellow.
My firm belief is, that Charlotte worries herself with straws—
she's afraid for her own sake of losing Alnwick."

And Mrs. Darling replied by a deprecating gesture. Rose
always would have the last word, and always did have it.

But ah! how false were these hopes. Charlotte St. John
arrived at Belport; and from the first moment that Mrs.
Darling threw her eyes upon the child, she saw that his days
were numbered. There was no particular disease; neither
had there been any in the case of his father; he was simply
wasting gradually away; almost imperceptibly so to those who
were about him.

"Oh, Charlotte! how thin and worn he looks. He is like a
shadow."

Mrs. Darling's incautious greeting broke from her in the first
startled moment. He *was* like a shadow; like nothing else.
His face was wan and thin, his cheeks and his blue eyes were
unnaturally bright, his little hands were transparent, and his
fair and pretty curls looked damp and dead.

"It is because he is tired," said Charlotte. "He will be all
right to-morrow."

Was she really deceived as to the truth, or did she but wilfully deceive herself? Mrs. Darling thought it was the former; she had not yet admitted to herself the possibility—not yet *seen* it—of the boy's death. *She* was changed, if you will; changed even more than George; her beautiful cheeks were haggard and crimson, her eyes had a wasting fire in them. She was quite well, she said; and so far as bodily health went, there might be no reason to doubt the assertion. Her disease lay in the mind.

The meeting took place at the Hôtel du Nord, for Mrs. St. John declined to accept of her mother's hospitality, even could space have been found in that lady's apartments for their accommodation. Rose had accompanied her mother to the hotel: Mrs. Darling was ever indulgent to Rose over the other two sisters.

"Do you know who I am?" cried Rose, lifting the little boy upon her knee; and so fragile did he seem, that a tremor ran through her, lest he should fall to pieces. "I have never, never seen you, George; do you know my name?"

George looked up at the smiling face; he raised his poor little weak hand, and pushed away the blue ribbons of her pretty bonnet from her chin; he touched the golden hair.

"No, I don't know you," he said.

"Of course not," returned Rose, in resentment. "Charlotte—your mamma would not talk to you about me, I suppose? I am your Aunt Rose, Georgy; your mamma's sister."

"Will you come along with us when we go away?" he asked, much taken with his new aunt. "I wish you would."

"I wish I could," said Rose; "though I don't know whether I should get on with—with every one. But I can't; I am at school; is not that a shame, Georgy? And I am going out on a visit in a day or two."

A pause ensued. Georgy was silent, and breathing, oh, so quickly; Mrs. Darling stood as one not at ease; Charlotte, apathetical as ever, save for the restless fire in the eyes, was looking down into the street between the crimson curtains of the somewhat high salon. Presently George spoke, looking at Rose.

"I want to go back to Alnwick. I want Benja."

"Oh, child!" exclaimed Rose, in a sort of awe. "Benja is not there."

"He's gone to heaven," continued George; "but I *might*

see him, you know. Mamma sees him sometimes. She saw him
the other night when she cried out: she squeezed hold of me
so that she hurt me."

Rose cast an involuntary glance at her impassive sister.
Believe she saw a ghost!—she, Charlotte, the mocker! No,
no; it could not have come to that.

"I should have all Benja's playthings; I should ride his
pony," went on Georgy. "I should see Brave, Aunt Rose. I
want to go home to Alnwick."

"And the best place for you, my little darling," answered
Rose. "Charlotte, do you hear? This child says he would
like to go back home. I'm sure I should think it is only the
worry of his being hurried about so from place to place that
makes him thin. He is nothing but a bag of bones."

"I have come to think that Alnwick is not healthy," observed
Charlotte, with her usual equanimity. "All the St. Johns die
there."

"Don't you intend to go back to it?" asked Rose, breathlessly.

"Not at present; when George shall have grown strong
again."

"Alnwick, his native air, might be the very place where he
would grow strong," cried Rose, persistently. "Wouldn't I go
to it if it were mine. Healthy or not healthy, I'd reign there,
with the county at my feet."

She laughed merrily; Mrs. Darling seemed uneasy. Indeed,
there is little doubt that the appearance of both Charlotte and
the child had seriously disturbed her. She moved past the
crimson sofa to the side of her daughter, who was still looking
listlessly into the street below.

"Do you think it well, Charlotte, to abandon Alnwick Hall
so entirely to servants? I don't."

"You may go and live in it yourself, mamma, if you choose.
I'm sure I don't care who lives there. The servants keep it in
order, I suppose—in readiness for my return? It is all my
own now; that is, it's Georgy's; and I am responsible to no
one."

She spoke quietly, indifferently, smoothing back the braids
of her most luxuriant hair. But for the strange fire in her eyes,
the consuming hectic of her cheek, it might have been affirmed
that she took no interest in any earthly thing.

"I am glad to see you have left off your widow's caps, Charlotte," resumed her mother. "They always look sad upon a young woman."

"There was no help for leaving them off; we could not get any abroad. Prance contrived to manage them in some way as long as I wore them, but they were never tidy. Where's Honour?" she suddenly exclaimed, turning her eyes, ablaze with sudden angry fire, on Mrs. Darling.

Mrs. Darling positively recoiled. And some feeling, which she did not stay to account for, and perhaps could not have accounted for, prompted her to withhold the fact that Honour had been taken in at Castle Wafer.

"She procured some other situation, I believe, Charlotte, after quitting the Hall. I have never heard from her."

"A situation! Where? Not at Alnwick?"

"Oh dear no; not at Alnwick; in a different county; not very far, I think, from her native place."

"Mamma, if ever you see her, ask her whether the boy's spirit comes and haunts her in the night? It may; for she murdered him. She ought to suffer on the scaffold for her work. I wish she could; I might be more at rest."

"Oh, Charlotte! Charlotte!" soothingly spoke Mrs. Darling from the depths of her fearful heart,—fearful she knew not of what.

"Come and look here!" interrupted Rose in a whisper.

They both turned. The little lad had fallen into a light doze on her lap, his wan hand clasping Rose's blue ribbons, and the upright line on his pale forehead seeming to denote that he had gone to sleep in pain.

"Charlotte," said Rose, earnestly, "I'm not used to children, and don't pretend to understand them as you must do; but my belief is, that this child wants rest—repose from travelling. It cannot be good for him to be hurried about incessantly. It is wearing him out."

"You do *not* understand them," returned Mrs. St. John. "It is for him that I move about. He grows so languid whenever we settle down. What should you know about children, Rose? Are you a nurse, or a doctor? You are not a mother. A chacun son métier."

"Comme vous voulez," returned Rose, with her pretty shrug. "Charlotte, I am going to visit where I shall see something of a sort of cousin of yours—Mr. St. John."

"Mr. St. John of Castle Wafer?" quickly asked Mrs. St. John, with more interest than she had yet displayed.

"The heir to Castle Wafer, Frederick."

"Oh—he," slightingly returned Mrs. St. John, and she relapsed into apathy.

"How long shall you remain at Belport, Charlotte?" asked Rose, speaking softly, not to awaken the child.

"I don't know yet; I shall see how the place suits George. Do you happen to know of a good sick-nurse here, Rose—English? I hear they abound."

"I know of one," said Rose, rather eagerly. "And she is excellent in these cases of—of——" Rose caught back the ominous word she had so nearly uttered—consumption; substituting one for it, however, that proved little better—"of wasting away. It is her *spécialité.*"

"Who says he is wasting away? Who says it?"

"Nay," said Rose, "I only thought it, seeing him so thin. I dare say it's natural to children to be thin. She is a most excellent nurse, Charlotte; a Mrs. Brayford. I saw her several times in the spring, when she was nursing Adeline de Castella."

"What was her complaint?"

"They feared she was going into a decline. Mrs. Brayford nursed her into perfect health, and she is as strong and well now as I am. I should think she would be the very nurse to suit you, and she is a pleasant sort of woman."

"Where can I find her?"

"Well, I don't know," said Rose. "It can readily be ascertained, though. The concierge at Signor de Castella's is sure to know her address. Of course, she may not be at liberty just now, Charlotte; neither may she be inclined to take a place that involves travelling."

"Is she one of those monthly nurses?" asked Mrs. St. John. "I don't like them."

"No; I believe not. I will get you her address, Charlotte, and you can send to her or not, as you please. How this child starts!"

"He would lie more comfortably on a bed," interposed Mrs. Darling, lifting him gently from Rose's knee. "I'll take him to Prance."

It was what she had been longing to do—to get to Prance. For ten minutes' conversation with the serving-woman, Mrs. Darling would have given an earldom. The servant met her at the chamber-door, and the child was laid on his bed without awaking.

"Prance, he is surely dying," breathed Mrs. Darling, as they stood over him.

Prance glanced round, making sure there were no other listeners. "He is as surely dying, ma'am, as that his father died before him; and of the same complaint—wasting away. A month or two longer, and then—the end."

"Your mistress does not seem to see it. *Does* she see it, do you think?"

"I think not. I think she really believes that he will get well."

"Why does she go about from place to place in this restless manner?"

The woman stooped to brush a fly from George's forehead, and she answered with her head and eyes bent down.

"She says it is for the benefit of the child: that he gets more languid and fretful when we stay quietly in a place than when we are moving about. But in her anxiety, she a little overdoes it: there's a medium in all things. In some of the towns she has not liked the doctors, and then she has gone away immediately."

"I wish she would come back to Alnwick," lamented Mrs. Darling. "Pym knows the constitution of the St. Johns. No one could treat the child so well as he."

"I wish she would!" heartily acquiesced Prance. "I wish you could persuade her——"

Prance stopped, and hastily busied herself straightening George's petticoats. Mrs. St. John had entered the room.

But there was no persuading her to Alnwick—or to put a stop to this incessant travelling. Only a few days and she had quitted Belport again, taking her retinue with her, amidst whom was the nurse, Mrs. Brayford.

How strangely do the links in that chain we call fate, fit themselves one into the other, unconsciously to ourselves.

CHAPTER XXII.

THE invitation sent to the young ladies by Madame de Castella had been given at the pressing instigation of Adeline. The nervous, anxious tones of the little notes enclosed from herself, praying them to accept it, at once proved the fact to Mary Carr.

The return of Signor de Castella to Beaufoy, and consequently the visit of the Baron de la Chasse, had been subjected to another postponement of a week; but then the time was positively fixed, and Adeline knew it would be kept. Her suspense and fears were becoming intolerable. How avoid being often in the society of the baron, when he would be the only visitor in the house? It was this grave question that suggested to her the thought of asking for the presence of her schoolfellows. Madame de Castella fell all innocently into the snare, and acquiesced at once. Adeline had ever been an indulged child.

It was almost impossible for Adeline to conceal her terror as the days drew on. She knew her father's haughty, unbending character, his keen sense of honour. He would have been the last to force her into an unpalatable union, and had Adeline expressed the slightest repugnance to M. de la Chasse when it was first proposed, the affair would have been at an end. But she had cheerfully consented to it; the deeds of betrothal were signed on both sides, and M. de Castella's word and honour had been pledged. Never, Adeline feared, would he allow that betrothal, that word to be broken; never would he consent to entertain proposals for her from another.

Now that her eyes were opened, she saw how fearfully blind and hazardous had been the act by which she consented to become the wife of the Baron de la Chasse, a personal stranger. There are thousands who consent in the same unconscious haste, and know not what they do, until it is too late. It is gratifying to a young girl's vanity to receive an offer of marriage; to anticipate an establishment of her own; to leave her companions behind. Marriage is to her a sealed book, and she is eager to penetrate its mysteries. If a voice from a judicious friend, or a still small voice in her own conscience, should whisper a warn-

ing to wait, to make sure she is on the right path ere she enter
its enclosures irrevocably, both are thrust aside unheeded. So
the wedding-day comes surely on; and soon the once eager
careless girl awakes to her position, and beholds herself as she
really is—sacrificed. She is the wife of one whom she cannot
love; worse still, perhaps not respect, now that she knows him
intimately: there is no sympathy between them; not a feeling,
not a taste, it may be, in common. But the sacrifice was of
her choosing, and she must abide by it. Deliberately, of her
own free will, she tied herself to him, for better for worse, for
richer for poorer, until death shall them part. She has linked
herself to him by a chain which divides her from the rest of the
world; every thought of her heart belongs, of right, to him;
she is his companion and no other's, and must obey his behests;
at uprising and down-sitting, at the daily meals and in the
midnight chamber she is his, his own, for evermore.

A strong impression, call it a presentiment if you will, had
taken hold of Adeline, that the very first word of disclosure to
her father, though it were but a hint of it, would be the signal
for her separation from Mr. St. John. She spoke of this to him,
and she wrung a promise from him that he would be for the
present silent; that at least during this few days' visit of the
Baron's he should continue to appear as he did now—an
acquaintance only. Rose would be there, and St. John's
intimacy with the family, his frequent presence at Beaufoy,
might be accounted for by his relationship to her. No relationship whatever in point of fact, as the reader knows; but
Adeline chose to construe it into one. Mr. St. John at first
hesitated to comply with her wish. It is true that he would
have preferred, for reasons of his own—his debts and his
estrangement from his brother—not to speak to Signor de
Castella just yet; but he was given to be ultra honourable, and
to maintain silence in such a case, though it were but for a
week or two, jarred against his nature. Only to her imploring
petition, to her tears, did he at length yield, and then con-
ditionally. He must be guided, he said, by the behaviour of
de la Chasse. "Should he attempt to offer you the smallest
endearment, should he begin to whisper tender speeches in
your ear, I should throw prudence to the winds, and step between you."

"Oh, Frederick!" she answered, her cheek a burning red,
her face bent in its maidenly confusion: "endearment—tender

speeches—they are not known in France, in our class of society.
Of such there is no fear. The Baron will be as politely ceremonious to me as though we were ever to remain strangers."

And Adeline was right.

Late in the afternoon of as hot and brilliant a day as the
July sun ever shone upon, the carriage, containing the young-
lady guests, which had been sent to Odesque to meet them,
drew up at the château, in the very jaws of the lions. Mary
Carr looked out. There, on the broad steps, in the exact spot
where she had last seen him, looking as though not an hour
had passed over his head since, stood Mr. St. John.

He assisted them to alight, and Adeline ran out to receive
them, so charmingly lovely in her white morning dress and pink
ribbons. Madame de Castella also appeared, and after a
cordial welcome, ordered the coachman to speed back with
haste to Odesque, or he would not be in time for the arrival of
the Paris train.

"I expect my husband and M. de la Chasse," she explained,
addressing her visitors. Mary Carr looked involuntarily at
Adeline. She met the gaze, and a burning crimson rushed over
her face and neck.

Before six the party had re-assembled, including Mr. St. John.
They were in the yellow drawing-room, a very fine apartment,
kept chiefly for show and ceremony, and one that nobody ever
felt at home in. The windows overlooked the approach to the
château ; every one was gazing for the first appearance of the
momentarily expected travellers, Adeline growing more pale,
more agitated with every minute ; so pale, so agitated, that she
could not escape notice.

"See, see!" exclaimed old Madame de Beaufoy, hobbling
to the window. "Is not that the carriage ?—far off, there ;—
at the turn by the windmill."

It was the carriage : the aged eyes were the quickest, after
all : and it came speedily on. Two dusty-looking figures were
in it, for they sat with it open. Madame de Castella and her
sister hastened to the hall to receive the travellers, and the old
lady thrust her head out at one of the windows. Adeline had
risen in terrible agitation, and was leaning on the back of a
chair. Her very lips were white. Mr. St. John advanced and
bent over her.

"My dearest love," he whispered, "you are ill, and I dare
not protect you as I could wish. Be under no apprehension of

any unwelcome scene with him: sooner than suffer it I will declare all."

He took up a flacon of eau de Cologne, and saturated her handkerchief. Mary Carr was looking on. She could not hear his words; but she marked his low, earnest voice, his looks, his actions, she saw how it was from that hour. "There will be tribulation in the house, ere this shall be over!" was her mental exclamation. But she little anticipated the deep tribulation that was indeed to come.

The Baron did not make his appearance until he had been to his dressing-room. He looked very presentable when he came in, though his hair was shorter than ever, and the curled corners of his yellow moustache were longer. His greeting of Adeline was in this fashion: advancing quickly towards her until he came within three paces, he there made a dead stand-still, and placing his feet in the first position, as dancing-masters say, slowly bowed his head nearly down to the ground, and in ceremonious words, "hoped he had the honour of finding mademoiselle in perfect health." That was all: he did not presume even to touch her hand: any such familiarity would, in good French society, be deemed the perfection of bad taste. Rose just smothered a scream of delight when she saw the bow, and gave Mr. St. John such a pinch on the arm, that the place was blue for days afterwards. But what a bow St. John received the Baron with when they were introduced—distant, haughty, and self-conscious; conscious of his own superiority. Certainly, in outward appearance, there was a wide contrast, and Mr. St. John, on this particular evening, seemed quite aware of his own personal gifts. De la Chasse was superbly dressed: a blue satin vest, curiously-fine linen of lace and embroidery, with various other magnificent et ceteras. St. John was in slight mourning attire; black clothes, a plain white waistcoat, and not a bit of finery about him; but he looked, as Rose Darling said, fit for a prince.

Dinner was announced. The Baron de la Chasse advanced to the aged mistress of the house, St. John to Madame de Castella, and Signor de Castella to Rose. Miss de Beaufoy, Adeline, and Mary Carr, went in together. It was a formal dinner, and Adeline was sick at heart.

It happened, in the course of the following morning, that the three young ladies and the Baron were alone in the western drawing-room—the one, you may remember, opening to the colonnade. The conversation flagged. De la Chasse, though a sensible man, did not shine in that flowing, ready style of converse so natural to Frederick St. John ; and Adeline seemed utterly spiritless. Mary Carr went upstairs to her chamber, but before she had been there five minutes, Rose came dancing in.

"Where have you left Adeline?" inquired Miss Carr.

"Where you did—with the Baron. I thought I might be *de trop*, and so came away. It is not pleasant to reflect that you may be spoiling a scene, all tenderness and sweetmeats, as Charlotte Singleton calls it. I say, though, Mary, did you see St. John whispering last night to her at the piano, whilst he was pretending to be engaged turning over for me? It's satisfactory to have two strings to one's bow."

Before another word could be said, in rushed Adeline, in high excitement. "Mary! Rose!—Rose! dear Mary! never you leave me alone with that man again! Promise it!—promise it to me!"

"What is it? What has he done?" they asked, in excessive astonishment.

"He has done nothing. But I dare not be alone with him, lest he should talk of the future. He has been inquiring after the engagement-ring. Hush! do not ask me any questions now," concluded Adeline. "I wish to Heaven, Rose, you could induce the Baron to fall in love with you!"

"Much obliged for the transfer," said Rose, with a laugh. "Perhaps you'll get him first to dye those appendages to his face : yellow is not a favourite colour of mine."

De la Chasse intended to remain but a week. He purposed leaving on Tuesday morning. His visit was passing quietly enough : there had been no outbreak between him and St. John, only excessive coolness. Had de la Chasse been an Englishman, an explanation could scarcely have been avoided; for an Englishman would inevitably, by speech, manner, or action, have shown that he was the young lady's lover : but in France these things are managed differently.

Madame de Beaufoy issued invitations for Monday evening to as many neighbours as were within driving-distance. A soirée dansante, the cards said, when they went out.

On the Monday afternoon, when the three young ladies were in the western drawing-room together, the Baron entered, and addressing Adeline, formally requested her to grant him the honour of a few minutes' conversation.

A strange rising in the throat; a dread, that caused her frame to quiver; a terrified, imploring, but unavailing look at Rose and Mary; and the door closed on them, and Adeline and her acknowledged lover were left alone.

She need not have feared. The Baron did not say a word to her that he might not have said to her mother. But he produced from his pocket the engagement-ring, which had been taken to Paris to be made smaller—it was a plain circlet of gold—and requested she would grant him the honour of allowing him to replace it on her finger.

Without a word of remonstrance—for what could she say? —and sick at heart, Adeline held out her hand; and the Baron ventured ceremoniously to touch it, while he slipped on the ring: in the very act and deed of doing which, the door opened, and into the room strode Mr. St. John, twirling in his hand a French marigold.

He saw them standing together, Adeline's hand stretched out, and meeting both of his; and he looked black as night. It has been said, in this book or another, that Frederick St. John was of quick temperament: on rare occasions he gave way to violent explosions of passion. It is probable that an outburst would have come then; but the Baron, with a polite bow to Adeline, quitted the room. And Mr. St. John, though certain as man could well be that he had no cause for jealousy, gave way to the irritation of his hasty spirit.

"So, Mademoiselle de Castella," he broke forth, "you have been enjoying a stolen interview with your lover! I must beg your pardon for having unintentionally interrupted it."

She turned deprecatingly to him; she did not speak, or defend herself from the charge; but the look of anguish on her countenance was so keen, the glance at himself so full of pure, truthful love, that the gentleman's better nature revolted at the temper he had shown, and he caught her to his heart.

"But they were cruel words," she sobbed; "and just now I have enough to bear."

"Let this be my peace-offering, my darling," he said, placing in her hand the French marigold.

St. John had long ago heard the tale of the French marigold, and Miss Rose Darling's sombre forebodings touching himself. He had been assiduously cultivating the flower in the garden at the Lodge, and this, that he now gave to Adeline, was the first which had appeared.

"This ring, Adeline," he said, drawing it from her finger. "He placed it there, I suppose?"

"You saw him doing so," she answered.

He slipped it into his waistcoat pocket, and then drew out his watch.

"Give me back the ring, Frederick."

"No, Adeline. It shall never encircle your finger again."

"But what am I to say if its absence is noticed? He said mamma had given him permission to replace it. She will be sure to ask where it is."

"Say anything. That it fell off—or wear a glove until evening. I will then tell you what to do. I cannot stay longer now."

When Mary Carr was dressed for the evening ball, she went into Adeline's room. Louise was putting the finishing strokes to her young lady's toilette, and very satisfactory they were, when Madame de Castella entered, holding in her hand a small circular case.

"Look here, Adeline," she said, opening it and displaying a costly bracelet, one of beauty and finish so rare, that all eyes were riveted on it. Exquisitely wrought, fine gold links, in the different crossings of which were inserted brilliants of the purest water, with pendant chains flashing with brilliants and gold.

"Oh, mamma!" was the enraptured exclamation. "What a lovely bracelet!"

"It is indeed, Adeline. It is yours."

"Ciel!" ejaculated Louise, lifting her hands.

"Mamma, how can I thank you!" she exclaimed, taking the jewels.

"You need not thank me at all, Adeline. It is the Baron's present. Make your acknowledgments to him."

Had the bracelet been a serpent, Adeline could not have dropped it quicker, and, but for Mary Carr, it would have fallen to the ground. Madame de Castella thought it was an accident.

"Don't be careless, child. Put it on. You must wear it to-night."

"Oh no, no, mamma!" she returned, her cheek flushing. "Not to-night."

"What nonsense!" exclaimed her mother; "you are as shy as a young child. When the Baron presented it to me for you, he said, 'Un petit cadeau pour ce soir.' Clasp it on, Louise."

"Mamma," she implored, a great deal more energetically

than Madame de Castella thought the case could demand, "do not oblige me to appear in this bracelet to-night."

"Adeline, I *insist* on its being worn. Persons who know you less well than we do, would suspect that affectation, more than delicacy, induced your refusal to wear a gift from one who will soon be your husband."

"Not my husband yet," faltered Adeline. "Not until next year."

"Indeed he will, Adeline," said Madame de Castella. "Before we go to the South."

Her colour came and went painfully. She sat down, gasping out rather than speaking, the words that issued from her white lips.

"We go to the South in two months !'

"Dear child," laughed Madame de Castella, "don't look so scared. There's no reason for it : a wedding is quite an every-day affair, I can assure you. This week I write to order your trousseau."

Louise fastened the bracelet on Adeline's arm, and she went down to the reception-rooms as one in a dream. If the younger guests, as they gazed on her excessive beauty, could but have read the bitter despair at her heart, the strife and struggle within, they would have envied her less. A single string of pearls was entwined with her hair, and she wore a pearl neck-lace ; no other ornament, save this conspicuous bracelet of de la Chasse's. But in the bosom of her low white dress, almost hidden by its trimmings of lace, was enshrined St. John's French marigold.

The guests had nearly all arrived, and Adeline had done her best towards greeting them, when in passing in the direction of the colonnade, the Baron came up to her. She was longing for a breath of the evening air—as if that would cool the brow's inward fever !"

"Permit me to exchange this flower with the one you have there, mademoiselle," he said, holding out a white camellia of rare beauty. And, with a light, respectful touch, he removed the French marigold from the folds of the lace.

Did de la Chasse suspect who had been the donor of that cherished French marigold? Did he remember seeing it in St. John's hand that same afternoon ? It is impossible to tell ; but he seemed more urgent over this trifling matter than a Frenchman in general allows himself to be.

"Sir, you forget yourself!" exclaimed Adeline, angry to excitement. "Return me my flower."

"It is unsuitable, mademoiselle," he rejoined, retaining his hold of the French marigold. "A vulgar, ordinary garden-flower is not in accordance with your dress to-night—or with you."

"You presume upon your position," retorted Adeline, pushing aside the white camellia, and struggling to keep down her anger and her tears. "Do not insult me, sir, but give me back my own flower."

"What is all this?" demanded M. de Castella, coming up. "Adeline, you are excited."

"I have incurred your daughter's displeasure, it would seem, sir," explained the Baron, showing symptoms of excitement in his turn. "Mademoiselle appeared in the rooms wearing this flower—a worthless, common garden-flower!—and because I wished to present her with one more suitable, she seems to imply that I only do it by way of insult. I don't understand, ma foi!"

"Nor I," returned M. de Castella. "Take the camellia, Adeline," he added, sternly and coldly. "Caprice and coquetry are beneath *you*."

The Baron put the camellia in her now unresisting hand, and amused himself with pulling to pieces the petals of the other flower. Adeline burst into a violent paroxysm of tears, and hurried on to the colonnade."

And all about a stupid French marigold!

"Let her go and have a cry to herself," said M. de Castella, walking off with the Baron; "it will bring her to reason. The coquetry of women passes belief. They are all alike. It appears I was mistaken when I deemed my daughter an exception."

Adeline, in her tears and excitement, rushed across the lawn. It was certainly a senseless thing to cry about, but, just then, a straw would have ruffled her equanimity. She had been compelled to wear the hated bracelet: she had been told that she would very speedily be made the wife of de la Chasse; she had stood by him, recognized by the crowd of guests as his future wife; and, blended with all this, was a keen sensation of disappointment at the non-appearance of Mr. St. John. She stood with her forehead pressed against the bark of a tree, sobbing aloud in her anguish where none could hear her. Presently, her ear caught the sound of footsteps, and she prepared to dart further away: but they were some that she knew and loved too well. He was coming through the shrubbery at a rapid pace, and she stood out and confronted him.

"Why, Adeline!" he exclaimed, in astonishment. And, then, the momentary restraint on her feelings removed, she fell forward in his arms, and sobbed aloud with redoubled violence.

"Oh, Adeline, what ails you? What has happened? Be calm, be calm, my only love! I am by your side now: what grief is there that I cannot soothe away?"

He became quite alarmed at her paroxysm of grief, and, half leading, half carrying her to the nearest bench, seated her there and laid her head upon his arm, and held her gently to him, and spoke not a word until she was calmer.

By degrees she told him all. The gift of the bracelet, her mother's threats of the coming marriage—*threats* they sounded to Adeline—and the dispute with the Baron. Upon this last point she was rather obscure. "I had a simple flower in my dress, and he wanted me to replace it with a rare one, a camellia." She did not say it was the one he had given her; she would rather have led him to think that it was not: never, until she should be indeed his, could she tell him how passionately and entirely she loved. But he divined all; he required no telling. And yet, knowing this; knowing, as he did, how her very life was bound up in his; how could he, only a few weeks later, doubt, or profess to doubt, of this enduring love?

"Adeline," he said, as he paced the narrow path restlessly in the moonlight, she still sitting on the bench, "I have done very wrong: wrong by you and your friends, wrong by myself, wrong by de la Chasse. I see it now. I ought to have declared all before he came to Beaufoy. I will see M. de Castella to-morrow morning."

She shivered, as if struck by a cold wind. "Remember your promise."

"It must be done," he answered. "I yielded too readily to your wishes, perhaps to my own motives for desiring delay. But for you to be looked upon as his future wife—condemned to accept and wear his presents—this shall not be. It is placing us all three in a false position; you must see that it is. Neither did I know that the marriage was being hastened on."

"He goes away to-morrow morning, and all immediate danger will be over," she urged. "Do not yet speak words that might—nay, that *would*—lead to our separation! Let us have another week or two for consideration ; and of—of happiness."

"I cannot imagine why you entertain these gloomy anticipations," he rejoined; "why think that my speaking to your father will be the signal for warfare. Believe me, Adeline, the St. Johns of Castle Wafer are not accustomed to find their overtures for an alliance despised ; they have mated with the noblest in their own land."

"Oh, it is not that ; it is not that ! Frederick, you know it is not.—Hark !" she suddenly broke off, starting from her seat as if to fly. "There are footsteps approaching from the house. If it should be papa !—or de la Chasse !"

"And what if it be ?" he answered, drawing her hand within his arm and raising himself to his full height, in the haughty spirit that was upon him, to stand and confront the intruders. "I will explain all now : and show that you are doing neither wrong nor harm in being here with me, for that you are my affianced wife."

But the footsteps, whosesoever they might be, passed off in a different direction : and they strolled on, talking, to the borders of the miniature lake. It was nearly as light as day, very warm, very beautiful. White fleecy clouds floated around the moon ; the air, redolent with the odour of flowers, was one balmy breath of perfume ; and Adeline forgot her trouble in the peaceful scene.

"What made you so late ?" she asked. "I had fancied you would come early."

"I have been to Odesque."

"To Odesque !"

He was drawing a small paper from his waistcoat pocket. Adeline saw that it contained a ring of plain gold. Motioning to her to take her glove off—and she obeyed mechanically —he proceeded to place it on her finger ; speaking solemn words :

"With this ring I will thee wed : with my body I thee worship ; with all my worldly goods I will thee endow, until death us do part : and thus do I plight unto thee my troth."

She knew the slightly altered words were in the English Protestant marriage-service, for she had heard Rose, and some of the other schoolgirls as foolish as Rose was, repeat them in their thoughtless pastime. There was a solemnity in Mr. St. John's voice and manner which imparted an awe to her feelings, never before experienced. The tears of deep emotion rose to her eyes and her frame trembled : she could not have been more strongly moved, had she in very truth been plighting her troth to him before the holy altar.

"Take you care of it, Adeline. Let none remove it from your finger as I removed the other. It shall be your wedding-ring."

"It is not the same ring?" she whispered, unable quite to recover herself. "His."

"*His!* Look here, Adeline."

He took another ring from his pocket as he spoke. It was cut in two parts; and he threw them into the water.

"There goes his ring, Adeline. May his pretensions go with it!"

"It is for this you have been to Odesque?"

"It is."

They turned to the house, walking quickly now, neither caring for Adeline's absence to be so prolonged as to attract notice. Long as it may have seemed to take in the telling, she had yet been away from the house but a few minutes. Adeline could not quite forget her tears.

"If mamma could only be kept from ordering the trousseau!" she suddenly exclaimed, more in answer to her own thoughts than to him.

"Where's the necessity of preventing her?"

She looked up wonderingly, and caught his smile full of meaning, all apparent in the moonlight.

"The things ordered and intended for Madame de la Chasse —will they not serve equally well for Mrs. Frederick St. John?"

"Oh—but "—and her downcast face felt glowing with heat "nothing will be wanted at all yet for—any one."

"Indeed! *I* think they will be wanted very soon. Do you suppose," he added, laughing, "I should be permitted to carry you away with me to the South without an outfit?"

"I am not going to the South now," she quickly said.

"Yes, Adeline. I hope you and I shall winter there."

"I am quite well now."

"I know you are : and that it will be almost a superfluous precaution. Nevertheless, it is well to be on the safe side. My darling!" and he bent over her, "you would not be dismayed at the prospect of passing a whole winter alone with me?"

Dismayed! To the uttermost parts of the earth with him, and for a whole lifetime Father, mother, country, home—what were they all, in comparison with him?

As they gained the open lawn, a dark figure swept across their path. Adeline shrank at being seen alone with Mr. St. John. It was Father Marc, the officiating priest of the little neighbouring chapel, and the family confessor, a worthy and very zealous man. He turned and looked at Adeline, but merely said, "Bon soir, mon enfant," and took off his hat to Mr. St. John. Mr. St. John raised his in return, saying nothing, and Adeline bent low, as one in contrition.

"Bon soir, mon père."

She glided onwards to a side door, that she might gain her chamber and see what could be done towards removing the traces of emotion from her face. Whilst Mr. St. John strode round to the front entrance, and rang such a peal upon the tinkling old bell that half-a-dozen servants came flying to the door.

And as Adeline stood by his side that night in the brilliant ball-room, and watched the admiration so many were ready, unsought, to accord him, and marked the cordial regard in which both her father and mother held him, and remembered his lineage and connections, the fortune and position that must eventually be his, she almost reasoned that overtures for her from such a man could never be declined.

But the Baron saw that she had thrown away the white camellia. "Petite coquette!" he exclaimed to himself, in tolerant excuse: not in anger. It never entered into the French brains of the Baron de la Chasse to imagine that the young lady, being under an engagement to marry him, could have the slightest wish to marry any one else.

CHAPTER XXIII.

JEALOUSY.

THE grey walls of the Château de Beaufoy basked idly in the evening sun. In the western drawing-room, M. and Madame de Castella, the old lady, and Agnes de Beaufoy were playing whist. Its large window was thrown open to the terrace or colonnade, where had gathered the younger members of the party, the green-striped awning being let down between some of the outer pillars. Mary Carr and Adeline were seated, unravelling a heap of silks, which had got into a mess in the ivory work-basket; Rose Darling flitted about amongst the exotics, her fine hair shining like threads of gold when, ever and anon, it came in contact with the sunlight, as she flirted—it was very like it—with Mr. St. John. But Rose began to turn cross, for he teased her.

"Did you write to England for the song to-day?" she asked. "Ah, don't answer: I see you forgot it. Most of the writing you are guilty of goes to one person, I expect. No wonder you forget other matters."

"Indeed! To whom?"

"I won't betray you now," glancing at Adeline. "I will be compassionate."

"Pray don't trouble yourself about compassion for me, ma belle," returned Mr. St. John, in a provokingly slighting manner. "It will be thrown away."

"Compassion for *you*, Mr. St. John! Don't flatter yourself. I was thinking of another."

Adeline looked up: a sharp, perplexed glance.

"You are mysterious, Rose," said he, laughing.

"Yes. But I could speak out if I would."

"I dare you," answered Mr. St. John. "Speak away."

"You know there is one in England, who monopolizes all your letters—not to speak of your dreams."

"Rose!" exclaimed Mary Carr, a dim shadow of Rose's meaning darting uneasily across her. "How can you talk this nonsense to Mr. St. John?"

"He asked for it. But he knows it is true. Look at his conscious face now!" she saucily continued.

"The only lady in England honoured with my correspondence," said he, in a more serious tone than he had hitherto spoken, "is Mrs. St. John."

"That's almost true," cried the provoking girl—"almost. She is not Mrs. St. John yet, only *to be*."

A strange wild spasm caught Adeline de Castella's heart. Would Rose have continued, had she known it? Did St. John suspect it?

"I spoke of my mother, Rose," he said. "She is the only lady who claims, or receives, letters from me."

" Honour bright?" asked Rose.

" Honour bright," repeated Mr. St. John: "the honour of her only son."

" Oh, faithless that you are then!" burst forth Rose. "Will you deny that there is one in England to whom your letters are due, if not sent; one whose shadow you were for many, many months—if not years—one, beautiful as a painter's dream?"

" Bah, Rose!" he said, his lips curling with a proud, defiant smile, " you are lapsing into ecstasies."

" Shall I tell her name—the name of his own true lady-love?" asked Rose, turning round, a world of triumph on her bright, laughing brow. " Mary Carr knows it already."

" You are out of your senses!" exclaimed Mary Carr, all too eagerly. " Don't impose your fabulous tales on us."

" Shall I tell it?" repeated Rose, maintaining her ground and her equanimity.

" Tell it," said Mr. St. John, carelessly. Did he think she knew so much!

" Tell it," repeated Adeline, but it was the motion of the syllables, rather than the words, that came from between her white and parted lips.

" Sarah Beauclerc."

A transient surprise crossed Mr. St. John's countenance, and was gone again. *Adeline saw it:* and from that wild, bitter moment, a pang of anguish took root within her, which was never to be erased during life.

" You are under a slight misapprehension, Rose," said Mr. St. John, with indifference.

" Am I? The world was under another, perhaps, when it asserted that the honour of Mr. St. John's hand would fall to Sarah Beauclerc."

" That it certainly was—if it ever did assert it. And I might believe it possible, were the world peopled with Rose Darlings."

" Look here," exclaimed Rose, snatching his pocket-handkerchief from a gilt cage, where he had thrown it to protect the beautiful bird from the rays of the setting sun. " Look at this, ' Frederick St. John,' worked in hair!"

It happened to be the handkerchief they had picked up that first morning in the painting-room. Rose talked on, in the recklessness of her spirits; and Adeline sat, drinking-in her words.

"*She* did this for him, I have not the least doubt. Look how elaborately it is worked, even to the finishings of the crest. It is her hair, Sarah Beauclerc's."

A random assertion. Rose neither knew nor cared whether she was right. In her present humour she would have stood to anything. It is possible: not likely, but barely possible: that she had stumbled on a bit of fact. Mr. St. John remained supremely indifferent, denying nothing. She talked on in her access of gaiety.

"This is his favourite handkerchief: I have noticed that. The others are marked with ink. I dare say she *gave* the handkerchief, as well as marked it. Let it alone, Mr. St. John: I shall show it round, if I like. A rather significant present from so lovely a girl! But it's known she was *folle* after him. He reciprocated the compliment then: he was always at the dean's. I don't know how it may be now," she added, after a pause, and there was a significant meaning in her tone as she looked to Adeline. Then, with a saucy glance at Mr. St. John, she sang out, in her clear, rich voice, to a tune of her own,

> "It is well to be off with the old love,
> Before you are on with the new."

Adeline rose, and passed quietly into the drawing-room, her step self-possessed, her bearing calm : the still exterior covers the deepest suffering. But Mr. St. John suspected nothing.

"Rose," he said, quoting a French axiom, "vous aimez bien à rire, mais rien n'est beau que le vrai."

"Ah," she answered, with another, "ce n'est pas être bien aise que de rire." Perhaps the deepest truth she had uttered that evening.

With outward calmness *there*, but oh! the whirlwind of despairing agony which shook Adeline's frame as she sank down by the bedside in her own chamber! That in one short minute, desolation so complete should have swept over her heart, and she be able to endure it and live! I tell you no false story: I am writing of one of those sensitive hearts which must thus suffer and be shaken. To have given up her whole love to one, in a passion little short of idolatry; to have forgotten early ties and kindred in the spell of this strong devotion—and now to be told there was *another* to claim his vows, another to whom they had first been offered!

The dream in which she had been living for months was

over—or, at least, it had been robbed of its golden colouring.
The serpent DOUBT had found its entrance into her heart: the
fiend JEALOUSY had taken possession of it, never to be wholly
eradicated.

Frederick St. John was certainly one of earth's favoured
people, with his manly beauty and his master intellect. It
seemed to her that the world might worship him without a
blush. He had made her life the Elysium that poets tell of;
and now she found that he loved, or had loved, another. Like
an avalanche falling down the Alps and crushing the hapless
traveller, so had these tidings fallen upon her heart, and
shattered it.

Adeline de Castella smoothed her brow at last, and returned
downstairs. She had taken no account of the time; but, by
the advanced twilight, it would seem she had been away an
hour, and Rose inquired whether she had been buried.

Following Adeline on to the colonnade, where the whole party
were now seated, came the old Spanish servant, Silva, bearing
a letter for Mr. St. John. The ominous words, "très pressée,"
written on it, had caused Madame Baret to despatch it with
haste to the château.

"Does any one wait?" he inquired.

"Si, Señor."

"It is well," he said, and retreated inside the room.

"You have received bad news!" exclaimed Madame de
Castella, when he reappeared.

"I have," he said, with controlled emotion. "I must
depart instantly for England." And it was well the shades of
evening were gathering, or they would inevitably have seen the
death-like pallor on Adeline's stricken face.

Mr. St. John handed them the letter to read. A dangerous
accident had happened to his mother. The horses of her
carriage took fright, and she opened the door and jumped out.
The physicians feared concussion of the brain.

"Are you going?" exclaimed M. de Castella, as St. John
held out his hand.

"Yes. I feel every moment wasted that does not speed me
on my journey."

And in another instant he was gone. Without a word more
of adieu to Adeline than he gave to the rest. There was no
opportunity for it.

"I don't know that I would have angered him, had I foreseen

this," cried Rose, candidly, as she lingered on the terrace with Adeline.

"*Did* you anger him?"

"I think I did. A little bit. He should not have dared me to it."

Adeline looked over the balustrades as she listened, seeing nothing. A painful question was upon her lips; but her poor sensitive heart—how unfit it was for the wear and tear of life !—beat so violently that she had to wait before she put it.

"What you said was not *true*, Rose?"

' "What did I say?" rejoined Rose, whose thoughts had veered to fifty other things in her light carelessness.

"That he loved—what was the name?—Sarah Beauclerc.'

The pretty assumption of forgetfulness! "What was the name?" As if the name, every distinct letter of it, had not engraved itself on her brain in letters of fire, when it was first spoken! Rose answered impulsively.

"It was quite true, Adeline. He knows that it is true. I as certainly believed that he loved her, as that we are standing here. People say she would have been his wife before this, but for the dispute, or estrangement, or whatever it is, between him and his brother. He can't marry until his debts are cleared : and he is living quietly to clear them. You should hear what Margaret says about it; she told me a great deal the very day before I came here."

Her crushed heart fluttered against her side. "She is nice-looking, you say?"

"Nice-looking! she's beautiful! One of the loveliest girls in society. A fair, proud face, just as proud as his own. Georgina Beauclerc is very pretty; but she's nothing beside her."

She could have cried aloud in her anguish as she listened to these praises of her rival : and how she schooled her voice to maintain its calm indifference, she knew not.

"Who is Georgina Beauclerc?"

"Her cousin. She's the daughter of the Dean of Westerbury : Fred St. John's native place, you know. Sarah is the daughter of the dean's brother, General Beauclerc. Her mother's dead, the Lady Sarah ; and since then she has lived with the dean. In point of family it would be a suitable match; and I dare say in point of fortune." .

"And in point of love?"

There was a peculiar sound in the hesitation, a tremor which struck on Rose's ear. She turned her face full on Adeline's.

"I believe with all my heart, from what I've heard, that there *was* love between them," answered Rose. "Perhaps *is*. Adeline, I don't say this in ill-nature, but because it may be good for you to know it. I am careless and random in general, but I *can* be serious ; and I am speaking seriously now. He is a gay-mannered man, you know, a general admirer ; those attractive men usually are so ; but I have little doubt that his love was given to Sarah Beauclerc."

Rose went into the room with the last sentence. She had really spoken from a good motive. Believing that Adeline was getting to like Frederick St. John more than was good for her, consistently with her engagement to the French baron, a word in season might act as a warning. Little did Rose suspect how far things had gone between them.

An hour passed. All save Adeline were gathered in the lighted room. Some were playing chess, some écarté, some were telling Father Marc, who had dropped in, of the young Englishman's sudden departure for England and its cause. Rose was at the piano, singing English songs in a subdued voice. Never was there a sweeter voice than hers : and old Madame de Beaufoy could have listened always to the bygone songs of her native land.

Adeline had not stirred from the terrace ; she was leaning still on its balustrades, gazing forth apparently into the night. But that Madame de Castella did not observe her absence, she had been called in long ago, out of the night air.

> "Oh, beware, my lord, of jealousy !
> It is a green-eyed monster, which doth make
> The food it feeds on."

That reader of the human heart never put forth a greater truth, a more needed warning. How vainly ! We can smile now, we can wonder at the "trifles" that once mocked us ; but we did not smile at the time. It is asserted that where there is love, impassioned love, there must be jealousy ; and who shall venture to dispute it ? Love is most exacting. Its idol must not listen to a tender word, or bestow a look of admiration on another. The faintest shadow of a suspicion will invoke the presence of jealousy ; what then when facts and details are put forth, as they had been by Rose ? It had aroused the most refined torments of the distressing passion ;

and let none doubt that they were playing their part cruelly on Adeline's heart. Not that she believed quite all: the hint that he might be intending to marry Sarah Beauclerc but touched her ear and fell away again. She knew enough of his honourable nature to be certain that he would never have spoken of marriage to herself, had he been under the slighest obligation of it to another. But that he loved the girl with deep intensity, or had loved her, Adeline never doubted. And so she stood on : bitterly giving way to this strange anguish which had fallen on her; wondering how long he would stay in England, and how often during his stay there he would see her beautiful rival. The very fact of his having gone without a loving word of adieu seemed a knell of unlucky omen.

But what is that movement which her eye has caught at a distance? Who or what is it, advancing with a hasty step from the dark trees? Ah! the wild rising of her pulse has told her, before the outlines of his form become distinct, as he emerges into that plot of pale light! It was *he*—he whom she thought to have looked upon at present for the last time ; and the ecstatic feeling which rushed over her spirit was such as almost momentarily to obliterate the cruel doubts that oppressed her. He had changed his dress, and was habited in travelling costume. His tread over the lawn was noiseless, and little less so as he ran up the steps to the colonnade.

"How fortunate that you are here, Adeline!" he whispered. "I could not go without endeavouring to obtain a word with you, though I doubted being able to accomplish it."

Adeline, painfully agitated, trembling to excess, both in her heart and frame, murmured some confused words about the time he was losing.

"I am not losing one precious moment," he explained. "My own preparations were soon made : not to those necessary to convey me to Odesque. As it always happens in these emergencies, the spring chaise—and there's nothing else to take me—had been lent out to Farmer Pichon. Baret is gone for it, and will come on with it here, which is all in the way. We shall catch the first train. Why do you tremble so, my love?" he added, as the fit of ague, which seemed to possess her, shook even his arm. "Are you cold?"

Cold! But most men would have had but the same idea.

"Now, Adeline, for one moment's grave consultation. Shall

I write, and lay my proposals before M. de Castella, or shall they wait until I return?"

"Oh, wait to do so!" she implored. "In mercy, wait!"

"I would prefer it myself," said Mr. St. John, "for I feel I ought to be present to support you through all that may then occur. But, Adeline, should I be detained long, there will be no alternative: the preparations for your wedding will soon be actively begun, and render my speaking an act of imperative necessity."

She laid her head upon his arm, moaning.

"Cheer up," he whispered: "I am only putting the worst view of the case. I trust that a few days may bring me back to you. Write to me daily, Adeline: everything that occurs: I shall then be able to judge how long I may be absent with safety. I was thinking, Adeline, as I came along, that it might be better if my letters to you are sent under cover to Rose or Mary. You are aware that I do not mention this for myself— I should be proud to address you without disguise—but for your own peace. Were I to write openly, it might force explanations on you before my return."

Ever anxious for her! Her heart bounded with gratitude. "Under cover to Mary Carr," she said.

"We must part now," he whispered, as a faint rumbling broke upon their ears from the distance, "you hear my signal. It is fast approaching."

"You will come back as soon as you are at liberty?" she sighed.

"Ay, the very instant. Need you question it, Adeline?"

He strained her to his heart, and the painful tears coursed down her cheeks. "God bless you, and take care of you, and keep you in peace until I return; my dear, my dear, my only love!" And when he had passed away, Adeline asked herself if that last lingering farewell kiss, which he had pressed upon her lips—she asked herself, with burning blushes, if she were sure it had not been returned.

And during the brief moments of this sudden interview, she had lost sight of the torment about Sarah Beauclerc.

The second evening after Mr. St. John's departure, before they had risen from the dinner-table, Silva brought in the letters. Two from England amongst them, bearing on their seals, as Rose Darling expressed it, the arms and quarterings of all the St. Johns. The one was addressed to Madame de Castella; the other was handed to Miss Carr.

Mary looked at it with unqualified surprise. The fact was, Adeline, not expecting they could hear from Mr. St. John till the following day, had put off the few words of explanation she meant to speak, feeling shy at the task.

"Why should Mr. St. John write to me?" exclaimed Mary Carr. But Adeline, who was sitting next her, pressed her hand convulsively, under cover of the tablecloth, to prevent her opening it. Miss Carr began dimly to understand, and laid the letter down by the side of her dessert-plate.

"Why don't you open it, Mary?" repeated Rose, impatiently.

"No," said Miss Carr, in a half-joking manner, "there may be secrets in it that I don't care to read before people." And Rose, whose curiosity was excited, could have boxed her ears.

"Mr. St. John writes that his mother is better," said Madame de Castella; "the injuries prove less serious than they were at first supposed. By the next post, he hopes to send us word that she is out of danger."

"This letter, Adeline," exclaimed Mary Carr, when they were alone—"I fancy it may not be meant for me."

"You can open it," replied Adeline, timidly. "Perhaps—I think—there may be one for me inside it."

Mary Carr opened the letter. It contained a few polite words from Mr. St. John, requesting her to convey the enclosed one to Adeline at a convenient opportunity.

"You see how it is?" faltered Adeline to her.

"I have seen it long, Adeline."

Adeline carried the letter to her chamber to read, bolting the door that she might be free from interruption. It was a long letter, written far more sensibly than are love-epistles in general, for it was impossible to Mr. St. John to write otherwise; but there was a vein of impassioned tenderness running through it, implied rather than expressed, which surely ought to have satisfied even Adeline. But the bitter doubts imparted by Rose that fatal night cast their shadow over all. Not a moment of peace or happiness had she known since. Her visions by day, her dreams by night, were crowded by images of Frederick St. John, faithless to her, happy with another. Nor did Sarah Beauclerc want a "shape to the mind." The day after St. John's departure, they were looking over the last year's "Book of Beauty," when Rose suddenly exclaimed, as she came to one, "This is very like Sarah Beauclerc!"

" It was great nonsense, Rose, that tale you were telling us!"
cried Adeline, with a desperate struggle to speak calmly.

" It was sober sense, and sober truth," retorted Rose.

" Not it," said Mary Carr. " It was but a flirtation, Rose."

" Very likely," assented Rose, volatile as usual. " Being an
attractive man, Mr. Frederick St. John no doubt goes in for
the game, roaming from flower to flower, a very butterfly,
kissing all, and settling upon none." And she brought her
careless speech to a conclusion with the first lines of an old
song, once in great vogue at Madame de Nino's :—

> " The butterfly was a gentleman
> Of no very good repute ;
> And he roved in the sunshine all day long,
> In his scarlet and purple suit.
> And he left his lady wife at home
> In her own secluded bower,
> Whilst he, like a bachelor, flirted about,
> With a kiss for every flower."

Adeline gazed at the portrait. It was that of a fair girlish
face, wearing a peculiarly sweet look of youth and innocence,
blended with pride. No impartial observer could have pronounced it so lovely as her own, but the jealous film just now
before her eyes caused her to take an exaggerated view of its
charms, and to see in it something more than loveliness. It
may have been little, if at all, like the young lady to whom
Rose compared it ; but no matter : to Adeline it was Sarah
Beauclerc and no other, and from that moment the image
fixed itself indelibly in her mind as that of her envied rival.
And yet she believed in Mr. St. John ; she knew he was seeking
to win *herself* for his wife ! Truly they are unfathomable, the
ways and fears of jealousy.

At length, in her intolerable misery and suspense, she took
courage, in one of her letters to him, to hint at his former intimacy with Sarah Beauclerc. What he answered was never
disclosed by Adeline ; but that it must have been satisfactory,
dispelling even *her* strong jealousy, may be judged from the
significant fact that her face grew radiant again.

Meanwhile Mr. St. John lingered at his mother's bedside in
London. All danger was over ; and in point of fact the
accident had not been so severe as was at first feared. Lady
Anne Saville was with her. Isaac St. John was ill at Castle
Wafer. It was Frederick's intention to pay his brother a visit
ere he returned to France, and get his sanction to the pro-

posals he intended to carry back to M. de Castella. But this visit was frustrated.

One afternoon the inmates of Beaufoy were startled by the unexpected arrival of the Baron de la Chasse. Wishing to consult M. de Castella on a little matter of business, he explained, he had done himself the honour and pleasure to come personally, instead of writing. All expressed themselves delighted to see him, except one; and *she* was nearly beside herself with consternation. Terrified and dismayed Adeline indeed was; and she wrote to Mr. St. John before she slept.

An evening or two later, the whole party were assembled in the billiard-room; soon about to separate for the night. A night of intense heat, but there was a strong breeze, and it blew in through the open windows, fluttering the lights and causing the wax to drop. It was nearly eleven o'clock: the last game was being finished—but the Baron was a remarkably slow, deliberate player—when, without the slightest preparation, the door opened, and Mr. St. John walked in. Adeline started from her seat, scarcely suppressing an involuntary cry; she had not thought he would be back so soon. It seemed that her letter had surprised him in the act of setting out for Castle Wafer. He turned his steps to the Continent instead.

He looked very well; very handsome. It seemed to strike them all, after this short absence, though he had no advantages from dress, being in his travelling attire. How could Adeline be blamed for loving him? A hundred inquiries were made after Mrs. St. John. She was quite out of danger, he answered, and progressing towards recovery.

"Will you allow me the honour of half-an-hour's interview with you to-morrow morning, sir?" he said, addressing M. de Castella, in a tone which the whole room might hear.

"Certainly," returned M. de Castella. But he looked up, as if surprised. "Name your hour."

"Ten o'clock," concluded Mr. St. John. And he took his leave.

The interview the following morning in Signor de Castella's cabinet lasted an hour. An hour!—and Adeline in suspense all that time. She could not remain for an instant in one place—now upstairs, now down. She was crossing the hall, for about the hundredth time, when the cabinet door opened, and Mr. St. John came out. He seized her hand and took her into the yellow drawing-room. She trembled violently from head to foot, just as she had trembled the night of his departure for England. It was the first moment of their being alone together, and he embraced her tenderly, and held her to his heart.

"You have bad news for me!" she said, at length. "We are to be separated!"

"We will not be separated, Adeline. Strange! strange!" he continued, as he paced the room, "that people can be so infatuated as to fancy an engagement of form must necessarily imply an engagement of hearts! M. de Castella does not understand—he cannot understand that your happiness is at stake. In short, he laughed at that."

"Is he very angry?"

"No; but vexed. I have not time now to relate to you all that passed, liable as we are to interruption. I told him that the passion which had arisen between us was not of will—that I had not purposely placed myself in your path to gain your love—that we had been thrown together by circumstances, and thus it had arisen. I pointed out that no blame could by any possibility attach to you, though it might be due to me; for I did not deny that when I saw an attachment was growing up between us, I might have flown before it was irrevocably planted, and did not."

"Did you part in anger?" she asked.

"On the contrary. M. de Castella is anxious to treat the affair as a jest, and hinted that it might be dropped as such. I do believe he considers it one, for he asked me to dinner."

"Frederick! You will surely come?"

"I shall come, Adeline, for your sake."

"Oh!" she exclaimed, with a shiver, "how will it end?"

"My dearest," he said earnestly, "you must be calm. Fear nothing, now I am by you. Rely upon it, you shall be my wife."

"Mr. St. John," cried Rose, as they went into the west drawing-room, "you have brought some music for me, a writing-case for Mary Carr, but what have you brought for Adeline?"

"Myself," he quietly answered.

"There's many a true word spoken in jest," said Rose, with a laugh. "You don't think you have been taking *me* in all this time, Mr. St. John, with your letters to Mary Carr, and her envelopes back again? Bah! pas si bête."

She went, waltzing, on to the colonnade.

Mr. St. John turned to Miss Carr, and thanked her for the very thing Rose had named. "I presume you know," he said, "that our correspondence was perfectly justified, though I did not wish it declared until my return—that we are affianced to each other?"

"I have feared it some time, Mr. St. John."

"*Feared* it?"

"Yes. Adeline is promised to another: and the French look upon such engagements as sacred."

"In a general way. But there are cases of exception. We have your good wishes, I hope?"

"Indeed you have. For I fear it may be a matter of life or death to Adeline—according as it may be decided. She is a sensitive plant."

"And shall be cherished as one."

It was a most uncomfortable dinner that day. Mr. St. John was present, looking quiet and resolute ; de la Chasse furious. During the afternoon some inkling of the pretensions of Mr. St. John had oozed out, and de la Chasse aspersed him in his absence before them all. After dinner, Signor de Castella led the way to the billiard-room, hoping, probably, that the knocking about of balls might dissipate the constraint. But it came to an open rupture. Some difference of opinion arose about the game. St. John was haughty and unbending : de la Chasse gave way to his anger, and so far forgot himself as personally to attack, by words, Mr. St. John. "A spendthrift, who had run through his own fortune, to come hunting after Adeline's——"

"Vous êtes menteur !" shouted Mr. St. John, forgetting his manners, and turning short upon the Baron. But what further he might have said was stopped by Adeline, who, terrified out of self-control, darted across the room, and, touching St. John's arm, whispered him to be calm for her sake. De la Chasse advanced and offered his hand to remove Adeline, but St. John held her by him in haughty defiance.

"Mademoiselle, you are degrading yourself !" said M. de la Chasse. "Come from his side."

There was no answer from St. John, save a quiet smile of power, and his retaining hold of Adeline. The Baron looked at M. de Castella, but the scene had really passed so quickly that the latter had found no breath to interfere. "Is it fit that my promised wife should thus be subjected to insult in my presence, sir?" he asked.

"Adeline," interposed M. de Castella, sternly, "return to your mother."

"She is *my* promised wife," said Mr. St. John to the Baron, "and I have a right to retain her here—the right of affection. A right that *you* will never have."

De la Chasse was foaming—presenting a very contrast to the cool equanimity of Mr. St. John. "I will not bandy words with him : I will not. Signor de Castella, when your salon shall be freed from that man, I will re-enter it."

Wheeling round upon his heel, he went out, banging the door after him. For a moment there was silence : St. John, his hold still on Adeline, remained at the far end of the room ; Signor de Castella, half paralyzed with the scandal, was near the billiard-table ; the rest were in a group by the crimson ottoman, Agnes de Beaufoy crossing herself perpetually, Madame de Castella the very image of dismay.

"Mademoiselle," spoke the Signor to his daughter, who was sobbing aloud in her terror and agitation, "do you dare to disobey me? I told you to go to your mother."

"*She* does not disobey you, sir, and never would do so willingly," returned Mr. St. John. "The fault was mine."

He released his hold on Adeline as he spoke, took her hand with almost ceremonious politeness, and conducted her across the room to the side of her mother.

"These scenes must be put a stop to, Mr. St. John," cried the Signor. "You received my answer this morning on the subject."

"Only to re-enter upon it, sir. The particulars which I spared then, I will relate now."

"I do not wish to hear them," said Signor de Castella, speaking irritably.

"Sir," calmly interposed Mr. St. John, "I demand it as a right. The Baron has been freely remarking upon me and my conduct to-day, I understand, in the hearing of all now present, and I must be permitted to justify myself."

"You must allow for the feeling of irritation on the Baron's part. You are neither devoid of cool judgment nor sound sense, Mr. St. John."

"That is just what I have allowed for," replied Mr. St. John, frankly. "He feels, no doubt, that he is an injured man ;

and so I have been willing to show him consideration. Any other man, speaking of me as de la Chasse has done, would have—have—been treated differently."

"Let this unpleasant matter be dropped, Mr. St. John," was the resolute answer.

"Sir, I beg you to listen to my explanation; I ask it you in courtesy: it shall be given without disguise. When I came of age, I obtained possession of a handsome fortune. It is all dissipated. I was not free from the faults of youth, common to my inexperience and rank, and I was as extravagant as my worst enemy could wish. But I solemnly assert that I never have been guilty of a bad thought, of a dishonourable action. There is not a man or woman living, who can bring a word of reproach against me, save that of excessive imprudence in regard to my money—and a good part of that went to help those who wanted it worse than I do. Well, about a twelve-month ago, I was cleared out, and had liabilities to the amount of a few thousands besides——"

"Pray do not enter upon these details, Mr. St. John," interrupted Signor de Castella.

"Sir, I must go on—with your permission. My brother, Mr. Isaac St. John, sent for me to Castle Wafer. He pointed out to me the errors of my career: bade me reflect upon the heedless course I was pursuing. I *had* been reflecting on it, had become quite as awake to its ills as he could be, and I had firmly resolved that it should end: but to a man deep in debt, good resolutions are sometimes difficult to carry out. My brother offered to set me free; making it a condition that I should marry. He proposed in that case to give up to me Castle Wafer—it has always been his intention to do so when I married—and a very liberal settlement he offered to make on my wife, whom they had already fixed upon——"

"Was it Sarah Beauclerc?" interrupted Rose, who never lost her equanimity in her life.

"It was my cousin Anne," resumed Mr. St. John, with scarcely a glance at Rose. "But the marriage suited neither her nor me. She was engaged, unknown to her friends, to Captain Saville, and I was keeping her secret. I took upon myself all the brunt of the refusal—for Captain Saville's position, at that period, did not justify his aspiring openly to Lady Anne St. John—and informed my brother I could not marry Anne. High words rose between us; we parted in

anger, and I returned to London. Just then my mother's
sister died, leaving me some money. It was not very much;
but it was sufficient to pay my debts, and to this purpose it is
being applied, as it is realized. By next November every
shilling I owe will be discharged. I should have preferred not
appearing again before my brother until I was a free man, but
circumstances have ordered it otherwise. I was about setting
out for Castle Wafer the day information reached me that
de la Chasse had again made his appearance here, and I
came off at once, without the credentials I should otherwise
have brought with me. But you cannot doubt me, M. de
Castella ? ”

“ Doubt what ? ”

“ My ability—my power—to offer a suitable position to your
daughter.”

“ Sir, the question cannot arise. Though I should very much
doubt it. My daughter is not Lady Anne St. John.”

“ I should have added that Lady Anne is married; a change
having occurred in Captain Saville's prospects; and she has
cleared up the past to Isaac. My brother is most anxious to
be reconciled to me. And I can take upon myself to say that
all the favourable projects and settlements he proposed for
Lady Anne, will be renewed for Adeline.”

“ Then you would take upon yourself to say too much, Mr.
St. John : you cannot answer for another. But to what end
pursue this unprofitable conversation? My daughter is promised to the Baron de la Chasse, and no other man will she
marry.”

“ Sir,” cried Mr. St. John, speaking with agitation, “ will you
answer me one question? If I were in a position to offer
Adeline ample settlements; to take her to Castle Wafer as her
present home—and you know it must eventually descend to
me—would you consider me a suitable *parti* for her?”

“ It is a question that never can arise.”

“ I pray you answer it me—in courtesy,” pleaded Mr. St.
John. “ Would you deem me eligible in a worldly point of
view ? ”

“ Certainly. It is an alliance that a higher family than mine
might aspire to.”

“ Then, sir, I return this night to England. And will not
again present myself to you, until I come armed with these
credentials.”

"Absurd! absurd!" ejaculated Signor de Castella, whilst Adeline uttered a smothered cry of fear. "I have allowed this conversation to go on, out of respect to you, Mr. St. John, but I bég to tell you, once for all, that Adeline never can be yours."

"I will not urge the subject further at present," said Mr. St. John, as he held out his hand to bid adieu to Madame de Castella. "We will resume it on my return from England."

"You surely do not mean to persist in this insane journey?" abruptly spoke M. de Castella.

"Signor de Castella," said Mr. St. John, his pale face and his deliberate manner alike expressive of resolute firmness, "I will not resign your daughter. If I could forget my own feelings, I must remember hers. To marry her to de la Chasse would be to abandon her to the grave. She is not strong; you know it; not fitted to battle with misery. Adeline," he added, turning to her, for she was sobbing hysterically, "why this distress? I have repeatedly assured you, when your fears of these explanations were great, that I would never resign you to de la Chasse, or to any other. Hear me repeat that assertion in the presence of your parents—by the help of Heaven, my love, you shall be my wife."

"Meanwhile," said M. de Castella, sarcastically, "as you are yet, at least, under my authority, Adeline, permit me to suggest that you retire from this room."

She rose obediently, and went towards the door, sobbing.

"A moment," cried Mr. St. John, deprecatingly, "if it is from my presence you would send her. I am going myself. Adieu to all."

He opened the door, and stood with it in his hand, glancing hesitatingly at Adeline. Her feelings were wrought to a high pitch of excitement, control forsook her, and darting forward she clung to the arm of Mr. St. John, sobbing out hysterically.

"You will return—you will not desert me—you will not leave me to *him*?"

He laid his hand tenderly on her shoulder, just as though they had been alone. "It is only compulsion that takes me from you, Adeline," he answered. "Be assured I will not let the grass grow under my feet. When three days shall have passed, look every minute for my return: and then, my darling, we shall part no more."

Lower yet he bent his head, and kissed her fervently. Then resigned her, turned, and was gone. He was a bold man.

Adeline flung her hands over her crimsoned face. To describe the astonished consternation of the spectators, would be a difficult task : a kiss upon a young lady's lips in France is worse than the seven cardinal sins. Madame de Castella escorted Adeline at once to her chamber, and Miss de Beaufoy's grey hair stood on end.

"Bah!" said the dear old lady. "He is a good and honourable man, Ferdinand," turning to her son-in-law—"and he means no harm. It is nothing, in English manners. I've had a kiss myself in my young days, and was none the worse for it."

CHAPTER XXIV.

FOILED !

A MOST uncomfortable night; a still more uncomfortable morning. Adeline lay in bed with headache ; and the Baron departed for Paris at mid-day. He believed, with Signor de Castella—though it may be questioned if the latter did believe it, except in speech—that Mr. St. John had taken himself to England for good. He did not cast blame on Adeline : his rage was vented on St. John. As to any affection Adeline might be suspected of entertaining for Mr. St. John, the Baron neither thought of it nor would have understood it.

The banns of the marriage were put up at the Mairie, and would shortly be published in the newspapers, according to the custom of the country,—"Alphonse Jean Hippolite, Baron de la Chasse, and Adeline Luisa de Castella." The wedding plan was already sketched out : and there is no doubt that this trouble regarding Mr. St. John was hastening matters on. The religious ceremony was to take place at the neighbouring chapel, the civil one at the Mairie at Odesque. A banquet would be given at Beaufoy in the evening, and on the following morning the bride and bridegroom would leave the château for Paris. In the course of a few days, Signor and Madame de Castella would join them there, and all four would proceed to the South together.

Rose was gratuitously free in her remarks on the programme.

" I'd have seen them further, Adeline, with their French ideas, before they should have made such arrangements for me ! "

Three days passed, and no Mr. St. John.   Adeline was in a sad state of excitement.   Good Father Marc, who had loved her since she was a little child, and had her interest warmly at heart, looked at her with deep concern whenever they met. On the evening of this third day he spoke.

" My child, I am grieved to see you unhappy.   This young Englishman was attractive, and it is natural, perhaps, that you should regret him : but his departure renders your course of duty all the more easy."

The priest thought he had gone for good, then ! Adeline was silent : but she could have thrown herself on the good priest's breast and wept out her sorrow.

" It is well that he should thus have terminated it, my poor child.   Nothing but fruitless dissatisfaction could have attended his remaining.   Never, under any circumstances, could you have allowed yourself to espouse one of the heretical faith. Best as it is, my child !   May the care of all the saints be given to you ! "

When the fourth morning arose and did not bring St. John, Adeline's state grew distressing.   To what compare her restless anxiety?   You are all familiar with the old tale of Bluebeard. " Sister Anne, Sister Anne, do you see anybody coming ? "

" Alas, my sister, I see only the dust from a flock of sheep."

" Sister Anne, Sister Anne, can you see anybody coming ? "

Thus it was with Adeline.   When her eyes ached with look- ing out, and she retired momentarily to ease them, it would be, " Rose, Rose, do you see him coming ? "

" No, I don't see a soul."

And then, " Mary ! go to the window.   Can you see him coming ? "

And the day passed like the others, and he never came.   It was, indeed, an anxious time with her.   Left to herself, the marriage would inevitably take place, for, unsupported by St. John, she should not dare to oppose her father.   But, on the fifth morning—ah, what relief !—he returned.   Adeline, dear girl, look at him : what do you read?   A self-possessed step of triumph, a conscious smile on his fine features, a glance of assured satisfaction in his truthful eye.   He comes, indeed, as St. John of Castle Wafer.

Miss de Beaufoy, Adeline, and Mary were alone : the rest

had gone over to the farm. He took Adeline's hands in his: he saw how she had been suffering. "But it is over, over," he whispered to her; "I shall never leave you more."

"It was unwise of you to come back, Mr. St. John," said Aunt Agnes, as she shook hands with him.

"It was wise of me to go," he cried, a happy flush of triumph on his brow. "Ah, dear Miss Beaufoy, you will soon pay us a visit at Castle Wafer. Where is Monsieur de la Chasse?"

"He has left for Paris."

"I am sorry for it. He styled me an adventurer—a hunter after Adeline's fortune. Had he remained until to-day, he might have eaten his words."

"What is there to hope?" Adeline could not help whispering.

"Hope all, hope everything, my love," was his reply. "*I* tell you to do so."

St. John, like an ambassador, had brought his credentials with him. All that he had so confidently asserted to M. de Castella was realized. His brother had received him with open arms, joying over the reconciliation. Solicitors were at once employed to liquidate Frederick's remaining debts, and to set free his property. Castle Wafer would be resigned to him on his marriage, and a brilliant income. He had represented Adeline in glowing colours to his brother, not enlarging on her beauty, which he said would speak for itself, but on her numerous endearing qualities of mind and heart. And Isaac, as he listened, became reconciled to the frustration of the marriage with Lady Anne St. John, and wrote to Adeline that he was prepared to love and welcome her as a daughter. His offered settlements for her were the same as those proposed for Lady Anne, and undeniable.

Never had Signor de Castella been so thoroughly put out. We are apt to believe what we wish, and he had been suffering himself to assume that Mr. St. John would really not return. Matters seemed to be becoming serious. With a bad grace he received the letter presented to him from Mr. Isaac St. John. It contained formal proposals for Adeline, with an explanatory detail of what has been stated above, submitting the whole to Signor de Castella's approval. The letter also preferred a request, which Frederick was to urge in person, that the Signor and his family would at once visit Castle Wafer and become acquainted with the home to which he consigned his child. The marriage could then take place as soon as was convenient, either in England or France, as might be agreed upon; after which, Frederick would take her to a warmer clime for the winter months.

Annoyed as M. de Castella was, he could not but be flattered at the honour done him, for he well knew that Isaac St. John of Castle Wafer might aspire, for his brother, to a higher alliance than this would be. But he showed his vexation.

"You have acted improperly, Mr. St. John, both towards me and towards your brother. Pray, did you tell him that Adeline was all but the wife of another?"

"I told him everything," said Mr. St. John, firmly; "and he agreed with me, that for Adeline's own sake, if not for mine, she must be rescued from the unhappiness which threatens her."

"You are bold, sir," cried M. de Castella, a flush of anger rising to his brow.

"I am," returned Mr. St. John, "bold and determined. You must pardon the avowal. It would ill become me to be otherwise, when so much is at stake."

M. de Castella wheeled back his easy-chair as he sat, the only diversion from the uncomfortable straight-backed seats which graced his cabinet. "Listen to me," he said; "I hope finally. Your journey to Castle Wafer, as I warned you it would be, has been worse than profitless: our conversation is the same. No human entreaty or menace—could such be offered me—would alter my determination one iota. Adeline will marry de la Chasse."

"I have abstained from urging my own feelings," said Mr. St. John, warmly, "but you must be aware that my happiness is at stake. My whole future, so to speak, is bound up in Adeline."

"You do well not to urge them; it would make no difference. I am sorry; but it would not. This must end, Mr. St. John. I have already expressed my acknowledgments to you for the honour done me in your wish for an alliance; I shall express them presently to your brother. And I have no objection to confess, that, under other circumstances, I might have been tempted to entertain it, in spite of the difference in our faith. But the barriers between you and Adeline are insuperable."

"Oh, M. de Castella, pray reflect. I have been bred with as nice a sense of honour as you: I venture to say it: and I trust I shall never be guilty of aught to tarnish that honour. But I should deem it an unrighteous thing to sacrifice to it a fellow-creature's happiness, and she an only child."

"Oh, tush! Sacrifice!—happiness! These chimeras of the imagination are not recognized by us. Adeline may rebel in spirit—may repine for a week or two, but when once she is married to the Baron, she will settle down contentedly enough."

"You are killing her," exclaimed St. John, in some excitement. "You may not see it, but what I tell you is true. The painful suspense and agitation she has been exposed to lately, if continued, would kill her."

"Then if such be your opinion, Mr. St. John," returned the Signor, sarcastically, "you should put an end to it by with-drawing yourself."

"I will not withdraw; I will not give up Adeline. I am more worthy of her than he is."

"You have been highly reprehensible throughout the affair. You knew that Adeline was promised to another, and it was your duty to fly the place, or at least absent yourself from her, when you found an attachment was arising."

"I don't know that I was awake to it in time. But if I had been, most likely I should not have flown. Had I been needy, as that man called me, or one whose rank were inferior to hers, then my duty would have been plain; but the heir to Castle Wafer has no need to fly like a craven."

"Not on that score—not on that score. Had Adeline been but a peasant and engaged to another, you should have respected that engagement, and left her free."

"I did not set myself out to gain her love. I assure you, Signor, that the passion which grew up between us was unsought on either side. It was the result of companionship, of similar tastes and sympathies; and it was firmly seated, I am convinced, in both our hearts, before I ever uttered a word, or gave way to an action that could be construed into a wooing one. And you will forgive me for reminding you, that had Adeline regarded de la Chasse with the feelings essential to render a marriage with him happy, she must have remained indifferent to me."

"Our conference is at an end," observed M. de Castella, rising: "I beg to state that I can never suffer it to be renewed. Finally: I feel obliged, flattered, by the honour you would have done Adeline, but I have no alternative but to decline it."

"You have an alternative, Signor de Castella."

"*I have none.* I have none, on my honour. Will you be the bearer of my despatch to Castle Wafer?"

"No. I shall remain where I am for the present."

"I cannot pretend to control your movements, Mr. St. John, but it will be well that you absent yourself until after my daughter's marriage. Where you to come in contact with the Baron, much unpleasantness might ensue."

"He is not here. Therefore at present that question cannot arise."

"I have no wish that our friendship should terminate : I may add that I do not wish it even to be interrupted, if you will but be reasonable. You must be aware"—and for a moment the Signor relapsed into a tone of warm cordiality—"that we have all liked you very much, Mr. St. John, and have enjoyed your society in an unusual degree. Indeed it is this very feeling for you which has thrown difficulties in the way : but for that, the house would have been closed to you on your first rejection. You may stay where you are, and welcome; you may come still and see us, and welcome ; provided you will exercise common sense, and allow matters to take their proper course."

Mr. St. John made no reply whatever. He said good morning, and left the cabinet, nearly running against Father Marc, who was waiting to enter it.

After that there ensued what might be called a lull in the storm. St. John came occasionally to Beaufoy, sometimes met Adeline, by chance as it seemed, out of doors ; but nothing more was heard of his pretensions. Meanwhile active preparations for the wedding went on : and the two young lady visitors prolonged their stay, having obtained leave from home and from Madame de Nino to do so.

And now we have to approach a phase of the history upon which it is not pleasant to touch. Mr. St. John made one final effort to shake the resolve of Signor de Castella ; or, rather, attempted to make it, but was met by a peremptory command never to introduce the subject again. After that, it appeared to him that there was only one alternative, and he cautiously ventured to break it to Adeline—that of flying with him. It was received with terror and reproach—as was only natural ; she felt indeed inexpressibly shocked, not only at the proposition itself, but that he should make it. But Mr. St. John persevered. He attempted reason first : if she did not take this step, how would she avoid the marriage with de la Chasse ?

He brought forth arguments of the most persuasive eloquence :
and reasoning eloquence is convincing, when it comes from
beloved lips.

Let us give St. John his due. He truly thought, in all honour,
that he was acting for the best, for Adeline's welfare. It could
scarcely be called an elopement that he was urging, since he took
measures for it to be countenanced and assisted by his family.
He told them the whole case, the entire truth; he implored
them, for Adeline's sake, to save her. To follow the progress
of the matter day by day, step by step, would be useless : it is
sufficient to say that he at length wrung a tardy and most ·
reluctant consent from Adeline.

It wanted but three days to that fixed for the grand wedding,
when she stood with him in the shrubbery in the twilight of the
hot evening. There was indeed little time to lose, if she was
to be saved. He put into her hand a letter addressed to her
by his mother.

"MY DEAR MADEMOISELLE DE CASTELLA,

"Frederick writes me word that you demurred to
the arguments of my last letter, as being used only out of
courtesy to you. You judge perfectly right in believing that I
look upon elopements with a severe eye; every gentlewoman
does so, if she be conscientious. But your case appears to be
a most peculiar one. Your whole future happiness, perhaps
life, is at stake; and I really do think Frederick is right in
saying that it is a duty before Heaven to save you from this
obnoxious marriage that is being forced upon you. It is a
cruel thing to sacrifice you merely to the pledging of a word—
and that is so, if I understand the matter rightly. Signor de
Castella has stated (in his letter to my step-son, Mr. Isaac St.
John) that were it not for this unlucky previous contract to
which he is plighted, he should be proud of the alliance with
Frederick ; that to him personally he has no sort of objection.
To tell you the truth, it appeared to me, from the wording of
this letter (which my step-son sent up for my perusal) that your
father would be glad of a pretext for breaking the contract, but
that it seemed to him a simple impossibility that any such
pretext could be found. It is this fact—though it may be better
to call it opinion—which was my chief inducement to countenance the step now contemplated by Frederick. And if it
must take place (and, as I say, I see no other way of escape

for you), it is better that it should be done with my sanction: which will absolve you afterwards in the judgment of the world.

"I am not sufficiently recovered to travel to the coast, as Frederick wished, but Lady Anne Saville has offered to supply my place. She leaves with her husband for Folkestone the day after to-morrow, and will receive you there from Frederick's hands. She will conduct you at once to London, to my house, where you will remain my guest until the marriage, which of course must take place at once; after which, you will leave for Castle Wafer, and pass there a brief sojourn before you start for the South. The settlements are here, waiting for your signature and Frederick's: Mr. Isaac St. John has already affixed his, and he will be in London before you arrive.

"I am impatient to receive and welcome you. Believe me, my dear child, that I will always endeavour to be to you an affectionate mother.

"Selina St. John."

"You will be in readiness to-morrow night," he whispered, as she closed the letter.

"When are we to be married?" she asked, after a pause. She might well bend her sweet face downwards as she asked it.

"Adeline, you see what my mother says. I have written to procure a special licence, so that the Protestant ceremony shall be performed on our arrival, securing us from separation. Should the forms of your own religion require any delay, which I do not anticipate, you will remain with my mother until they can be completed. My home in town is at Mivart's."

"You—you will be kind to me?" she faltered, bursting into tears. "I am leaving a happy home, my mother, my father, the friends of my childhood, I am leaving all for you; you will be ever kind to me?"

"Adeline," he interrupted, "how can you ask the question? I am about to make you my dear wife; I will cherish you as you never yet were cherished. Your parents have loved you dearly, but not with such a love as mine. Heaven helping me, your life shall be one dream of happiness. No mother ever watched over her first-born, as I will watch over and cherish you."

Save for the wild beating of her heart, as his hand lay against it, he might have thought her cold, so still did she stand. It was the impassioned repose of all-perfect love, too deep, too pure for utterance.

"You are leaving this home for one more beautiful," he continued: "you will forgive me for saying so when you see Castle Wafer. A home where you will reign its idol. I speak not now of myself. Its retainers are tried and faithful: they have been ours from generation to generation. They served my father, they have served my brother, they will serve me; and you, their mistress, will be revered and worshipped. It will be a happy home. We may sojourn occasionally in foreign lands; mingle in the gaieties of the world; but we shall return to it with a zest that in time will render us loth to quit it. There we will bring up our children, training them to goodness; there we will learn to live, so that we may become worthy to inherit a better world : the mode of worship may be different, but the faith and end are the same—one hope, one heaven, one God. Oh, Adeline, put away all fear for the future, all doubt of me, if indeed you could have such! I would bid another trust to my honour, I conjure you to confide in my love."

As they turned to the house, after a few hasty moments given to the arrangement of their plans, a sudden cough, sounding very near, startled them. St. John stepped aside a few paces, and saw, seated on a bench, Father Marc. Could he have been there long? If so, he must have heard more than was expedient, for he understood English. St. John bit his lip with vexation.

"Are you there, father?"

"I have this instant sat down, my son. I am no longer young, and my legs pain me when I walk far. My course this evening has been a long one."

"He may have come up only now," was the mental conclusion of Mr. St. John.

"Is that Mademoiselle with you?" resumed the priest—for Adeline, in her vexation, did not come prominently forward. "Should the child be abroad in the night-air?"

"No. I am going to take her indoors. But it is not night yet."

Not yet: it was twilight still: but a dampness was already arising, the effect of the day's heat. The weather was very sultry, even for the close of August, the days being one blaze of sunshine. Adeline hastened in : she had been away not much more than five minutes, but she dreaded being missed.

The plan for getting away was this. On the following night Adeline was to retire to her chamber early, under plea of headache, or some other slight indisposition; and, after dismissing Louise, to habit herself as she deemed suitable for her journey. She was then to steal downstairs and out of the house, before it was locked up for the night, and join Mr. St. John in the garden, who would be awaiting her. The same nondescript vehicle, which was a sort of long gig with a white calico head to it, that had served Mr. St. John on a previous occasion, and was both light and fleet, would be in readiness to convey them to Odesque. There they would take the night-train from Amiens to Boulogne and go at once on board the Folkestone steamer, Mr. St. John having taken care to ascertain that the tide served at a suitable hour for them, the steamer starting early in the morning. Once at Folkestone, he resigned her into the charge of Captain and Lady Anne Saville. By these means they hoped to get a whole night's start before the absence of Adeline was discovered at Beaufoy. The scheme appeared feasible enough in theory. But—in practice? that remained to be proved.

The eventful day arose; and what a day it was for Adeline! Not only was Adeline de Castella a bad one to carry on any sort of deception, but she looked upon the act she was about to commit, the quitting clandestinely her father's home, as a very heinous crime indeed. It was not her love for Mr. St. John that took her: swayed by that alone, she had not dared to do it: it was her intense horror of becoming the wife of Alphonse de la Chasse. Could she only have changed natures for that one day with Miss Rose Darling!

But the day was got through somehow, even by Adeline, and evening drew on. After dinner they were sitting in the favourite room, the western drawing-room, when Mr. St. John came in. Some of them looked up in surprise: his visits latterly had been rare. He was unusually silent and thoughtful, and little was said by any one. Signor de Castella was playing chess with Agnes, and did not speak to him after the first greeting. Old Madame de Beaufoy was playing écarté with Mary Carr.

An ominous spirit of dulness seemed to sit upon them all. The room seemed so intensely still. Rose, who hated dulness as she hated poison, started up and opened the piano, hoping perhaps to dispel it, and began to look amidst the pile of music. She chose an old song; an out-of-date by-gone song that she had not sung for months, perhaps years. *How* came she to hunt it up ? It was a strange coincidence ; little less than a fatality. The song was "Kathleen Mavourneen." Had any one asked Rose to sing it, she would have cast back a sarcasm on the "perverted taste," on "English ideas," "vandalism," and commenced instead some new Italian or German thing, and screamed it through in defiance. On this night she began the song of her own accord ; and I say it was a fatality.

> " To think that from Erin and thee I must part—
> It may be for years, and it may be for ever—— "

Thus far had Rose sung, when deep sobs startled her. They came from Adeline. She had been leaning back in her grand-mamma's fauteuil, pale and quiet, but full of inward agitation. The song seemed singularly applicable to her, and she had listened to its words as they went on with an oppressed heart. Singularly applicable ! She was leaving her country, her home, and her dear parents, it might be for years, or it might be for ever. In these moments of sadness, a straw will unhinge the outward composure. Adeline's sobs burst forth with violence, and it was entirely beyond her power to control them. The whole room looked up in amazement, and Rose brought her song to a sudden standstill.

Mr. St. John, who was near the piano, strode forward impulsively towards Adeline ; but arrested his steps half way, and strode as impulsively back again. Anxious inquiries were pressed upon Adeline, and her mother laid down her embroidery and went to her. Adeline seemed to recover herself by magic, so far as outward calmness went. She excused herself in few words : it was a fit of low spirits ; she had not felt well all day, and Rose's song had affected her ; the feeling had passed now. Mr. St. John whispered to Rose to begin another song, and she did so. He then wished the party good night, and left. By-and-by, Adeline, pleading fatigue, said she would go to bed.

"Do so, dear child," acquiesced her mother ; "you don't seem very well."

"Good night, dear, dear mamma," she said, clinging round her mother's neck, while the rebellious tears again streamed from her eyes. She would have given half the anticipated happiness of her future life for her mother to have blessed her, but she did not dare to ask it. She approached her father last, hesitatingly ; kissed him—a most unusual thing, for he was not a man to encourage these familiarities, even from his daughter—and left the room struggling convulsively to suppress her sobs.

After sitting in her chamber a few minutes, to recover serenity, she rang for Louise. Up came that demoiselle, in open surprise that her young lady should have retired so early. Adeline said she had a headache, let her take off her dress, and then dismissed her.

Adeline bolted the door and began to look around her. Shock the first: her wardrobe was locked and the key gone. The dress and bonnet she meant to wear were in it; so she had to ring again.

"I want the key of the wardrobe," she said, when Louise entered. "It is locked."

Louise felt in her pocket, brought forth the key, and threw the doors back on their hinges. "What should she give to mademoiselle?"

This was difficult to answer. At any other time Adeline would have ordered her to leave the wardrobe open, and go. But her self-consciousness and dread of discovery caused her to hesitate then.

"I want—a—pocket-handkerchief," stammered Adeline.

Sharply the doors were flung to again, locked, and the key returned to Louise's pocket. "Parbleu, mademoiselle," was her exclamation, turning to a chest of drawers, "as if your handkerchiefs were kept in the wardrobe!"

Adeline knew they were not as well as Louise, but just then she had not her wits about her. She was growing desperate.

"One would think we had a thief in the house, by the way you keep places locked," she exclaimed. "Leave the wardrobe open, Louise."

"Indeed, and we have something as bad as a thief," answered Louise, grumblingly. "If Susanne wants anything for madame, and thinks she can find it here, she makes no scruple of coming and turning about mademoiselle's things. Only three days ago it took me an hour to put them straight after her."

"Well, leave the wardrobe open for to-night," said Adeline: "you can lock it again to-morrow, if you will." And Mademoiselle Louise swung the doors back again, and quitted the room.

Adeline proceeded to dress herself. She put on a dark silk

dress, a light thin cashmere shawl, and a straw bonnet trimmed with white ribbons. She also threw over her shoulders a costly silk travelling cloak, lined and trimmed with ermine. It had been a present to her from Madame de Beaufoy against her journey to the South. She was soon ready, but it was scarcely time to depart. She was pale as death; so pale that the reflection of her own face in the glass startled her. Her head swam round, her limbs trembled, and she felt sick at heart. She began to doubt if she should have strength to go. She sat down and waited.

The minutes passed rapidly: it would soon be time, if she went at all. She felt in her pocket: all was there. Her purse, containing a few Napoleons; her handkerchief; a small phial of Cologne water; and a little case containing *his* gifts and letters.

She arose and placed her hands upon the lock of the door; but, too ill and agitated to proceed, turned round, drank a glass of water, and sat down again. The longer she stopped, the worse she grew; and, making a desperate effort, she extinguished the light, opened the door, and glided to the top of the stairs.

All seemed quiet. She could hear the murmur of the servants' voices in their distant apartments, nothing else, and she stole noiselessly down the staircase, and across the lighted hall. As she was opening the front door, some one came out of the western drawing-room, and Adeline, with a quick, nervous effort, passed through, before whoever it was should be in sight, pulling the door gently after her.

Oh, misery! oh, horror! Planted at the foot of the steps, right in front of her, as if he had stopped on the spot and fallen into a reverie, was the priest, Father Marc. He glided up the steps, and seized her arm; and Adeline cried out, with a shrill, startled cry.

It was heard by Mademoiselle de Beaufoy, who was crossing the hall, and she came running out. It was heard by Mr. St. John from his hiding-place, behind one of the lions of the fountain, and he hastened forward.

"Oh, Adeline, mistaken child, what is this?" exclaimed her aunt. "You would leave your home clandestinely! you, Adeline de Castella!"

"Aunt! aunt! have mercy on me! I—I do believe I am dying! I would rather die than go through what I have gone through lately!"

"And better for you," was the stern reply. "Death is preferable to dishonour."

She was interrupted by the appearance of Mr. St. John. Adeline broke from her aunt and the priest, and fell forward in his arms, with a smothered cry: "Oh, Frederick! Frederick! protect me in this dreadful hour!"

Agnes de Beaufoy flew into the drawing-room, crying out that Mr. St. John was running away with Adeline, and they all went flocking out. St. John's first effort was an attempt to soothe Adeline: his second to bear her into the house. The priest, a kind-hearted man, went away in the direction of his chapel.

For some time all was astonishment and confusion. Every one seemed to be talking at once, reproaching Mr. St. John. *She* still clung to him, as if to part with him would be to part with life; and he protected her valiantly. The first distinguishable words were from Signor de Castella.

"So this is the recompense we receive from you! basely to betray her! to lead her to dishonour!"

St. John was paler than they ever remembered to have seen him, but his voice and bearing were perfectly calm. "I was leading her away to happiness," he answered; "ere many hours had elapsed she would have been my honoured wife. Had my mother been well, she would have received her at Folkestone, but she is unable yet to quit her room, and Lady Anne Saville, than whom one of higher character and consideration does not exist, is there awaiting her, accompanied by her husband. My brother vacates Castle Wafer for her reception; the settlements, as they were proposed to you, are drawn up, awaiting our signatures; and until the marriage could have taken place—had there been but an hour's delay—Adeline would have remained under my mother's roof and protection, conducted to it by Lady Anne. There are the vouchers for what I assert," he added, throwing some letters on the table. "*I* lead her to dishonour! Had you, Signor de Castella, evinced the consideration for her happiness, that I have for her honour, there would not now be this dispute."

"And you, shameless girl, thus to disgrace your name!"

"Reproach her not," interrupted Mr. St. John. "I will not suffer a harsh word to her in my presence. For this step I alone am to blame. Adeline was resolute in refusing to listen or accede to it, and she never would have done so but for the

countenance afforded to her in it by my family. Signor de
Castella, this is no moment for delicacy: I therefore tell you
openly she shall be my wife. Our plans of to-night are
frustrated, and should we not be able to carry out any other
for her escape, Adeline must renounce at the altar the husband
you would thrust upon her."

"You are insolent, sir," said M. de Castella.

"Not insolent," he replied, "but determined."

There is no time to pursue the discussion. It was long and
stormy. Madame de Castella cried all the time, but old
Madame de Beaufoy was a little inclined to favour St. John.
Not that she approved of the attempted escapade, but he was
so wondrous a favourite of hers, that she could not remain in
anger with him long, and she kept rapping her stick on the
floor at many things he said, to indicate approval, something
after the manner of a certain house of ours, when it cries out
"Hear, hear !" Adeline stood by Mr. St. John, shaking with
convulsive sobs, her white veil covering her face, the costly
cloak falling from her shoulders and sweeping the ground.
Her father suddenly turned to her.

"Adeline de Castella, are you determined to marry this
man ?"

"Speak out, Adeline," said Mr. St. John, for no answer came
from her.

"I—cannot—marry de la Chasse," she faltered.

"And you are determined to marry him—this Protestant
Englishman ?"

"If I may," she whispered, her sobs growing violent.

"To-morrow morning I will discuss with you this subject,"
proceeded M. de Castella, still addressing his daughter. "At
the conclusion of our interview, you shall be free to choose
between—between the husband I marked out for you, and him
who now stands by your side."

"On your honour ?" exclaimed Mr. St. John, surprised by
the remark.

"My word, sir, is valuable as yours," was the haughty reply.
"When my daughter shall have heard what I have to say, she
shall then be free to follow her own will. I will not further
influence her."

"You will permit me to receive her decision from her own
lips ?"

"I tell you I will not further control her. She shall be as

free to act as I am. And now, Mr. St. John, good night to you."

"Would to Heaven I might remain and watch over you this night!" he whispered, as he reluctantly released Adeline. "You need all soothing consolation, and there are none to offer it. Yet be comforted, my dear love, for if M. de Castella shall keep his word, it is our last parting."

"He is a noble fellow, with all his faults," mentally ejaculated Agnes de Beaufoy, as she watched Mr. St. John's receding form. And "all his faults," what were they? That he would have interfered in another's marriage contract, and stolen away the bride, to make her his own.

"I did not think Adeline had it in her!" exclaimed Rose, in a glow of delight, partly to the company, chiefly to herself. Rose had stood in a rapture of admiration the whole time. Adeline and Mary could not cast old scores at her, now.

CHAPTER XXV.

A CRISIS IN A LIFE.

THE dreaded interview with M. de Castella was all but over, and Adeline leaned against the straight-backed chair in the cabinet, more dead than alive, so completely had her father's words bereft her of hope and energy.

When Mr. St. John first opened the affair, Signor de Castella had felt considerably annoyed, and would not glance at the possibility of breaking the contract with de la Chasse. But the Signor, cold as he was in manner, was not, at heart, indifferent to Adeline's happiness. And when he found how entirely she was bound up in Mr. St. John, and the latter brought forth his munificent proposals and departed for England to get them triumphantly confirmed, then he began in secret to waver. But now stepped in another.

You, who read this, are of course aware that in many Roman Catholic families, especially foreign ones, the confessor exercises much influence over temporal matters as well as spiritual. And though the confessor to the Castellas, Father Marc, had not hitherto seen cause, or perhaps had opportunity, to put himself forward in such affairs, he felt himself bound to do so now. But you must not jump to a mistaken conclusion, or fancy he was one of those overbearing priests sometimes represented in works of fiction. That there are meddlers in all positions of life—in the Romish Church as well as in our Reformed one—every one knows. But Father Marc was not one of these. He was a good and conscientious man, and though an over-rigid Romanist, it was only in zeal for the Faith of his country, the religion to which he had been born and reared. No other Faith, according to his tenets, to his firm belief, would lead a soul to Heaven: and he deemed that he was acting for the best, nay, for the immortal interest of Adeline. Do not blame him! He loved the child, whom he had watched grow up from infancy. He honestly believed that to suffer Adeline to marry an Englishman and a heretic and make her home in Protestant England, would be to consign her to perdition. He therefore placed his veto upon it, a veto that might not be gainsaid, and forbid the contract to be interrupted with de la Chasse. If he interfered, with what may appear to us desperate measures, he believed the cause to be desperate which justified them; and he acted in accordance with the dictates of his own conscience; with what he deemed his duty to Adeline, to his religion, and to God.

She knew it all now : the secret of her father's obstinacy, and why she must give up Mr. St. John and marry de la Chasse. She knew that if her father consented to her heretical marriage, or if she of herself persisted in contracting it, the Curse of the Church was to alight upon her, and upon her father's house. *The Curse of the Church !* Adeline had been reared in all the belief and doctrines of the Romish faith, and she could no more have dared to act in defiance of that awful curse, than she would have dared to raise her hand against her own life. She leaned her head back on the uncomfortable chair, and moaned aloud in her overwhelming anguish. It might be cruel of Father Marc to have whispered of such a thing, but he had done it in his zealous love. Desperate diseases require desperate remedies.

"The alternative of a convent," she gasped, "cannot that be given me ?"

"No," replied M. de Castella, who was painfully frigid throughout the interview, perhaps as a guard to his own feelings. "You must marry. Your mother and I cannot consent to lose you from our sight, as, in the will of Providence, we lost Maria. You must choose between this Englishman and him to whom you are betrothed. If you marry the Englishman, you—and I, Adeline—will be put beyond the pale of Heaven. · Marry him who expects, ere three days, to be your husband, and you will lead a tranquil life here, with sure hope of a Hereafter."

"Does my mother know of this?" she asked.

"No. She will know it soon enough if your decision be against us."

"Oh papa, papa!" she burst forth, in momentary abandonment to the feelings that seemed to be killing her, "can I not live on with you and mamma always, unmarried?"

"You cannot, Adeline. The only child that is left to us must fulfil woman's appointed destiny on earth. And not shrink from it," he sternly added.

There was little more to be said, nothing more to be understood. She comprehended it all, and the situation she was placed in. She knew that, for her, all of peace and joy on earth was over. A mirror of the future flashed before her mind's eye: she saw herself battling with its waves, and it was one broad sea of never-ending agony. Her heart fluttered violently, as it had never before fluttered: there was a strange sensation within her, as of some mighty weight, some torment rushing to her brain. She tottered as she rose from the chair, and laid hold of the table to steady herself. "There—there is nothing more?" she whispered.

"Nothing, Adeline. Save to give your reply to Mr. St. John."

She was passing to the door when a word arrested her. She leaned against one of the secrétaires as her father spoke.

"I do not ask what your decision will be, Adeline. I have laid the case before you, as it exists, without circumlocution and without disguise. I said last night I would not bias your choice by a word of mine, and I will not."

The words sounded in her ear very like a mockery, and wild thoughts came across her, as she stood, of falling at her father's feet, and beseeching him to have mercy. But she remembered that mercy, for her, did not rest with him.

Signor de Castella became alarmed at her ghastly look. He went forward and took her hands, speaking with more emotion than he had ever betrayed.

"Adeline, may our holy Mother support you through this!

I have but your welfare at heart, and were your temporal interests alone in question, I would not oppose your inclinations. Child, I would give the half of my fortune, now, to ensure your happiness here. But—when it comes to pass that the interests of Eternity are at stake, no choice, as it seems to me, is left us. The Church has you in its keeping, and must be obeyed: I, at least, have no alternative: act, you, as you please. I have said that I would not coerce you; I do not. If your decision be against us, you shall depart for England to-day under the protection of your Aunt Agnes, who will remain and see you married. Hush! do not tell your decision to me; indeed, I am trying to keep my promise of leaving it entirely to you. Make your choice, and then give it to Mr. St. John."

He had released her as he was speaking. She was laying her hand upon the door, when her father spoke again. She turned towards him.

"There is one thing, Adeline. Whatever be your decision you must not impart the nature of the impediment to Mr. St. John."

"Not tell him the cause!" she gasped—and the very words spoke all too plainly of what the decision would be—"not tell him!"

"Holy saints, no!" he rejoined, his voice rising between surprise, anger, and emotion. "I had scarcely thought it necessary to caution you. Not a word must be breathed. Our Church permits not her modes of dealing to be revealed to—to heretics."

He had made a pause at the last word, as if unwilling to speak it. With all his coldness and his bigotry, he was an essentially courteous man at heart. Adeline clasped her hands in piteous beseeching, but he interrupted the prayer hovering upon her lips.

"*It must not be, Adeline:* Mr. St. John is not one of us. Surely you are not growing disaffected!" he continued, in a sharp tone. "It has occurred to me at times that I may have done wrong in allowing you to be so much here in your grandmother's home. When she married she quitted her Protestant faith and embraced ours, but I doubt whether she has ever been zealous in it at heart."

The tears shone in her eyes at the accusation, but she was too miserable, too agitated to let them fall.

"Only a hint to him, papa!" she implored. "Permit it to me in mercy. Only a hint!"

"Not a hint; not a word," he sternly rejoined. "I forbid it. The Church forbids it. Promise this."

"I promise," she faintly said, yielding to the compulsion.

"Kiss the crucifix."

He took down the small, beautiful image of our Saviour, in carved ivory, that was wont to hang over the mantelpiece, and held it to her lips. She did as she was told, and so sealed the secret.

There was nothing more. Adeline, a very ghost of despair, quitted the cabinet. Outside she encountered Rose.

"What a long time you have been in there!" was the young lady's eager exclamation. "Your wedding-dress is come, with lots more things, nearly a fourgon full, Louise says. They are gone upstairs to inspect them, and I have been waiting for you, all impatience. No reason why we should not admire them, you know, though matters are cross. But—Adeline!"

Adeline lifted her eyes at the sudden exclamation.

"How ill you look!"

"Is Mr. St. John in the drawing-room?" was the only rejoinder.

"He has been there this half-hour. I left him there, 'all alone in his glory,' for I could stay away from the view no longer. I shall go upstairs without you, if you are not coming."

"I will follow you presently," she murmured.

"Adeline, let me into a secret. I won't tell. Will the dress be worn for the purpose it was intended—de la Chasse's wedding?"

"Yes," she feebly answered, passing on to the west drawing-room.

Rose arrested her impatient steps, and gazed after her.

"Whatever is the matter? How strangely ill she looks! And she says the marriage is to come off with de la Chasse! I wonder whether that's gospel: or nothing but a blind? When the wedding-morning comes, we may find Jock o' Hazeldean enacted in real life. It would be glorious fun!"

Mr. St. John was pacing the room when Adeline went in. He met her with a sunny smile, and would have held her to him. But Adeline de Castella was possessed of extreme rectitude of feeling: and she now knew that in two days' time she should be the wife of the Baron de la Chasse. Alas! in spite of the fears that sometimes assailed her, she had, from the beginning, too surely counted on becoming the wife of Mr. St. John. She evaded him, and walked forward, panting for breath.

He was alarmed as he gazed upon her. He saw the agitation she was in; the fearful aspect of her features, which still wore the ghastly hue they had assumed in the cabinet. He took one of her hands within his, but even that she withdrew.

"In the name of Heaven, Adeline, what is this?"

She essayed to answer him, and could not. The palpitation in her throat impeded her utterance. The oppression on her breath increased.

"Adeline! have you no pity for my suspense?"

"I—I—am trying to tell you," she gasped out, with a jerk between most of her words. "I am going—to—marry *him*— de la Chasse."

He looked at her for some moments without speaking. "You have been ill, Adeline," he said at length. "I saw last night the state you were in, and would have given much to remain by you."

"I am not wandering," she answered, detecting the bent of his thoughts. "I am telling you truth. I must marry him."

"Adeline—if you are indeed in full possession of your senses —explain what you would say. I do not understand."

"It is easy enough to be understood," she replied, leaning against the side of the large window for support. "On Saturday, their fixed wedding-day, I shall marry him."

"Oh, this is shameful! this is dreadful!" he exclaimed. "How can they have tampered with you like this?"

"They have not tampered with me, Frederick. I decide of my own will."

"It is disgraceful! disgraceful!" he uttered. "Where is Signor de Castella? I will tell him what I think of his conduct. *He* talk of honour!"

She placed her hand upon his arm to detain him, for he was turning from the room. "He can tell you nothing," she said. "He does not yet know my decision. Do not blame him."

"He said last night that you should be free to choose," impatiently returned Mr. St. John.

"And I am free. He—laid"—(she hardly knew how to frame her words and yet respect her oath)—"he laid the case fully before me, and left me to decide for myself. Had I

chosen you, he said my Aunt Agnes should accompany us
to-day to England, and see me married. But—I—dared not
—I "—(she burst into a flood of most distressing tears)—" I
must marry de la Chasse."

" Explain, explain." He was getting hot and angry.

" I have nothing to explain. Only that my father left it to
me, and that I must marry him : and that my heart will break."

When he perfectly understood her, understood that there was
no hope, the burst of reproach that came from him was terrible.
Yet might it not be excused? He had parted from her on the
previous night in the full expectation that she would be his
wife : now could he think otherwise after all that had occurred,
and the concluding promise of M. de Castella? Yet now,
without preface, without reason, she told him that she re-
nounced him for his rival. A reason, unhappily, she dared
not give.

Oh, once more, in spite of her resistance, Mr. St. John held
her to his heart. He spoke to her words of the sweetest and
most persuasive eloquence; he besought her to fly with him,
to become his beloved wife. And she was obliged to wrest
herself from him, and assure him that his prayers were wasted ;
that she was compelled to be more obdurate than even her
father had been.

It was a fault, you know, of Mr. St. John's to be hasty and
passionate, when moved to it by any great cause ; but perhaps
a storm of passion so violent as that he gave way to now, had
never yet shaken him. His reproaches were keen : entirely
unreasonable : but an angry man does not weigh his words.

" False and fickle that you are, you have never loved me !
I see it all now. You have but led me on, to increase at the
last moment the triumph of de la Chasse. It may have been
a planned thing between you ! Your true vows have been
given to him, your false ones to me."

Adeline placed her hands on his, as if imploring mercy,
and would have knelt before him ; but he held her up, not
tenderly.

" If I thought you did not know your words are untrue, it
would kill me," she faltered. " Had we been married, as,
until this day, I thought and prayed we should be, you would
have known how entirely I love you ; how the love will endure
unto death. I can tell you this, now, because we are about to
separate, and it is the last time we must ever be together in

this world. Oh, Frederick! mercy! mercy!—do not profess to think I have loved another."

"You are about to marry him."

"I shall marry him, hating *him*; I shall marry him, loving *you*: do you not think I have enough of misery?"

"As I am a living man," spoke Mr. St. John, "I cannot understand this! You say your father told you to choose between us?"

"I feel as if I should die," she murmured; "I have felt so, at times, for several weeks past. There is something hanging over me, I think," she continued, passing her hand across her forehead, abstractedly.

"Adeline," he impatiently repeated, "are you deceiving me? *Did* your father give you free liberty to choose between us?"

"Yes; he gave it me—after placing the whole case before me," she was obliged to answer.

"And you tell me that you have deliberately chosen de la Chasse? You give me no explanation; but cast me off like this?"

"I dare not give it. That is"—striving to soften the words that were wrung from her—"I have no explanation to give. Oh, Frederick, *dearest* Frederick—let me call you so in your presence, for the first and last and only time—do not reproach me? Indeed, I must marry him."

"Of your own free deliberation, you will, on Saturday next, walk to the altar and become his wife?" he reiterated. "Do you mean to tell me that?"

She made a gesture in the affirmative, her sobs rising hysterically. What with her confused state of feeling, and the anxiety she was under to preserve inviolate the obligation so solemnly undertaken, she was perhaps even less explanatory than she might have been. But who, in these moments of agitation, can act precisely as he ought?

"Fie upon you! fie upon you!" he cried, contemptuously. " *You* boast of loving! you may well do so, when you had two lovers to practise upon. I understand it all, now; your objection to my speaking, until the last moment, to M. de Castella; you would keep us both in your train, forsooth, incense to your vanity! You have but fooled me by pretending to listen to my love; you have led me on, and played with me, a slave to be sacrificed on *his* shrine! I give you up to him joyfully. I am well quit of you.

"Mercy! mercy!" she implored, shrinking down, and clasping her hands together.

"Fool that I was to be so deceived! Light and fickle that you are, you are not worthy to be enshrined in an honourable man's heart. I will thrust your image from mine, until not a trace, not a recollection of it, is left. I thank God it will be no impossible task. The spell that bound me to you is broken. Deceitful, worthless girl, thus to have betrayed your false-heartedness at the last: but better for me to have discovered it before marriage than after. I thank you for this, basely treated as I have been."

She made an effort to interrupt him, a weak, broken-hearted effort; but his fierce torrent of speech overpowered it.

"I go now; and, in leaving this place, shall leave its memories behind. *I will never willingly think of you again in life.* Contemptuously as you have cast off me, so will I endeavour in my heart to cast off you, and all remembrance of you. I wish you good-bye, for ever. And I hope, for de la Chasse's sake, your conduct to him, as a wife, may be different from what it has been to me."

There was a strange, overwhelming agony, both of body and mind, at work within her, such as she had never experienced or dreamt of; a chaos of confused ideas, the most painful of which was the conviction that he was leaving her for ever in contempt and scorn. A wild desire to detain him; to convince him that at least she was not the false-hearted being he had painted her; to hear some kinder words from his lips, and *those* recalled, crowded to her brain, mixing itself up with the confusion and despair already there.

With his mocking farewell he had hastened from the room by way of the colonnade; it was the nearest way to the path leading to his home, and he was in no mood to stand upon ceremony. Adeline went after him, but his strides were quick, and she did not gain upon his steps. She called aloud to him, in her flood-tide of despair.

He turned and saw her, flying down the steps after him. One repellent, haughty gesture alone escaped him, and he quickened his pace onwards. She saw the movement of contempt; but she still pressed on, and got half-way across the lawn. There she sank upon the grass, at first in a kneeling posture, her arms outstretched towards him, as if they could bring him back, and a sharp, wailing cry of anguish escaping from her lips.

Why did he not look round? There was just time for it, ere he was hidden in the dark shrubbery: he would have seen enough to drive away his storm of anger. But waxing stronger in his wrath, he strode on, without deigning to cast another glance behind.

They were in the chamber over the western drawing-room, examining the things just arrived from Paris. Rose happened to be at the window, and saw Adeline fall. Uttering an exclamation, which caused Mary Carr also to look, she turned from it, and ran down to her. Mary followed, but her pace was slow, for she suspected nothing amiss, and thought Adeline had but stooped to look at something on the grass. When Mary reached the colonnade, Rose was up with Adeline, and seemed to be raising her head.

What was it? Miss Carr strained her eyes in a sort of bewildered wonder. Of their two dresses, the one was white, the other a delicate lilac muslin, and strange spots appeared on each of them, spots of a fresh bright crimson colour, that glowed in the sun. Were they spots of—*blood?* And—was Adeline's mouth stained with it? Mary turned sick as the truth flashed upon her. Adeline must have broken a blood-vessel.

Terrified, confused, for once Mary Carr lost her habitual presence of mind. She not only rang the bell violently, but she shrieked aloud, crying still as she hastened to the lawn. The servants came running out, and then the family.

Rose was kneeling on the grass, pale with terror, supporting Adeline's head on her bosom. Rose's hair, the ends of her long golden ringlets, were touched with the crimson, her hands marked with it; and Adeline—— Madame de Castella fell down in a fainting-fit.

Yes, she had broken a blood-vessel. The anguish, the emotion, too great to bear had suddenly snapped asunder one of those little tenures of life. Ah! the truth flashed upon more than one of those standing around her in their consternation— those frail lungs had but been patched up for a short time; not healed.

They bore her round, gently as might be, from the lawn into the yellow drawing-room, avoiding the steps of the colonnade, not daring to carry her up to the bed-chambers, and laid her on the costly, though somewhat old-fashioned and large sofa. What a sight she looked! the white face, the closed eyes, telling scarcely of life, and the red stains contrasting with the amber-velvet pillows. A groom went riding off to Odesque at full gallop—that is, as much of a gallop as French by-roads will allow—to bring back the Odesque doctor, the nearest medical man. He was also charged to send a telegraphic message to Belport for the French gentleman who had attended her in the spring; and *he* was requested to bring with him an English physician.

How prone are we to cheat ourselves! that is, to try to cheat ourselves. Signor de Castella, the first shock past, affected to talk cheerfully—cheerfully for him—of its being only a little vessel that had given way on the chest, not the lungs. Adeline lay on the sofa, passive. She was quite conscious, fully awake to all that was passing around her; as might be seen by the occasional opening of the eyes. Madame de Castella, really ill, as these impressionable natures are apt to be, was in her room, falling from one fainting-fit into another. Madame de Beaufoy sat with her; and the Signor, a most devoted husband, made repeated pilgrimages to the chamber. The poor old lady had taken one look at Adeline, and been led away by her maid, wringing her hands in shuddering dismay. So that in point of fact the yellow drawing-room was left very much to the two sympathizing, but terrified young ladies, the upper women-servants, and Aunt Agnes. As she lay there, poor child, the angry indignation cast upon her ever since the previous night calmed down. Better perhaps that they had let her go to her runaway wedding. It would not have much mattered either way: a loving bride, or a disappointed, unhappy girl, life for her could not last very long. How far the sense of shame, so ripe in her mind for the last few hours, had contributed its quota to the attack, will never be known. The most indignant of them all had been Agnes de Beaufoy; and *she* could not quite recover it yet.

Adeline turned her head as Rose was passing near her. "Am I dying?" she asked.

"Oh, Adeline, you must not speak!" was Rose's startled rejoinder. "The doctor will be here soon. Dying! of course you are not."

"Where's papa?"

"*Pray* don't attempt to speak! He was here a minute or two ago: he will be here again."

"Rose," came the soft whisper, in spite of the injunction,

"I think I am dying. I should like to see Frederick St. John. Only for a minute, tell him."

Rose, consulting no one, penned a hasty note to Mr. St. John, her tears dropping all the time : *she* also thought death was at hand. It was written in her own rather wild fashion, but was clear and peremptory. Louise was called out of the yellow drawing-room and despatched with it. And the time passed slowly on.

The most perfect quiet, both of mind and body, was essential for Adeline ; yet there she lay, evidently anxious, inwardly rest-less, her eyes seeking the door, expecting the appearance of Mr. St. John. But he did not come ; neither did Louise. Had Rose done well to pen that note ? Adeline was exhausted and silent, but not the less excited.

In came Louise at last, looking, as usual, fiery hot, her black eyes round and sparkling. Her proper course would have been to call Rose from the room ; but she stalked direct into the presence of Adeline, bringing her news. It happened that none of the elders were in the room at the moment : Signor de Castella had again gone to his wife's chamber ; and Miss de Beaufoy was outside the large entrance-door, looking in her impatience for signs of the doctor from Odesque. Louise had made haste to Madame Baret's and back, as desired, and came in at once, without waiting even to remove her gloves, the only addition (except the parapluie rouge) necessary to render her home-costume a walking one. What would an English lady's-maid say to that ? In her hand she bore a packet, or very thick letter, for Adeline, directed and sealed by Mr. St. John. Adeline followed it with her eyes, as Rose took it from Louise.

"Shall I open it ?" whispered Rose, bending gently over her.

Adeline looked assent, and Rose broke the seal, holding it immediately before her face. It was a blank sheet of paper, without word or comment, enclosing the letters she had written to him. They fell in a heap upon her, as she lay. Rose, at home in such matters, understood it as soon as Adeline, and turned with a frown to Louise.

" Did Mr. St. John give you this ?"

"Ah, no, mademoiselle. Mr. St. John is gone."

"Gone !"

"Gone away to England. Gone for good."

Rose gathered the letters into the sheet of paper, as if in abstraction, amusing herself by endeavouring to put together

the large seal she had broken. Truth was, she did not know
what to say or do. Adeline's eyes were closed, but she *heard*
—by the heaving bosom and crimsoned cheeks, contrasting
with their previous ghastly paleness. Louise, like a simpleton,
continued in an undertone to Rose, and there was no one by
to check her gossip.

"He had not been gone three minutes when I got there——
Oh, by the way, mademoiselle, here's the note you gave me for
him. Madame Baret was changing her cap to bring up the
thick letter, for Mr. St. John had said it was to be taken special
care of, and given into Mademoiselle Adeline's own hands, so
she thought she would bring it herself. She's in a fine way at
his going, is mother Baret, for she says she never saw any one
that she liked so much."

"But what took him off in this sudden manner?" demanded
Rose, forgetful of Adeline in her own eager curiosity.

"Madame Baret says she'd give her two ears to know," responded Louise. "She thought something must have happened
up here—a dispute, or some unpleasant matter of that sort.
But I told her, No. Something had occurred here unfortunately, sure enough, but it could have had nothing to do with
Mr. St. John, because he had left the château previously. She
then thought he might have received ill news from England;
though no letters came for him in the morning. But whatever
it might be, he was in an awful passion. He has spoilt the
picture."

"Which picture?" quickly asked Rose.

Before recording the answer, it may be well to explain that
Adeline's portrait had been finished long ago, and taken to the
château. But on the return of M. de Castella from Paris, he
had suggested some alteration in the back-ground and in the
drapery, so it was sent back to the Lodge. Events had then
crowded so fast, one upon another, coupled with Mr. St. John's
two visits to England, that the change was not at once effected.
During the last few days, however, St. John had been at work,
and completed it. Only the previous evening, when he was
secretly expecting to leave with Adeline, he had given orders
that it should be conveyed the next day to Beaufoy.

"Which picture?" was the impatient demand of Rose.

"Mademoiselle's likeness that he had been taking himself,"
answered Louise. "He went into the painting-room after he
got home just now, and began flinging his things together.

Madame Baret heard sounds and went to look who was there; but she only peeped in at the door, for she had not changed her night-cap, and there she saw him. There was some blue paint on a palette at hand, and he dabbed a wet brush in it and smeared it right across the face. My faith ! the way he must have been in, to destroy his own work. And such a beautiful face as he had made it ! "

A pause. Rose, in her astonishment, could only stare. She knew nothing, be it remembered, of the breach between him and Adeline. No one did know of it.

" I knew he could be furiously passionate on occasions," was her first remark. " I told him so one day."

" It was a shame, Madame Baret said in telling me, to vent his anger upon *that*," resumed Louise. " So senseless : and quite like an insult to Mademoiselle Adeline—just as if she had offended him. Of course I agreed with the Mère Baret that it *was* a shame, a wicked shame : and then, if you'll believe me, mademoiselle, she flew out at me for saying it, and vowed that nobody should speak a word against Mr. St. John in her hearing. He was of a perfectly golden temper, she went on, he always behaved like a prince to everybody, and she was sure something out of common must have occurred to shake him, for he seemed to be quite beside himself—to know no more what he was doing than a child."

Rose glanced at Adeline, whom, perhaps, she suddenly remembered. The crimson had faded on the wan cheeks ; the quivering eyes were closed. What effort might it be costing her, let us wonder, to lie there and make no sign ?

" I am sure *I* don't want to speak against him," continued Louise, in an injured tone, meant as a reproach for the absent mistress of the Lodge. " I only chimed in with the Dame Baret for politeness' sake—and what had taken her, to be so capricious, I can't think : one mood one minute, another the next. Mr. St. John was a thorough gentleman, always behaving like one to us servants : and you know, besides, Mademoiselle Rose, he spoke French like a true angel."

"Comme un vrai ange," were the maid's words. It may be as well to give them. Rose nodded.

" Which is what can't be said of most Englishmen," added Louise.

" But what has he gone away for so suddenly ? " questioned Rose.

"Nobody knows, mademoiselle. As he was going in, he met Victor—that lazy fellow Père Baret keeps about the place; *I* wouldn't—and ordered a horse to be got ready for him and brought round. Then he went into the painting-room, where Madame peeped in and saw him, but didn't show herself on account of her cap. He was in there ever so long, and then he went up to his chamber. By the time he came out his anger was over, and he was never more calm or pleasant than when he called to Dame Baret and gave her the packet for Mademoiselle Adeline, asking her to oblige him by bringing it up herself. Then he told her he was going to leave. She says you might have knocked her down with a whiff of old Baret's pipe. And I don't wonder at it; what with the unexpected news, and what with the consciousness of her cap, which she hadn't had time to change. It's not once in six months that Madame Baret's coiffure is amiss, but they have the sweeps to-day."

"Let her cap and the sweeps alone," cried Rose, impatiently. "I wish you'd go on properly, Louise."

"Well, mademoiselle, when Dame Baret had recovered the shock a little, she asked him whether he was going away for long, and when he should be back. He told her he should never come back; never; but would write and explain to M. d'Estival. He thanked her for all her attention, and said she and M. Baret should hear from him. With that he rode off; giving orders that his clothes and other things should be packed and sent after him, and leaving a mint of money for all who had waited on him."

"And where is he gone?" questioned Rose. "To England?"

"Mother Baret supposes so, mademoiselle. It's where his things are to be sent, at any rate. He is riding to Odesque now, so he must be going to take the train either for Paris or the coast."

It is impossible to say how much more Louise would have found to relate, and Rose to listen to, but the clattering hoofs of a horse were heard outside, and Louise hastened to the window, hoping it might be the surgeon from Odesque. Hazardous, perhaps, it had been for Adeline to listen to this: and yet well. As he *had* gone, it was better that she should know it; and be, so far, at rest.

The surgeon from Odesque it proved to be. Ah! how strangely do things fall out in this world! When the two horsemen had met in the road some half-hour before, each of them spurring his steed to its fleetest pace, and had exchanged a passing salutation of courtesy, how little was Mr. St. John conscious that the surgeon was speeding to her whom he had quitted in anger, against whom he was even then boiling over with resentment; speeding to her in her sore need, as she lay a-dying!

Not dying quite immediately; not that day, perhaps not for some short weeks; but still dying. Such was the fiat of the surgeon, as whispered to Miss de Beaufoy; from whom it spread to the awe-struck household. Some of them refused to receive it: M. de Castella for one; Rose for another. Well, the doctor answered, it was his fatal opinion; but no one would be more thankful than he to find it a mistaken one; and he was truly glad that other medical men were telegraphed for; he felt his responsibility.

He assisted to carry Adeline upstairs to her chamber. Very gently was she borne to it: and Rose carried the packet up after her, and put it away safely in the sight of Adeline. Of course the chief thing was to keep her perfectly quiet, mentally and bodily, the doctor said. If further hemorrhage could be prevented and the wound healed, she might—might go on. He spoke the words in a hesitating manner, as if himself doubting it: and Rose, who had stolen into the conference, which was taking place downstairs, said afterwards she should have liked to gag him.

Late in the evening, arrived the two doctors from Belport, le Docteur Dorré and an English physician. They were more reticent than the surgeon of Odesque had been, not saying that Adeline was in any sort of danger; not thinking it, so far as could be seen. The Englishman was old, the Frenchman comparatively young. Adeline was considerably better then, to all appearance: perhaps they did not really detect cause for alarm. She lay quite tranquil, smiled at them, and talked a little; neither did she look very ill, except that she was pale; and all traces of the sudden malady had been removed. Indeed the wild commotion of the morning had given place to a very different state of things. All was tranquil; and Madame de Castella was about again, and cheerful.

After the doctors had seen Adeline, they retired to a room alone, emerging from it after a few minutes' consultation. The chief thing, as the other one had said, was to keep her still and quiet; no talking, no excitement. One person alone must be in the room with her at a time; and that, as they strongly recommended, should be a sick-nurse. Madame de Castella assented eagerly, hanging, as it were, upon the very words that issued from their lips. Dr. Dorré spoke of the Englishwoman who had attended her in the spring: she had struck him as being one of the best and most efficient nurses he had ever in his life seen.

"I'll inquire after her the first thing to-morrow morning," said the young doctor; "I think I know her address: and I'll send her over."

They were to be over themselves also on the morrow, to meet the doctor from Odesque; for *their* visits could not be frequent. Belport was too far off to allow of their coming daily.

"See after Nurse Brayford!" exclaimed Rose, when this item of intelligence reached her ears after the doctors had departed. "It will be of no use, dear Madame de Castella. She went away with my sister, Mrs. Carleton St. John. They are travelling somewhere in Germany. Did I not tell you Charlotte had taken her?"

"But has she kept her all this time? The nurse may have returned."

"She *may*," replied Rose, speaking slowly in her deliberation. "I don't think she has, though. The last time I heard from London, from mamma, she said she feared dear Charlotte was being tried sadly, for that she never could get a letter from her now. Charlotte was always first and foremost with mamma, the rest of us nothing. It's more than she was with me, though," added Rose, lifting her nose in the air as she shook back her golden ringlets. "A domineering thing!"

"If the little child has got better, the nurse may have been dismissed," observed Madame de Castella, who now remembered to have heard the circumstances under which Nurse Brayford had been taken.

"But I fear he has not got better," answered Rose. "I fear he is getting worse. Mary Anne said so when she wrote to me. About the nurse we shall see: I hope, for Adeline's sake, she is back again."

It should have been mentioned that Signor de Castella had sent an express to the Baron de la Chasse, to arrest his journey to Beaufoy. But he came, nevertheless: much concerned, of course. He saw Adeline for a few minutes in the presence of her mother and aunt. It was on the very day they were to have been married. He was excessively shocked at her death-like appearance—to which there's not the least doubt the sight of himself contributed—but endeavoured to express many a kind hope of her speedy recovery, hinting that he was an interested party in it.

"She is very ill!" he exclaimed to Rose, when they met downstairs, before his departure.

"Very," lamented Rose. "And to think those beautiful wedding things, that were to have been worn to-day, are shut up out of sight in drawers and boxes!"

"Where's that presuming Anglais?" asked the Frenchman.

"Oh, he's gone back to his own country," replied Rose, carelessly. "Ages ago, it seem now. I don't think you and he need have quarrelled over her, Monsieur le Baron."

He detected her meaning—that Adeline would not live to belong to either—and he bent his head in sorrow, and stroked his silky yellow moustache, and began to speak in a feeling, thoughtful manner of her illness; of the mischief of the spring which had broken out again, when they had all deemed it cured. *He* had no idea, and never could have any, that this had been brought on by the misery and emotion that were too great to bear.

Meanwhile Mrs. Brayford had been sought for in vain. She was still absent from Belport, in attendance on the little heir of Alnwick. A French nurse came to Beaufoy to occupy her place. A tall, thin, dark-eyed, quick woman, dressed in black; kind enough, and very capable; but with a gossiping tongue that rivalled at least that of Louise.

CHAPTER XXVI.

THE SICK CHAMBER.

"DRAW aside the curtain, Rose," said Adeline de Castella, feebly. "The sun has passed."

You can take a look at her as she lies. Some few weeks have passed since the sad occurence just related, but there is no visible improvement in her appearance. Her face is wan, thinner than it was then, and dark circles have formed round

her eyes. There had been no recurrence of the alarming
symptoms from the lungs: indeed, the hurt seemed to have
healed itself immediately; but a great deal of fever had supervened, and this had left her in a sad state of weakness. The
doctors seemed a little puzzled at this condition of fever and
its continuance; some of those around her were not, but knew
it for the result of her unhappy state of mind. That consumption had set its seal upon her, there was no longer any
doubt, but it was thought probable the disease might linger in
its progress.

Rose and Mary were with her still. Adeline could not bear
to hear of their leaving. "They must spare you to me until
the end," she said, alluding to their friends, and the young
ladies seemed quite willing to accept the position. They were
her chief companions; the French nurse remained, but her
office was partly a sinecure, and just now she was occupied with
Madame de Beaufoy, who was confined to her bed with illness. Signor de Castella was in Paris on business—he always
seemed to have business on hand, but no one could ever quite
find out what it was. Agnes de Béaufoy sat much with her
mother. Madame de Castella was almost as ill as Adeline;
grieving, fretting, repining continually. She paid frequent
visits to Adeline's room, but seldom stayed in it long, for she
was apt to suffer her feelings to get ahead, and to become
hysterical. A frequent visitor to it was Father Marc; the
most cheerful, chatty, pleasant of all. He brought her no end
of entertaining anecdotes of the neighbourhood, and sometimes
succeeded in winning a smile from her lips. He never entered
with her upon religious topics, so far as the two young ladies
saw or heard; never appeared to anticipate that the end of
life's race was entered upon. Rose had put aside much of her
giddy vanity, and they all loved her. She was in bitter repentance for her unnecessary and exaggerated revelations
touching Sarah Beauclerc;—*there*, in her knowledge of that,
lay the keenest sting of Adeline's misery. Adeline remained
silent as to her inward life, silent as the grave; but something
had been gathered of it. She had more than once fallen into
a sort of delirium—I don't know any better name for it; partly
sleep, partly a talking and waking dream, and some painful
thoughts had been spoken in it. It always occurred at the
dusk of evening, and Adeline herself seemed unconscious of it
when she woke up to reality. You may meet with such a case

yourselves; when you do, suspect the patient's state of alarming bodily weakness.

Adeline's former chamber had been changed for one with a southern aspect. The bed was in a recess, as is customary in the country, or rather in a smaller room, for there were windows and two doors in it. A large cheerful chamber, or sitting-room, the chief, the windows lofty, the fire-place handsome, the little Turkey-carpet mats, scattered on the polished floor, of bright colours. Adeline's sofa just now faced the windows; it was light, and could be turned easily any way on its firm castors; Madame de Castella leaned back in an easy-chair, nearly as pale and worn as Adeline; Mary Carr was working; Rose listlessly turned over the leaves of one of the pretty books lying on the large round table.

"Draw aside the curtain, Rose," Adeline said. "The sun has passed."

Rose drew it aside. An hour or so before, the weak, watery sun had come forth from behind the lowering grey clouds and sent his beams straight into Adeline's eyes, so they had shut him out. Diminished in force though the rays were, they were yet too bright for the invalid's sight. Surely, when you come to think of it, there was a singular affinity between the weather and Adeline's health and happiness. Cold, wet, boisterous, and gloomy had it been in the spring, during the time of her long illness, up to the period, within a few days, of her arrival at Beaufoy and commencing intimacy with Frederick St. John; warm, brilliant and beautiful it was all through the months of that intimacy; but with its abrupt termination, the very day subsequent to the miserable one of his departure and of Adeline's dangerous accident, it had abruptly changed, and become cold, wet, dreary again. Weeks, as you have heard, had elapsed since, and the weather still wore the same gloomy aspect, in which there seemed no prospect of amendment on this side winter. A feeling of awe, almost of superstition, would creep over Mary Carr, as she sat by Adeline's bedside in the dim evenings, listening to the moaning, sighing wind, as it swept round the unprotected château and shook off the leaves from the nearly bare trees on the western side. It sounded so like a dirge for the dying girl who was passing from them! The watchers would look up with a shiver, and say how dreary it was, this gloomy weather, and wish it would change, forgetting that the sweetest summer's day, the brightest skies, cannot bring joy to a house where joy exists not, or renew the peace of a heart from which hope has flown. Very fanciful all this, no doubt, you will say; what has the weather to do with events in this busy world of ours? Nothing, of course. Still, it had been a curious year; winter, summer, and now winter again; but neither spring nor autumn.

As Rose drew aside the curtain, humming a scrap of a song at the same time, for she was always gay, and nothing could take it out of her, Adeline left the sofa where she had been lying, and sat down near the fire in any easy-chair of white dimity.

"Mamma," she said, catching sight of Madame de Castella's lifeless, sickly aspect, "why do you not go out? It is not raining to-day, and the fresh air would do you good."

"Oh, Adeline," sighed the unhappy mother, "nothing will do me good while I see you as you are."

"Now, Madame de Castella!" remonstrated Rose. "You persist in taking a wrong view of things! Adeline is getting better and stronger every day."

True, in a degree. But would it last? Perhaps Rose herself, in her inmost heart, knew that it would not. Madame de Castella rose abruptly, and quitted the room; and Rose gave a shrug to her pretty shoulders. There were times, as she privately confided to Mary Carr, when she could have shaken Madame for her line of conduct. She vented her anger just now on the pillow behind Adeline's back, knocking it unmercifully, under the plea of smoothing it to comfort.

"I'm putting it straight for you, Adeline."

"No matter, dear Rose. It will do very well. Thank you all the same."

"I wish you'd taste this jelly; it's delicious."

"But I don't care for it; I don't care to eat," was the apathetic reply.

"Shall I read to you?" asked Rose.

"As you will, dear Rose; it seems all one to me. But thank you very much."

Thus had she been all along; thus she continued. Quiet, passive, grateful for their cares, but showing no interest in any earthly thing. No tidings whatever had been heard of Mr. St. John since he left; what quarter of the known world he might be in, whether or not he was aware of Adeline's state, they could not conjecture. It was assumed that he was in London;

Adeline, for one, never thought of doubting it. All this while, and not a single remembrance from him!

Rose went to the table, turned over the books collected there, and took up a volume of Tennyson.

"Not that," said Adeline, quickly glancing up with a faint colour. "Something else."

No, not that. *He* had given her the book, and been accustomed to read it to her. How could she bear to hear it read by another?

Rose tried again: Béranger. "That won't do," she said. "A pretty laugh you would have at my French accent!"

"Your accent is not a bad one, Rose."

"It may pass in conversation. But to read poetry aloud in any language but one's own, is—— What's this?" continued Rose, interrupting herself as she opened another volume; which she as quickly dropped again. It was Bulwer's "Pilgrims of the Rhine."

"That will do as well as another," said Adeline.

"No," shortly answered Rose, avoiding the book with a gesture that was half a shrug and half a shudder. Adeline stretched out her hand and drew her near, speaking in a low murmuring tone.

"You fear to remind me of myself, Rose, in telling of Gertrude. Indeed, there is no analogy to be traced between the cases," she added, with a bitter smile, "save in the nature of the disease; and that we must both die. One might envy *her* fate."

"I don't like the book," persisted Rose.

"I do," said Adeline. "One tale in it I could never be tired of. I forget its title, but it begins, 'The angels strung their harps in Heaven, and the——'"

"I know," interrupted Rose, rapidly turning over the pages. "Here it is. 'The Soul in Purgatory; or, Love stronger than Death.' It is a tale of woman's enduring love."

"*And its reward*," sighed Adeline. "Read it. It is very short."

Rose began her reading. It was quite impossible to tell whether Adeline listened or not: she sat silent, in her chair, her hand over her face; and, when it was over, she remained in the same position, making no comment, till the nurse came in to give the medicine.

"I'm not wanted in there just now," said she, with that

freedom of manner which is so characteristic of the depen-
dents in a French family, but which is never offensive, or even
borders on disrespect; "so I'll sit here a bit."

"You can wheel the sofa nearer to the fire, nurse," said
Adeline.

It was done, and Adeline lay down upon it. Rose began
another tale, and read till dusk.

"Shall I stir the fire into a blaze, Adeline, and finish it now;
or wait until candle-light?"

There came no answer. Mary Carr stole forward and bent
over Adeline. She had fallen asleep. Stay: not sleep; but
into one of those restless, dreamy stupors akin to it. The
thought had more than once crossed them—did that Odesque
doctor, who chiefly saw to the medicine, put laudanum in it,
and were these feverish wanderings the result? The uncertain
light of the wood fire played fitfully upon Adeline's face, re-
vealing its extreme beauty of feature and its deathly paleness.
Rose closed her book; and Mary left Adeline's sofa, and stood
looking through the window on the dreary night. The nurse,
who had dropped into a doze herself, soothed by the monotonous and incomprehensible tones of the foreign tongue, rose
and went downstairs for some wood.

Mary Carr had laid her finger with a warning gesture on
Rose Darling's arm, for sounds were heard from Adeline.
Turning from the darkened window where they had been hold-
ing a whispered colloquy, they held their breath to listen.
Very distinct were the words in the silence of the room:

"Don't say it! don't say it!" murmured Adeline. "I tell
you there is no hope. He has been gone too long: one—two
—three—four—do you think I have not counted the weeks?—
Why does he not come?—Why does he not write?—What's
this? My letters? thrust back upon me with scorn and insult!
—What is he whispering to Sarah Beauclerc? Oh, mercy!
mercy!"

The nurse re-entered the room, her arms laden with wood.
By some mishap she let a log fall to the floor, and the noise
aroused Adeline. Rose ran to the sofa, her eyes full of tears.

"Oh, Adeline," she sighed, leaning over her, "you should not
take it so heavily to heart. If things were at an end between
you and Mr. St. John, there was something noble rather than
the contrary in his returning you your letters. Indeed, we have
always seen him honourable in all he does. Another might

have kept them—have boasted of them—have shown them to the world. I only wish," broke off Rose, going from Adeline's affairs to her own, in the most unceremonious way, "that I could get back all the love-letters I have written! What a heap there'd be of them!"

"What do you mean?" demanded Adeline, sitting up on the sofa in her alarm. "Have I been saying anything in my sleep?"

"Not much—only a few words," said Mary Carr, stepping forward and speaking in a calm, soothing tone, a very contrast to Rose's excited one. "But we can see how it is about Mr. St. John, Adeline. He left in ill-feeling, and the inward grief is killing you by inches. If your mind were at rest, time might restore you to health; but, as it is, you are giving yourself no chance of life."

"There is no chance for me," she answered; "you know it. If I were happy as I once was, as I once thought I should be; if I were even married to Mr. St. John, there would be no chance of prolonged life for me; none."

Mary Carr did know it; but she strove to soothe her still.

"I might have expected all that has happened to me," smiled Adeline, trying to turn the subject to a jest, the first approach to voluntary smile or jest they had marked on her lips. "Do you remember your words, Rose, on that notable first of January, my ball-night—that some ill-fate was inevitably in store for me?"

"Rubbish!" said Rose. "I was an idiot, and a double idiot: and I don't remember it."

But Rose did remember it, all too vividly. She remembered how Adeline had laughed in ridicule, had spurned her words, then; in her summer-tide of pride and beauty. It was winter with her now!

There could be no further erroneous opinions on the point. Physically, she was dying of consumption, as a matter of course, and as the doctors said: but was she not just as much dying of a broken heart? The cruel pain was ever torturing her: though her lungs had been strong and healthy, it might have worked its work.

I hardly know how to continue this portion of the history, and feel a great temptation to make a leap at once to its close. Who cares to read of the daily life of a sick-chamber? There is so little variation in it: there was so little in hers. Adeline better or worse; the visits of the doctors, and their opinions; a change in her medicine, pills for mixture, or mixture for pills; and there you have about the whole history. Which medicine, by the way, was ordered by the English physician. A French one never gives any. He would not prescribe one dose, where the English would choke you with five hundred. It is true. Pills, powders, mixture; mixture, powders, pills: five hundred at the very least, where a Frenchman would give none. Warm baths and fasting in abundance they order, but no medicine. They are uncommonly free with the lancet, however; with leeches; with anything else that draws blood. The first year Eleanor Seymour (if you have not forgotten her) was at school at Madame de Nino's, an illness broke out amidst the pupils, and the school medical attendant was sent for. It was this very Dr. Dorré, now attending Adeline de Castella. Five or six of the younger girls seemed heavy and feverish, and there were signs of an eruption on the skin. Monsieur le docteur thought it would turn out to be measles or scarlatina, he could not yet pronounce which; and he ordered them to bed and to take a few quarts of eau sucrée: he then sent for the rest of the pupils one by one, and bled them all round.* "A simple measure of precaution," he said to Madame.

If this history of the sick-chamber is to be continued, we must borrow some extracts from the diary of Mary Carr. A good thing she kept one: otherwise there would have been little record of this earlier period in the closing scenes of life.

Meanwhile it may be as well to mention that a sort of wild wish—in its fervour it could be called little else—had taken hold of Adeline: she wanted to return to Belport. Every one at first opposed it. The cold would be greater in the seaport town than it was at Beaufoy; and the journey might do her harm. There appeared to be only one consideration in its favour; but that was a strong one: they would be on the spot with the doctors. She seemed to get better and stronger. Signor de Castella came home and was astonished at the improvement. Perhaps it was what he had not looked for.

EXTRACT FROM THE DIARY OF MARY CARR.

Nov. 3rd.—What *can* make her so anxious to return to Belport? She is growing feverish about it, and the Signor and

* A fact, in all its details.

Madame see that she is. Rose has been offering to bet me a pair of gloves that it will end in our going. I hope it will. This house seems to be dedicated to illness. Madame de Beaufoy does not improve, and one of the servants has taken gastric fever.

Belport, Belport! It is the one wish of her existence; the theme of her daily prayer. Has she an idea that she may there be in the way of hearing of *him*, perhaps of seeing him? Or is it that she would bid adieu to this place, hoping to bid adieu at the same time to its remembrances?

She is so much better! She comes downstairs now, dressed as she used to be, except the hair. It is braided under a pretty little lace cap: the French are such people for keeping the head warm! Often on her shoulders she wears a light cashmere shawl: the one she put on the night when she attempted to go away with Mr. St. John. "I wonder if she thinks of it?" I said yesterday to Rose. "What a donkey you are!" was the complimentary reply: "as if she did not think of that miserable night and its mishaps continually!"

We now know that Mr. St. John is in London. In looking over the *Times*—which comes regularly to Madame de Beaufoy —I saw his name amidst a host of others, as having attended a public meeting: Frederick St. John, Esq., of Castle Wafer. I put the paper into Adeline's hand, pointing to the list, and then quitted the room. On my return to it the journal was lying on the table, and her face was buried amidst the cushions of the armchair.

Is this improvement to turn out a deceitful one? It might not, but for the ever-restless, agitated mind. A calm without, a torrent within! The weakness is no longer apparent; the cough is nearly gone. But she is inert and indifferent as ever; buried within herself. This apparently languid apathy, this total indifference to life and its daily concerns, is set down by her friends to bodily weakness; and so they let it remain unchecked and unaroused, and she indulges, unmolested, in all the bitter feelings of a breaking heart.

6th.—These last few fine days have afforded the pretext for complying with Adeline's wish, and here we are, once more, at Belport, she wonderfully improved. Still better, still better! for how long? Rose has resumed her wild gaiety of spirits, and says she will sing a *Te Deum* for having left the dreary old château and its ghosts behind us.

A bed has been placed on the first-floor for Adeline, in the back drawing-room. This is better; for she can now reach the front drawing-room, where we sit, without being exposed to the cold air of the staircase. And should she be confined to her room at the last, as may be expected, it will be more convenient for the servants; and indeed in all respects.

7th.—Madame de Nino called to-day, bringing two of the elder girls. Adeline asked them innumerable questions about the school, and seemed really awakened to interest. Many other friends have also called; compared with the gloomy solitude of the château, each day since our arrival has been like a levee. The doctors apparently see no impropriety in this, for they don't forbid it. *I* think Adeline is better for it: she has not the leisure to brood so entirely over the past. She is still silent on the subject of her misery, never hinting at it. Mr. St. John's name is not mentioned by any one, and the scenes and events of the last six months might be a dream, for all the allusion ever made to them. Never was she so beautiful as she is now; delicate and fragile of course, but that is a great charm in woman's loveliness. Her features are more than ever conspicuous for their exquisite contour, her soft brown eyes are of a sweeter sadness, her cheeks glow with a transparent rose colour. Visitors look at her with astonishment, almost question the fact of her late dangerous illness, and say she is getting well. But there is no exertion: listless and inanimate she sits, or lies, her trembling, fevered hands holding one or other of the English journals—looking in them for a name that she never finds.

Yesterday Rose was reading to her in a volume of Shelley, when a letter from England was brought in, its superscription in the handwriting of Mrs. Darling. Adeline looked up, eager and flushed, signing to Rose to open it. Madame de Castella has stared in her ladylike way at this betrayed emotion whenever letters come for Rose. *We* understand it: and Rose always reads them to her. The Darlings are in London, know people that Mr. St. John knows, and Adeline thinks there may be a chance that his name will be mentioned in these letters. "The letter will keep," said Rose, glancing cursorily into it; and she laid it down and resumed her book.

> "I love, but I believe in love no more,
> I feel desire, but hope not. Oh, from Sleep
> Most vainly must my weary brain implore
> Its long-lost flattery now: I wake to weep,

> And sit, the long day, gnawing through the core
> Of my bitter heart——"

I looked up at her, involuntarily, it was so applicable; Rose also made a momentary stop, and her glance wandered in the same direction. Adeline's eyes met ours. It was one of those awkward moments that will happen to all; and the flush on Adeline's cheek deepened to crimson. It was very applicable:

> " I wake to weep,
> And sit, the long day, gnawing through the core
> Of my bitter heart."

Alas! alas!

Rose's letter contained ill news of the Darling family. Her quick sight saw what it was, and she hastened to put the letter up, not caring to speak of it at once to Adeline. Really she is growing more cautious than she used to be! That poor little child, the heir, in whose life was bound up so much of worldly prosperity, is dead: he died more than a week ago. Rose is in a state of what she is pleased to call "dumps." Firstly, for the child's own sake: she never saw him but once, this summer at Belport, but took a real liking for the little fellow; secondly, because Rose has orders to put herself into mourning. If Rose hates one thing in this world more than another, it is a black bonnet.

Adeline was standing by the fire to-day when the English physician came in. He was struck with the improvement in her looks. "You are cheating us all," he said. "We shall have a wedding yet."

"Or a funeral, doctor," quietly answered Adeline.

"I speak as I think," he seriously said. "I do believe that now there is great hope of your recovery. If we could but get you to the South!"

"Adeline," I exclaimed, as the physician went out, and she and I were alone, "you heard what he said. Those words were worth a king's ransom."

"They were not worth a serf's," was her reply. "I appreciate his motives. He imagines that the grave must of necessity be a bitter and terrible prospect, and is willing to cheer me with hopes, whether they prove true or false: as all doctors do; it is in their trade. But he knows perfectly well that I must die."

"How calmly you speak! One would think you *coveted* the approach of death!"

"Well—I don't know that I regret it."

"Has life no longer a charm for you? Oh, that you had never met Frederick St. John!"

"Don't say so! He came to me in mercy."

A burst of tears succeeded to the words, startling me nearly out of my senses.

"There! that's your fault," she cried, with a wretched attempt at gaiety. "In talking of regret, you made me think of my dear papa and mamma. Their grief will be dreadful."

"Oh, Adeline, *don't* try to turn it off in this way," I stammered, not knowing what to say, and horribly vexed with myself. "What do you mean—that he came to you in mercy with this wretchedness upon you, the crushed spirit, the breaking heart? I see what you go through day by day, night by night. Is there any cessation to the pain? Is it not as one never-ending anguish?"

Adeline was strangely excited; her eyes glistening, her cheeks a burning crimson, and her white, fragile, feverish hands fastening upon mine.

"It is all you say," she whispered. "And now he is with another!"

"I can understand the misery *that* thought brings."

"No, you can't. If my heart were laid bare before you, and you saw the wretchedness there as it really is, it would appear to you all as the mania of one insane; and to him as to the rest."

"And yet you say this has come to you in mercy!'

"It has—it has. I see it all now. How else should I have been reconciled to die? The germs of consumption must have been in me from the first," she concluded, after a pause. "You schoolgirls used to tell me I inherited all the English characteristics; and consumption, I suppose, made one of them."

9th.—Miss de Beaufoy is here for a day or two, and we had a quiet little soirée yesterday evening. Aunt Agnes, in the plentitude of her delight at the improvement visible in Adeline, limped down, poor lady in a splendid canary-coloured silk gown, all standing on end with richness. Who should come in unexpectedly after tea, but Monsieur le Comte le Coq de Monty! (I do love, after the fashion of the good Vicar of Wakefield, to give that whole name—*I*, not Miss Carr). Business with the Sous-Préfet brought him to Belport. He inquired very *mal à propos*, whether we had recently seen or heard of Mr. St. John ; and while we were opening our mouths, deliberating what to say, Rose, always apt and ready, took upon herself evasively to answer that he was in England, at Castle Wafer. Adeline's face was turned away, but the rest of the family looked glum enough. De Monty, very unconsciously, but not the less out of time and tune, entered into a flowery oration in praise of Mr. St. John, saying he was the most attractive man he ever came in contact with ; which, considering St. John is an Englishman, and de Monty French, was very great praise indeed.

She looked so lovely this morning, as she sat in the great chair, that I could not forbear an exclamation. But it is all the same to her, admiration and indifference ; nothing arouses her from that dreamy apathy.

"Ours is a handsome family," she answered. "See how good-looking papa is ! I have inherited his features."

Not the slightest sign of gratified vanity as she spoke. All *that* had passed away with Frederick St. John.

That Signor de Castella was excessively handsome, I did not deny ; but she was much more so.

"The complexion makes a difference," said Adeline, in answer. "Papa is pale ; sallow you may term it, and in complexion I am like mamma. She owes hers, no doubt, to her English origin. You never saw a Frenchwoman with that marvellous complexion, at once brilliant and delicate."

I marvelled at her wondrous indifference. "You were formerly sufficiently conscious of your beauty, Adeline ; you seem strangely callous to it now."

"I have outlived many feelings that were once strong within me. Vanity now for *me* !"

"Outlived ? It is a remarkable term for one of your age."

"It is appropriate," she rejoined, quickly. "In the last few months I have aged years."

"Can this be ?"

"You have read of hair turning grey in a single night," she whispered ; "it was thus with my feelings. *They* became grey. I was in a dream so blissful that the earth to me was as one universal paradise ; and I awoke to reality. That awaking added the age of a whole life to my heart."

"I cannot understand this," I said. And I really can't.

"I hope you never will. Self-experience alone could enlighten you, nothing else; not all the books and arguments in the world."

"You allude to the time when Mr. St. John went away in anger."

"Not so," she murmured, scarcely above her breath. "When I learnt that he loved another."

"I think it is fallacy, that idea of yours, Adeline," I said, determined to dispute it for her own sake. "How could he have cared for Sarah Beauclerc and for you at the same time? He could not love you both."

"No, he could not," she said, a vivid, painful flush rising to her cheeks. "But he knew her first, and he is with her now. Can you draw no deduction?"

"We don't know where he is," I said. "Was your sister good-looking, Adeline?"

"Maria was beautiful," she replied. "We were much alike, resembling papa in feature, and mamma in figure and complexion."

"And she also died of consumption. What an insidious disease it is! How it seems to cling to particular families!"

"What is running in your head now, Mary? Maria died of scarlet fever. She was delicate as a child, and I believe they feared she might become consumptive. I don't know what grounds they had to judge by: perhaps little other than her fragile loveliness."

"If consumption is fond of attacking great beauties, perhaps Rose will go off in one."

"Rose!" answered Adeline—and there was a smile on her lip—"if Rose goes off in anything, it will be in a coach-and-four with white favours."

And so the days pass on; Adeline, I fear, not really better. To look at her, she is well—well, and very lovely; but so she was before. If they could but get her to the South! But with this winter weather it is impossible: the doctors say she would die on the road. If they had but taken advantage, while they might have done it, of the glorious summer weather! If!—if! —if! These "ifs" follow too many of us through life; as they may henceforth follow the Signor and Madame de Castella.

CHAPTER XXVII.

THE LITTLE CHILD GONE.

You have not failed to notice the one item of news in Miss Carr's diary—the death of a little heir—or to recognize it for the young heir of Alnwick.

Since quitting Belport, Mrs. Carleton St. John had pursued the same course of restless motion until within two or three weeks of the final close. Whether she would have arrested her wandering steps then of her own accord, must be a question; but the sick-nurse, Mrs. Brayford, interfered. "You are taking away every chance for his life, madam," she said, one day. "If you persist in dragging the child about, I must leave you, for I cannot stay to see it. It will surely prove fatal to him before his time."

A sharp cry escaped from Mrs. St. John as she listened. The words seemed to tear the flimsy make-believe veil from her eyes: the end was very near: and who knows how long she had felt the conviction? They had halted this time at Ypres, a city of Belgium, or West Flanders, famous for its manufactures of cloths and serges. Handsome apartments were hastily procured, and George was moved into them. Not very ill yet did the child appear; only so terribly worn and weak. Mrs. St. John's anguish, who shall tell of it? She loved this child, as you have seen, with a fierce, jealous love. He was the only being in the world who had filled every crevice of her proud and impassioned heart. It was for his sake she had hated Benja; it was by Benja's death—and she alone knew whether she had in any shape contributed to that death, or whether she was wholly innocent—that he had benefited. That some dread was upon her, apart from the child's state, was evident—clinging to her like a nightmare.

The disease took a suddenly decisive form the second day after their settling down at Ypres, telling of danger, speaking palpably of the end. He could not have been moved from Ypres now, had it been ever so much wished for. Mrs. St. John called in, one after another, the chief doctors of the town; she summoned over at a great expense two physicians from London; she sent an imperative mandate to Mr. Pym; and

not one of them saw the slightest chance of saving the boy's
life.   She watched his fair face grow paler; his feverish limbs
waste and become weaker.   She never shed a tear.   For days
together she would be almost unnaturally calm; but once or
twice a burst of anguish had broken from her, fearful in itself,
painful to witness.   One of these paroxysms was yielded to in
the presence of the child.   Yielded to? Poor thing! perhaps
she could not help it!   George was frightened almost to death.
She flung herself about the large old foreign room as one
insane, tearing her hair, and calling upon the child to live—
to live.

"Mamma, don't, don't!" panted the little lad, in his terror.
"Don't be so sorry for me!   I am going to heaven, to be with
Benja."

At his first cry she had stopped and fallen on her knees
beside him.   Up again now; up again at the words, and
darting about as if possessed by a demon, her hands to her
temples.

"Oh, mamma, don't frighten me," shrieked the child.   "I
shall be glad to go to Benja."

Cease, Georgy, cease! for every innocent word that you utter
seems but renewed torture to your poor mother.   Look at her,
as she sinks down there on the floor, and groans aloud in her
sharp agony.

It was on the day of this outbreak, an hour or two after it,
that Mr. Pym arrived.   The good man, utterly innocent of
French, and not accustomed to foreign travel—or indeed to
much travelling of any sort, for he was quite a fixture at
Alnwick—had contrived to reach Ypres some two days later
than he should have done; having been taken off, perplexity
alone knew whither.   In the first place, he had called the town
"Wypers"—which was not the surest way of getting to Ypres.
However, here he was at last, a little ruffled certainly, and confused in mind, but on the whole thankful that he was found,
and not lost for good.

George was lying on some pillows when the surgeon entered;
a very wan, white, feeble George indeed—a skeleton of a
George.   But he held out his little transparent hand, with a
glad smile of welcome at the home-face.

"I've not forgotten you!" he panted, his poor breath very
short and laboured now.   "Mamma said you were coming;
she thought you'd come yesterday."

"Ay, so did I. But I—lost my way, Georgy."

Mr. Pym drew a chair close to the boy, and sat looking at him. Perhaps he was thinking that in all his practice he had rarely seen a child's frame so completely worn. But a few days of life were left in it; perhaps not that. The blue eyes, large and lustrous, were cast up at the surgeon's face; the hot fragile hand lay passively in the strong firm palm.

"Did you see Benja's pony?"

"Benja's pony!" mechanically repeated the doctor, whose thoughts were far away from ponies. "I think it is still in the stable at Alnwick."

"I was to ride it when I went home. Prance said so. Grandmamma said so. I wanted to go home to ride it; and to see Brave; but I'm not going now."

"Not just yet," said the surgeon. "You are not strong enough, are you, Georgy? How is mamma?"

"I'll tell Mrs. St. John that you are here, sir!" interposed a respectable-looking woman, rising from a chair at the other end of the large room.

It startled Mr. Pym. He had not observed that any one was present. She went out and closed the door.

"Who was that, George?"

"It's Mrs. Brayford!"

"Oh, ay; Nurse Brayford. I heard of her from Mrs. Darling."

"Mamma won't let her be called nurse. She said I did not want a nurse. We call her Brayford. Have you seen Benja?" continued the lad, speaking better, now that the excitement arising from the doctor's entrance had subsided; but with the last words his voice insensibly dropped to a low tone.

"Seen Benja!" echoed Mr. Pym, in his surprise. "Do you mean Benja's tomb? It is a very nice one: on rather too large a scale, though, for my taste, considering his age."

"No," said George; "I mean Benja."

"Why, child, how could I see Benja? He is gone away from our eyes; he is safe in heaven."

"Mamma sees him."

"Oh no, she does not," said Mr. Pym, after a slight pause.

"But she does," persisted Georgy. "She sees him in the night, and she lays hold of me and hides her face. She sees the lighted church; it blazes up sometimes."

There was a curious look of speculation in Mr. Pym's eyes as he gazed at the unconscious speaker. "Mamma dreams," he said; "as we all do. Do you remember my old horse Bob, Georgy? Well, he died this summer, poor fellow, of old age. I dream of him some nights, Georgy; I think he's carrying me along the road at a sharp trot."

Georgy's imaginative young mind, quickened by bodily weakness, took hold of the words with interest. "Do you see his saddle and bridle, Mr. Pym?"

"His saddle, and bridle, and stirrups, and all; and his old mane and tail. They had grown so grey, Georgy. He was a faithful, hard-working servant to me: I shall never have his like again."

"Have you got another horse? Is his name Bob?"

"I have another, and his name's Jack. He's not a second Bob, Georgy. When he has to stand before people's doors in my gig, he gets impatient and begins to dance. One day when I was on him, he tried to throw me, and we had a fight for the mastery: another day, when I wanted him to turn down Bell-yard, he wished to walk into the brush-shop, and we had another fight."

Georgy laughed, with all the little strength left in him. "I wouldn't keep him. Benja's pony never did all that."

"Well, you see, Georgy, I am trying to train him into better ways; that's why I keep him. But he's a naughty Jack."

"Why shouldn't you have Benja's pony? I'm sure mamma would give it you: she says she doesn't care what becomes of anything left at Alnwick. It was for me; but I'm not going back now; I'm going to heaven."

"Ah, my little generous lad, Benja's pony would not carry me; I'm heavier than you and Benja. And what about the French tongue, Georgy? Are you picking it up?"

"It's not French they talk here," said Georgy; "it's Flemish. We have two Flemish servants, and you should hear them jabbering."

Mr. Pym stroked back the child's flaxen hair: to his touch it felt damp and dead. In mind, in speech, he seemed to have advanced quite three years, though it was not yet a twelvemonth since he quitted Alnwick.

The door opened, and Mrs. St. John came into the room. Not the anguished excited woman who had gone into that insane paroxysm an hour or two before; but a cold high-bred gentlewoman, whose calm exterior and apparently impassive feelings were entirely under self-control. Her dark hair, luxuriant as ever, was elaborately dressed, and her black silk gown was of rich material and the most fashionable make.

"I have been expecting you these two days," she said as she advanced. "I thought this morning you must have given up all intention of coming, and I looked for a letter instead."

"Ah," said Mr. Pym, holding out his hand to her, "I got lost, as I have been telling Georgy. Never was abroad before in my life : never got puzzled by any language but once, and that was in Wales."

She heard nothing in the sentence except the one word, "Georgy."

"How do you think he is looking, Mr. Pym?"

"Well—there might be more flesh upon his bones," was all the surgeon answered, his tone bordering upon jocularity rather than dismay. Doubtless he knew what he was about.

"I thought, if any one could do him good, it was you," said Mrs. St. John. "The doctors here say they cannot; the physicians I had over from London said they could not, and went back again : and then I sent for you."

"Ah, yes," answered Mr. Pym, in an unmeaning tone. "I'm glad to see my little friend again. Georgy and I always got on well together, except on the score of physic. Do you remember those powders, Georgy, that you and I used to have a battle over?"

"Don't I!" answered Georgy. "But you won—you made me take them."

The surgeon laughed.

"Can you give him some powders now?" asked Mrs. St. John; and there was nothing of eagerness in her voice and manner, only in her glittering eyes.

"I'm not sure that it is exactly powders he requires now," was the answer, spoken in evasion. "We'll see."

Mrs. St. John walked to the distant window and stood there. For a moment her face was pressed against its cold glass, as one whose brow is in pain; the next, she stood up—tall, haughty, commanding; not a symptom of care upon her handsome face, not a shade of sorrow in her resolute eye. It is very probable that this enforced self-control, persisted in as long as Mr. Pym was at Ypres, cost her more than even he dreamt of.

Turning her head, she beckoned to the surgeon. Mr. Pym, waiting only to cover George with the silken coverlet, for the boy had settled down on his pillow exhausted, and seemed inclined to sleep, approached her. The house on this side faced the green fields; there was no noise, no bustle; all that was on the other side. A quaint old Flemish tower and clock, from which the hands were gone, stared them in the face at a field's distance : the Flemish cook had tried to make Prance understand that it was about to be taken down, when that fastidious lady's-maid protested against its ugliness.

"I have sent for you for two purposes, Mr. Pym," began Mrs. St. John, taking a seat, and motioning the surgeon to another, both of them beyond the reach of George's ears. "The medical men I have called in to him, say, or intimate, that he cannot live; they left one by one, all saying it. The two who attend him regularly were here this morning. I saw them go out whispering, and I know *they* were saying it. I have sent for you to confirm or dispute this : you know what is the constitution of the St. Johns, and are acquainted with his. Must George die ? "

Not a sign of emotion was there about her. *Could* this be the same woman whose excitement for months had been a world's wonder, whose anguish, when uncontrolled, had been a terror to her servants ? She sat with an impassive face, her tones measured, her voice cold and calm. One very small sign of restlessness there was, and it lay in her fingers. A thin cambric handkerchief was between them, and she was stealthily pulling at one of its corners : when the interview was over, the fine texture of threads had given way, leaving a broad hole there.

Mr. Pym knew that the child must die : it had required but one moment's glance to see that the angel of death was already on the wing; but to say this to Mrs. St. John might be neither kind nor expedient. He was beginning some evasive reply, when she stopped him peremptorily.

"I sent for you to know the truth, and you must tell it me. Must George die ? "

That she was in no mood to be trifled with, the surgeon saw. To attempt it might not be wise. Besides, the signs on George's face were such this day, that she must see what the truth was as clearly as he saw it.

"I think him very ill, Mrs. St. John. He is in danger."

"That is not a decisive answer yet. *Can't* you give me one? —you have come far enough to do it. Will he die?"

"I fear he will."

"He has gone too far to recover? He will shortly——"
A momentary pause, but she recovered instantly. "A few hours will see the end?"

"I do not say that. A few days will no doubt see it."

Mrs. St. John looked across at the handless clock, as if asking why it did not go on. The surgeon glanced at her face, and was thankful for its composure. She resumed:

"Then the other motive with which I sent for you need scarcely be entered upon. It was, that you, who have watched him from his birth, might perhaps suggest some cure that the others could not."

"Some mode of treatment, I dare say you mean, Mrs. St. John. No, I fear nothing would have been effectual. I could not save his father; there is no probability that I could have saved him."

"Why is it that the St. Johns of Alnwick die in this way?" she returned, her voice taking a passionate tone.

"Nay," returned Mr. Pym, soothingly, "none may question the will of God. It is not given to us always to discern causes: we see here through a glass darkly. Of one thing we may ever rest assured, Mrs. St. John—that at the Great Final clearance we shall see how merciful God has been, how all happened for the best."

"Is he dying of the same wasting disease that his father died of?" she resumed after a pause. "Or of—of—of what he took the evening of the birthday dinner?"

"What did he take the evening of the birthday dinner?" returned Mr. Pym, asking the question in surprise. "He took nothing then, that I know of."

"He took a fright—if nothing else. *I* have never understood what it was that ailed him."

"Pooh! A momentary childish fright, and a fit of indigestion," said the surgeon, lightly. "They are not things to injure a boy permanently."

"He has never been well since," she said, in low tones. "Never for an hour."

"The disease must have been stealing upon him then, I suppose, and the little derangement to the system that night brought out its first symptoms." observed Mr. Pym. "Who knows but he might have caught it from his father during the latter's illness?"

"You think, then, that nothing could have saved him?"

"I think it could not. Where there is a strong tendency to hereditary disease, it is sure to show itself."

"And—I have not taken him about too much? It has not injured him?"

"I hope not," cheerfully replied Mr. Pym. Where was the use of his saying it had, whatever his opinion might be?

She had her finger right up through the hole in the handkerchief now, and was looking at it—at the finger, not the hole. Mr. Pym watched every turn of her features, seeming to keep his eyes quite the other way.

"What right had George St. John to marry?" she suddenly cried. "If people know themselves liable to any disease that cuts off life, they should keep single; and so let the curse die out."

"Ay, if people would! Some have married who had a less right to do so than George St. John."

The remark seemed to have escaped him unwittingly. Mrs. St. John turned her eyes upon him, and he hastened to resume:

"No blame could attach to your husband for marrying, Mrs. St. John. When he did so, he was, to all appearance, a hale, healthy man."

"He might have suspected that the waste would come upon him. It had killed the St. Johns of Alnwick who had gone before him."

"It had killed one or two of them. But how was George St. John to know that it would attack him? He might have inherited his mother's constitution: hers was a sound one."

"And why—and why—could not Georgy inherit mine?"

The pauses were evidently made to recall calmness, to subdue the rebellious breath, which was shortening. A very peculiar expression momentarily crossed the surgeon's face.

"All is for the best, Mrs. St. John. *Rely upon it.*"

A little feeble voice was calling out for mamma, and Mr. Pym hastily quitted his seat at the sound. Any one might have said he was glad of the interruption. The child's sweet blue eyes were raised as the surgeon bent over him, and his wan lips parted with a smile.

"Best as it is; oh, thank God, best as it is!" he murmured to himself, as he gently drew the once pretty curls from the

white and wasted brow, and suffered his hand to rest there.
"A short time, and then—one of God's angels. *Here*, had he
lived—better not think of it. All's for the best."

The surgeon remained twenty-four hours at Ypres, and then
took his departure. Not once, during all that time, was Mrs.
St. John off her guard, or did she lose her self-possession.

The hour came for the child to die, and he was laid in his
little grave in Belgium. For a day or two, Mrs. St. John was
almost unnaturally calm, but the second night, at midnight, her
cries of despair aroused the house, and a violent scene came on.
Prance shut herself up in the room with her, and silence at
length supervened. So far as Mrs. Brayford could make out
—but that was not very much, through Prance's jealous care—
the unhappy lady laboured under some perpetual terror—fancying she saw a vision of Benja coming towards her with a lighted
church. These paroxysms occurred almost nightly: and Mrs.
St. John grew into a terribly nervous state from the very dread
of them. She sometimes drank a quantity of brandy, to the
dismay of Prance: not, poor thing, from love of it, but as an
opiate.

What would be her career now? It would seem that the old
restlessness, the hurrying about from place to place, would form
a feature in it. No sooner were the child's remains removed
from her sight, than the eagerness for change came on. It had
been thought by all around her that George would have been
taken to Alnwick, to be interred with his forefathers, but it had
not pleased Mrs. St. John to give orders to that effect. Indeed,
she gave no orders at all; and but for Prance, the tidings had
not been conveyed even to Mrs. Darling. The blow fallen,
all else in the world seemed a blank to the bereaved mother.
Apart from the child's personal loss, his death took from her
state and station; and she was not one to disregard those
benefits. That the boy had been more precious to her than
heaven, was unhappily too true; and all else had died with
him. If she had indeed any sin upon her conscience connected with that fatal night, what terrible retribution must now
have been hers. Were Benja living, she would still be in the
enjoyment of wealth, pride, power; would still be reigning at
the once much-coveted Hall of Alnwick, its sole mistress. With
the death of the children, all had gone from her. No human
care or skill could have saved the life of her own son; but
Benja?—Heaven did not call *him*.

It seemed that the ill-fated boy's image was rarely absent from her. Not the burning figure, flying about and screaming (as there could be no reasonable doubt he did fly about and scream), but the happy child, marching to and fro in the room, all pleased with his pretty toy, the lighted church. After George's death, when grief was telling upon her system and calling forth all of nervousness inherent in it, she hardly dared to be alone in the dark, lest the sight should appear to her; she dreaded the waking up at night, and Prance's bed was removed into her room. A little time to renew her strength of body, and these nervous fancies would subside; but meanwhile there was one great comprehensive dread upon her—the anniversary of the fatal day, the 10th of November,—St. Martin's Eve. It was close at hand,—the intervening hours were slipping past with giant strides; and she asked herself how she should support its remembrances. "Oh, that he had lived! that he were at my side now! that I could give to him the love I did not give him in life!" she murmured, alluding to poor Benja.

From Ypres she hastened away to Lille, and there spent a day or two; but she thought she would go back to England. That renowned saint's vigil was dawning now, for this was the ninth. Should she spend the tenth in travelling?—or remain where she was, at rest, until the eleventh? *At rest!*—while this state of mind was upon her? It were mockery to call it so. Rather let her whirl over the earth night and day, as the fierce raven whirled over the waters on being set loose from the Ark; but not again let her hope for rest!

The tenth day came in, and she was to all appearance calm. But a fit of restlessness came upon her in the course of the morning, and she gave orders to depart at once for a certain town on the coast—a town belonging to France now, but whose population still cling to their Flemish tongue. A steamer was about to leave the port of this town for London that night, and the sudden idea had taken her that she would go by it—to the intense indignation of Prance, who had never in all her life heard of civilized beings crossing the Channel except by the short passage.

They quitted Lille, and arrived at the town about four in the afternoon, putting up at the large hotel. Mrs. Brayford was still in her train: her services had been useful during the recent excited state of Mrs. St. John; but she was not to attend her to England, and here they would part company.

"Will Madame dine in her salon, or at the table-d'hôte?" inquired the head-waiter of the man-servant, in sufficiently plain English.

"At the table-d'hôte, no doubt," was the man's reply, speaking in accordance with his own opinion. "Madame has lost her two children, and is in low spirits, not caring to be much alone. To-day is the anniversary of the eldest's death."

"Tiens!" returned the waiter. "To-day is the eve of St. Martin. All the children in the town will be gay to-night."

"Yes, it's the eve of St. Martin," assented the servant, paying no attention to the other remark, and not in the least understanding it.

The domestic proved correct in his surmises. At five o'clock, when the bell rang for table-d'hôte, Mrs. Carleton St. John entered the dining-room. Very few were present; all gentlemen, except herself, and mostly pensionnaires; the hotels on the coast are empty at that season. The dinner was excellent, but it did not last long; and the gentlemen, one by one, folded their large serviettes, and quitted the room.

She was seated facing the mantelpiece, its clock in front of her. The hands were approaching six—the very hour when, twelve months before, while she sat in her dining-room at Alnwick, Benja was on fire with none near to rescue him. Nervousness tells in various ways upon the human frame, and it seemed to Mrs. St. John that the striking of the hour would be her own knell. Every symptom of one of those frightful paroxysms was stealing over her, and she dreaded it with an awful dread. As long as the rest of the dinner-guests were present, endurance was possible, though her brain had throbbed, her hands had trembled. But they were gone, those gentlemen. They had gazed on her beauty as she sat before them, and wondered that one so young could be so wan and careworn. A choking sensation oppressed her; her throat seemed to swell with it; and that sure minute-hand grew nearer and nearer. Invalids have strange fancies; and this poor woman was an invalid both in body and mind.

The agitation increased. She glanced round the large space of the darkened room—for the waiter, as was his custom, had put out the side-lamps now that dinner was over—almost believing that she should see Benja. The hands were all-but pointing to the hour; the silence was growing horrible, and she suddenly addressed an observation to the waiter at the sideboard behind her; anything to break it. There was no answer. Mrs. Carleton St. John turned sharply round, and became aware that the man had gone out; that she was alone in that dreary room. Alone! The nervous climax had come; and with a cry of horror, she flew out at the door, and up the broad lighted staircase.

What is it that comes over us in these moments of superstitious fear? Surely we have all experienced this sensation: ay, even we who pride ourselves upon our clear consciences—the dread of looking behind us. Yet look we must, and do. The unhappy lady had only taken a few steps up the stairs, when she turned her head in the impulse of desperation, and there—*there*—at the foot of the stairs, as if he had but stepped in through the open doors of the courtyard, stood the indistinct form of a boy, bearing a lighted church; the very facsimile of the one that other boy had borne on his birthday night, while a dull, wild, unearthly sound, apparently proceeding from him, smote upon her ear.

She knew not how she got up the stairs, how she burst into her chamber in the long corridor. Prance ought to have been there; but Prance was not: there was only the wood-fire in the grate; the two wax lights on the mantelpiece.

And at the same moment she became conscious of hearing a strange noise; the wildest sounds that ever struck on the ear of man. They seemed to come from the street; the very air resounded with them; louder and louder they grew; loud enough to make a deaf man hear, to strike the most equable mind with a vague sense of momentary terror. The same basilisk impulse that had caused her to glance round on the staircase, drew her now to the window. She dashed it open and leaned out—perhaps for company in her desperate loneliness, poor thing! But—what was it she beheld?

In all parts of the street, in every corner of it, distant, near, nearer, pouring into it from all directions, as if they were making for the hotel, as if they were making for *her*, flocking into it in crowds,—from the Place Jean Bart, from the Rue de l'Eglise, from the Rue Nationale, from the Rue David-d'Angers, from the Place Napoleon,—came shoals upon shoals of lighted churches, toys, similar to the one she had just seen below, to the one carried by that unfortunate child a year ago, at Alnwick. Of all sizes, of all forms, of various degrees of clearness and light, a few were red and a few were green, came on these conspicuous things : paper models of cottages, of houses, of towers, of lanterns, of castles, and many models of churches ; on, on they pressed ; accompanied by the horrible din of these hollow and unearthly sounds. With an awful cry, that was lost in the depths of the room—what could be heard amidst that discordant babel ?—Mrs. St. John turned to fly, and fell to the floor in convulsions. She had only *imagined* that she saw Benja in those previous nervous dreams of hers : now it seemed that the dream had passed into reality, and these were a thousand Benjas, in flesh and blood, come to mock at her.

And where was Prance ? Her mistress had said to her on going down to dinner, " Wait for me in my room ; " but Prance for once neglected to observe the mandate. For one thing, she had not supposed dinner would be over so soon. Prance was only in the next chamber : perfectly absorbed, both she and Mrs. Brayford, in this strange sight, which was all real ; not supernatural, as perhaps poor Mrs. St. John had been thinking. They stood at the window both of them, their necks stretched out as far as they could stretch, gazing with amazed eyes at all this light and din. Nothing of the supernatural did it bear for them : they saw the scene as it was, but wondered at its cause and meaning. It was a wonderfully novel and pretty sight, though the two women kept petulantly stopping their ears and laughing at the din. The lighted toys, lanterns, churches, or whatever you please to call them, were chiefly composed of paper, the frames of splinters of wood ; a few were of glass. They were borne aloft on long sticks or poles, chiefly by children ; but it seemed as if the whole population had turned out to escort them ; as indeed it had. The Flemish maids, in their white caps, carried these toys as well as the children, all in a state of broad delight, except when one of the lanterns took fire and was extinguished for evermore. It was a calm night : it generally is so, the inhabitants of that town will tell you, on St. Martin's Eve. The uproar proceeded from *horns ;* cows' horns, clay horns, brass horns, any horns ; one of which every lad under twenty held to his lips, blowing with all his might. Prance, who rarely exhibited curiosity about any earthly thing, was curious as to this, and sought for an explanation amidst the servants of the hotel. The following was the substance of it—

When the saint, Martin, was on earth in the flesh, sojourning in this French-Flemish town, his ass was lost one dark night on the neighbouring downs. The holy man was in despair, and called upon the inhabitants to aid him in his search. The whole population responded with a will, and turned out with horns and lanterns, a dense fog prevailing at the time. Tradition says their efforts were successful, and the lost beast was restored to its owner. Hence commenced this annual custom, and most religiously has it been observed ever since. On St. Martin's Eve and St. Martin's Night, the 10th and 11th of November, as soon as darkness comes on, the principal streets of the town are perambulated by crowds carrying their horns and lanterns. It is looked upon almost as a religious fête, and is sanctioned by the authorities. Police keep the streets clear; carriages, carts, and horses are not allowed to pass during the two or three hours that it prevails; and, in short, every consideration gives way to the horns and lanterns on St. Martin's Eve and Night.

It was a strange coincidence that had taken thither Mrs. St. John; one of those inexplicable things that we cannot explain, only wonder at. The women, their number augmented by two of the Flemish maid-servants, remained at the window, enduring the din, admiring some particularly tasty church or castle; laughing at others that took fire, to the intense irritation of their bearers. In the midst of this, Prance suddenly bethought herself of her mistress, and hastened into the adjoining room.

A sharp cry from Prance summoned Nurse Brayford. Their lady was lying on the floor, to all appearance insensible.

CHAPTER XXVIII.

MRS. BRAYFORD'S BELIEF.

THE deceitful improvement in the state of Adeline de Castella still continued. Herself alone (and perhaps the medical faculty) saw it for what it was—a temporary flickering up of the life-flame before going out. Now and then she would drop a word which betrayed her own convictions, and they did not like to hear it.

Rose had put on her mourning, as slight as was consistent with any sort of decency; but she heard few particulars of the last days of the little heir, except that he died at Ypres, and was buried there. "Ypres! of all the places in the world!" ejaculated Rose, in astonishment. Mrs. St. John had gone to England, but not to Alnwick. Alnwick had passed into the hands of the other branch—the St. Johns of Castle Wafer.

"What a miserable succession of misfortunes!" mused Rose, one day, upon reading a letter from her mother. "All Charlotte's grandeur gone from her! First her husband, then the little stepson, next her own boy, and now Alnwick."

"Has she nothing left?" asked Adeline. "No fortune?"

"Just a pittance, I suppose," rejoined Rose. "About as adequate a sum to keep up the state suited to the widow of George St. John of Alnwick, as five pounds a year would be to find me in bonnets. There was something said about George St. John's not being able to make a settlement at the time of the marriage. Most of his money had come to him through his first wife, and his large fortune in prospective has not yet fallen in."

"Will it fall to your sister?"

"Not now. It passes on to Isaac St. John. How rich he'll be, that man!"

Adeline was looking so well. She sat at the table, writing a note to one of the girls at Madame de Nino's. Her dress was of purple silk; its open lace cuffs, of delicate texture, shading her wrists; its white collar, of the same, falling back from her ivory throat. And the face was so lovely still! with its delicate bloom, and its rich dark eyes. Madame de Castella came in.

"Adeline, that English nurse is downstairs—the one who nursed you in the spring," she said. "Would you like to see her?"

"What, Nurse Brayford!" exclaimed Rose, starting up. "*I* should like to see her. I shall hear about little Georgy St. John."

"Stay a minute, Rose," said Madame de Castella, laying her hand upon the impulsive girl. "Adeline, this person is very skilful; her judicious treatment did you a great deal of good in the spring. I feel inclined to ask her to come here now for a week."

Adeline looked up from her writing, the faint colour in her cheeks becoming a shade brighter.

"Surely, mamma, you do not think I require two nurses! It has seemed to me of late that the one already here is superfluous."

"My dear child! don't suppose I wish her to come here as a nurse. Only for a few days, my child! it would be the greatest satisfaction to me. I'll say a word of explanation to the *garde*," added Madame, "or we shall make her jealous. These nurses can be very disagreeable in a house, if put out."

She rang the bell as she spoke, and Rose made her escape, finding Mrs. Brayford in one of the downstairs rooms. Rose, a very Eve of curiosity, liking to know every one's business, whether it concerned her or not, as her mother did before her, poured out question upon question. Mrs. Brayford, not having the slightest objection to answer, told all she knew. Rose was rather indignant upon one point: why had they left the poor little fellow at Ypres? Why was he not taken to Alnwick? The nurse could not tell: Prance had been surprised too. She supposed Mrs. St. John was too much absorbed by grief to think of it."

"Does Charlotte—does Mrs. St. John feel it *very* much?" asked Rose.

"Oh, miss! my firm belief is, that"—the woman stopped, glanced over her shoulder to see that they were alone, and lowered her voice to a whisper—"the sorrow has turned her brain."

"Nonsense!" uttered Rose, after a pause. "You don't mean it!"

"It's the truth, Miss Darling, I'm afraid. She was always having visions of—did you know, miss, that the eldest little boy died through an accident, a paper church taking fire that his nursemaid had left him alone with?"

"Of course I know it," replied Rose. "That nursemaid ought to have been transported for life!"

"Well, miss, poor Mrs. St. John used to fancy that she saw the boy with his lighted church. I heard of this first from little George; but after his death she was worse, and I witnessed one of these attacks myself. She seemed to have an awful dread of the vision. If her brain's not affected, my name's not Nancy Brayford."

"I never heard of such a thing," cried Rose. "Fancies she sees—— Oh, it can't be."

"It *is*, miss. I've not time to tell you now, excepting just the heads, but we had such a curious thing happen. At the last place we stopped at, where Mrs. St. John went to take the steamer direct for London, there was a street show at night,

consisting of these very churches and lanterns, all lighted up
and carried about on poles. It's their way of keeping St.
Martin's Eve ; and I don't say it wasn't pretty enough, but of
all the noises ever heard, which was caused by about a thousand
horns, all being blowed together, that was the worst. We
found Mrs. St. John on the floor in her room in a sort of fit ;
and when she came to, she said the wildest things—about
having, or not having, we couldn't make it out, set fire herself
to the child. She was as mad that night, Miss Darling, as
anybody ever was. The sight of the lighted things had put
the finishing touch to her brain."

Rose hardly knew whether to recoil in fear, or to laugh in
derision. The tale sounded very strange to her ear.

"Prance was frightened, for once," went on the woman,
"and it's not a little that can frighten *her*—as perhaps you
know, miss. She telegraphed to Mrs. Darling, and we got
Mrs. St. John on board the London boat—which was starting
at three in the morning. She was calm then, from exhaustion,
and seemingly sensible. Prance brought her up one or two
of the lanterns and a horn to show her that they were real
things and quite harmless."

"She is very well, now," said Rose. "I had a letter from
mamma this morning ; and she says how glad she is that
Charlotte is recovering her spirits."

" Ah, well, miss, I'm rejoiced to hear it," was the answer, its
tone one of unmistakable disbelief. "I hope she'll keep so.
But that she was mad in the brain then, I could take my
affidavit upon. Bless you, miss, I've seen a great deal of it :
the notions that some sick people take up passes belief. I've
known 'em fancy themselves murderers and many other things
that's bad,—delicate ladies, too, who had never done a wrong
thing in their lives."

"My sister was always so very calm."

" And so she was throughout, except at odd moments ;
quite unnaturally calm. She—but I'll tell you more about it
another opportunity, Miss Darling," broke off the woman, as
Madame de Castella entered the room. "It's no disparage-
ment to the poor young lady—and she is young : sick folks are
not accountable for the freaks their minds take."

Rose returned a slighting answer, as if the words had made
little impression on her. But as the hours went on, she somehow could not get rid of their remembrance ; they seemed to

grow deeper and deeper.   What a horrible thing if the wom
were right! if the grief and trouble should have turn
Charlotte's brain!

EXTRACT FROM MISS CARR'S DIARY.

Dec. 10*th.*—Oh this deceitful disease! all the dread
weakness has returned.   Adeline cannot go downstairs nc
She just comes from her chamber into the front room, and l
on the sofa the best part of the day.   Madame de Castel
who fully believed in the amendment, giving way more th
any one of us to the false hopes it excited, is nearly beside h
self with grief and despair.   She is perpetually reproachi
herself for allowing Nurse Brayford to leave.   The wom
stayed here for a few days, but Adeline was so well it seemec
farce to keep her, and now she has taken another place a
cannot return.   I am glad she's gone, for my part.   She cou
not do Adeline the slightest good, and she and the *garde* ke
up an incessant chatter in strange French.   Brayford's Fren
was something curious to listen to: 'Le feu est sorti,' s
said one day, and sent Rose into a screaming fit.   Signor
Castella we rarely see, except at dinner; now and then at t
second déjeûner; but he is mostly shut up in his cabinet.
it that the sight of his fading child is more than he can bea
Cold and reserved as he has always been, there's no dou
that he loves Adeline with the deepest love.

15*th.*—Five days, and Adeline not out of her bedroo:
The cough has come back again, and the doctors say she m
have taken cold.   I don't see how she could; but Dr. Don
as cross as can be over it.

A fancy has taken her these last few days to hear Rose si
English songs.   On the first evening, Rose was in the fr
room, the intervening door being open, singing in a sweet, l
voice to amuse herself; but Adeline listened and asked
more.   More songs, only they must be English.

"I think I have come to the end of my stock," answei
Rose; "that is, all I can remember.   Stay!—what was tl
long song so much in request this year at school?   Do y
remember the words, Mary Carr?"

"How am I to know what song you mean?" I asked.

"Some of us set it to music,—a low, soft chant.   L
spring it was, after Adeline had left.   You must remember

It was strummed over for everlasting weeks by the whole set of us. It begins thus," added Rose, striking a few chords.

I recollected then. They were lines we saw in a book belonging to that Emma Mowbray, an old, torn magazine, which had neither covers nor title-page. Some of the girls took a violent fancy to them, and somebody—Janet Duff, was it?—set them to music.

"I have it," cried Rose, striking boldly into the song. Nearly with the first words Adeline rose into a sitting posture, her eyes strained in the direction of Rose though she could not see her, and eagerly listening.

> " When woman's eye grows dim,
>   And her cheek paleth ;
> When fades the beautiful,
>   Then man's love faileth.
> He sits not beside her chair,
>   Clasps not her fingers,
> Entwines not the damp hair
>   That o'er her brow lingers.
>
> " He comes but a moment in,
>   Though her eye lightens,
> Though the hectic flush
>   Feverishly heightens,
> He stays but a moment near,
>   While that flush fadeth ;
> Though disappointment's tear
>   Her dim eye shadeth.
>
> " He goes from her chamber, straight
>   Into life's jostle :
> He meets, at the very gate,
>   Business and bustle.
> He thinks not of her, within,
>   Silently sighing ;
> He forgets, in that noisy din,
>   That she is dying."

"There is another verse," I called out, for Rose had ceased.

"I know. there is," she said, "but I cannot recollect it. Only its purport !"

"Try, try," exclaimed Adeline ; "sing it all."

Rose looked round, astonished at the anxious tone, as was I. What was the matter with her?—she who never took interest in anything.

"Mary Carr," said Rose, "do you recollect the last verse ?"

"Not a word of it."

Rose struck the notes of the chant upon the piano, murmuring some words to herself, and stopping now and then.

Presently she burst out, something after the manner of an improvisatrice—

> "And when the last scene's o'er,
>   And cold, cold her cheek,
> His mind's then all despair,
>   And his heart like to break.
> But, a few months on,—
>   His constancy to prove—
> He forgets her who is gone,
>   And seeks another love."

"They are not exactly the original words," said Rose, "but they will do."

"They will do, they will do," murmured Adeline, falling back on the sofa. "Sing it all again, Rose."

And every evening since has this song been sung two or three times to please her. What is it she sees in it?

23rd.—I fear the day of life is about to close for Adeline. All the ominous symptoms of the disease have returned : pain oppresses her continually, and now she experiences a difficulty in breathing. Ah, Mr. St. John, if you were to come now and comfort her with all your love, as of yore, you could not restore her to health, or prolong her life by one single day. How strange it is we never hear of him ! Is he in London ?—is he at Castle Wafer ?—is he abroad ?—where is he ?

26th.—It is astonishing that Madame de Castella continues to cheat herself as to Adeline's state—or, rather, *make believe* to cheat herself, as the children do at their play. She was determined there should be only one dinner-table yesterday, Christmas Day ; so it was laid in the drawing-room, and Adeline went in, the nurse and Louise making a show of dressing her up for it. But all the dress, and the dinner, and the ceremony, could not conceal the truth—that she was dying. Madame de Castella was in most wretched spirits ; her silent tears fell, in spite of her efforts, with every morsel she put into her mouth. The Signor was gloomy and reserved ; latterly he had never been otherwise. Had it not been for Rose, there would have been no attempt at conversation ; but Rose, with all her faults, is a downright treasure in a house, always gay and cheerful. We gathered round the fire after dinner, Rose cracking filberts for us all.

"Do you remember our Christmas dinner last year?" she said to Adeline.

"At Madame de Nino's? Quite well."

"And our sly draw at night at Janet Duff's cards, and the French marigold falling, as usual, to you?"

Adeline answered by a faint gesture, it may have been of assent, it may have been of denial, and Rose bit her repentant tongue. She had spoken without reflection: does she ever speak with it?

29th.—A dark, murky day has this been, but one of event for Adeline. The lights were brought in early in the afternoon, for Rose was reading to her, and it grew too dusk to see. It was the second volume of a new English novel, and Rose was so deeply interested in it, that when Susanne came in with a letter for her, she told her to "put it down anywhere," and read on.

"Not so," said Adeline, looking eagerly up; "open your letter first. Who is it from?"

"From Mary Anne, of course: Margaret never writes to me, and mamma but seldom," replied Rose, breaking the seal. And, not to lose time, she read it out at once. Mrs. Darling and her family are spending Christmas with old Mrs. Darling, in Berkshire.

"MY DEAR ROSE,

"We arrived here on Christmas Eve, but I have found no time to write to you until now. Grandmamma is breaking fast; it is apparent to us all: she has aged much in the past twelve months. She was disappointed you did not make one of us, and particularly hopes you have grown steady, and are endeavouring to acquire the reserve of manner essential to a gentlewoman." ("Or an old maid," ejaculated Rose, in a parenthesis.) "Charlotte is here: she has recovered her spirits wonderfully, and is as handsome as ever. Frank joined us on Christmas morning: he has only got leave for a fortnight. He reports Ireland—the part he is now quartered in—as being in a shocking state. For my part, I never listen to anything he may have to say about such a set of savages. Frank lays down the law beautifully—says he only wishes they would make him Viceroy for a spell: he'd do this, and he'd do that. I don't doubt he does wish it.

"In your last letter you ask about Frederick St. John——" Rose looked off, and hesitated; but Adeline's flushed, eager gaze, the parted lips, the breathless interest, told her there was nothing for it but to continue. "We met him lately at one of the Dowager Revel's assemblies—very crowded it was, considering the season. It was whispered last year that he was ruined, obliged to leave the country, and I don't know what. People ought to be punished for inventing such falsehoods. Instead of being ruined, he enjoys a splendid income, and has not a single debt in the world. It is reported that his brother has made over to him Castle Wafer, which I should think to be only a report : it may be true, though, now he has come into Alnwick. He is again the shadow of Sarah Beauclerc ; at least he was her shadow this evening at Lady Revel's, and I should think it will inevitably be a match. I wish we knew him ; but did not dare ask for an introduction, he looks so haughty, and mamma was not there. Grandmamma sends her love, and——"

I went forward and raised Adeline on her pillows. The emotion that she would have concealed was struggling with her will for mastery. Once more the burning red spot we thought gone for ever shone on her hollow cheeks, and her hands were fighting with the air, and the breath had stopped.

"Oh, Adeline !" cried Rose, pushing me aside without ceremony, "forgive, forgive me! Indeed I did not know what there was in the letter until I had entered upon the words : I did not know his name was mentioned. What is to be done, Mary? this excitement is enough to kill her. La garde, la garde !" called out Rose in terror; "que faut-il faire. Mademoiselle se trouve malade !"

The nurse, who was in the next room, glided up with a rapid step ; but, in regaining her breath, Adeline's self-possession returned to her. "It is nothing," she panted ; "only a spasm." And down she sank on her pillow, whispering for them to remove the lights.

"Into the next room—for a little while—they hurt my eyes."

The nurse went out with the tapers, one in each hand, and I knelt down by the sofa.

"What of your deductions now, Mary?" she whispered, after a while, referring to a former conversation. "He is with his early love, and I am here, dying."

"Adeline," I said, "have you no wish to see him again ? Did I do wrong in asking it?"

She turned her face to the wall and did not answer.

"I know that you parted in anger, but it all seems to me a

great mystery. Whatever cause he may have had for estrang-
ing himself, I did not think Mr. St. John was one to forsake
you in this heartless way, with the grave so near."

"He forsook me in health," she said, and her voice now had
assumed that hollow tone it would never lose in this world;
"you might admit there was an excuse for him if you knew all.
But—all this time—never to make inquiry after me—never
to seek to know if I am dead, or living, or married to another!
Whilst to hear of him, to see him, I would forfeit what life is
left to me."

New Year's Day.—And a fearful commotion the house has
been in, by way of welcome. This morning Adeline was taken
alarmingly worse; we thought she was dying, and doctors,
priests, friends and servants, jostled each other in the sick
chamber. The doctors gained possession, expelled us all in a
body, and enforced quiet. She will not die yet, they say, if
she is allowed tranquillity—not for some days, perhaps weeks,
but will rally again. I think they are right, for she is much
better this evening. Adeline is nineteen to-day. This time
last year! this time last year! it was the scene and hour of her
brilliant ball-night. How things have changed since then!

Yesterday Adeline showed her hands to young Docteur
H——. It has struck her as being very singular that their
nails should have turned white. It strikes me so too. He
seemed to intimate that it was a very uncommon occurrence,
but said he had seen it happen from intense anxiety of mind.
"Which," he added, "cannot be your case, my dear Mademoiselle de Castella." Adeline hastily drew her hands under
the blue silk sofa cover, and spoke of something else.

Jan. 5th.—"Could you not wheel the chair into the other
room—to the window?" Adeline asked suddenly to-day. "I
should like to look out on the world once more."

Louise glanced round at me, and I at the nurse, not knowing
what to do. But the nurse made no objection, and she and
Louise wheeled the large chair, with as little motion as possible,
to one of the drawing-room windows, and then raised her up,
and supported her while she stood.

It was no cheering prospect that she gazed upon. A slow,
small rain was falling; the snow, fast melting on the housetops,
was running down in streams of water, and patches of snow
lay in the streets, but they were fast turning into mud and
slop. Through an open space a glimpse of the distant country

was obtained, and there the snow lay bleak, white, and dreary. What few people were passing in the street hurried along under large cotton umbrellas, some as red and round as Louise's, the women with their heads tied up in blue and yellow kerchiefs. "Dreary, dreary!" she murmured as she gazed; "dreary and void of hope, as my later life has been!"

Old Madame G——'s cook came out of their house with an earthen pan, and placed it underneath the spout to catch the water.

"Is that Madame G—— herself?" cried Adeline, watching the movement. "Where can her two servants be?"

"It's nobody but old Nannette, with white bows in her cap," said Louise, laughing. "Mademoiselle's eyes are deceiving her."

"Is not that M. de Fraconville?" resumed Adeline, pointing to a gentleman who had just come in view, round the opposite corner.

"Something must have taken your eyesight to-day, Adeline," exclaimed Rose, who was at the other window; "it's a head and half too tall for M. de Fraconville."

"You say right," meekly sighed Adeline; "my sight is dim, and looking on the white snow has rendered it more so. Take me back again."

It will be her last look at out-door life.

They wheeled her into the other room, and settled her comfortably on her chair, near the fire, her head on the pillows and her feet on a footstool. Rose followed, and took up a light work to read to her.

"Not that," said Adeline, motioning away the volume in Rose's hands; it is time I had done with such. There is ANOTHER Book there, Rose."

In coming in from church last Sunday, I laid my Bible and Prayer-book down in Adeline's room, and forgot them. It was towards these she pointed. Rose took up the Bible.

"Where shall I read?" she asked, sitting down. Adeline could not tell her. The one was almost as ignorant as the other. The Bible, to Adeline, has been a sealed book, and Rose never opens it but as a matter of form. Rose turned over its leaves in indecision. "So many chapters!" she whispered to me, pleadingly, "Tell me which to fix upon."

"Take the Prayer-book," interrupted Adeline, "and read me your Service for the Burial of the Dead."

Rose found the place at once, for she knew it was close to the Marriage Service, and began :

"'I am the resurrection and the life, saith the Lord : he that believeth in me, though he were dead, yet shall he live : and whosoever liveth and believeth in me shall never die.'"

There she stopped, for the tears were falling, and she could not see the page ; and, just then, Miss de Beaufoy came into the room, and saw what Rose was reading. For the first time, in our hearing, she interfered, beseeching Adeline to remember she was a Roman Catholic, and recommending that a priest should be sent for.

"Dear Aunt Agnes," exclaimed Adeline, impressively, "when you shall be as near to death as I am, you will see the fallacy of these earthly differences,—how worse than useless they must appear in the sight of our universal Father, of our loving Saviour. There is but one heaven, and I believe it is of little moment which form of worship we pursue, so that we pray and strive earnestly in it to arrive there. I shall be none the worse for listening to the prayers from this English book : they are all truth and beauty, and they soothe me. The priests will come later."

A bold avowal for a Roman Catholic, and Agnes de Beaufoy crossed herself as she left the room. Rose read the Burial Service to the end.

And so, existence hanging as it were upon a thread, the days still struggle on.

There will be no more extracts from this young lady's diary. And indeed but little more of anything ; this portion of the history, like Adeline's life, draws near its close.

CHAPTER XXIX.

LOUISE'S WHISPERED WORDS.

You could see at a first glance that it was only a temporary bed-chamber—a drawing-room converted into one, to serve some special occasion. Its carpet was of unusual richness ; its chairs and sofa, handsomely carved, were covered with embossed purple velvet ; its window-curtains, of white flowered muslin, were surmounted by purple velvet and glittering yellow cornices; and fine paintings adorned the walls. The bed alone seemed out of place. It was of plain mahogany, a French bed, without curtains, and was placed in the corner which made the angle between the two doors, one of which opened on the corridor, the other on the adjoining room, a large, magnificent drawing-room, furnished *en suite* with the one in which the bed was.

On a couch, drawn before the fire, she lay, her sweet face white and wasted. The sick-nurse sat near the sofa, and the lady's-maid, Louise, was busy with the pillows of the bed. Adeline was about to be moved into it, but as they were disrobing her, she suddenly fell back, apparently without life or motion.

"She has fainted," screamed Louise.

"She is taken for death," whispered the nurse.

Louise flew into a fit of anger and tears, abusing the nurse for her hard-hearted ideas. But the nurse was right.

"You had better summon the family, Mademoiselle Louise," persisted the nurse; "they must have done dinner; and let the doctors be sent to,—though they can do nothing for her, poor young lady."

"She has not fainted," whispered Louise. "She is conscious."

"No, no, it is no fainting-fit," was the brief answer. "I have seen more of these things than you have. She will rally a little, I dare say."

No one went to bed that night at Signor de Castella's: it was a general scene of weeping, suspense, and agitation. Adeline was tranquil, except for her laboured breathing.

Early in the morning, she asked to see her father. He remained with her about twenty minutes, shut up with her alone. What passed at the interview none can tell. Did she beg forgiveness for the rebellion she had unintentionally been guilty of in loving one whom, perhaps, she ought not to have loved? Or did *he* implore pardon of her, for having been instrumental in condemning her to misery? None will ever know. When Signor de Castella left the chamber, he passed along the corridor on his way to his cabinet with his usual measured, stately step; but there were traces of emotion on his face—they saw it as he strode by the drawing-room door. Mary Carr opened the door between the two rooms, and went

ın, knowing that Adeline was alone, and she gathered a little
of the interview. Adeline was sobbing wildly. She had heard
the last words of impassioned tenderness from her much-loved
father—always deeply loved by her ; tenderness that he would
never have given vent to in the presence of a third person, or
under any circumstances of less excitement : but when these
outwardly-cold natures are aroused, whether for anger or for
tenderness, their emotion is as that of the rushing whirlwind.
Adeline had clung round him with the feeble remnant of her
strength, whispering how very dear he had always been to her,
dearer far than he had ever suspected : and the Signor had
given his consent (now that it was too late) to the true facts of
the separation being disclosed to Frederick St. John.

The day grew later. The nurse, for the twentieth time, was
arranging the uneasy pillows, when Susanne went in to tell her
to go to dinner, taking herself the nurse's place, as she in
general did, during her absence. Madame de Castella, quite
exhausted with grief, had just gone away for a little repose.
Adeline, though comparatively free from pain, was restless to
an extreme degree, as many persons are, in dying. When not
dozing, and that was rare, she was never still for two minutes
together, and the pillows and bedclothes were continually misplaced. Scarcely had the nurse left the room, when Miss Carr
had to lean over her to put them straight.

"Who is that?" inquired Adeline, in her hollow voice, her
face being turned to the wall. She detected, probably, the
difference of touch, for in this the sick are very quick.

"It is I—Mary. Nurse has gone down to her dinner."

She took Miss Carr's hand, and held it for some time in
silence. "I have been wanting—all day—to speak to you—
Mary—but I—have waited." She could say now but few
words consecutively.

"What is it you would say, dearest Adeline ?"

"Who is in the room ?"

"Susanne. No one else."

"Tell her to go. I want you alone."

"She does not understand our language."

"Alone, alone," repeated Adeline. "Susanne."

The lady's-maid heard the call, and went to the bedside.

"Help me to turn round, Susanne. I have not strength."

With some difficulty they turned her, for they were not so
clever at it as the nurse. Adeline then lay looking at them, as

she panted for breath. Susanne wiped the cold dew from her pale forehead, and some tears from her own face.

"Leave us alone, Susanne. I have something to say to Mademoiselle Carr."

"Stay in the next room, within call, Susanne," whispered Miss Carr to the servant. It may seem strange, but dearly as Mary Carr loved Adeline, she experienced an indescribable awe at being left alone with her. She did not stay to analyze the sensation, but it must have had its rise in that nameless terror which, in the mind of the young, attaches itself to the presence of the dead and dying.

"I am about to entrust you with a commission to *him*, Mary," she panted. "You will faithfully execute it?"

"Faithfully and truly."

And, stretching out her white and wasted hand, she held out the key of her writing-desk. "There is a secret spring in the desk, on the right, as you put in your hand," she continued; "press it."

With some awkwardness, Mary Carr did as she was desired, and several love-tokens were disclosed to view. Two or three trinkets of value, a few dried flowers, and some letters, the edges much worn.

"Throw the flowers in the fire," murmured Adeline, "and put all the rest in a parcel, and seal it up."

"How the notes are worn, Adeline!" exclaimed Mary. "One would think them twenty years old."

"Yes," she said, "until I took to my bed I carried them *here*," touching her bosom. "They are his letters."

Miss Carr speedily made up the packet, and was about to seal it.

"Not that seal," said Adeline. "Take my own; the small one, that has my initials on it. Mary, do you think I could direct it?"

"*You* direct it!" exclaimed Miss Carr, in surprise. "I don't see how."

"If you could raise me up—and hold me—it would not take more than a minute. I wish to write the address myself."

"Let me call Susanne."

"No, no, I will have no one else here. Put the letter before me on a book, and try and raise me."

It was accomplished after some trouble, Mary Carr was nervous, and feared, besides, that the raising her up might do some injury : but she knew not how to resist Adeline's beseeching looks. She supported her up in bed, and held her, whilst she wrote his name, "Frederick St. John." No "Mr.," no "Esquire;" and written in a straggling hand, all shakes and angles, bearing not any resemblance to what Adeline's had been. Mary laid her down again, and Adeline, in a few words, explained the secret of their being parted, and charged her to enlighten him.

"Tell him I have returned all except the ring, and that will be buried with me. That it has never been off my finger since he placed it there."

" What ring ? " exclaimed Mary Carr, surprised, even at such a moment, into curiosity. " The ring you wear is de la Chasse's engagement-ring," she continued, looking down at the plain circlet of gold, that was only kept on Adeline's emaciated finger by the smaller guard worn to protect it.

She shook her head feebly. "*He* will know."

"What else, Adeline ? "

"Tell him my heart will be faithful to him in death, as it ever was in life. Nothing more."

" Why did you not write to him—" asked Mary Carr, " a last letter ? "

"He might not have cared to receive it. There is *another* now."

The close of the afternoon came on. The nurse was sitting in her chair on one side the fireplace; Louise silently see-sawed herself backwards and forwards upon another; Mary Carr was standing, in a listless attitude, before the fire, her elbow lodging on the mantelpiece ; and Rose Darling sat on a low stool, half asleep, her head resting against Adeline's bed. They were all fatigued. In the next room were heard murmurings of conversation : M. de Castella talking with one of the medical men. Adeline, just then, was quiet, and appeared to be dozing.

" I say, la garde," began Louise, in a low whisper, "is it true that mademoiselle asked old H—— this morning how many hours she should live ? "

The nurse nodded.

" Chère enfant ! " apostrophized Louise, through her tears. "And what did he say ? "

" What should he say ? " retorted the nurse. " He does not know any more than we do."

. "What do *you* think ?"

The nurse shook her head, rose from her seat, and bent ove
the bed to look at Adeline, who was lying with her face turned
away.

"She sleeps, I think, nurse," observed Rose, whom the
movement had disturbed ; and her own eyes closed again as
she spoke.

"I suppose she does, mademoiselle. I can't see her face
but, if she were not asleep, she wouldn't remain so quiet."

"I heard a word dropped to-day," cried Louise, in a mys
terious voice, as the nurse resumed her chair.

"What word ?"

But there Louise stopped, pursed up her mouth, and dried
her eyes, which, for the last fortnight or so, had been generally
overflowing.

"I don't know," resumed Louise. "It mayn't be true
and I am sure, if it should turn out not to be, *I* shouldn'
choose to say anything about it. So I had better hold my
tongue."

Now the most effectual way to induce Louise *not* to hold her
tongue, was to exhibit no curiosity as to anything she might
appear disposed to communicate. The garde knew this, and
for that reason, probably, sat silent. After awhile, Louise
began again.

"But it can do no harm to mention it amongst ourselves. I
was Susanne told me, and of course she must have gathered i
from madame. She said—you are sure she's asleep?" broke
off Louise, looking round at the bed.

"She's asleep, fast enough," repeated the nurse ; "she is too
quiet to be awake." And Louise resumed, in the hushed
peculiar tone she had been using; it sounded awfully myste
rious, taken in conjunction with her subject, through the space
of that dying room.

"Susanne thinks that mademoiselle will be exhibited."

"*What ?*" ejaculated the nurse, in a startled tone.

"Qu'elle sera exposée après sa mort." (I prefer to give
this sentence in the language in which the conversation wa
carried on.)

"What in the world do you mean?" demanded Rose, waking
up from her semi-sleep.

"That Mademoiselle Adeline will hold a reception afte
death, mademoiselle."

"Louise, what *do* you mean?" persisted Rose, opening her eyes to their utmost width.

But Mary Carr had taken in, and understood, the full meaning of the words; she was more generally acquainted with French manners and customs than Rose: and as her eye caught the reflection of her own face in the large pier-glass, she saw that it had turned of a ghastly whiteness.

"You don't follow this fashion in your country, mademoiselle, so I have learnt," whispered the nurse, addressing Rose. "Neither is it kept up here as it used to be. We scarcely ever meet with a case now. But I have heard my mother say—she was a sage-femme, mademoiselle, as well as a garde-malade—that when she was a girl there was scarcely a young gentlewoman of good family, who died unmarried, but what held her reception after death. And in my time, also, I have seen many splendid exhibitions."

"Oh, nurse, nurse," shivered Mary Carr, "*don't* talk so."

"What's the matter, mademoiselle?" asked the woman, kindly gazing at Miss Carr's scared face. "You look ill."

"I feel sick," was Mary Carr's faint answer. "I cannot help it. I think what you are talking of is *horrible.*"

"Do explain what it is you *are* talking of," interrupted Rose, impatiently. "La garde! what is it all?"

"I will tell you one instance, mademoiselle," said the woman, "and that will explain the rest. My aunt was housekeeper in Madame Marsac's family. Madame was a widow with three children, and lived in a grand old château near to our village. The eldest, Mademoiselle Marsac, was married to an officer in the army, and had gone away with him, the Saints know where, but a long way off, for it was in the time of Napoleon, and we were at war with half Europe then. Young Marsac, the only son, was a captain in the same regiment; he was also away with it; and Mademoiselle Emma was the only one left at home, and madame her mother doted on her. A fine, blooming young lady she was, with a colour like a rose: you might have taken a lease of her life. But, poor thing, she fell suddenly ill. Some said she had taken cold, others thought she had eaten something that did her harm, but an inward inflammation came on, and she was dead in a week. Madame was nearly crazed, and my aunt said it was pitiful to hear her shrieks the night after the death, and her prayers to the good Virgin to be taken with her child. But madame's sister came to the château with the early light, and she forthwith gave orders that poor Mademoiselle Emma should be exhibited."

"Do go on, nurse," pleaded Rose, whose cheek was getting as white as Mary Carr's, the woman having stopped, in thought.

"I was but a little child then, mademoiselle, as you may suppose, for it was in 1812; but my aunt suddenly sent for me up to the château, to assist. They did not keep many servants; my aunt had only one under her, besides the old gardener, for Madame Marsac was not rich; so I was put to do what I could. My faith! I shall never forget it: it was the first thing of the sort I had seen. They dressed the corpse up in rich white robes, as if for her bridal, with flowers and jewels, and white gloves, and white satin shoes. And then she was placed upright at the end of the grand salon, and all the neighbouring people for miles round, all the rich, and as many of the poor as could get admission, came to visit her. My aunt slipped me into the room, and I was there for, I should think, five minutes. It had the strangest effect! That dressed-up dead thing, at one end, and the live people, all dressed up in their best too, and mostly looking white and awestruck, coming in at the other. There was a long table going down the room, and they walked once round it, looking at her as they passed, and going out in silence. I don't think it was the thing, mademoiselle, for that aunt of mine to send a timid young child of five or so, as I was then, to see such a sight; but she was always indulgent to me, and thought it would be a treat. I could scarcely keep down my terror whilst I stayed in the room, and I am sure I must have looked as white and shocking as Mam'selle Mary looks just now. I did not dare to go about in the dark for long afterwards, and I could not overcome the feeling for years. Though I have seen many such a sight since, none have stayed upon my memory as that first did. I did not seem to see much, at the time, either: I never looked, but once, to—to that part of the room where the bridal robes were."

"But why dress them in *bridal* robes?" questioned Rose, breathlessly.

"As a symbol that they are going to be the bride of Heaven. At least, that is the interpretation I have always put upon it, mademoiselle," answered the woman.

"The first one *I* ever saw," interposed Louise, jealous that the nurse should have all the talking, "was a young priest who died at Guines. Stay—I don't think he was quite a priest, but would have been one if he had lived. His name was Théodore Borne. He died of an accident to his hand, and they made him hold a reception after death. I have never seen but two beside him. One was the sister of the Count Plessit, a lady about forty, but she had never been married; and the other was a young girl in this very town, the daughter of a couple who kept a general-furnishing shop, hired out, and sold furniture, and that; and a mint of money they had made. Wasn't she dressed out, that girl! She was an only child, poor thing, and they spared no money on her reception. Her veil was real Brussels; and her dress was half covered with Brussels lace, and little sprigs of orange-blossoms, and bows of white satin ribbon. Their shop faced the market-place, and they stuck her up at the window, looking down on to the Place.* It was market-day, and the Place was full of people; crowds of them, for the news spread, and everybody came. It was a wet day, too. Many children were frightened at the sight. Susanne had not met with the custom till she came to these parts : she says they never heard of it where she comes from, just beyond Paris; at least, *she* never did. That Théodore Borne——"

At this moment, Adeline stirred. Louise's tongue stopped as still as if it had been shot through, and the nurse made a quiet rush to the side of the bed. She was awake, and wanted her mouth moistened.

As the nurse was putting down the tea and the teaspoon, Dr. Dorré, who had been talking in the other room, came in to look at Adeline before he quitted the house. She was quite sensible, and said she felt easy. In the bustle of his leaving, the nurse going out to attend him to the staircase, Adeline put out her hand and touched Mary Carr, who was now standing by the bed. Her voice was very faint, and Mary had to lean close to hear.

"I—was not asleep—when Louise said—*that*. I heard it. Mary ! do not let it be done."

Miss Carr felt much distressed. She knew not what to say.

"I—I am sure nothing will be done that you do not wish, Adeline," she stammered. "I think it must have been a misapprehension on the part of Louise. Shall I speak to Madame de Castella ?"

* A fact

"Not now. When I am dead—you will see if they are making preparations—speak to mamma then."

"Do not let this distress you, Adeline," proceeded Mary, wishing Louise had been at the bottom of the sea before she had introduced so unfitting a subject in Adeline's hearing. "Rely upon it, every wish of yours will be sacredly respected."

"It does not distress me," was the feeble reply. "But I would rather be left in peace after death."

Madame de Castella came down, but soon went away to her chamber again, for her hysterical grief disturbed Adeline; Agnes de Beaufoy remained with her sister, endeavouring, by persuasions and remonstrances, to keep her there. Old Madame de Beaufoy was expected; and, a little before five, M. de Castella went to the railway station to receive her. Rose and Mary were in the drawing-room then, drinking some tea, when the old servant, Silva, came in with a letter on a salver.

"Pour qui !" demanded Mary.

"Pour Mademoiselle Rose Darling," responded the old man.

Rose, who was sitting before the fire, her feet on the fender, took the letter, without turning her head to look at it, and threw it on the table.

"That worrying Mary Anne! There's no end to her letters: and they are nothing but prosy lectures of admonition. If they think I am going to answer all she chooses to write, they'll find their mistake. If mamma made it a condition for a double allowance for me, I wouldn't do it."

"It is not your sister's handwriting," observed Mary Carr.

"No?" And Rose condescended languidly to turn her eyes towards the epistle. "Why, I do believe it is from Frank!" she exclaimed, snatching it out of Mary's hand. "What can he have to write about? Perhaps grandmamma's dead, and has left us all a fortune! But it's a red seal."

And, breaking the red seal, she skimmed hastily over it.

"Good Heavens! how singular! Mary! Mary!"

Miss Carr looked at her in wonder. Her countenance, which had been pale all day with anxiety and the previous night's watching, was now glowing with colour and excitement.

"He is coming to Belport. How passing strange! Mary, can it be some unknown sympathy that attracts him hither at this hour?"

"Your brother !"

" He ! Do you think his coming here could put me out like this ? What a stupid you are, Mary Carr ! Do listen :—

"My dear Rose,
    " Our dear and venerable grandmother, whom may all good angels preserve—though her long life does keep us an unreasonable time out of our own—entrusted me with a mission concerning you upon my coming to London two days ago. She had made, or purchased, or in some way prepared for you, a splendid article, but whether it is intended to represent a purse or a bag, I am unable to say, being, in my uninitiated opinion, too large for the one, and too small for the other. A magnificent affair it is, redolent of silver beads and gleaming silks, and it was *lined* with her usual Christmas present to you. Being in a generous mood myself, I slipped in another lining, knowing your partiality for feathers and laces, and any other sort of trumpery that costs money. This *cadeau*, duly prepared for transportation, and directed for you to the care of Madame de Nino, I brought to town, and was to have handed over to a quondam schoolfellow of yours, Miss Singleton, who was returning to Belport. Now you have frequently honoured me by saying I have a head that can retain nothing, and in this instance certainly the bag and the commission slipped clean out of it. In packing my carpet-bag this morning, preparatory to starting for Ireland, for which delectable spot of the globe I am bound, what should I come upon but this unlucky parcel. What was to be done ? I called a hansom, and galloped to Miss Singleton's address, invoking blessings on my forgetfulness all the way. No result. Miss Singleton and the archdeacon had started for Belport. I was walking down Brook Street, on my return, wondering what I should do with the money, and who, amongst my fair friends in Ireland, would come in for the bag, when I nearly ran over Fred St. John, or he over me, coming out of Mivart's.

"'Why, where have you been buried ?' said I.

"'At Castle Wafer, for nearly the last month. And I am off to-morrow for Paris. Any commands ?'

"'I should just think I had, if your route lies through Belport.' And forthwith I delivered to him the unlucky parcel and its history.

"So the long and short of it is, Rose, that you may expect to receive your bag safe and sound. Not so sure, though, as to the day, for St. John is proverbially uncertain in his movements.

"I hope your friend Mademoiselle de Castella's health is improving. I would beg my remembrance to her, but have no doubt I have long since gone out of hers. She has my best wishes for her recovery.

"Your affectionate brother, dear Rose,

"F. DARLING."

"What news for Adeline! Get out of the way, Mary Carr."

"Rose," said Miss Carr, in a tone of remonstrance, "it will not do to tell her."

"Not tell her!" exclaimed Rose.

"She is resigned and quiet now. Let her die in peace. News of him will only excite and disturb her."

"Don't talk to me! Let me go!" for Mary had laid hold of her dress to detain her.

"Rose, you are doing very wrong. She is almost in the last agony. Earthly hopes and interests have flitted away."

"You don't understand these things," rejoined Rose, with a curl upon her lip—"how should you? Has she not for months been yearning to see him—has not the pain of his cold neglect, his silence, his absence, hastened her to the grave—and, now that he is coming, you would keep it from her? Why, I tell you, Mary Carr, it will soothe her heart in dying."

She broke away impetuously, and went into the bed-chamber. Adeline unclosed her eyes at her approach. What Rose said, as she leaned over her and whispered, Mary Carr could not hear; but even in that last hour, it brought the red hectic to her faded cheek. How wildly and eagerly she looked up!

"But it is too late," she sighed, in a troubled whisper—"it is too late; I shall be gone. If he had but come a day earlier!"

She closed her eyes again, and remained silent. The next words she uttered, some time afterwards, were to Miss Carr.

"Mary—you—that which Louise was saying to-day——"

"Yes. I understand."

"If mamma wishes it—do not prevent it. I—I—should like him to see me—the wreck I am. And then he could come—you would bring him."

Rose assented eagerly, before Mary Carr could speak.

"And otherwise—if he had not been here—I have been

reflecting—that it would answer no end to oppose my mother —what can it matter to me, then? If I—had a child—and she died—it is possible I might wish the same. Don't interfere. But—you will bring *him ?* "

" Dearest Adeline, YES," cried Rose, " if he is to be found. I promise it to you solemnly."

" And now—dear friends of my girlhood, Rose! Mary ! " she breathed, holding out her hands, " I have but to say farewell. All things are growing dim around me. You know not how grateful I have been for your care of me. You will think of me sometimes in after-life."

The pause that ensued was only broken by Rose's sobs. Mary Carr's aching grief was silent.

" Remember—you especially, Rose—that life—will not last for ever—but—there is one beyond it; *that* will. Endeavour to inherit it. Will you not kiss me for the last time ? "

They leaned over her, one by one, their aching hearts beating against the counterpane, the tears raining from their eyes.

" You—will—come—to me—in heaven ? "

Barely had the words left her lips—and they were the last that either of them heard her utter—when Louise, with a solemn face, full of mighty importance, threw the corridor door wide open, and whispered something which only the nurse caught. She jumped up, thrust her chair behind her, and dropped down upon her knees where she stood.

" What in the world has taken her ? " ejaculated Rose.

" Don't you understand ? " was Mary's hurried answer, drawing Rose after her, and escaping to the drawing-room.

They saw it through the open door. The line of priests, in their white robes, coming up the stairs ; the silver crucifix borne before them ; the " Bon Dieu " sacredly covered from observation. Louise sank on her knees in the passage, as the nurse had done in the room, and they swept past her with solemn step, towards Adeline's chamber, looking neither to the right nor left. They had come to bestow absolution, according to the rights of the Roman Catholic faith—to administer to her the Sacrament of the dying.

CHAPTER XXX.

THE RECEPTION OF THE DEAD.

It was a sad day to describe—that next one. Adeline had died a little before midnight, fully conscious to the last, and quite peaceful; all her relatives, and they only, surrounding her bed.

Not only a sad day to describe, but a strange one; and I hardly know how to do it. You may look upon its chief incident as a disagreeable fiction; but it was sober fact, truthful reality. Perhaps you have never met with the like in your experience? I will transcribe it for you as exactly and faithfully as I can. The anecdotes of the same nature mentioned in the last chapter, were all facts too.

Louise was right: the corpse of Adeline de Castella was to hold a reception.

It was rumoured in the house that Signor de Castella was averse to the exhibition, but yielded the concession to his broken-hearted wife. Old Madame de Beaufoy made no secret of being against it; every English idea within her revolted from it. But Madame de Castella carried her point. There was perhaps a negative soothing to her wild grief in the reflection that before her beautiful and idolized child should be hidden away for all time, the world would once more look upon her, arrayed in all the pomp and splendour of life.

Early in the morning—the printers had been set to work betimes—the black-bordered death-circulars went forth to Belport.

"Monsieur et Madame de Castella; Madame de Beaufoy; Mademoiselle de Beaufoy:

"Ont l'honneur de vous faire part de la perte douloureuse qu'ils viennent de faire en la personne de Mademoiselle Adeline Luisa de Castella, leur fille, petite fille, et nièce; décédée à Belport le 8 Janvier, à l'age de 19 ans.

"Priez pour elle."

The invitations to the reception—or it may be more correct to say the intimations that it was to be held, for no invitations went out—were conveyed privately to the houses of friends by one or other of the Castella servants; by word of mouth, not officially. And I can tell you that it caused a commotion in the town, not forgotten yet.

It was about midday when Silva came to a little boudoir on the ground-floor, tenanted by Rose and Mary only, for the family kept their chambers. He said one of Madame de Nino's maid-servants was asking to see Miss Darling.

"She can come in, Silva," said Rose, getting up from her low chair by the fire, and passing her hand across her heavy eyes.

The woman came in—Julie. She handed a packet to Rose, which the latter divined at once must be the one her brother had written about. "It was left at the school for you this morning, mademoiselle."

"Who left it?" asked Rose.

"A tall handsome Englishman, for I happened to answer the gate myself," responded Julie. "He inquired for you, made-moiselle, and when I said you were not with us now, but visiting in the town, he handed in his card. You'll see it if you turn the parcel, Mademoiselle Rose: I slipped it inside the string for safety, coming along."

Rose scarcely needed to look at the card. She knew it was Frederick St. John's."

"Did he say where he was staying?—at what hotel?"

"He said nothing else, mademoiselle, but just left the parcel and card, with his compliments. Madame charged me to ask you, mesdemoiselles, at what hour it would be best for her to come to see the poor young lady?" continued Julie, dropping her voice.

"It begins at two, Julie. Any time between that hour and five."

"I wish I might come and see her too!" cried Julie. "I think us servants who served her so long at Madame de Nino's, might be allowed it."

"I dare say you might," said Rose. "Of course, you might. Tell Madame I say so."

"Julie," interposed Mary Carr, "I shall see her, of course; it would be looked upon as a slight in the house if I did not; but I can tell you I would rather walk ten miles away from it."

"But think of the beautiful sight it will be, Mademoiselle Carr!" remonstrated Julie. "We hear she is to wear her real wedding-dress—to be adorned with flowers and jewels. Ah, poor, poor thing!" broke off the girl, giving way to her ready tears. "But a few months ago, well and happy, and going to be married; and now, dead."

"Mary," said Rose, when they were alone, "I shall go out and find him, now I know he is in the town. Will you come?"

Mary Carr hesitated. "Would it be a proper thing, Rose, for us to go about to hotels, inquiring after gentlemen? I don't much like it."

"We have to do many things in this life that we 'don't like,'" was Rose's sarcastic answer. "Do you fear the hotels would eat you?"

"It is *not* the thing."

"Not for you, I dare say, so you can stay away: I'm sorry I asked. I promised that poor girl I would bring him to see her, were there any possibility of doing it; and I *will*."

"Then I shall go with you."

"Oh," retorted Rose.

The preparations for the great event were all but completed. *The preparations!* I feel nearly as ill, now that I am writing it, as I felt then; and some years have gone by. The large salon, next to the room in which she died, was laid out for the visitors, part of the furniture removed, and a barrier placed down the middle—a space being left clear at either end. It was a very long, large room, and so far suitable. She—Adeline —was placed against the wall at the far end, upright, standing, facing the company who were to come in, as if waiting to receive them and give them welcome. I cannot tell you how they fixed and supported her: I never asked then; I would as little ask now; I knew none of the details; the broad facts were enough.

As Mary Carr went creeping upstairs to put on her bonnet, she heard voices in the death-chamber, and looked in. They were dressing Adeline. The French nurse was standing before the upright corpse, supporting it on her shoulder, her own face turned aside from it; and the hairdresser stood behind, dressing the hair. Louise seemed to be helping to hold the dead weight; Susanne handed hair-pins to the man. If ever there was a revolting task on earth, that seemed one; and Mary Carr turned sick as she hastily closed the door again, and leaned against the wall to recover, if that might be, from her faintness.

"What hotel do you mean to try?" she inquired, when she went out with Rose into the broad daylight, a welcome relief from the darkened house and what was being transacted in it.

"I shall try them all in succession, until I find him," returned Rose. "I think he must use the Hôtel des Bains. I know Frank does."

Rose bent her steps towards that renowned hostelry, and turned boldly into the yard. A man came forward with a cloth on his arm, waiter fashion.

"Monsieur de Saint John," she began, "est-il descendu ici?"

The man stammered something in wretched French, "comprenais pas," and Rose found he was a very native Englishman.

Mr. St. John was staying there, but was going on to Paris in the evening. He was out just then.

"Out!" cried Rose, not expecting this check to her impatience. "Where's he gone?"

Of course the waiter could not say where. Rose intimated that her business was of importance; that she must see him. The group stood looking at each other in indecision.

"If you would like to go to his room and wait, ladies, I have the key," suggested the man. "It is only on the first floor."

"What is to be done, Mary Carr?" cried Rose, tapping her foot in pettish annoyance.

"Don't ask me. It is your expedition, not mine."

What Rose would have done, is uncertain. She was looking at the man in hesitation, perhaps thinking of the room and the key, when who should turn into the yard with a light quick step but Mr. St. John himself.

Not changed—not a whit changed. The same high bearing, the same distinguished form and face, the same frank manners, possessing for all so irresistible a fascination.

Rose, in a somewhat confused, anything but an explanatory, greeting—for she would not tell him the truth of what she wanted, lest he should decline it—said she had come to request him to accompany her for a short time. He answered that he was at her service, and in another moment the three were walking down the street together.

"Of all the sticklers for etiquette, I think Mary Carr's the worst," began Rose. "I wonder she does not apply for a post as maid-of-honour at court. The man asked us to go and wait in your rooms, and I should have gone had you not come in. She looked fit to faint at the bare idea."

Mr. St. John laughed; his old low musical laugh.

"Where would have been the harm?" went on Rose. "We are cousins, you know."

"Of course we are," said Mr. St. John. "I thought you both expected to have been in England before this?"

"We shall be there shortly now. At least, I shall. Mary, I believe, is going first to Holland. And you? You are going to Paris, we hear."

"Yes, but not to stay. My old roving love of travel has come upon me, and I think I shall gratify it. A friend of mine leaves Paris next week for a prolonged exploration of the Holy Land, and I feel inclined to accompany him."

"It does not look as though he were on the point of marrying Sarah Beauclerc," thought Rose to herself. For a wonder, she did not put the question.

But not a word of inquiry from him after Adeline! And yet, only a few months before, they had been on the nearest and dearest terms, but a few hours removed from the closest tie that can exist in this world—that of man and wife. Oh, the changes that take place in this transitory world of ours. *She* was dead, sleeping well after life's fitful fever; and he was walking there in all the pomp and pride of existence, haughtily indifferent, never unbending so far as to ask whether she was married to another, whether she was living or dead.

And so they reached the residence of Signor de Castella, and entered the courtyard, St. John unconscious where he was going. He had never gone to the house but once, and then it was at night, and in Sir Sandy Maxwell's carriage. The hall-door was placed wide open. Silva stood on one side of it, bareheaded, another servant opposite to him, and as the various visitors passed between them, they bowed to each group in silence. It was the manner of receiving them. Mr. St. John, talking with Rose, advanced close to the door; but when he caught sight of Silva, he drew back. The old man looked at him with a pleasant look: St. John had always been a favourite with the Castella servants. Mary Carr left them then, and ran upstairs.

"Why have you brought me here?" he demanded of Rose. "This is Signor de Castella's!"

"I have not brought you without a motive, Mr. St. John. Pray come in with me."

"You must excuse me," he said, very coldly.

"I cannot," answered Rose. "Do you think I should go dancing after you to the hotels, shocking Mary Carr and the waiters out of their notions of propriety, without an urgent motive? Pray come along : we are obstructing the entrance."

Mr. St. John indeed saw that a group of several ladies were gathered close behind him, waiting to go in. He stepped inside the hall—he had no other alternative—and so allowed them to pass. They moved noiselessly towards the broad staircase ; but he drew aside with Rose.

"Rose, this is beyond a joke," he said. "Why did you bring me here? I will wish you good morning."

"Indeed," she murmured, clasping her agitated hands on his arm, in her fear lest, after all, he should escape her, "this is no joke. Do you suppose Mary Carr would lend herself to one? and she came with me. Pray come upstairs with me, Mr. St. John."

"You forget," he began, in answer more to her evident excitement than to her words, "that—putting aside any objection I may experience—my presence here may not be acceptable to the family."

"You will not see the family. They are not visible to-day."

"Who are all these people going up the stairs?" he said, looking on in amazement, as more groups were silently bowed in by Silva. "It seems like a reception."

"It is one," said Rose : "nevertheless the family do not hold it. There comes Madame de Nino ! She is directing those strict eyes of hers towards us, and I shall catch a sharp lecture for standing whispering with you. Do come, Mr. St. John."

"I cannot understand this, Rose. These visitors, flocking to the house, while, you say, the family are not visible ! Why do they come, then? Why do you wish me to go up?"

"There's—there's—a show upstairs to-day," stammered Rose "That is why they come. And I want you to see it."

"A flower-show?" said Mr. St. John, somewhat mockingly.

"A faded one," murmured Rose, as she took his hand, and drew him towards the staircase.

His manner was hesitating, his step reluctant ; and but for the young lady's pertinacity, which he could not resist without downright rudeness, he had certainly retreated. Involuntarily, he could not tell why or wherefore, the remembrance of a past scene came rushing to his mind ; when he, Frederick St. John, had in like manner forced a resisting spirit up the stairs and into the room of a college-boy who was dying.

At the head of the stairs they met Mary Carr, who held out a small sealed packet.

"A commission was intrusted to me yesterday, Mr. St. John," she said, "that I would deliver this into your own hands. I have also a message——"

"Which you can give him presently," interrupted Rose.

He glanced at the packet ; he glanced at the seal, "A. L. de C. ;" he looked at the other side, at the strange, sprawling address.

"Not a very elegant superscription," he observed, carelessly, as he slipped the parcel into the breast-pocket of his coat. "I don't recognize the handwriting."

"Yet you were once familiar with it, Mr. St. John.'

"Oh, never ! " answered he. "Not, certainly, to my recol-lection."

They were now at the door of the drawing-room. Rose, feeling a sick terror at the thought of what she was going to behold, laid her hand momentarily on Mr. St. John, as if doubting her own capability to support herself.

"Are you ill?" he inquired, looking at her pale face.

"A slight faintness," she murmured. "It will go off."

It was in front of them, at the other end of the room as they entered. *It!* But they could not see it distinctly for a moment together, so many persons were pushing on before them. Mr. St. John, who was taller than most persons pre-sent, obtained a more distinct view than Rose.

"Who is that—standing yonder—receiving the company ? " he asked hastily. "It looks like—— no ; it cannot be. *Is* it Adeline ? "

"Yes, it is Adeline de Castella," replied Rose, under her breath, her teeth chattering. "She is holding her reception."

Adeline *de Castella*. Did the name strike oddly upon Mr. St. John ? But if it did, how then came he not to ask why it was not Adeline de la Chasse?

"You have deceived me, Miss Darling," he said in severe tones ; "you assured me the family were not here. What means all this ? "

"They are not here," whispered Rose, whose face and lips were now as white as those of the dead.

"Not here! There stands Adeline."

"Yes, true; Adeline," she murmured. "But she will not speak to you. You—you will pass and look at her: as we look at a picture. You can't go back now, if you would: see the throng. Trust me for once," she added, as she seized his arm: "Adeline will not speak to you—she will not, as I live and breathe."

Partly from the extreme difficulty of retreating, for they were in the line of advance, not in that formed for returning according to the arrangements of the room, partly in compliance with Rose Darling's agitated earnestness, and partly yielding to his own curiosity, which was becoming intensely excited, Mr. St. John continued his way, ever and anon catching a glimpse of the rigid form opposite, before which all were filing.

"It cannot be Adeline!" he exclaimed, involuntarily. "And yet it is like her! Who is it? *What* is it? How strange she looks!"

"She has been ill, you see," shivered Rose, "and is much attenuated. But it is Adeline."

They were nearly up with her. Rose, in her faintness, not having yet dared to look at the sight, clung to the arm of Mr. St. John. He was gazing on her—Adeline; and his face, never very rosy, had turned of a yet paler hue than common.

Oh, the rich and flowing robes in which they had decked her! white satin, covered with costly lace; white ribbons, white flowers, everything about her white; the festive attire of a bride adorning the upright dead, and that dead worn and wasted! A narrow band of white satin was passed tightly under the chin, to keep the jaw from falling, but it was partly hidden by the hair and the wreath of flowers, and the veil that floated behind her. Never, in health, had those beautiful ringlets been seen on Adeline as they were set forth now, to shade those hollow cheeks: but all the richness of her dress and the flowing hair, all the flowers and the costly lace, could not conceal the ghastliness of the features, or soften the fixed stare of the glazed eyes. Yet, in the contour of the face, there was something still inexpressibly beautiful. To a stranger entering the room, unsuspecting the truth, as Mr. St. John, she looked like one fearfully ill, fearfully strange: and how was Mr. St. John, who had never heard of the custom, to divine

the truth? Did the idea occur to him that Adeline was standing in the very spot where he had first met her, a year before,
when the French marigold in his button-hole was accidentally
caught by her? Did the strange gloomy silence strike ominously upon him; putting him in mind of a funeral or a lying-
in-state, rather than a gay reception?

He went close up, and halted in front of her: Rose by him,
shaking from head to foot. Forgetting, probably, what Rose
had said, that she would not speak to him, or else obeying the
impulse of the moment, he mechanically held out his hand to
Adeline: but there was no answering impulse on her part.

He stood rooted to the spot, his eyes running rapidly over
her. They glanced down on the flounces of the rich lace
dress, they wandered up to her face—it was the first close, full
view he had obtained of it. He saw the set, rigid features, the
unmistakable stare of the glassy eye; and, with a rushing
sensation of sickening awe and terror, the terrible truth burst
upon his brain.

That it was not Adeline de Castella, but her CORPSE which
stood there.

He was a strong-minded man—a man little given to betray
his feelings, or to suffer them to escape beyond his own control: yet he staggered now against the wall by her side, in
what seemed a fainting-fit. Rose, alarmed for the consequences of what she had done, burst into tears, knelt down,
and began to rub his hands.

"Open the windows—give some air here," called out little
Monsieur Durante, who had come all the way from Ostrohove
to see the sight. "Here's a gentleman in an attack."

"Nothing of the sort," returned an Englishman, who made
one of the company; "he has nearly fainted, that's all.
There's no cause for alarm, young lady. I suppose he came
in, not knowing what he was going to see, and the shock
overpowered him. It *is* an odd fashion, this. See: he revives
already."

Consciousness came to Mr. St. John. He rose slowly, shook
himself out of a shuddering-fit, and with a last wild yearning
glance at the dead, fell into the line of the retreaters. But it
was Miss Carr who now detained him: Adeline's message had
yet to be given.

"The address on the packet was in *her* handwriting, Mr. St.
John," she whispered; "she wrote it yesterday, only a few

hours before she died. She charged me to say that everything is there, except the ring, which has never been off her finger since you placed it there, and will be buried with her ; and to tell you that she had been ever faithful to you ; as in life, so unto death."

Mr. St. John listened, and nodded in reply, with the abstracted air of one who answers what he does not hear, touching unconsciously the breast-pocket of his coat, where lay the packet.

"There was something else," continued she, " but I dare not venture to breathe that here. Later, perhaps ? "

Again he nodded with the same look of abstraction, never speaking ; and began to follow in the wake of the crowd, who had taken their fill of gazing, and were making their way from the room.

"He is a fine young man, though," exclaimed M. Durante, looking after St. John with eyes of admiration. "But he is very pale : he has scarcely recovered himself."

"To think that he should have dropped at seeing a corpse, just as one might drop a stone, a fine strong man like him ! " responded a neighbouring chemist, who had stepped in to have a look at the reception. "Qu'ils sont drôles, ces Anglais-là ! "

CHAPTER XXXI.

UNAVAILING REPENTANCE.

ROSE DARLING struggled out of the room with Mr. St. John : not caring to remain in it, possibly, without his sheltering presence. They went downstairs with the crowd—all silent and well-behaved, but still a crowd—and then Rose drew him into the small snug room that had been her abiding place and Mary's for the day.

Mr. St. John sat down, and leaned his head upon his hand. In a shock like this, he could not make believe not to feel it, or to gloss it over ; indeed he was an independent man at all times, utterly refusing to give in to the false artificialities of society. Rose slipped away, and brought him a glass of wine ; but he shook his head, declining to take it. Mary Carr had not come with them; it turned out afterwards that she thought he had left the house.

"When did she die?" was the first question he presently asked.

"Last night; a few minutes before twelve."

"Just as I was stepping on board the steamer at Folkestone," he murmured to himself. "Why is she—*there*, Rose? —dressed—in that form? Are they mad?"

"It is a custom they have in France, as it seems; but I had never before heard of it," answered Rose. "Hark at the people passing up still!"

A shiver of remembrance took him, but it was conquered immediately. Rose untied the black string of her straw bonnet, and put it on the table.

"I suppose we are both in mourning for the same person," she remarked, in allusion to the narrow band of crape on his hat: "little George St. John."

"Yes," he shortly answered. "What did she die of?"

"Of consumption: at least, that is what the doctors would tell you. I won't say anything about a broken heart."

Mr. St. John made no reply. Rose resumed:

"From the moment that blood-vessel burst, there has been, I suppose, no real hope, no possibility of cure. But she rallied so greatly, and seemed so well, that I, for one, believed in it."

He looked at Rose; the words seemed to arouse his curiosity. "When did she burst a blood-vessel?"

"It was at Beaufoy. It was—why, yes, it was the very day you were last there, Mr. St. John, almost in your sight. You remember the morning you quitted the house, and never came back again?—did you notice Adeline running down the steps of the colonnade after you, imploring you to stop?—did you notice that she sank down on the grass, as if from fatigue?"

"I think I did," he answered, in allusion to the last question. "I know she followed me down the steps."

"It was then the blood-vessel broke; through emotion, no doubt. Had you but looked back once again, you might have seen what was amiss. I never shall forget the sight. Just at first I had thought her foot slipped and threw her down, next I thought she was kneeling for a joke: but when I reached her, I saw what it was. One minute longer, and you would have seen the whole house gathered round her on the lawn. She was got indoors, and the doctors were sent for.

What a house it was! She thought she was dying; and I believe the chiefest wish of her heart then was to see you."

"Why did you not send for me?"

"We did send. I wrote to you, and Louise took the note at once to the Lodge. But you had already gone—turning Madame Baret's brains upside down with the shock."

"You might have sent it after me to England."

"Of course I might—if I had only known you were gone to England. How *was* I to know it? I might be wishing to get a note to some one in the moon, but not see my way clear to writing the address. It was weeks, and weeks, and weeks, Mr. St. John, before we ever heard a syllable of you, whether you were in England or in any other part of the known world, or whether you were at the bottom of the sea."

"And she never married de la Chasse?"

The words seemed spoken as a remark, not as a question. Rose, who seemed to have a touch of one of her ironical moods coming on, answered it:

"Would you have had her marry him when death had set in? After the doctors had met that day, it was known throughout the house that nothing could save her. At least, they said so. The old malady of the spring had but been lying dormant; it was in her still; and the terrible trouble she went through had brought it forth again. Under the very happiest circumstances, had she married you, even—and I suppose that might have been *her* idea of happiness," added Rose, satirically—"she could not have lived long. De la Chasse saw her for a few minutes on the day they were to have been married, and expressed himself very much concerned, and all that, as a matter of course; I don't suppose he broke his heart over it."

"And she has been ill ever since?"

"Ever since. The disease has fluctuated, as you may imagine; some weeks she would be at death's door, some weeks comparatively well; but it has all the while been progressing on gradually to the ending. Frederick St. John"—and Rose stepped up to him in her excitement—"I don't believe you were ever absent for one minute from her mind; by day and by night it was filled with that miserable love for you; and the yearning wish, destined not to be gratified, was ever upon her—that you would come and see her before she died."

"*Why* did you not let me know it?—why could you not have written to me?" he asked, in a sharp tone of pain.

"For one thing, I tell you, I did not know where to write. For another, Adeline would not have let me. She had an idea that you did not care to come to her—that you perhaps would not, if summoned. And I"—Rose paused a moment, and angrily compressed her repentant lips—"I could wish my tongue had been bitten out for a share I took in the past. There's not the least doubt that one ingredient in Adeline's cup of bitterness was worse than all the rest—the thought of Sarah Beauclerc."

He uttered an exclamation.

"And of your love for her. And I say I wish Sarah Beauclerc had been smothered, and I with her, if you like, before I had ever breathed her name to Adeline. But for that, but for deeming that *she* was your true love, and would some time be your wife, Adeline would have sent to the far ends of the earth after you for a parting interview."

He sat, leaning his head upon his fingers, looking into the fire.

"What a miserable business it seems altogether! Nothing but cross-purposes, the one with the other. Sarah Beauclerc!"

"Are you still engaged—perhaps at a moment like this I may be pardoned for asking it—to Sarah Beauclerc?"

"I never was engaged to Sarah Beauclerc. I had once a sort of passing fancy for her; I don't know that it was more. I have had no thought of her, or of any one else, since I parted from Adeline."

"In a letter I had from London, not very long ago," resumed Rose, slowly, "your name was coupled with Miss Sarah Beauclerc's. It said you were her shadow."

"Who said it?"

"Never mind. It was a lady."

"Your correspondent laboured under a mistake, Rose; you may tell her so, for her satisfaction. Sarah Beauclerc will very soon be a wife, but not mine."

"Who is she going to marry?"

"Lord Raynor."

Rose exhausted her surprise in ejaculations. She had thought Sarah Beauclerc would be Frederick St. John's chosen wife; had felt utterly certain of it in her own mind. He sat in silence, never heeding her. Remembrances of the past were crowding upon him. That he had been very near loving Sarah Beauclerc, was indisputable: and but for the meeting with Adeline, this might have come to fruition: there was no knowing now. At Lady Revel's—the evening spoken of to Rose by Miss Mary Anne Darling—he had learnt that she, Sarah, was going to be married to the Viscount Raynor, a man who, as Captain Budd, had been attached to her for years. She herself told him of this. In her calm, cold, cutting manner, she spoke of *his* contemplated marriage to Mademoiselle de Castella: was any covert reproof intended in this? any secret intimation that *that* justified her own engagement? However that might be, all chance of their being one in this world, had any such chance ever existed, was at an end; and Frederick St. John had no regret left in regard to it. All his regrets were for another.

"If Adeline had but known it!" murmured Rose, genuine tears of vexation filling her eyes. "Did you not know she was dying, Mr. St. John?"

"No. I knew nothing about her."

"Have you been in England ever since you quitted us that day?"

"I went straight to London from Beaufoy, saw my brother Isaac, explained matters to him, and then accompanied him to Castle Wafer. Subsequently I went to Scotland, deer-stalking; running over once to London from thence, to see my mother. Before Christmas, I was again for a week in London, and then I escorted my mother to Castle Wafer. Now you know what my movements have been, Rose. I heard nothing of Adeline."

"Perhaps you kept yourself out of the way of hearing of her?"

"I did."

"That was your temper!"

"Just so. Our faults generally bring their own punishment."

"We heard you were in an awful passion at Madame Baret's," remarked Rose, who plunged into things irrelevant without mercy.

"I thought I had cause to be. I thought so then. I do not know the reason now why she rejected me."

"Mary Carr will tell you that. Ill-fated Adeline! She would have given her poor life to have been allowed to whisper it to you then, to justify herself in your eyes. The fact is," added Rose, after a pause, "the Church interfered to prevent the marriage, and Adeline was sworn to silence on the crucifix. *I* did not know it until to-day. She thought of you until the last, Mr. St. John, and in her dying moments got permission from her father for the truth to be disclosed to you. Mary was charged with it."

Mr. St. John's eyes blazed up with an angry light. "Then I know that was the work of Father Marc!"

"I dare say it was. He was very fond of Adeline, and no doubt thought her marriage with a heretic would be perdition here and hereafter. I don't see that you can blame him : you would have done the same in his place, had you been true to your creed. Father Marc's one of the best gossipers living. We saw a great deal of him in Adeline's sick-room, after you left. I fell in love with the charming old père."

Would she ever be serious! The question might have crossed Mr. St. John at a less bitter moment.

"And I think his gossip did Adeline good," continued Rose. "It was a sort of break to her misery. How could you have doubted her—have doubted for a single moment, whatever your passionate rage might have been, that her whole love was yours?"

How indeed? But perhaps in his inmost heart he never had doubted it. He sat there now, bearing the bitter weight of remembrance as he best might, his eyes looking back into the past, his delicate lips drawn in to pain.

"They have no portrait of her," went on Rose, not in her mercilessness, but in her giddy, gossiping lightness. "And the one you took of her, you defaced."

"Don't, Rose!"

The words came from him with a wail. His remorse wanted no feeding; it was already as great as he well knew how to bear. Rose was not quite without feeling, and the words and their tone checked her. She sat thinking how unkind she had been, and began flirting the strings of her bonnet about, as it lay near her on the table.

But it was not in her nature to remain silent long. Something, perhaps the black ribbon, took her thoughts to another subject : and in truth she did not like to say more of Adeline.

"Does it not seem like a fatality? All three of them to have died, one after the other!"

Mr. St. John came slowly out of his pain, and looked at her for an explanation. "Three of whom?"

"Oh, I was thinking of Alnwick.   Mr. Carleton St. John first and then his two boys.   I suppose you have inherited?"

"My brother has.   Yes, it is a very sad thing.   Quite a fatality, as you say."

"What fortune has Charlotte now?   Much?"

"I really do not know.   I fear not much."

"She reckoned so surely—I know she did—upon being Lady St. John!"

"That seems to be a chief portion of life's business, I think," he remarked: "the reckoning upon things that never come to pass."

"I suppose you have not seen her since?"

"Mrs. Carleton St. John?   Yes, I have.   I heard she was staying with Mrs. Darling in town, the week I spent there before Christmas, and I called."

"How was she looking?   How did she seem?" asked Rose, rather eagerly.

"She seemed quite well, and she looked well.   Very thin: but in good health and spirits."

"There was no—excitement in her manner, was there?"

"On the contrary.   She struck me as being one of the calmest, quietest-mannered women I ever saw."

"Did you think her pretty?"

"No.   I thought her handsome."

"What did mamma say to you about me?—and Margaret and Mary Anne?   No good, I know.   They are always abusing me."

"I did not see them.   Mrs. Carleton St. John said they had all gone out to call on some old friend."

"You had no loss.   Mamma you know; I don't say anything against her, though it was a shame of her to keep me at school so long; but Mary Anne and Margaret are the primmest old creatures you can picture.   Why, they are going on for thirty! I sent them over a cap apiece the other day, in return for a little interference of theirs.   Lottie Singleton took the parcel. Didn't it make them wild!"

A faint smile parted his lips.

"Where is Charlotte going to live?" resumed Rose.   "Have you heard?"

"I have heard nothing.   I believe my brother wrote to beg of her to go back to Alnwick, and remain there as long as she chose.   But she declined."

"I know one thing—that I hope she'll not live with us," cried Rose, tossing back her golden curls. "Charlotte always was so domineering, and now—especially—— You are *sure* you observed no undue excitement of manner?" she broke off, after a pause.

"Why do you ask it? To me she appeared to be almost unnaturally calm."

"I think I'll tell you why," said thoughtless Rose. And forthwith she disclosed to Mr. St. John all she had heard from Nurse Brayford. It was lamentably imprudent of her, without doubt; but she meant no harm. And the notion she herself had gathered from the story was, that the trouble had temporarily touched Charlotte's brain, just as a passing fever will touch it. That was all the real thought of her heart; but her expressions were exaggerated as usual, meaning less than they implied. It had the effect of fully arousing Frederick St. John from his own care: and Rose was surprised to see him make so much of it.

"That Charlotte—that your sister at the time of the child's death was *mad!*" he repeated. "Surely not, Rose!"

"It was nothing less. How else could she fancy she saw all sorts of visions of the child? Not her child; I don't mean him: the little heir, Benja. He was always walking before her with the lighted toy, the church; the one that caused his death, you know. She had awful fits of this terror, frightening Georgy nearly to death."

Mr. St. John made no reply. His eyes were fixed on Rose, and he was revolving what she said.

"It was Mrs. Brayford told me this; the nurse who was with Adeline in the spring. You heard that she had gone from Belport with Mrs. Carleton St. John to watch George. But I don't think the woman told me quite all," added Rose, casting her thoughts back: "she seemed to reserve something. At least, so it struck me."

"It must have been a sort of brain fever," remarked Mr. St. John.

"It must have been downright madness," returned Rose. "They hold a curious custom, it seems, in one of the towns of France: on St. Martin's Eve every one turns out at night with horns and lighted paper lanterns, which they parade about the streets for a couple of hours. It happened that Charlotte was there this very night: she had gone to the town to take the steamer for London. The lanterns were of various forms and devices, many of them being churches; and Charlotte was in her room when the show began, and saw it all. She had a sort of fit from terror," continued Rose in a whisper. "She was quite mad when she came to, fancying it was a thousand Benjas coming after her to torment her. Prance had always locked Brayford out of the room before, when these attacks came on; but she couldn't do it that night, for Charlotte had to be held; she was raving."

"It is very strange," said Mr. St. John.

"That is why I asked you whether you saw anything unusual in her manner,—any excitement. Of course I can't write and ask; I can't hint at it. They *say* Charlotte is well, but if she were not I know they would never tell me, and I like to be at the top and bottom of everything. I'm mamma's true daughter for that."

"Rose, I wish you had not told me this."

"Why?" exclaimed Rose, opening her eyes very wide.

He seemed to have spoken involuntarily. The retort and its surprised tone woke him from his dream, and all his senses were in full play again.

"It is not pleasant to hear of women suffering. I can't bear it. Your sister must have gone through a great deal."

"Oh, poor thing, yes she must. I'll not call her hard names again. And I do hope and trust the brain trouble has really left her."

"She seemed quite well. I saw no trace whatever of the mind's being affected. It must have been a sort of temporary fever. Rose, were I you, I think I would never talk of this."

"I don't. I only said it to you. I assure you I wouldn't say a word of it to mamma to be made Empress to-morrow. She'd box my ears for me, as she used to do when I was a little girl."

Mr. St. John rose to leave. "There's nothing more you have to say, Rose?"

She knew as well as he that he alluded to Adeline. "There was nothing more, just then," she answered. "Mary Carr would, no doubt, see him later."

He shook hands with Rose and was leaving the room, when Miss Carr came in. She uttered an exclamation of surprise.

"I thought you had gone," she said. "Will you come with me and see old Madame de Beaufoy? I was in her room just now, and told her you had been here; she thought I ought to have taken you up to her; and she cried when she said how great a favourite you had been in those happy days, now gone by for ever."

With some hesitation—for he did not care to see the family again, especially on that day—Mr. St. John suffered himself to be conducted to her room. The show people were still silently jostling each other on the staircase, passing up and down it.

Madame de Beaufoy was in her chamber: it is the custom you know to receive visitors in the bed-chambers in France: a handsomely furnished room, the counterpane a blue satin, richly quilted, and the large square pillows, lying on it, of the finest cambric edged with choice Mechlin lace. As she held Mr. St John's hand in greeting and drew him to the fire, the tears coursed freely down the fine old face.

"Ah, my friend, my friend!" she said, speaking in English, "if they had but suffered her to marry you, she might not be lying low this day. A hundred times I have said to Maria, that she should not have been severed from Frederick St. John. But Maria, poor thing, had no hand in it; she is not a dévote; it was the Church that did it. And we must suppose all's for the best, though it sacrificed her."

No tears shone in his eyes, his grief was too deep for that. It could be read in every line of his face, of his rigid features.

"I wish to Heaven things had been allowed to take a different course," he answered in low tones. "But they tell me that no care, no amount of happiness could have saved her."

"Tush!" returned the old lady. "The greatest mistake they made was in not taking her to a warmer climate while they had the opportunity. Had that been done, and had you been allowed to marry her, she might have enjoyed years of life. I don't say she could have lived to be old: they insist upon it that she could not: but she would have had some enjoyment of this world, poor child, and not have been cut off from it, as she is now."

The thought crossed him—and it came in spite of his regrets, and he could not help it—that all things might still be for the best. Had she lived to bear him children—and to entail upon them her fragility of constitution——

"You did love her, Mr. St. John."

"With my whole heart and soul."

"Ay, ay; and she was bound up in you. I don't see why

you should have been parted—and we all liked you. For my part," continued the tolerant old lady—"but you know it doesn't do to avow such sentiments to the world—I think one religion is as good as another, provided people do their duty in it. She had as sure a chance of going to heaven as your wife, as she had if she had married that de la Chasse, whom I never liked."

"Indeed I trust so."

" I became a Roman Catholic to please my husband and his family, but I was just as near to heaven when I was a Protestant. And I say that Adeline need not have been sacrificed. You have been in to see her, I hear."

"Yes. Not knowing what I was going to see."

"Was ever such a barbarous custom heard of! But Maria would listen to no sort of reason : and Agnes upheld her. I wonder the Signor allowed it. They will not get me in. I shall see the dear lost one in her coffin to-night ; but I will not see her the actor in all that mummery."

The old lady was interrupted by the entrance of Madame de Castella. She did not know St. John was there ; and her first surprised movement was that of retreat. But a different feeling came over her, and she stepped forward sobbing, holding out both her hands.

A few broken sentences of mutual sorrow, and then the scene became disagreeably painful to Mr. St. John. Madame de Castella's sobs were loud and hysterical, her mother's tears rained down quietly. He took his leave almost in silence.

" Would you like to attend the funeral ? " asked the old lady. " It takes place to-morrow."

"To-morrow !" he echoed : the haste striking upon his English ideas as unseemly.

" To-morrow at eleven."

"Perhaps Mr. St. John would not like it ? " interposed Madame de Castella between her sobs. " The Baron de la Chasse is coming for it."

"And what if he is !" cried her mother. " Surely their animosities must have ended now. Be here a quarter before eleven, my friend, if it would be any satisfaction to you to see the last of her."

Ah yes, all animosities had ended then, and St. John did not fail to be there. It was one of the grandest funerals ever seen in Belport. Amidst the long line of priests was Father Marc : and he recognized St. John and saluted him courteously and cordially, as if entirely oblivious of the past, and of the share he had taken in it. Signor de Castella walked bareheaded after the coffin; de la Chasse and another near friend were next. St. John was lost amid the crowd of followers, and his companion was Monsieur le Comte le Coq de Monty.

"So happy to have the honour of meeting you again, though it is upon this melancholy occasion!" cried the Comte, who was very fond of talking and had hastened to fasten himself on Mr. St. John. "What a sad thing that consumption is! And de la Chasse is here! How he must feel her loss! the engaging, beautiful demoiselle that she was!"

The procession moved on. To the church first, and then to the grave. But amidst all its pomp and show, amidst the tall candles, the glittering crucifixes, the banners of silver and black, amidst the array of priests and their imposing vestments; through the low murmurs of their soothing chant, lost in the echoes of the streets; even beyond that one dark mass, the cheaf feature of the pageant, borne by eight men with measured tread, through his regrets for what was in it—his buried love—there came something else, totally foreign to all this, and uncalled for by will, floating through the mind of Mr. St. John.

The curious tale whispered to him by Rose Darling the previous day, touching the fancies of Mrs. Carleton St. John, was connecting itself, in a haunting fashion, with certain words he had heard dropped by Honour at Castle Wafer.

CHAPTER XXXII.

SOME MONTHS ONWARDS.

IT was August weather. The glowing sunlight of the day had faded, and the drawing-rooms were lighted at Castle Wafer. A small group of guests had gathered there; it may almost be said a family group; had been spending there some five or six weeks. Changes have taken place since you met them last. Its master has come into the inheritance so coveted by Mrs. Carleton St. John for her own child : and he is also in stronger

health than he has been for years. Look at him as he sits in
the remotest corner of the room, his table covered with books
and bearing a small shaded reading-lamp. But he is not reading now; he is listening with a fond smile to a charming girl in
white evening attire, as she sits close to him and talks in a low
voice. Her great eyes, of a blue grey, are raised to his face,
and the gold chain glistens on her fair white shoulders as she
bends towards him, and she seems to be petitioning some
favour; for he keeps shaking his head in the negative, as if to
tantalize her; but the kindly look in his eyes, and the sweet
smile on his face are very conspicuous. You have met her
before : it is Miss Beauclerc, the daughter of the Dean of
Westerbury.

Unpleasantly conspicuous, that smile and that tender look,
to one of the distant group. The glittering chandelier—and
only one chandelier has been lighted to-night, as is usual on
these quiet evenings—is reflected as in a thousand prisms by
the wax-lights, and the glitter shines full on the face of this one
lady, who sits back in the satin chair unnoticed, her dark eyes
disagreeably fierce and eager. Is she a young girl? She really
looks like one, in her black silk dress with its low simple body
and short sleeves, edged only with a narrow ruching of white
crape; looks almost as young as Miss Beauclerc. But she is
not young; she has passed her thirtieth year, and more than
that; and you have met her before, for she is the widow of
George Carleton St. John of Alnwick. They call her here at
Castle Wafer Mrs. Carleton, in a general way, as her additional
name would interfere with Mrs. St. John's. We had better do
the same. Sometimes they call her Charlotte; and she likes
that best, for she hates the name of Carleton, simply because
it was the name of her late husband's first wife.

Right underneath the chandelier, both of them at some sort
of work, sit Mrs. St. John and Mrs. Darling. Mrs. St. John
has recovered the accident of a year ago; it left a languor
upon her which she is rather too fond of indulging. Isaac St.
John is glad that visitors should be staying at Castle Wafer, for
they divert his step-mother, whom he greatly esteems and
respects, from her own fancied ailments. That accident would
seem to have aged her ten years, and you would take her to be
nearly sixty. Lastly, talking and laughing at the open glass
doors, now halting inside, now stepping forth on the terrace in
the balmy summer's night, are Rose Darling and Frederick St.

John. Frederick has been but a few days arrived, after an
absence of many months, chiefly spent in the Holy Land; the
rest have been for six weeks at Castle Wafer.

Six weeks, and they went for only one! Isaac pressed the
visit upon Mrs. Carleton, whose position he much pitied, and
politely invited Mrs. Darling to accompany her with any of the
Miss Darlings she might like to bring. Mrs. Darling accepted
the invitation and brought Rose. The other two were staying
with old Mrs. Darling in Berkshire, who was flourishing and
seemed likely to live to be a hundred. It almost seemed to
Isaac St. John, in his refined sensitiveness, that *he* had committed a wrong on Charlotte St. John, by succeeding to the
property that would have been her husband's and then her
son's, had they lived. Could he have done it with any sort of
delicacy, he had made over to her a handsome yearly income.
Indeed, he had hinted at this to Mrs. Darling, but that lady
said she felt sure it could not be done with Charlotte's proud
spirit. Isaac hoped still : and meanwhile he pressed Charlotte
to *stay* with them at Castle Wafer, not to run away, as her
mother talked of doing. Mrs. Darling had been talking of it
this month past; and her departure was now really fixed for
the morrow. She was going with Rose to Paris; but Charlotte
had accepted the invitation to remain.

Her fate really deserved sympathy. Bereft of her husband,
of her cherished son, bereft not only of the fortune but also of
the position she had thought to secure in marrying the master
of Alnwick, she had perforce retired into a very humble
individual again, who could not keep up much of an establishment of her own. In health she was perfectly well : all that
dark time seemed to have passed away as a dream : she was
better-looking than ever, and the inward fever that used to
consume her and render her a very shadow, did not waste her
now. Mrs. Darling had spoken to her seriously of what her
future plans should be : that lady herself would probably have
desired nothing better than to keep her favourite daughter with
her always : but her other daughters rose rather rebelliously
against it, and some unpleasantness had been the result.

Rose spoke out freely, as was her custom. If Charlotte did
remain with them, she should not stand any domineering; and
Mary Anne and Margaret Darling intimated that they should
not leave grandmamma until home was free for them. Charlotte
had brought this ill-will upon herself by the very line of con-

duct Rose spoke openly about—domineering. Mrs. Darling was a little perplexed: but she was an easy-tempered woman, and was content to let trifles take their chance. There was no immediate hurry: Charlotte's visit at Castle Wafer was to be extended, against the wish of Mrs. Darling, and might be continued for an indefinite time. Who knew but that Charlotte might captivate its bachelor master? *And who knew but Charlotte herself was entertaining the same possibility?* Mrs. Darling feared so; and, in all cases where Charlotte was concerned, she was a keen observer. What, though Isaac St. John had a hump upon his back, he was, apart from that, a lovable man—a man that even an attractive woman might covet for her own.

Mrs. Darling's employment this evening was some intricate working of gold beads on canvas. And every time she looked off to take up a bead upon the long needle, she seized the opportunity to glance at Charlotte. How entirely still she was!—leaning back in the armchair; her delicate hands lying motionless on her lap. But for the eyes, directed to one part of the room, and the angry glare beginning now to shine in them, Mrs. Darling had deemed her entirely at rest. She, Mrs. Darling, moved her chair, apparently to get some better light for the beads, and the change of position enabled her to look towards the spot herself.

Miss Beauclerc, her fair face bending forward in its eagerness, her wide open, fine grey eyes raised to his, had laid her two hands on Isaac St. John's; and he had playfully made prisoner of them and was keeping them fast. In the stillness of the room their voices were distinctly heard.

"You *will* promise it to me, then!"

Isaac laughed and shook his head. "You don't know how incorrigible the man has been, Georgie."

"All the more reason for your forgiving him."

"If the dean were here, I'm not sure that he would say so. He has had the greatest trouble with him, Georgina."

"That's just why I'm asking you," cried the girl prettily and saucily. "Papa might refuse me; you must not. You know you *can't*."

"What will you give if I say yes?"

"I'll give you——" she dropped her voice and laughed. Isaac bent and kissed her crimson cheek. Kissed it as a father might kiss a child; but she drew back shyly, and blushed to her fingers' ends, half glancing towards the window.

Something like a faint sound of anger came from Charlotte. It was smothered beneath a sudden cough. No ears heard it save those of the anxious mother; no eyes, save hers, saw the involuntary clenching of the impassive hands. She—Mrs. Darling—sat upright in her chair and turned her eyes in the direction where her daughter's were fixed.

"Did you obtain that information to-day, Sir Isaac?"

Sir Isaac was again laughing—oh, how much better in health was he now than of yore!—and did not hear the question.

"Are you speaking to me, Mrs. Darling?"

"That information you said you would obtain for me about the conjunction of the trains. Did you do so?"

"Brumm did. I thought he had given you the paper. He has all particulars set down, I know, in black and white. Perhaps he gave it to Miss Rose?"

"Who is taking my name in vain?" cried Rose, looking in, her bright face aglow with mirth.

Mr. St. John had been standing for the last few minutes inside the room, Rose on the threshold. As he talked to her, his eyes had unconsciously rested on the face of Mrs. Carleton; and the strange expression in hers, their look of fierce anger, had struck him with amazement; even the movement of the hands, telling of suppressed pain, was not wholly hidden from him. With a rush and a whirl there came back to his mind certain facts connected with Mrs. Carleton St. John, which had almost faded out of his remembrance. But what could be the cause of her antipathy to Miss Beauclerc? And there *was* antipathy in those eyes, if he ever read eyes in this world.

It was over directly,—quick as a flash of lightning,—and the relative situations of the parties changed. Georgina Beauclerc came to the table with a light step, as gay and careless as Rose; Sir Isaac followed more slowly, and sat down by Mrs. Carleton.

"You look pleased, my dear," observed Mrs. St. John, glancing up at Georgina.

"I have been teasing Sir Isaac, and I have gained my wish. But—you didn't see"—and she bent her lips with a smile— "I had to give him a kiss for the concession."

"Rather a hazardous favour to grant in a general way," observed Mrs. Darling, whose ears the whispered words had reached. "Some gentlemen, in the bachelor position of Sir Isaac, might deem the gift significant."

She put down her beads and her canvas, and looked full at
Georgina, expecting a protest against such motives. But in
this she was mistaken. Georgina only threw back her pretty
head with a laugh; and in it—at least to Mrs. Darling's ears—
there was a sound of triumph.

"What was your petition to him, my dear?" asked Mrs. St.
John.

"Ah, that's a secret; it's something between himself and
me;" and Miss Georgina Beauclerc went dancing towards the
window, as if desiring a breath of the fresh night air.

The scene was almost more lovely than by day, with that
moon, brighter than you often see it in August, shining on the
landscape, and bringing out its light and its shade. Mrs.
Carleton, every vestige of dissatisfaction removed, talked to
Sir Isaac St. John. The tones of her voice were low and
tender; the pale, passive countenance was singularly attractive.
Sir Isaac had grown to like her very much indeed; and she
knew it. But, what perhaps she did, not know, liking with
him had hitherto been confined to respect, esteem, friendship,
—as the case might be. *Never* had the probability of its going
further occurred to any one. He had always expressed a determination to live and die unmarried, and it was accepted as a
matter of certainty.·

Mr. St. John leaned against the wall, partly shaded by the
blue satin window-curtains. He was watching her keenly.
All that old gossip which had reached him, creating a strange
suspicion in his mind, was rising up bit by bit. *She* mad!
Surely not! In that low, modulated voice; in that composed,
self-controlled countenance; in those dark eyes, lighted now
with a pleasant smile, there was no madness to be traced, past,
present, or to come,—not a symptom of it. What had Rose
meant by taking up the idea seriously?—by speaking of it to
him? Nay, *his* was the fault for having listened to her.
Rose! vain, giddy, careless as of old. Mr. St. John had
wondered two or three times this past week what she was
coming to.

As he looked, an idea flashed over him. He had noticed
this last week, since his residence with them, little odds and
ends in Mrs. Carleton's conduct. How she strove incessantly
to make herself agreeable to Sir Isaac; how she walked out
with him, drove out with him, sat with him oftentimes in his
morning-room, how *suave* she was to Mr. Brumm; how, in

short, she seemed to have one object in life—and that, to devote herself to Sir Isaac. It was very kind of her—very considerate, had been Frederick's only thought until now, and he felt grateful to her, though rather wondering; he felt grateful to any one who appreciated his brother; but now the truth seemed to have opened his eyes, and removed the scales that were before them. She was hoping to become Lady St. John.

Every feeling of Frederick St. John rose up in arms against it. Not against his brother marrying. If it would be for his comfort and happiness, Frederick would have been glad to see him marry on the morrow. But to marry *her*—with that possibility of taint in her blood? Any one in the wide world, rather than Charlotte Carleton. The room suddenly felt too hot for him, and he turned from it impetuously, his hand lifted to his brow.

"Who's this? Don't run over me, Mr. St. John."

He *had* nearly run over her; she was so still; gathered there against the wall, just beyond the window.

"I beg your pardon, Georgina; I was deep in thought."

"Is it not a lovely night?"

"Yes, I suppose so. How long"—he dropped his voice—"is Mrs. Carleton going to remain here? Do you know?"

"Not I. How should I? Mrs. Darling and Rose leave to-morrow."

There was a pause. He held out his arm to Georgina, and began slowly to pace the terrace with her. She looked very fair, very lovely in the moonlight.

"How came Mrs. Carleton to prolong her stay beyond that of her mother and sister?"

"As if I knew! Sir Isaac pressed it, I think. I heard him say to her one day that as Mrs. St. John intended to spend the winter at Castle Wafer, she could not do better than promise him to remain also. Don't you like her?"

"Not very much, I think."

"I did like her. I cannot tell you how much I pitied her. It seems so hard a fate to lose her husband and her two children, and now to have lost Alnwick. But she won't let me like her; she is so very distant with me; repellant might be the better word; and so I think she is making me *dis*like her. I like Rose."

He laughed. "No one can help liking Rose; with all her

faults she is open as the day. Do you know, Georgina, I used at times to think Rose very much like you."

"In face?"

"No. And yet there may be a certain resemblance even there: both of you are fair, and both—pretty. You need not fling away from me as if it were treason to say so. But I meant in manner. You were once as wild as Rose is now."

"You saw a great deal of her this time last year, did you not, when she was staying with Adeline de Castella?"

"Yes," he laconically answered.

Georgina Beauclerc turned to the terrace railings, and leaned over them, looking far away. He stood by her side in silence.

"Do you think I am wild in manner now?" she presently asked.

"No; you have greatly changed."

"Those old, old days in Westerbury—and I know I *was* wild in them—have faded away as a dream. It seems so long ago!—and yet, marked by the calendar, it is only a short time. One may live years in a few months, Mr. St. John."

With the privileged freedom of his boyhood he turned her face towards him, and saw what he had suspected. The blue eyes were filled with tears.

"What is it, child?"

"Nothing. Past days are often sad to look back to."

"Do you know that you *have* changed—wonderfully changed?"

"From my wildness? Yes, I think I have been tamed."

"And what has tamed you?"

"Oh,"—there was a slight pause—"nothing but my own good sense."

"And now please tell me why you call me Mr. St. John. You have been doing it all the week."

The tears vanished, and a slight smile parted the pretty lips.

"You are Mr. St. John now."

"Not to you, I should have thought."

"I remember the lecture you once gave me for calling you Fred."

"No doubt. I gave you little else than lectures then; some of them in earnest, some in fun. The lecture you speak of was of the latter description."

"I know how vexed you used to get with me. You must have hated me very much."

"Wrong, young lady. Had I cared for you less, I should not have lectured you. We don't get vexed with those we dislike. I should lecture you still, if I saw cause to do it."

Georgina laughed. They were again pacing the terrace, for he had placed her arm in his.

"I always believed in you, Georgina, though you did require so much keeping in order. You were as wild a young damsel as I ever wish to see. It is well your mood has changed."

"I dare say you mean to say my manners."

"Call it what you will. I like you best as you are. What's that, shooting up like a bonfire?"

They paused and watched the appearance he spoke of: a flaming light in a distant field.

"I know," cried Georgina. "Old Phipps is burning that dead tree of his. Sir Isaac told him this morning not to let it lie there across the path."

"Were you there with Isaac this morning? So far off as that!"

"He and I and Mrs. Carleton had walked there. He is a famous walker now."

"A little bird whispered a tale to me about you, Georgina, as I came through London," he said, resuming their walk. "Shall I tell it?"

"Tell it if you like. What is it?"

"That you might, at no very distant time, be mistress of Hawkhurst. His lordship——"

"What a wicked untruth," she burst forth, as impulsively as ever she had spoken in former days. "Who told it you? It was Sarah, I'm sure; and she knows I refused him."

"I'm sure he is a well-meaning young man; easy, good-tempered, and very fond of you."

"He is as stupid as an owl," returned Georgina, in her anger. "Oh—I see: you are only laughing at me."

"Tell me why you would not have him. We used to tell each other mutual secrets in bygone days. Do you remember that real secret—that accident—when you nearly set the deanery on fire, by placing the lamp too close to the window-curtains, and I burnt my hands in putting the fire out, and then took down the curtains afterwards, to remove all traces of fire from them? I suppose the dean does not know the truth to this day."

"Mamma does not; and that is a great deal more to the purpose. She still believes the curtains were mysteriously stolen. They were fortunately very beautiful."

"Fortunately! But you have not told me why you dismissed Hawkhurst and his coronet."

"I wouldn't have him if he had ten coronets. I wouldn't have any one."

"Do you intend never to marry, Miss Georgina?"

"Never, never. Papa and mamma have no one but me, and I shall not leave them."

Her blushes were conspicuous even in the moonlight. But she raised her head, as if in defiance of the emotion, and looked straight out before her.

"So you did see Sarah as you came through London! She has made a good marriage, has she not?"

"Very good, in all senses of the word. She has rank, wealth; and her husband, for a Viscount, is really a superior man."

"For a Viscount! What next? Is Sarah as beautiful as ever?"

"Well—no. She was both thin and pale. She'll get up her looks again by-and-by, I dare say."

"I'm sure she's happy, and that's the chief thing. They are to come to us at Westerbury next winter. Talking of Westerbury," continued Georgina, "Rose Darling had a letter from Westerbury this morning."

"Indeed! I was not aware that Rose was acquainted with Westerbury, or any one in it. Here she comes."

She had been standing outside the window, and came forward as he spoke. She had caught the sound of her own name, and wanted to know—as she had just before, in the drawing-room—why they were taking it in vain.

"Miss Beauclerc says you heard from Westerbury this morning."

"Well, so I did," cried Rose. "The letter was from Mary Carr. She is staying with some friends there: what's their name?—Mr. and Mrs. Travice Arkell."

"Ah, yes," said Mr. St. John. "I heard from Travice not long ago."

"Did he mention Lucy?" asked Georgina.

"He said Lucy had sent her love to me, and that that was all he could get out of her, for she was rapturously absorbed in her new toy, the baby."

St. Martin's Eve.   25

"Mary Carr says you are to be its godfather," remarked Rose.

"Oh, are you?" cried Georgina. "Which is it—a boy or a girl?"

Mr. St. John considered, and then laughed. "I declare I don't know," he said; "it's one of the two. Travice told me, I think, but I forget. Knowing who the godmother is to be, I forgot all about the baby."

"And who is it to be—Mrs. Dundyke?"

"Not at all. It is a lady of a great deal more importance—in size, at any rate. Miss Fauntleroy."

Georgina laughed. Rose was a little puzzled: the bygone histories were strange to her. And she was feeling cross besides. Where Rose took a fancy—and she had taken one long ago to Frederick St. John—she did not like to see attentions given to any one but her own sweet self. She tossed her head, throwing back her blue ribbons and golden curls.

"Is your sister going to make a long stay with us, Rose?" he quietly asked.

"My opinion is, that she'll make it just as long as you choose to ask her: for ever and a day if Sir Isaac should please. Take care of her, Frederick St. John! I never saw Charlotte put forth her attractions as she is doing now."

She spoke at random—in her wild carelessness: she had never given a suspicion to the truth—that her sister was purposely trying to attract Isaac St. John. Cold, proud, arrogant; to do so, would be against Charlotte's nature, as Rose had always believed.

Mrs. Darling and Rose took their departure from Castle Wafer, leaving Charlotte and Georgina Beauclerc its only guests. It was lovely weather, and the weeks went on. The mornings were chiefly spent out of doors. Isaac St. John, so much stronger than he used to be, had never gone about his grounds as he was going now. His companions were always Charlotte Carleton and Georgina; Frederick often strolling by their side. In the afternoon one or other of them would be driven out by Sir Isaac in his low pony-carriage, and the other would be with Mrs. St. John, sitting at home with her or going out in the close carriage, as the case might be. As to Frederick, he was apparently leading a very idle life. In point of fact, he was secretly busy as ever was a London detective, watching Mrs. Carleton. He had been watching her closely ever since the departure of Mrs. Darling and Rose, now three weeks ago, and he persuaded himself that he did detect signs of incipient madness.

One thing he detected in which there could be no mistake— her hatred of Georgina Beauclerc. Not by any ordinary signs was this displayed, by rudeness, by slight, or anything of that sort. On the contrary, she was studiously polite to Georgina, even cordial at times. But every now and then, when Georgina crossed her, there would blaze forth a wild, revengeful fire in the eye, there would be an involuntary contraction of the long thin fingers, as though they were tightening on somebody's throat. It would all pass in a moment and was imperceptible to general observation : but Frederick was *watching*.

He also observed that whenever she was put out in this way, it was always with reference to Isaac. One day in particular, it almost came to open warfare.

Sir Isaac had ordered round his pony-carriage in the morning, having to go farther than he could walk. Frederick and Mrs. Carleton were in the morning-room, and it was somehow arranged, in haste, that Mrs. Carleton should accompany him. Frederick had not been particularly attentive at the moment : he was writing letters : but he thought it was Mrs. Carleton herself who offered to go, not Isaac who asked her. Be that as it might, she put on her things, and came back to the room. At almost the same moment, Georgina flew in, a mantle and bonnet in her hand.

"Are you going out?" asked Mrs. Carleton, drawing her shawl more closely around her slender and stately form.

"I am going with Sir Isaac," replied Georgina : and Mrs. Carleton made an almost imperceptible pause before she spoke again.

"*I* am going with Sir Isaac."

"That I'm sure you are not," cried Georgina, in her spoilt, girlish way. "Sir Isaac is going to Hatherton, and knows why I must go there with him : why he must take me in preference to any one else. Don't you, Sir Isaac?" she added, entwining her arm within his.

"You petted child!" he fondly said. "Who told you I was going to Hatherton?"

"Brumm. I asked him what the pony-carriage had come round for this morning. You will take me?" she continued, her voice and manner irresistible in their sweetness.

"I suppose I must," he answered. "If Mrs. Carleton will allow me—will excuse the trouble she has had in putting on her things. There! put on your bonnet, my wilful, troublesome child; you would charm a bird from its nest."

That any feeling of *rivalry* could be entertained by either, never once crossed the brain of Sir Isaac St. John. He had watched Georgina Beauclerc grow up from a baby, and he looked upon her still as a child: he gave way to her moods as we give way to those of a child who is very dear to us. He loved her fondly; he would have liked her for his daughter: and since the project of marrying Frederick to Lady Anne St. John had failed, he had cherished a secret and silent wish down deep in his heart, that Lady Anne might be supplanted by the dean's daughter. But he was cautious not to breathe a hint of this, not to further it by so much as lifting a finger. If it came to pass, well and good, but he would never again plot and plan, and be made miserable by failure, as he had been in the case of Lady Anne. That Mrs. Carleton could be seriously annoyed at his disappointing her for Georgina, did not occur to him: it never would have occurred to him that she could look on the young lady as anything but a lovable and loving child.

They went out to the pony-carriage, Georgina on his arm and prattling in her pretty way. Sir Isaac placed her in, solicitous for her comfort, and took his seat beside her. Her bright face and its sparkling grey eyes were beaming with triumph, and she turned back with a saucy farewell.

"Don't expect us home until you see us."

Let us give Georgina Beauclerc her due. She never suspected, any more than did Sir Isaac, that Mrs. Carleton could by any possibility regard her as a rival. Had she been told that Mrs. Carleton was laying siege to the master of Castle Wafer, Georgina had retired to a respectful distance and looked on. From her light-hearted youth, they appeared very old to her. Mrs. Carleton was a widow, who had lost all she cared for in life; Sir Isaac was a second father to her, looking older, in his hump, than her own, and she was at liberty to be free and familiar with him as a daughter.

Mrs. Carleton stood at the window as they drove off. She was wholly mistaking matters, as we all do when ill-nature or prejudice is upon us. The triumphant look in the girl's face and eyes, really shining forth in her warm-hearted joyousness, and unsuspicious of offence to any, was regarded by Charlotte Carleton as a displayed triumph over *her;* the saucy farewell, which was more saucy in tone than in words, and which was meant for no one in particular, but for Frederick if any one, was taken by the unhappy lady to herself. That strange evil look arose in her eyes as she gazed after the carriage, and a shiver passed through her frame.

Frederick St. John was half frightened. If ever a woman looked mad, she looked so in that moment. Her long fingers quivered, her lips were drawn, her face was white as death. He rose silently.

"I beg your pardon, Mrs. Carleton : you are dropping your shawl."

In truth the shawl, which had become unfastened, was falling from her shoulders, and he made it an excuse for interfering, speaking in quiet, soothing tones, to be near her and prepared, should there be any act of violence. She turned and glared at him. No other word will express the blaze that was in her eyes at the moment. One whole minute did she so stand before she recollected herself, or seemed to know what she was looking at or where she was. Then she gathered up the shawl on her arm, and sat down quietly.

"Thank you," she said ; "this silk shawl is given to slipping off."

In a moment she had obtained perfect mastery of herself : her pale face was calm again, nay, impassive ; her eyes had lost their frightful expression, and were ordinary eyes once more. Frederick asked whether he should drive her out; there was Mrs. St. John's basket-carriage : if she would like a little fresh air, he was at her service.

At first she said no ; but recalled the negative and thought she would trouble him. It was so quiet indoors this morning without Sir Isaac, and that gay, foolish girl, Georgina. Yes ; if not interrupting those apparently important letters, she would accept his offer.

So the basket-carriage—rather a rickety affair, for Mrs. St. John never used it now, and it was given over to neglect—was ordered round. Mrs. Carleton put on her shawl again, and they started. And there he was, driving this, as he verily believed, half-mad woman, who was calm as an angel now ; conversing with him sensibly and placidly, a pleasant smile in her dark eyes.

But this morning's doings were an exception. In a general way it was Mrs. Carleton who was the companion of Isaac St. John. She walked with him in the morning; Georgina and Frederick generally falling into the background; she drove out with him in the afternoon; she sat by his side, speaking in soft whispers, at night. That she was either really in love with Isaac St. John, or striving to make him in love with her, there could no longer be any doubt on the mind of Frederick. He wondered whether it was apparent to others; but he could not tell.

Over and over again he asked himself the question—were these signs of madness, or not? People were rather in the habit of turning white with passion; he himself, to wit, on occasion; and jealousy and dislike of a pretty girl were nothing new. All that was as nothing: but he could not forget that awful look in the eyes, that movement of the hands, that peculiar shiver of the frame; and he believed that she, Charlotte Carleton, was either mad or in danger of becoming so. You see, the doubt had been already implanted in him by Rose Darling; but for that, he might never have so much as glanced at the possibility; and he very seriously pondered the question, whether this fear arose solely from that whispered communication, and had no place in reality.

It is possible the affair altogether might not have continued to trouble him, but for a word dropped by his mother. Mrs. Carleton sat by Sir Isaac that evening in the drawing-room, her low words breathed in the softest whisper. She was trying to learn, so ladylike and candid all the while, what business he and Georgina had had at Hatherton. Isaac made no very particular reply: and indeed there was none to make. A man lived at Hatherton who had been a protégé of the dean's, but he fell into evil habits, ill-treated his poor sick wife, and finally was discarded. It was for this man Georgina had been begging grace of Isaac—that Sir Isaac would take him on, and give him a trial; and it was to see the wife that Georgina went to Hatherton. No great news to tell; and Sir Isaac did not perceive that Mrs. Carleton was *anxious* to hear it. Presently Sir Isaac rose, went out, and sat down on the terrace; it was a sultry night, and every breath of air was grateful. Mrs. Carleton also went out and sat by him.

"Frederick," whispered Mrs. St. John, in the impulse of the moment, "should you be very much disappointed were Isaac to give Castle Wafer a mistress?"

So his mother had noticed it! "Not if the mistress were suitable."

"He might give it a worse, Frederick; I like her."

Frederick St. John drew in his breath. A worse! Surely, never a worse, if his fears were correct, than she; not though Isaac searched the whole world through. Mrs. St. John looked up at her son.

"You are silent, Frederick. Should you not like her?"

"I think not."

"It is only a suggestion that crossed me; it does seem next door to an impossibility that Isaac should marry, after all. Don't let it make you uncomfortable."

"Nay, mother mine, you mistake me," he said. "None would more heartily welcome the thought of a wife for Isaac, should such be his own desire; but I—I think I should not like the wife to be Mrs. Carleton."

He spoke calmly, but a flush passed over his brow at the thought, a chill to his heart. He quitted his mother and strolled outside.

Georgina was with Isaac then. She had edged herself between him and the arm of the bench, and was taking up his attention, to the exclusion of Mrs. Carleton. If the girl had only known the sin she was committing in that lady's sight! Luring him away in her pretty wilfulness to walk with her on the lower walks under the bright stars; and he went without so much as a word of apology or regret to Mrs. Carleton: and the sound of their voices as they paced together, came up with a joyous ring on the still night air. Frederick St. John watched *her* attentively under cover of the darkness; he saw the distorted countenance, the fearful eyes, and he decided that she was mad, and was meditating some revenge on Miss Beauclerc.

It troubled him greatly. At one moment he recalled all the queer and horrible tales he had heard of people killing or injuring others in their madness, previously unsuspected; the next, he asked himself whether he were awake or dreaming, that he should call up ideas so unlikely and fantastical. By-and-by, when they were all indoors again, Mrs. Carleton sat down to the piano, and sang some low, sweet music, charming their ears, winning their hearts. Had all the doctors connected with Bethlehem Hospital come forward then to declare her mad, people would have laughed at them for their pains; and Mr. St. John amidst the rest.

Have you ever observed with what a different aspect we see things in the morning from what we saw them at night? In the broad light of the bustling day, if we by chance glance back at our evening fancies—seeming true enough then—it is with a shrug of compassion at their folly. All the time Mr. St. John was dressing, the sun shining gaily into his chamber, he was feeling rather ashamed of himself. How *could* he have allowed those horrible thoughts to obtain a moment's ascendency the previous night? Was he not doing Mrs. Carleton an unpardonable injury? He had positively no grounds whatever to go upon, except that past communication made by Rose, which might have had no truth in it. "I've a great mind to go away!" quoth Mr. St. John, "and pick up some common sense before I come back again."

As he went along the corridor, Mrs. Carleton was coming out of her own room, pale, quiet, handsome, her head raised a little haughtily as usual. She held out her hand to Mr. St. John with a smile; and he, in his new fit of repentance, placed it within his arm, and led her downstairs.

"I have had a letter from Rose," she said. "Would you like to see it? She speaks of Paris as of an elysium."

She sat down to preside at the breakfast-table. Mrs. St. John rarely quitted her room until midday. The windows opened to the terrace, and he went out, the letter in his hand. Georgina was leaning on some railings, and did not turn to greet him. He asked her what she was looking at.

"I'm not looking: I am thinking. I was trying to recollect whether I really had an adventure in the night, or whether it was only a dream."

The words, without perhaps sufficient cause, seemed to sharpen every faculty he possessed. Crushing Rose's letter in his hand, as a thing of no moment, he asked Georgina to explain what she meant.

"Something awoke me in the middle of the night," she said; "and I saw, or thought I saw, a face bending over my bed, close to mine. I called out, 'Who is it? What do you want?' but there was no answer, only the curtain seemed to stir, and then the door closed very quietly, as if whoever it was had left the room. I don't think I was yet quite awake, but I ran to the door, opened it, and looked out. I saw—at least I fancied I saw—that quiet maid of Mrs. Carleton's, Prance; she was standing in the corridor in a white petticoat or nightdress, and I could have declared that I heard her speaking in an angry whisper. But the next moment I could see no trace of any one; and when my eyes grew accustomed to the grey light, I saw that all the chamber doors were shut."

He paused an instant before replying. "Are you sure it was Prance in the corridor? Did you see her distinctly?"

"I saw only the white things she was wrapped in; the outline of her figure. It was by that outline I took it to be Prance, and because she was standing at Mrs. Carleton's door, which was then open, or seemed to be."

"Could it have been Mrs. Carleton herself, standing there?"

"No. It was nothing like tall enough. If it was anybody, it was Prance; that is, if anything of the sort did take place, and it was not a dream; and she was speaking angrily to some one inside Mrs. Carleton's room."

"Do you, yourself, think it was a dream, Georgina?"

"I should have felt quite certain that it was not a dream, that it was all reality, only that Prance positively denies it. She says she never was out of the room at all last night after Mrs. Carleton came up to bed. She says, she thinks I must have had a nightmare."

"Where does Prance sleep? Somewhere at the back, I suppose."

"She sleeps in Mrs. Carleton's room. Did you not know it? There was a little bed put into the room for her the day they came. Mrs. Carleton does not like sleeping in a room alone."

"When did you speak to Prance about it?"

"Just now. I saw her in the corridor. I asked whether anything was the matter last night, but she did not seem to know what I meant, and I explained. She quite laughed at me, saying I must have been suffering from nightmare." ·

"And denying that she was in the corridor?"

"Entirely. She says it's not possible any one could have been there, for she slept very badly last night, and must have heard the slightest movement outside, had there been any, her bed being close to the door. What do you think?" concluded Georgina.

Mr. St. John did not say what he thought: he chose rather to treat it lightly. "It might have been a sort of nightmare."

"But I never had nightmare before in my life. I seemed to see the outline of a head and face over me, though indistinctly."

" Did you think the face was Prance's ? "

" It seemed to belong to somebody taller than Prance. I dare say it *was* a dream, after all.   Don't laugh at me."

" A dream, no doubt," he said.   " But Georgina, I would not mention this if I were you.   I'll not laugh at it, but others might : and Mrs. Carleton would not like the idea of her door being open, or supposed to have been open in the middle of the night.   If Prance has to sleep in her room, I suppose she must be of a timid nature, and she might be getting thieves and robbers into her head should she hear of this."

" I did not intend to say anything to her.   But Prance most likely will."

" Prance can do as she chooses.   There is another thing— I would advise you to lock your chamber-door just at present."

She looked up at him with surprise.   " Lock my chamber-door !   What for ? "

" Well," he answered, after a brief hesitation, " you could not then fancy that any one came in."

" I could not sleep with my door locked.   If a fire took place in the house, I might be burnt up before any one could arouse me."

" Georgina, trust me," he said, impressively, and he laid his hand upon her shoulder.   " *I* will take care of you in case of fire, and if your door is locked, burst it open.   Turn the key of your door just now, to oblige me."

" Tell me what you suspect—that you should thus caution me."

" I—think it—just possible—that some one may walk in their sleep.   Perhaps one of the maids."

" Oh !   I should not like that," exclaimed Georgina, unsuspiciously.   " I should be far more frightened if some one asleep came into my room in the night, than if they were awake."

" Just so : therefore you will lock your door.   Promise me."

" I promise, Frederick."

He turned from her, and crossed the terrace to enter the breakfast-room, she looking after him, a whole world of love shining unconsciously from her wistful eyes.   No, it was of no use : she had striven against her love ; but it was all in vain. Passionately as she had loved Frederick St. John in the old days, before he had given signs of liking any one—unless it had been her cousin Sarah,—before he ever saw Adeline de Castella, so passionately she loved him still.

CHAPTER XXXIII.

A TELEGRAM.

GEORGINA BEAUCLERC's revelation was a complete overthrow to Mr. St. John's more tolerant feelings of the morning. He fully believed it. He believed that the face leaning over the girl's bed must have been Mrs. Carleton's, that she had glided away when Georgina awoke; and that Prance, who must have suddenly discovered her absence from the room, had then come in search of her. Why did Prance sleep in her chamber? That seemed rather an odd thing to Mr. St. John. And—assuming that it was Mrs. Carleton—what motive could have taken her to Georgina's room?—have caused her to hang over her when asleep? Had she done it in restlessness?—become weary, and so have risen and prowled about the corridor and the rooms to while away the hours? Mr. St. John strove to think so: perhaps, rather, to deceive his own heart into thinking so. As to her having any intention of injuring Georgina, his mind shrank from entertaining the idea. He could not bear even to glance at it: apart from the horror of the thing, it partook too much of the sensational and romantic.

And how, indeed, could he think it? Look at her now. Sitting there so calm, so gentle, by Georgina's side, handing the cup of tea to Isaac she had just poured out, speaking with a sunny smile.

" I won't transgress this time, Sir Isaac, and give you too much sugar. Indeed, I forgot before. I must have thought I was sweetening for Mr. St. John."

" Ay, no doubt," replied Sir Isaac. " He can take any amount of sugar. Do you remember when you were a little fellow, Fred, I would half melt the lumps in my tea, and you would eat them for me?"

Frederick laughed. " I remember you indulged me in many things a great deal more than I deserved."

" I have had a letter from Alnwick this morning," observed Sir Isaac, turning to Mrs. Carleton. " Drake remonstrates against the Hall being left empty any longer. He says if I would only go to it for a week, it would be an earnest that it will sometime be occupied again. What should you all say to a week's visit there—provided Mrs. St. John shall think herself well enough to undertake the journey?"

No one replied. Mrs. Carleton gave one startled glance upwards, and then busied herself with her tea-making.

"The alterations in the conservatory are finished," continued Isaac: "a very nice thing they have made of it, Drake says. You remember that awkward-looking corner by the stove, Mrs. Carleton? That also has been remedied."

Mrs. Carleton looked up now, her face quietly impassive. "Sir Isaac, I would rather not hear anything about Alnwick. I try to put my past happiness from me as much as possible, and do not care to be reminded of it."

"I beg your pardon," cried Sir Isaac, in warm, considerate tones; "I ought to have remembered. Then you would not like to go there?"

"No. Not yet."

Of course that ended it, Sir Isaac intimated, and the conversation dropped. He was ever solicitous for the comfort of Mrs. Carleton, in small things as in great. This may have arisen solely from his sympathy with her position, from the feeling that he was in possession of the revenues she had once expected would be hers: but that she attributed it to a warmer sentiment, there could be little doubt.

"Will you go out with me in the pony-carriage this morning?" asked Sir Isaac. "I have not felt so strong the last day or two, and think, perhaps, I have been walking too much."

"I will go with you, dear St. Isaac," was Mrs. Carleton's honeyed answer; and Frederick St. John did not like to see the gratified look that illumined his brother's face as he thanked her.

They went out. Georgina disappeared within the apartments of Mrs. St. John, to write a long-delayed letter to her mother; and Frederick buried himself and his thoughts in the shadiest nook of his painting-room—for he had one at Castle Wafer. He had intended to go out shooting that morning, after breakfast, in his lazy fashion, for September was passing; but he felt in no mood for it now. A horrible dread had taken possession of him—that, not interfered with, his brother would be led on to marry her.

Not interfered with! Who was to interfere? In moments of difficulty we always think, "If the case were different, I could meet it." *He* was thinking so. "If I were not Isaac's heir, then I might speak out fearlessly. As it is—it would appear as though I interfered from interested motives; and I cannot do it."

Perhaps he was right. He might have seen his way more clearly, had there been tangible proof to bring forward concerning Mrs. Carleton's state of mind; but there was none. To say, "I fear she is not quite sane, or that she may hereafter become insane," would naturally be met by the question, "What grounds have you for thinking so?"—and he had really no good grounds to advance. And yet he felt that Isaac ought to be warned, lest he should compromise himself.

Grumbling at the untowardness of things, tired to death with worry, flinging a palette here, a painting there, striding the room with slow and uneven steps, Mr. St. John contrived somehow to live through the morning. Suddenly, when he was stretching himself, and rather wishing for wings that he might fly to the uttermost parts of the earth, it occurred to him that he would speak to Honour. The girl had once dropped some inadvertent words in his hearing, and she might be able to tell him more. It seemed that he would give half his own undoubted inheritance to set the question at rest.

He rang the bell, and told the servant who answered it to send Honour to him. He had not seen the girl, as far as he remembered, since his present sojourn at home. The fact was, Honour's duties had been changed, and lay downstairs now, instead of above. She had given up the place of housemaid, which she found did not suit her, to become assistant to the housekeeper, and was learning cooking and confectionery. Not once in six months now would her duties take her up the grand staircase, or bring her in contact with the guests.

"Where have you been hiding yourself?" asked Mr. St. John, when she appeared in obedience to his orders. "I never see you by any chance."

Honour explained now. She looked just the same as ever, and she still wore mourning for her beloved Benja.

"Honour, I want to ask you a question. And you must answer it, for it is essential that you should do so. But you may rely upon my discretion, and no trouble shall accrue to you from it. You once spoke a word or two which led me to infer that your late mistress, Mrs. Carleton St. John, was not altogether of sound mind. Did you mean what you said?"

Honour paused. Not from fear of speaking, but in doubt what to say. Mr. St. John, attributing it to the former motive, again assured her that she might trust him.

"It is not that, sir; it is that I don't well know how to answer you. I remember what I said—you were asking me about that dreadful night, saying that from the manner in which he had been burnt to death it looked as though some-body had done it for the purpose; and I answered, in the moment's haste, that nobody could have done that, unless it was Mrs. St. John in her madness."

"But did you mean anything, Honour? That is the point to be considered now."

"I did, and I didn't, sir. I had seen my mistress two or three times in a most awful passion; a passion, sir, that you would hardly believe possible in a lady, and I meant that if she had done it, it must have been in one of those mad fits of passion. But I did not really mean that she had done it," resumed Honour, "and I could have bitten my tongue out afterwards for answering so carelessly; it was the very thing Mrs. Darling warned me against. There was no reason for sup-posing the calamity to have been anything but pure accident."

"What had Mrs. Darling warned you against?"

"It occurred in this way, sir. After it was all over and the poor lamb buried, I had brain fever; and they tell me I made all sorts of wild accusations in it, amidst others that my mistress had set fire to Benja and bolted the door upon him. After I got well, Mrs. Darling told me of this. Nothing could be kinder than what she said, but she warned me never to breathe such words again. I should not have had such a thought, even in my delirium, but for the bolted doors; I couldn't get over that at the time; but I came to the same conclusion at last as other people—that poor Benja must have fastened the one to keep me out, and that the other was not bolted at all. It's likely enough, for I never was in such a flurry before, smelling the burning so strong."

"And in your delirium you accused your mistress of having caused the mischief?"

"So they tell me, sir. How I came to fancy such wicked thoughts is the wonder. It's true that she was always jealous of Benja after her own child was born, always hated him; and I suppose I remembered that, even in my unconsciousness. Not an hour before the accident she had beaten him cruelly."

"*Beaten* him!" interrupted Mr. St. John.

"She did, sir. It's over now, and I said nothing about it : where was the use? Well, all these things must have got jumbled together in my poor fevered brain, and caused me to say what I did. I was very sorry for it, sir, when I got well; I should never have thought of such a thing in my senses."

"Then—although you used the word 'madness,' you never had cause to think her really insane?"

"Oh no, never. In those frightful passions she was as one mad, sir, but they were over directly. "I hope you'll pardon me, sir, for having been so foolish as to say it."

"Nay, Honour, it is nothing to me. We all make slips occasionally in talking. That's all I wanted to ask you."

She turned to leave the room. Mr. St. John took a rapid summary in his mind of what he had heard. It seemed only to increase his difficulties. There was not the slightest corroborative testimony as to her possible insanity; but there were other hints which tended to render her a most unfit wife for Isaac. If——

His reflections were brought to a sudden conclusion by a scream outside. This studio of his was situated in an angle of the staircase, where it was rather dark. Honour had not yet closed the door : but the scream did not appear to have come from her. He hastened out.

It had come from Mrs. Carleton. Standing in the opposite angle, gathered closely against the wall, as if hiding from a ghost, her eyes were fixed with a glare of terror upon Honour, her face was white as death. She had just come in from the drive with Sir Isaac, and was on her way to her room to take off her bonnet for luncheon. Honour saw the effect her appearance caused, and stood irresolute, curtseying, not liking to go down, because she would have to brush past Mrs. Carleton. Before Mr. St. John had recovered from his astonishment, Prance came gliding up and took her mistress by the arm.

"It's only Honour Tritton, ma'am; do you not know her? You fool, why did you put yourself in her sight!" added the woman to Honour in whispered exasperation. "I told you to keep out of it—that she didn't know you were here. The sight of *you* cannot be pleasant to her remembrance."

Almost by force, as it seemed, she led her mistress away to her bedroom and closed the door. A good way down the

corridor Mrs. Carleton's white face was turned back on
Honour, with its look of wild, desperate fear.

Mr. St. John seemed equally stunned with Honour. "What
is the meaning of this?" he asked.

"I'm sure I don't know, sir," was the girl's answer, as she
burst into tears.

"Prance said she had warned you to keep out of Mrs. Carleton's sight. Is that true?"

"Yes, sir, it's true. She said her mistress did not know I
was at Castle Wafer, and I had better take care and not show
myself to her."

"But why?"

"I don't know, sir. All she said was that Mrs. Carleton St.
John was fearfully angry with me still, knowing that, but for
my carelessness in leaving the child he would be alive now. I
had kept out of her sight until to-day. But it seemed to me
now that she looked more terrified than angry."

As it had to Mr. St. John. Honour went out about her
business, and he felt bewildered with the complication of
events that seemed to be arising. There came down an
apology to the luncheon-room from Mrs. Carleton, delivered
by Prance. Her lady had a headache, brought on by being so
long in the hot sun without a parasol, and was now lying down.

"How sorry I am!" exclaimed Sir Isaac. "She complained of the sun when we were out."

Late in the afternoon, she came into the drawing-room,
dressed for dinner. Frederick happened to be there alone.
As a matter of politeness, he condoled with her on her indisposition, hoping it was gone.

"Not quite. To tell you the truth, Mr. St. John," she continued in quiet, confidential tones, "the sight of that woman,
Honour Tritton, had as much to do with my headache as the
heat. You know who she was, I presume—nurse to my poor
little step-son ; the woman to whose unpardonable carelessness
his death was attributable. I have never been able to think of
the woman since without horror, and the unexpected sight of
her—for I had no idea she was at Castle Wafer—was almost
too much for me."

"She is one of the servants here," observed Frederick, not
very well knowing what else to answer.

"As I hear. I wonder Sir Isaac should have engaged her.
However, of course, that is no business of mine. I hope she

will not come into my way again, for I have a perfect horror
of her. But for her wickedness, we might all still have been
happy at Alnwick."

She rose as she spoke, and went on the lawn. Mrs. St.
John was there. Sir Isaac was then in his own sitting-room,
and Frederick went in to him. The table was strewed with
papers, and he was writing rapidly.

"Look at this," he said to Frederick, holding out a letter,
and in his voice might be traced a sound of annoyance. "It
is incomprehensible how people can be so stupid."

"Are you writing to stop it?" asked Frederick, when he had
read the note.

"I am writing; but whether it will be in time to stop it, is
another matter. The letter only came by this afternoon's post."

"I should telegraph," said Frederick.

Sir Isaac laid down his pen. "It might be the better plan.
But you can say so little in a message."

"Do both," advised the younger brother. "I will go off at
once and send the message, and you can post your letter afterwards. You will then have the satisfaction of knowing that all
has been done that can be done."

"Yes, that will be better. If you don't mind the trouble.
But you will hardly be back by dinner-time."

"Yes I shall. And as to trouble, Isaac, I think it's doing
me a kindness. I have been in a cross-grained mood all day,
for want perhaps of something to do.'

Sir Isaac wrote the message, and Frederick started with it,
leaping down the slopes buoyant as a schoolboy. It was a
sensible relief, perhaps, to what he had called his cross-grained
mood. He had only a short walk; for the railway had now
been extended from Lexington, and its small station was not
far from the lodge gates of Castle Wafer.

Mr. St. John entered the little telegraph office. He gave in
his message, and was exchanging a few words with the clerk,
when the rustle of petticoats was heard, and a female voice
addressed the clerk in hurried accents. Mr. St. John at the
moment was behind the partition, and unseen by the new-
comer.

"Young man, can I send a telegraph off at once? It's in a
hurry."

"You can send a telegram," responded the clerk. "Where's
it to?"

St. Martin's Eve.   26

"Paris."

"What's the message?"

"I've wrote it down here, so that there may be no mistake. It's quite private, if you please, and must be kept so: a little matter that don't concern anybody. And be particular, for it's from Castle Wafer. Will it be in Paris to-night?"

"Yes," said the clerk, confidently, as he counted the words.

"What's to pay?"

"Twelve-and-sixpence."

"Twelve-and-sixpence!" repeated the voice. "What a swindle."

"You needn't pay it if you don't like."

"But then the telegram would not go?"

"Of course it wouldn't."

The clink of silver was heard, dashed down upon the counter. "I can't stop to argue about the charge, so I must pay it," grumbled the voice. "But it's a great shame, young man."

"The charges ain't of my fixing," responded the young man. "Good afternoon, ma'am."

She bustled out again as hurriedly as she had come in, not having seen Mr. St. John, or suspected that the wooden partition had any one behind it. He went to the door, looked after her, and recognized Prance: he thought he had not been mistaken in the voice. She was walking very fast indeed in the direction of Castle Wafer.

"I must see that message, Jones," said Mr. St. John, turning back into the little room.

Mr. Jones hesitated; but there was an air of quiet command in the words—and the speaker was the heir of Castle Wafer. He laid the written message on the desk.

"Mary Prance to Mrs. Darling.

"Please come back as quick as you can. I don't like her symptoms. I am afraid of something that I had better not write down here."

"Is it to go, sir?" asked the clerk.

"Oh yes, it is to go. Thank you. It's all right. I had a reason for wishing to see it."

He walked back to the house; not quickly, as Prance was doing, but slowly and reflectively. Sufficient food for reflection he had, in truth. They had not gone in to dinner; and

Georgina Beauclerc, her beautiful grey eyes sparkling with excitement, crossed the lawn to meet him, wearing a blue silk evening dress, and pearls in her hair.

"Oh, Frederick, guess the news! It has come to me only now. I won't tell it you unless you guess it."

He took both her hands in his, and gazed steadfastly into her excited face. The blushes began to rise.

"News—and I am to guess it? Perhaps it is that you are going to be a sober girl."

She laughed, and would have drawn her hands away. But he held them still.

"I can't wait: I must tell you. Papa and mamma are on their way home. They will be at the Rectory to-morrow night."

"How have you heard it?"

"They have had news at the Rectory and sent up to tell me. I am so glad! It seems ages and ages since I saw papa. Only think how I might have been spared the trouble of writing that long letter to mamma to-day, had I known?"

"I am glad too," he said, his tone changing to seriousness. "We shall get rid of you now."

One hasty glance at his face. What she saw there puzzled her. He really did look as though he meant it.

"Why do you say that?"

"Because it's the truth. I shall be glad when you are away from here, safe in the dean's charge again."

There was an earnestness in his tone which caused her large eyes to open.

"You have not been rude to me once this time until now," she pouted. "Sir Isaac would not say that."

"Rude?"

"It is rude to tell me you want to get rid of me. I never said a ruder thing to you than that, in my wildest days."

"I do want it," he answered, laughing. But he laid his hand upon her head as he spoke, and looked fondly at her. Her eyelids fell.

"You know I don't care for you, Georgina."

But the words were spoken as though he did care for her. Georgina ran away from him into the drawing-room. He followed, and found them going in to dinner, Charlotte Carleton leaning on the arm of Sir Isaac.

"What are you going to do with Alnwick, Sir Isaac?"

The question came from Mrs. Carleton, and it may be that it took Sir Isaac somewhat by surprise, after her previous avoidance of the subject. They were at dessert, not on this same day, but on the next, for four-and-twenty hours have gone on.

"In what way do you mean?" Sir Isaac asked, consideration very distinguishable in his tone. But it was called up by the subject alone.

"Shall you ever live at it?"

"I am not sure. I have a place in the North, you know, hitherto held in reserve should I leave Castle Wafer."

"But you would never leave Castle Wafer!"

"As its master, yes, should Frederick marry. It has always been my intention to resign it to him. But I dare say they would have me as their guest for six months of the year."

Her handsome face was bent downwards; her raven hair, with the perfumed white rose in it, was very close to her host.

"Is he likely to marry?"

"Not that I am aware of. I wish he was!"

"Let him take Alnwick as a residence, and remain yourself at Castle Wafer. The idea of your having to quit this beautiful place when you have made it what it is!"

Sir Isaac smiled. "Frederick says as you do, Mrs. Carleton. He protests he will never reign at Castle Wafer so long as I live. It may end in our living here together, two old bachelors; or, rather, an old bachelor and a young one."

"But shall you never marry?" she softly asked. "Why should you not form ties of your own? Oh, Sir Isaac, it is what every one would wish you to do."

Sir Isaac slightly shook his head. Frederick St. John's ears were strained to catch the conversation, although he was giving his attention to Miss Beauclerc.

"Do you know what I should like to do with Alnwick?"— and Sir Isaac's voice dropped to a whisper. "I should like to see *you* in it."

A streak of crimson crossed her cheek at the words. "I never, never could live again at Alnwick. Oh, Sir Isaac"— and the handsome face was raised pathetically to his—"think of the trouble it brought me! You could not expect me to go back to it."

He answered the look with eyes as pitying as her own.

"Give Alnwick to your brother, Sir Isaac. Remain yourself at Castle Wafer: never think of leaving it."

"You like Castle Wafer?"

"I never was in any place that I liked so much."

"Then you must not run away from it," said Sir Isaac, smiling.

"I don't want to run away from it," she answered, her eyes lifted pleadingly to his. "I have nowhere to run to. It is so hard—so very hard to make a fresh home! And I have so little to make one with. I lost all when I lost Alnwick."

A movement. Mrs. St. John was rising, and Frederick gave his mother a mental blessing as he opened the door. Sir Isaac passed the claret to him as he sat down, and he poured out a glass mechanically, but did not touch it. In the last twenty-four hours his doubts, as to Mrs. Carleton's designs on Sir Isaac, had become certainties, and his spirit was troubled.

"You have been inviting Mrs. Carleton to prolong her stay here, Isaac?"

"I invited her, when she first came, to stay as long as she liked," was Sir Isaac's reply. "I hope she will do so."

"Do you like her?"

"Very much indeed. I liked her the first time I ever saw her. Poor thing! so meek, so gentle, and so unfortunate! she has all my sympathy."

Frederick St. John took up his dessert-knife and balanced it on one of his fingers, supremely unconscious of his actions. He by no means saw his way clear to saying what he should like to say.

"She urges me to give you Alnwick as a residence, Fred."

"She is very generous," returned Fred: and Sir Isaac did not detect the irony of the remark. "I heard her say it would be a sin for you to quit Castle Wafer; or something to that effect. It has been always my own opinion, you know, Isaac."

"We shall see."

"Isaac, I am going to be rather bold, and attack one of your—I had almost said prejudices. You like Charlotte Carleton. I don't like her."

"Not like her!"

"No, I don't. And I am annoyed beyond measure at her staying on here, with no chance, as far as I can see, of her leaving. Annoyed, for—for your sake."

The words evidently surprised Sir Isaac. He turned his keen eyes upon the speaker. Frederick's were not lifted from the balancing knife.

"What do you see in her to dislike?"

"For one thing, I don't think she's sincere. For another——"

Down fell the knife on the dessert-plate, chipping a piece off its edge. The culprit was vexed. Sir Isaac smiled.

"The old action, Fred. Do you remember breaking that beautiful plate of Worcester porcelain in the same way?"

"I do: and how it vexed my mother, for it spoilt the set. They had better not put me a knife and fork; make me go without, as they do the children. I am sure to get playing with them."

"But about Mrs. Carleton? Go on with your catalogue of grievances against her."

When the mind is hovering in the balance, how a word, a tone, will turn it either way! The slight sound of amusement, apparent in Isaac's voice, was a very mockery to his listener; and he went on, hating his task more than before, almost inclined to give it up.

"For another thing, I was going to say, Isaac—I am not sure that she is *sane*."

"You are not sure of—what?"

"That Charlotte Carleton is quite in her sane senses."

Sir Isaac stared at his brother as though asking whether he was in *his*.

"Are you jesting, Frederick?"

"No. I am in sober earnest."

"Then perhaps you will tell me what grounds you have for saying this."

And here was Frederick's dilemma. What grounds had he? None. The reasons that seemed weighty enough to his own mind, were as nothing when spoken; and it suddenly struck him that he was not justified in repeating the gossip of a girl as careless as Rose.

"I have seen a strange look in her face more than once," he said; "a wild, awful expression in her eyes, that I don't believe *could* visit the perfectly sane. Isaac, on my honour I don't speak without believing that I have good reason—and that it lies in my duty to do so."

"I think you speak without grounds, Frederick," said Sir Isaac, gravely. "Many of us look wild enough at times. I have noticed nothing of this."

"She is on her guard before you."

"That is nonsense. Insane people are no more on their guard before one person than another. Did you go to sleep and dream this?"

Frederick winced. He saw that Isaac was laughing at him. "There are other indications," he said.

"What are they?"

Could he answer? Could he tell the doubt, spoken by Georgina—that the lady had been in her room in the night? Could he tell of the meeting with Honour on the stairs? Of the telegram he had surreptitiously read? And if he did, what proofs were they? Georgina might have had nightmare: Mrs. Carleton's horror at sight of Honour was not unnatural: and Prance's telegram need not refer to her mistress. No; it was of no use mentioning these: they might weaken rather than strengthen Isaac's belief.

"Isaac, I am almost sorry that I spoke to you," he resumed. "To my own mind, things are pretty conclusive, but I suppose they would not be so to yours."

"Certainly not, unless you have other grounds than 'looks' to go upon. Why did you mention the matter at all?"

Frederick was silent. The true motive—the fear that Isaac might be drawn into marrying her—he could not reveal. He might have been misconstrued.

"Did you enter on this to prejudice me against her?"

"Well—yes; in a sense I did."

"That you might get her away from Castle Wafer?"

"Yes, also."

"Then all I can say is, I don't understand you: unless, indeed, you are more insane than she is. She may stop here for ever if she likes. Remember, I enjoy the revenues that were once hers. And please don't attempt anything of this sort again, Frederick."

Sir Isaac left the dining-room as he spoke, and Frederick took his hat and went out, his veins tingling with a sense of shame and failure. He *could* not speak to more effect than he had spoken now; that wretched self-consciousness withheld him: and yet he felt that Isaac ought to be warned. Were he indeed to marry her, and find out afterwards that she was insane, Frederick believed that it would kill him.

Ill at ease, he strode on towards the Rectory, Georgina having exacted a promise from him that he would go and learn at what hour Dr. and Mrs. Beauclerc were expected. They had already arrived. The dean was in his study alone, his genial face bent over sundry letters he was opening. A few threads of silver mingled now with his light auburn hair, and his shoulders were slightly stooping; but his eyes, the very counterpart of his daughter's, were frank and benevolent as ever, and his hand was as cordial.

Losing his own father at an early age, and being much with Dean Beauclerc, it is possible that Frederick St. John had insensibly grown to look upon him almost in the light of a father. Certain it was, that as he shook hands now with the dean, an impulse came over him to confide his trouble to him. None would give him wiser and more honest counsel than this good man. With Frederick St. John to think of a thing was to do it impulsively; and, without an instant's deliberation, he entered on his story. Not, however, mentioning Georgina as in any way connected with it.

The dean listened attentively to its conclusion, and shook his head. "Very slight grounds indeed, my young friend, on which to suspect a woman of insanity."

"I know it," answered Frederick; "there lies my stumbling-block. Were they only a little stronger, I should feel more at liberty to pursue any course of action that might appear advisable."

"Your chief fear is—if I take your meaning—that this lady is making herself too agreeable to Sir Isaac."

"Yes; but pray don't misunderstand me, Dr. Beauclerc," was the eager rejoinder. "Were she a person likely to bring Isaac happiness, I would further the matter to the utmost; I would indeed. Do you not see how difficult it is for *me* to interfere? Ninety-nine persons out of a hundred would say I did so from interested motives; a fear of losing the inheritance. I declare before Heaven, that it is not so: and that I have only my brother's happiness at heart. He is one of the justest men living, and if he were to marry, I know he would first of all secure me an ample fortune."

"My opinion is that he never will marry," said the dean.

"I don't know. I have the fear upon me; the fear of *her*. Were he to marry her, and afterwards discover that she was not quite right, I believe it would kill him. You know, sir, his great sensitiveness."

"Just go over again what you have said," returned the dean. "I mean as to Mrs. Carleton's symptoms."

Frederick St. John did so. He related what Rose had told him; he mentioned the wild and excited looks he had himself observed in Mrs. Carleton; he spoke of meeting Honour on the stairs; of the telegram sent by Prance. Somewhat suspicious circumstances, perhaps, when taken together, but each one nothing by itself. "Nevertheless, I believe in them," he concluded. "I believe that she is not sane."

"I wonder if there has ever been insanity in her family?" mused the dean—who by no means saw things with Frederick's eyes. "Let me see—who was she?"

"She was a Miss Norris. Daughter of Norris, of Norris Court. Mrs. Darling——"

"Oh, to be sure," interrupted the dean, as recollection came to him. "I knew her father. I was once a curate in that neighbourhood."

Mr. St. John looked up at the high-church dignitary before him. "*You* once a curate!"

The dean laughed. "We must all begin as curates, Frederick."

The young man laughed also. "You knew Mr. Norris, then?"

"Yes; slightly. I once dined at his house. My church was on the confines of Alnwick parish, not very far from Norris Court. Mr. Norris died just as I was leaving. He died rather suddenly, I think. I know it took the neighbourhood by surprise. And, if I remember rightly, there seemed to be some mystery attaching to his death."

"What did he die of?"

"No one knew. It was in that that the mystery lay. Report said he died of fever, but Mr. Pym, the surgeon who attended him, told me it was not fever; though he did not say what it was."

"Is that Pym of Alnwick?"

"Mr. Pym was in practice then at Alnwick. He may be still, for aught I know."

"He is. I met him twice at Alnwick Hall when I went down to the funerals; George St. John's and poor Benja's. Isaac was too ill to go each time, and I had to represent him. Do you"—he paused a moment in hesitation, and then went on— "think it likely that Mr. Norris died insane? I am sure there is no insanity on Mrs. Darling's side."

"I have no reason for thinking so," replied the dean. "I

was in want of a servant at the time, and a man who had lived with Mr. Norris applied to me for the situation. It was the surgeon, Pym, who spoke to his character: Mrs. Norris was ill and could not be seen. I engaged him. He had been the personal attendant of Mr. Norris in his last illness."

"Did he ever say what Mr. Norris's disease was?"

"No. He was very reserved. A good servant, but one of the closest men I ever came across. I once asked him what illness his master had died of, and he said fever. I observed that Mr. Pym had told me it was not fever. He replied he believed the illness had a little puzzled Mr. Pym, but he himself felt sure it was fever of some description; there could be no doubt whatever about it."

"Is he with you now?"

"No, poor fellow, he is dead. My place was too hard for him, for I kept only one man then, and he left me for a lighter one. After that he went back to his late mistress, who had just married Colonel Darling. A little later I heard of his death."

Frederick St. John was paying no attention to this last item of explanation: he had fallen into a train of thought. The dean looked at him.

"Dr. Beauclerc, if any one could throw light upon this subject, it is Pym. I wish you would write and ask him."

"Ask him what?"

"What Mr. Norris really died of. It might have been insanity."

"People don't generally die of insanity."

"But there's no harm in writing. If you have no objection."

"I'll think it over," said the dean.

"And now I must go back," said Frederick, rising. "Will you walk with me, and see Georgina?"

"Ah, Frederick, you know how to tempt me! I would walk further than to Castle Wafer to see *her*. My only darling: I believe no one in the world knows her real worth."

They went out together. Looking into the drawing-room for a minute first of all, to tell Mrs. Beauclerc. She was there with Miss Denison, a middle-aged lady who had come home with them for a long visit, and who was one of the *bêtes noires* of Georgina's life.

Georgina was watching: whether for the possible sight of her father, or for the more certain one of his companion—there

she stood, half in, half out of the open French window.
Frederick stole a march upon her. He made the dean creep
round the corner of the house, so that she did not see them
until they were close upon her. He watched the meeting; he
saw the clinging, heartfelt embrace, the glad tears rising to
her eyes: never after that could he doubt the girl's loving
nature. Perhaps, with all her lightness, he had not doubted
it before.

"And where's mamma. Could she not also come?"

"I left her to entertain Miss Denison."

Georgina gave a scream. "Papa! You have never brought
her home!"

"Mamma has done so. She has come for two months,
Georgie."

Georgie groaned. "Then I shall remain at Castle Wafer."

"No, you won't," cried Frederick, and then hastened to
turn his apparent discourtesy into a laugh. "We wouldn't keep
you, Georgina."

"And I could not spare you," said the dean.

They entered the room, Georgina—who so proud as she?—
on her father's arm. Sir Isaac, who was playing chess with
Mrs. Carleton, rose to welcome him. Mrs. Carleton rose also.
She had never seen the Dean of Westerbury, and the introduction took place. Calm, impassive, perfectly self-possessed,
she stood; exchanging a few words of courtesy with the dean,
her handsome features looking singularly attractive, one of
the beautiful crystal chessmen held between her slender
fingers. Not a woman in the world could look much less
insane than did Charlotte Carleton; and the dean turned his
eyes on Frederick, in momentary wonder at that gentleman's
hallucination.

Georgina stole up to the master of Castle Wafer.

"You'll let me stay here, won't you, Sir Isaac?"

"You know I will. *Let* you stay!"

"But you'll ask papa to let me stay?"

"My dear, yes. Does he want to take you away?"

"Of course he will want it. And—do you know what
mamma has done? Brought home with her that horrible Miss
Denison. I wonder papa let her. The last time she was with
us—but that was at Westerbury—there was no peace in the
house for her. She was always quarrelling with me, and of
course I quarrelled with her again. Nothing that I did was

right; and one day she actually got mamma to lock me in my room for two hours, because she said I had been insolent to her. You'll get leave for me to stay, Sir Isaac?"

He gave her a reassuring smile, and sat down to chess again. The dean talked with Mrs. St. John, Georgina flitted incessantly from them to the chess-players, making every one as merry as she was; Frederick alone seemed quiet and abstracted. He sat apart, near the tea-table, a cup before him, as if tea-drinking was his whole business in life.

The evening wore on. When ten o'clock struck, the dean rose, saying he had not supposed it to be so late.

"You will spare Georgina to us a little longer?" said Sir Isaac. They were still at chess, of which it seemed Mrs. Carleton never tired; and he rose as he spoke to the dean.

"Until to-morrow. She must come home then."

"Oh, papa!" broke in the really earnest voice, "do let me stay longer. You know why I wish to—it's because of that Miss Denison."

The dean looked grave.

"Only a few days longer, papa; just a few days. Then I will come home. It will take me all that time to get over the shock."

But there was a merry twinkle in her eye; and the dean smiled. Whilst he was shaking hands with Mrs. Carleton, Georgina turned suddenly to Frederick. "Won't you say a word for me? You once called Miss Denison an old hag yourself."

"It must have been when I was a rude boy," he answered.

"But won't you?"

"No," he said, in a low and unmistakably serious tone. "I would rather you did not stay, Georgina."

While Georgina was recovering from her surprise, she became conscious of some commotion in the room. Turning, she saw a lady in travelling costume, and recognized Mrs. Darling. Her appearance was exciting universal astonishment: Frederick in particular rubbed his eyes to be sure he was not dreaming. How quickly she had answered the telegram!

It happened that the dean, the only one of the party not pressing forward either in surprise or welcome, was close to Mrs. Carleton, and had leisure to note her looks, though indeed chance alone caused his glance to fall upon her in the first instance. Instead of pressing forward, Mrs. Carleton drew back, seemed to stagger; her face turned livid, her eyes were ablaze with a wild, curious light; and one of the costly chessmen fell and was broken in pieces. It almost seemed to have been crushed in her hand. Another had seen it too, Frederick St. John. Was it a habit, then, of hers to be so unpleasantly excited under any surprise? Or were these indeed signs of incipient insanity? If the crystal had broken in her hand and not in the fall, she must possess a strength beyond that of ordinary women. He, Frederick St. John, had just time to see that the dean's gaze was riveted upon her, before the stir became universal, every one talking at once, Mrs. Darling laughing gaily.

She knew she should take them by surprise, she was saying, as she shook hands with one and another; had been enjoying it in anticipation the whole day. From a communication received from her cottage at Alnwick, she found her orders were wanted in some repairs that were being done; so had started quite on a moment's impulse; and—here she was, having determined to take Castle Wafer on her way, and see whether Charlotte was ready to return home. Rose? Oh, Rose was quite well, and staying with some friends in Paris, the Castellas. Darling Charlotte! How well she was looking!

Darling Charlotte had recovered from her emotion, and was herself again,—calm, sweet, impassive Charlotte. After submitting to the embrace of her mother, she turned in contrition to Sir Isaac. Frederick and Georgina were both stooping to gather up the broken crystal.

Would Sir Isaac ever forgive her? That lovely set of chessmen! And how it came to slip out of her hand, she could not imagine: how it came to break on the soft carpet (unless indeed it struck against the foot of the chess-table) she could not tell. In vain Sir Isaac begged her not to think more of so trifling a misfortune: it seemed that she could not cease her excuses.

"Mrs. Carleton! look at your hand. You must have broken the bishop yourself."

The words came from Georgina Beauclerc. The fair white hand had sundry cuts within it, and the red spots oozing from them had caught Georgina's gaze as she rose from the carpet. One angry, evil glance from Mrs. Carleton's eyes at the outspoken young lady, and then she resigned the white hand to Sir Isaac to be bound up.

"Strange, that we rarely can tell how these things happen," she said, with a genial smile. "Miss Beauclerc must have a curious idea of strength, to suppose my fingers could have broken that bishop. Thank you very much, Sir Isaac."

Frederick St. John went out with the dean. "I do hope you will write to Mr. Pym?" he said.

"I intend to," answered the dean.

CHAPTER XXXIV.

WALKING OUT TO DINNER.

IF Mrs. Darling's hurried visit to England was caused by the fact of the repairs in progress at her cottage, being at a stand-still, the repairs must be at a stand-still yet; for the lady did not go farther than Castle Wafer. On the morning following her arrival, Sir Isaac politely asked whether she would not remain a few days with them before going on; and Mrs. Darling took him at his word and did remain. Georgina also remained, and things seemed to go on very smoothly and quietly, but Mrs. Carleton remained a great deal in her own room; and to Mr. Frederick St. John's eyes her mother's face wore a strangely haggard, anxious look.

"Is Mrs. Carleton well?" he asked her one day.

"Quite well, thank you," responded Mrs. Darling, stooping, as she spoke, to pluck a geranium.

"I have not liked her look at times," continued Frederick, boldly. "I was fearing she was not in—altogether good health."

"She is in excellent health," was the reply, and Mrs. Darling faced the speaker with a look intended to express surprise. "Charlotte was always strong. She and Rose are like myself, blessed with rude health: I cannot say as much for the other two. I want to take Charlotte away with me; but she does not feel inclined to come, and was quite angry when she saw me arrive. She is very happy here."

No more was said, for Mrs. Darling sauntered leisurely away. Frederick St. John had gained nothing by his move.

The dean, who had written to Mr. Pym, received in due course that gentleman's answer. Mr. Norris, of Norris Court, had died *mad.* The widow, subsequently Mrs. Darling, had hushed the matter up for the sake of her child, and succeeded in keeping it secret. He, Mr. Pym, had never disclosed it to mortal ears; but the high character of the Dean of Westerbury was such that he knew he might safely confide the fact to him. Indeed, from the tenour of the dean's letter, he felt there might be some essential reason for not remaining silent.

"You see," cried Frederick, when the dean showed him the letter, "I was right."

"Nay," dissented the dean. "Right as to your suspicion that madness was in the family; but this does not prove that it has yet attacked Mrs. Carleton."

"I suppose it would not prove it to most minds; it does to mine, in a very great degree. You will at least admit that this renders her a most undesirable wife for Isaac."

"Granted. But, Frederick, my opinion is that Sir Isaac is in just as much danger from her as you are, and no more. Rely upon it he has no idea of marrying."

Frederick was silent. In a sense he agreed with the dean; but he knew how subtle is the constant companionship of a designing and attractive woman; and that the danger was all the greater where that companionship had been previously held aloof from, as in the case of Sir Isaac.

Two or three days passed on, and nothing occurred to disturb the peace even of fanciful Frederick St. John. The old routine of life was observed at Castle Wafer, varied with visits to the Rectory, or with the Rectory's visits back again. But for the suspicion he was making so great a trouble of, Mr. St. John would have felt supremely happy. A strangely bright feeling was stealing over him; a feeling whose source he did not question or analyze. The influence of Georgina was quietly making its way in his heart; perhaps, unconsciously to himself, it had ever in a degree lain there.

Mrs. Darling sat in her room, writing letters. Mrs. Carleton was with her, looking from the window, the folds of her silver-grey brocade rustling with every movement. She wore very slight mourning now.

"Charlotte, my dear child," suddenly cried Mrs. Darling, " I am writing to the cottage. Let me once again ask you when you will be ready to go with me?"

"Never—to Alnwick. When I left the cottage to become George St. John's wife, I left it, as a residence, for ever."

"Where *will* you go? Will you go into Berkshire?—will you go to London?—to Brighton?—to Paris? Only say where —I don't wish to force you to Alnwick."

"Mamma, I beg you not to worry me on this point. I am very comfortable at Castle Wafer, and you need not try to force me away from it. It is lost labour."

Mrs. Darling made no reply. It would have been useless. All her life she had found it "lost labour" to endeavour to force Charlotte to do anything against her will; and sometimes she felt the yoke upon her was a very heavy one. She bent over her writing again in silence. Presently Charlotte spoke, abruptly:

"How long is that girl going to remain here?"

Mrs. Darling's train of thought just then was roaming to many things, pleasant or unpleasant, and she thought "that girl" must mean Honour Tritton. Charlotte's eyes were ablaze with light at the mistake; and Mrs. Darling could have bitten her tongue out for her incaution in mentioning the name. What she next said, did not mend it.

"Charlotte, my darling, I really beg your pardon. I'm sure I don't know how I came to think of her, unless it was that I was talking to her this morning. You——"

"Talking to *her!*" came the imperative interruption. "I should like to know, mamma, what you can have to say to her. If every one had their deserts, Honour Tritton would be—would be—— What did she presume to say of me?"

"My dear Charlotte!" cried the unfortunate mother, half aghast at the tone in which the last sentence was spoken, "she did not presume to speak of you at all. It was only a casual meeting in one of the lower passages. She just dropped a curtsey, and asked how I was: that was all."

"She presumed to put herself in my way the other day, that woman; I know that," scornfully returned Mrs. Carleton. "But that it might be said I made too much of a trifle utterly beneath me, I should ask Sir Isaac to banish her from Castle Wafer."

"Oh, Charlotte! What, because she—she happened to meet you?"

"No. For the misery she wrought in the years gone by. I wonder what brought her *here*—why she came?"

Mrs. Darling had heard of the meeting with Honour on the

stairs, and knew as much of the scene as though she had been present. She passed to another topic.

"Then it was of Miss Beauclerc you spoke, Charlotte?"

"It was of Miss Beauclerc. *I want to know what she stops here for.*"

The low, impressive whisper in which this was spoken, astonished Mrs. Darling. What had Charlotte got in her head now?

"My dear, it cannot matter to you whether she stays here or whether she goes home."

"But it does matter: it matters very much. She is staying as a spy upon me."

"A spy? Charlotte!"

"She is. She is doing what she can to turn Sir Isaac against me."

"Oh, Charlotte! Indeed you are mistaken. I am quite sure she is doing nothing of the sort."

• "I tell you yes. Look there!"

Mrs. Darling rose in obedience, and glanced from the window in the direction in which Charlotte had pointed. Georgina Beauclerc, in her flowing dinner-dress of a clear white muslin, was marching about with Sir Isaac, both her hands clasped upon his arm, her pretty head and its silken hair almost touching his face as she talked to him. That Sir Isaac was bending down to the fair head, a great deal of tender love in his face, might be discerned even at this distance.

"He promised to ride out with *me* this afternoon; he was going on his pony, and I was to try Mr. St. John's grey horse, and she came and took him from me. He gave me up for her with scarcely a word of apology, and they have been away together for hours somewhere on foot. She cannot let him rest. The moment she is dressed for dinner, you see, she lures him to her side again. And you say she is not plotting against me?"

What could Mrs. Darling reply? The idea had taken possession of Charlotte, and she knew that no earthly argument would turn it by so much as a hair's-breadth. The shadow of a trouble that she should not have strength to combat fell upon her; and as Charlotte abruptly left the room, she took a letter from her pocket and read it with a gleam of thankfulness, for it told of the speedy arrival of one who might be of use.

St. Martin's Eve.   27

Mrs. Carleton descended, glancing to the left and right of the broad staircase, into all its angles, over the gilded balustrades down on the inner hall, as had been her custom since that encounter with Honour. Not with open look, but with stealthy glance, as if she dreaded meeting the woman again. She went into the drawing-room, and stood gazing through the open window with covert glances, partially shielding herself behind the blue satin curtains. Georgina was on the terrace with Sir Isaac, and on them her regard was fixed. A gaze, evil, bitter, menacing. Her eyes shone with a lurid light, her lips were pale, and her hands were contracted as with irrepressible anger. In the midst of these unwholesome signs, as if instinct whispered to her that she was not alone, she turned and saw, quietly seated at a table near, and as quietly regarding her, Frederick St. John.

She came up to him at once, her brow smoothed to its ordinary impassiveness.

"What a warm afternoon it has been, Mr. St. John!"

"Very warm."

"You are ready for dinner early," she said, in allusion to his notably late appearance for that meal; often coming in after they had sat down to table.

"I don't dine at home to-day. I am going with Miss Beauclerc to the Rectory."

"And Sir Isaac also?" she quickly asked.

"I think not."

Sir Isaac and Georgina approached the window. They, with Frederick, had walked to the Rectory that afternoon, and the dean asked them to come in to dinner. It was very dull, he said, with only Miss Denison, who generally contrived to act as a wet blanket. So it was arranged that Georgina and Frederick should go; but Sir Isaac could not promise. It appeared that Georgina was now urging him to accompany them. Her voice was heard in the room.

"It is very uncharitable of you, Sir Isaac. You know what papa said it was for him, with that statue of a woman there. If *you* were shut up in a house with a female Hottentot, and you asked papa to come in as a relief, he would not think of refusing."

"But I can't go," returned Sir Isaac, in laughing tones. "I told the dean that Mrs. St. John was not well enough to come down."

"And you will let me walk all that way without you! It's not kind, Sir Isaac. Suppose I get run away with? There may be kidnappers in the shrubbery."

"You will have a more efficient protector with you than I could make; one young and powerful—I am old and weak."

"Never old to me—never old to me. Oh, I *wish* you would come!"

"I wish I could, Georgina; you know that when you leave me, half my sunshine goes also. But I must head the table at home, in the absence of Mrs. St. John: I cannot leave my visitors."

"Tiresome people!" apostrophized Georgina, in allusion to the lady visitors. "I know you would rather be with us. I shall tell papa that if he is fixed with Miss Denison, you are fixed with Mrs. Carleton. I don't see how you would get through your days with her just now, if it were not for me."

She stepped into the room, a saucy expression on her charming face; a loving smile on Sir Isaac's. Mrs. Carleton was in time to catch a glimpse of each as she swiftly glided away in the distance; and neither had the remotest suspicion that their conversation had been overheard.

Frederick St. John rose. "I think we shall be late, Georgina."

"Shall we! I shall say it was your fault," cried the happy girl, as she caught up her white mantle and straw hat from a chair. "I'm ready now."

"Won't you put your cloak on?"

"No. I am only taking it to come back in to-night. You may carry it for me."

She placed it on his arm; and with her face shaded only by her little dainty parasol, they went out. Mrs. Carleton was at one of the other windows watching the departure.

"Do you know the time, Georgina?" he asked.

"Oh—more than five, I suppose."

He held his watch towards her. It wanted only twenty-five minutes to six. "Of course you can say it is my fault if you like; but Mrs. Beauclerc will be excessively angry with both of us."

"Not as angry as Miss Denison will be," returned Georgina, laughingly. "Fanciful old creature! saying she gets indigestion if she dines later than half-past five. If I were papa,

I should let her dine alone, and order the regular dinner at seven. See how quickly she'd come to her senses."

"If you were your papa you'd do just as he does" cried Frederick. "And when you have a house of your own, Georgina, you will be just as courteous as he is."

"Shall I? Not to Miss Denison. But I should take care not to have disagreeable people staying with me. I wouldn't have Mrs. Carleton, for instance."

"Do you think Mrs. Carleton disagreeable?" he asked. "I have heard you say you liked her."

"So I did at first. I pitied her. But she gets very disagreeable. She looks at me sometimes as if she would like to kill me, and—see what she did yesterday."

Georgina extended her wrist towards her companion. There was a blue mark upon it, as from pressure.

"How did she do this!" he exclaimed, examining the wrist.

"Not purposely, of course, that is, not intending to hurt me. I differed from her: it was about going out with Sir Isaac. She said it was too hot for me, and I said the hotter the pleasanter; and she caught me by the wrist as I was running away. I cried out with the pain; indeed it was very sharp; and Sir Isaac heard it outside and looked back. She laughed then, and so did I, and I ran away. This morning I saw that my wrist had turned blue."

"Did you tell Isaac of this?"

"I don't remember. Stay, though—I think I told him Mrs. Carleton had been preaching morality to me, as connected with sunstrokes and freckles," continued the careless girl. "Please loose my hand, Mr. St. John."

He released her hand, saying nothing. Georgina floated on by his side, her blue ribbons and her fair hair flashing in the setting sun as they passed through the shrubbery.

"I think she must be frequently out of temper," continued Georgina, alluding still to Mrs. Carleton. "Did you see her as we passed the window just now? She looked so cross at me."

"I presume she thinks she has cause for it," observed Mr. St. John.

"What cause?"

"She is jealous of you."

"Jealous of me?"

"Of you and Sir Isaac."

Georgina's grey eyes opened to their utmost width as she stared at the speaker.

"Jealous of me and Sir Isaac? Why, what could put such an idea into her stupid head? How *could* she be jealous of me, in relation to Sir Isaac? She might as well be jealous of papa."

"I suppose she thinks that she, as chief guest, ought to receive more of the host's attention than any one else," he said, not caring to be more explanatory. "And therefore she does not like your monopolizing Isaac."

"Oh!" cried Georgina, turning up her pretty nose. "I declare I thought you meant it in another light. I'll take up Sir Isaac's attention all to-morrow, just to tease her."

He made no reply. He was thinking. It had not been his fault that Georgina's stay at Castle Wafer was prolonged; but he had seen no feasible way of preventing it. And yet there was always an undercurrent in his heart—a wish that she was away from it, beyond the risk of any possible harm.

"Please put the mantle over my shoulders, Mr. St. John."

"Ah, you are getting cold! You should have put it on at first."

"Getting cold this warm afternoon! Indeed no. But in one minute we shall be in the Rectory grounds, liable to meet mamma or her charming guest. They would sing a duet all dinner-time at my walking here in nothing but my dinner-dress. Miss Denison comes out before dinner, and creeps round the paths for half-an-hour. She calls it 'taking her constitutional.' Thank you; she can't find fault now."

Mrs. Beauclerc was a fretful lady of forty-five; Miss Denison was a fretful lady of somewhat more: and Georgina was greeted with a shower of reproaches, for having kept dinner waiting. She laid the blame on Mr. St. John; and Miss Denison looked daggers at him to her heart's content.

"I could not make him believe you were dining at the gothic hour of half-past five," cried the imperturbable girl. "The more I told him to hasten the less he did so. And, mamma, Mrs. St. John says will we all go to Castle Wafer for the evening."

She stole a glance at him. He was standing calm, upright; a half-tender, half-reproving look cast upon her for her nonsense. But he contradicted nothing.

The dean and Mr. St. John were sitting alone after dinner, when a servant came in and said a gentleman was asking if he could see Dr. Beauclerc. The dean inquired who it was, but the servant did not know: when he requested the name, the gentleman said he would tell it himself to the doctor.

"You can show him in here," said the dean, who was one of the most accessible men living.

The servant retired, and ushered in a little grey-haired man in spectacles. The dean did not recognize him: Frederick St. John did, and with some astonishment. It was Mr. Pym of Alnwick.

He explained to the dean that a little matter of business had brought him into the neighbourhood, and he had taken the opportunity (following on the slight correspondence which had just taken place between them) to call on Dr. Beauclerc. Dr. Beauclerc—who was not addressed as "Mr. Dean" out of his cathedral city as much as he was in it—inquired how long he had been in the neighbourhood, and found he had only just arrived by the evening train,—had come straight to the Rectory from the station.

A suspicion crossed the dean's mind, and he spoke in accordance with it. "Did Mr. Pym come from Alnwick on purpose to see him?"

"No," said the little surgeon, taking the glass of wine the dean passed to him, but declining other refreshment. "I have been summoned to the neighbourhood of Lexington to see a patient; and as I was on the spot, I thought I would call upon you, Dr. Beauclerc. My chief motive in doing so," he added, after a brief pause, "was to inquire whether you had any particular reason for asking me those questions."

The dean looked at Frederick St. John, as much as to say, Shall we, or shall we not confide in this medical man?

"I do not inquire from motives of idle curiosity, Dr. Beauclerc," resumed the surgeon, marking the dean's hesitation. "Believe me, I have an urgent reason for wishing to know."

"Better tell him everything," cried Frederick, who had read the dean's look, and was vehement in his earnestness. "I am sure Mr. Pym may be trusted; and perhaps he can help us with his advice."

"Very well," said the dean. "But you know, Frederick, the suspicion is more yours than mine."

"Yes, yes; I take it all upon myself," was the young man's impatient answer, so fearful was he of losing this new ally.

"Mr. Pym, you have known Mrs. Carleton St. John all her life, have you not? She was Charlotte Norris."

"Yes, it may be said that I have known her all her life. I brought her into the world."

"Well, a disagreeable suspicion has recently come upon us in regard to her—upon me, that is. An awful suspicion; one that I do not like to mention."

"What is it?" cried the surgeon.

"I fear that she is showing symptoms of insanity."

Frederick St. John looked at Mr. Pym as he spoke, expecting a start of surprise. Far from evincing any, that gentleman quietly raised his wine to his lips, sipped it, and put the glass down again.

"Ah," said he. "Well?"

Then Mr. St. John poured forth his tale. He who was usually almost coldly impassive, who had every tone of his voice, every pulse of his veins under control, seemed this evening to have become all impulse and excitement. But in telling his story, he grew gradually calm and cool.

Mr. Pym listened in silence. At the conclusion of the story he waited a minute or two, apparently expecting to hear more, but the narrator had ceased. He spoke then.

"You are sure about that telegram—that it was Prance who sent it?"

"Quite sure. There can be no mistake about that."

"A cautious woman," observed the surgeon. "She mentioned no name. You see it might have applied to any one as much as to Mrs. Carleton."

"The very remark I made," interposed the dean, and it was the first word he had spoken. "I tell Mr. St. John that the symptoms and facts he thinks so much of are very slight."

"Too slight to pronounce any one insane upon," said the doctor. "Will you be so good as tell me, Mr. St. John, what *first* gave rise to suspicion in your mind? It is a rare thing, however eccentric our friends' actions may be, for us to take up the notion that they are insane."

"What first gave rise to the suspicion in my mind?" repeated Frederick. "Why, I don't suppose I ever should have thought of it but for—but I forgot to tell you that," he broke off, suddenly remembering that he had omitted to mention what Rose Darling had told him at Belport.

He related it now. The assertions of the nurse Brayford

that Mrs. Carleton was mad; her terror at the sight of the
lighted lanterns in the Flemish town on St. Martin's Eve.
Still Mr. Pym said nothing : he only took out a note-book and
entered something in it.

"Can you not help us, Mr. Pym? Do you not think she
must be insane?"

"I cannot say that. But I may tell you that I have always
feared it for her."

"Her father died mad, you wrote word to the dean."

"He died raving mad. You have confided in me, and I see
no reason why I should not tell you all I know—premising, of
course, that it must not be repeated. His madness, as I
gathered at the time, was hereditary; but he had been (unlike
his daughter) perfectly well all his life, betraying no symptoms .
of it. I was sent for in haste one night to Norris Court. I
was only a young man then—thirty, perhaps; I'm turned sixty
now. My predecessor and late partner, Mr. Jevons, had been
the usual attendant there, but he had retired from business,
and was very infirm. I thought I was wanted for Mrs. Norris,
whom I was to attend in her approaching confinement; but
when I reached the Court, I found what it was. Mr. Norris
had suddenly become mad; utterly, unmistakably mad; and
Mrs. Norris, poor thing, was nearly as much so with terror.
He had always been of a remarkably jealous disposition ; some
slight incident had caused him to become that day jealous of
his wife, without, I am certain, the least foundation, and after
an awful scene, he attempted her life with his razor. In her
endeavour to escape from him, she dashed her hand through a
mirror, whether accidentally or purposely she could not afterwards remember. Never shall I forget her dismay and terror
when I reached the Court. Her husband was tolerably quiet
then; exhausted, no doubt, from violence; and his own man,
James, was keeping guard over him. That night we had to
put him into a strait-waistcoat. Mrs. Norris, poor young
lady—and she was not twenty then—cried most bitterly as she
told me the tale of her husband's jealousy. She could not
imagine what had given rise to it. She had only received some
gentleman, a friend of theirs who had often called, and had sat
and talked with him in the drawing-room, as she would with
any other visitor; but the jealousy, as I explained to her, pre-
ceded the attack of madness. In three or four days the child
Charlotte was born. I took the baby in to Mr. Norris, thinking

it might possibly have a soothing effect upon him. It had just the contrary—though it is unnecessary to recall minor particulars now. He had seemed better that day, quite collected, and his servant had removed the strait-waistcoat. An accession of violence came on at sight of the child; he sprang out of bed and attempted to seize it; I put the baby down under the bed, while I helped James to overpower his master; but it was the hardest struggle I had ever been engaged in. Mr. Norris never was calm afterwards, and died in a few days, raving mad."

"But," interrupted the dean, "how was it possible to keep this state of things from transpiring in the house? The domestics understood, I believe, that their master died of fever."

"True, Dr. Beauclerc. Fortunately the room to which Mr. Norris was taken was shut in by other surrounding apartments, and no sound penetrated beyond it. The servants were kept away by a hint of infection; a confidential man from an asylum was had in to assist James and take turn in watching—the servants supposing him to be merely a sick-nurse. Poor Mrs. Norris entreated for her child's sake that the nature of its father's malady might be suppressed, if possible; and the secret was kept. Whether it was well in the long-run that it should be so kept, I have often asked myself."

Mr. Pym paused in thought. Frederick St. John interrupted it.

"You say this madness was hereditary?"

"Mr. Jevons managed to get to the Court when he found what had happened. It appeared that some near relatives of Mr. Norris—two, I think—had died abroad, insane. Mr. Norris was aware of this, and had been fond of talking of it to Mr. Jevons: the latter thought he had feared the malady for himself. He had used to say that he should never marry; and that resolution Mr. Jevons emphatically endorsed. However, he did marry, and, of course, Mr. Jevons had no power to prevent it. These particulars I learned of Mr. Jevons as I was driving him to the Court. Mrs. Norris begged to be made acquainted with all details; and after her husband's death Mr. Jevons disclosed them to her, suppressing nothing. What a changed woman she was from that time! and I believe would then have been thankful had her baby died. 'It must be my care to prevent its marrying, should it live to grow up,' she said to Mr. Jevons in my presence; and ten times over during that one interview she begged him to tell her whether he thought the child would inherit the fatal disease."

"But the child did marry," interrupted the dean. "Married Mr. Carleton St. John."

"Yes. I believe Mrs. Darling did try to prevent it, but it was of no use. Whilst she concealed the reason, arguments could not fail to prove powerless. It might have been better— I don't know—had she allowed her daughter to become acquainted with the truth. My opinion is, that Charlotte has more than once, even before her marriage, been on the verge of insanity. In her attacks of temper the violence displayed was very great for a person perfectly sane."

"Did Mrs. Darling ever attempt to excuse this violence to you?"

"Mrs. Darling has never spoken to me on the subject at all since her first husband's death," replied Mr. Pym. "She has ignored it. But for an expression at times in her face, I might suppose she fancied that all recollection of the tragedy had faded from my mind. When I heard that George St. John was about to marry Miss Norris, I called on Mrs. Darling, and in the course of conversation I said, incidentally, as it were, 'Will this marriage be for your daughter's benefit, think you?' and she seemed offended, and said, Of course it would—what did I mean?"

"Could you not"—Frederick St. John hesitated as he spoke —"have whispered a word of warning to Mr. George St. John?"

"I suppose not. The thought crossed me, but I could not see that I was justified in carrying it out. Had Mrs. Darling met me in a different manner, I might have ventured. I don't think it would have done any good, though. George St. John was in love with Miss Norris, or fancied himself so; and would most likely have married her in spite of caution."

"In her life, subsequently to her marriage, were there at any time indications of insanity?"

"I feel tempted to say there were, though I could not bear witness to it in a court of law," was the reply of Mr. Pym. "One thing is indisputable—that she inherited her father's jealousy of disposition. I don't know what it might have been in him; but in her it was in excess so great as to be in itself a species of madness. She was not, that I ever heard, jealous of her husband; it displayed itself in her jealous love for her child. Until he was born, I don't think she had one of those paroxysms of violence that those about her called 'temper.' George St. John could not understand them. These fits of passion, coupled with the fierce jealousy that was beyond all reason, all parallel in my experience, were very like madness."

There was a pause. Frederick St. John broke it with a question.

" Did you suspect—I mean, was there any cause to suspect —that she had a hand in the little boy's death—Benja's ? "

" I did suspect it. That is, I doubted whether it might not be so," said Mr. Pym, in low tones. " There was an ugly point in the matter that I have never liked—that of the doors being fastened. But I am bound to say there was no proof against her. Still I could not get rid of my doubts, and I think her mother entertained them also."

" Mrs. Darling ! "

" I think so. We both caught each other in the act of trying whether the bolt would slip when the door closed, in the manner asserted. You see, when a suspicion of insanity attaches to a man or woman, we are prone to imagine things that we should never think of doing under ordinary circumstances."

" Very true," emphatically assented the dean.

" The most bitter person upon the tragedy was Honour; it was only natural she should be so ; but even she did not suspect Mrs. Carleton. She spoke against her in her ravings, but ravings go for nothing. If Honour suspected any one, it was Prance rather than Mrs. Carleton."

" Prance ! " echoed Mr. St. John.

" She told some tale, at the time, of having seen Prance hiding in a niche of the corridor, opposite the nursery door. I did not think much of it, from the state of confusion in which Honour must then have been ; and Prance denied it *in toto :* said she had never been there."

" Then you cannot give me any help ? " said Frederick St. John, in tones of disappointment. " You are unable to bear out my suspicions of her present madness ? "

" How can I bear them out ? " asked Mr. Pym. " I have not seen her."

Frederick drummed for a minute on the table. " Don't you think it strange that Prance should telegraph for Mrs. Darling in the manner she did, and that Mrs. Darling should hasten to respond to it—on the wings of the wind, as one may say—and stay on at Castle Wafer?"

"I do," was the surgeon's reply: "assuming that the message related to Mrs. Carleton, of which I suppose there can be no doubt. Mrs. Carleton is not ill in body; therefore it must have had reference to her mind."

"I wish you could see her!" impulsively spoke Frederick, "and watch her as I have done."

"I intend to see her," said Mr. Pym. "I thought of calling at once on Mrs. Darling; now, as I leave you."

"Do so," cried Frederick. "Contrive to remain a few days at Castle Wafer. You can say that you are my guest. Stay; I'll give you the invitation in a careless sort of way before them all to-night, and you can accept it."

"We will see about that," said the surgeon, rising. "I had better be going, if Dr. Beauclerc will excuse me, or it may look late to call. Perhaps you will direct me the nearest way to Castle Wafer."

"I will go with you," said Mr. St. John. "The nearest way is through the shrubberies. We shall be there in five minutes."

They went out together, the dean saying he would follow with the ladies, as they were all to spend the evening at Castle Wafer. But when the dean reached the drawing-room he found they had already gone, and he did not hurry himself.

It was a lovely moonlight night, clear and bright, and Mr. St. John and the surgeon commenced their walk, talking eagerly. Mr. St. John told him, what he had not liked to mention before the dean—Mrs. Carleton's jealousy of Miss Beauclerc; the occasional wildness of her eyes when she looked at her, and the little adventure in Georgina's chamber at midnight. "It is an awful responsibility that rests upon us," he remarked. "I feel it so, Mr. Pym, now that I have heard your story to-night. If her father went mad from jealousy, and attempted the life of his wife, Mrs. Carleton may be attempting some violence to Miss Beauclerc."

"Miss Beauclerc is young and good-looking, I suppose."

"Both; and her manners are perfectly charming. She is just the girl that would be obnoxious to a rival."

"It is all fancy, I presume, on Mrs. Carleton's part. There is nothing between Miss Beauclerc and Sir Isaac?"

Frederick St. John broke into a laugh. "Sir Isaac loves

her as he would a child of his own; and she venerates him as a father. There is no other sort of love between them, Mr. Pym."

Mr. Pym took a side glance at the speaker. Something in the tone had struck him that some one else might be a lover of Miss Beauclerc's, if Sir Isaac was not.

"Even allowing that Mrs. Carleton has been sane hitherto, and my suspicion a myth, it would never do for her to marry Sir Isaac," resumed Frederick. "You would say so if you knew my brother and his extreme sensitiveness. The very thought of his wife being liable to insanity would be to him perfectly horrible."

"It would be to most people," said the doctor.

"I think he must be told now. I have abstained from speaking out hitherto, from a fear that my motives might be misconstrued. My brother, a confirmed old bachelor, has brought me up to consider myself his heir; and it would look as though I were swayed by self-interest."

"I understand," said the surgeon. "But he must be saved from Mrs. Carleton."

"I cannot bring myself to think that he is in real danger; I believe still that he has no thought of marrying, and never will have. But Mrs. Carleton is undeniably attractive, and stranger things have been known."

"The better plan would be to lay the whole case before Sir Isaac. It need not be yourself. I should suggest Dr. Beauclerc. And then——"

The surgeon ceased, arrested by the warning hand of Frederick. They had turned into the dark labyrinth of a place where the artificial rocks rose on the confines of the Rectory grounds. Georgina Beauclerc was walking very deliberately towards them. Not at her did Frederick lift his hand; but at a swift, dark figure, who was following her silently as a shadow, stealthily as an omen of evil. Frederick St. John sprang forward and clasped Georgina in his arms.

The dark figure turned suddenly and vanished; but not before its glaring eyes and its white teeth had been seen by the unwelcome intruder. He recognized Mrs. Carleton, her black lace shawl thrown over her head.

"Well, I'm sure!" exclaimed Georgina.

It all passed in an instant. Georgina had heard nothing, seen nothing; and she felt inclined to resent Mr. St. John's extra-

ordinary movement, when the first surprise was over. He held
her for a moment against his beating heart; beating more perceptibly than usual just then.

"What did you do that for? Were you going to smother
me?"

"I did it to shield you from harm, my darling," he whispered,
unconscious, perhaps, that he used the endearing term.
Rarely had Frederick St. John been less himself than he was
at that moment. Miss Beauclerc looked at him in surprise;
in the midst of her bounding pulses, her glowing blushes, she
saw that something had disturbed his equanimity.

"What are you doing out here alone?"

"You need not be cross"—and indeed his sharp quick
question had sounded so. "As if I could not take a stroll by
moonlight if I like! Perhaps you are afraid of the moon, as
mamma is."

"But what were you doing? Had you come from Castle
Wafer? You must not go out at night alone, Georgina."

"Oh indeed; who says so?" she returned, with wilful im-
pertinence; but it was all put on to hide the ecstatic rapture
his one word had brought to her. "If you must know, mamma
and Miss Denison kept up such a chorus of abuse of me as we
went to Castle Wafer, that I would not go on with them. I
came slowly back to meet you and papa."

He had drawn her arm within his own, and was leading her
back to the Rectory. She could hardly keep up with him.

"Where are you hurrying me to?"

"To the dean. He will take care of you to Castle Wafer."

It may be that she thought some one else might have taken
care of her. But she said nothing. Just before they reached
the Rectory door, Mr. St. John stopped under the shade of the
laurels.

"Georgina, I must say a serious word to you. Put away
nonsense for a minute, and hear me. I think I have saved
you from a great danger; will you make me a promise in
return?"

"From a great danger!" she repeated, the words rendering
her as serious as he was. "What danger? What can you
mean?"

"I cannot tell precisely what danger, neither can I say more
particularly what I mean. Nevertheless I think I am right.
It is not good for you to be about alone just now, whether

before nightfall or after it. You must give me your promise not to be so."

"What is there to harm me?" she whispered, involuntarily clinging more closely to his arm.

"Leave that with me for the present. Only trust me, and do as I say. Will you promise?"

"Yes, if there is a necessity for it. I promise you."

Her earnest face was raised in the moonlight. She had never seen him so solemn as now. He bent his head.

"Will you seal the compact, Georgina?"

Instinct, and the grave tender tone, told her what he meant. Her eyes filled with tears; but she did not draw her face away, and he left a kiss upon her lips.

"Mind, Georgina, that's as binding as an oath," he said, as he walked on. "Take care that you strictly keep your promise. There is urgent necessity why you should do so. Sometime I may tell you why, if you are good. I may be telling you all sorts of things besides."

Her face was bent to conceal its hot blushes. Heaven seemed suddenly to have opened for Georgina Beauclerc.

"Halloa!" cried the dean, as he met them in the hall. "I thought you had gone on with your mamma, Georgina."

"She came back to walk with you, sir," said Mr. St. John, only waiting to speak the words and then hastening away again.

Mr. Pym was standing near the rocks as he got up to him. "Where did you hide yourself?" cried Frederick. "You seemed to vanish into air. I could see you nowhere."

"I slipped behind here," answered the surgeon, indicating the rocks. "Was not one of those ladies Mrs. Carleton?"

"Yes."

"Well, I thought it might be as well for her not to see me here. I wish to call at Castle Wafer by accident, you understand."

Frederick St. John nodded. "Could you see her teeth and her glistening eyes? She was stealthily following Miss Beauclerc. *For what purpose?* I am thankful we were here."

"Where is Miss Beauclerc now?"

"She is coming on with the dean. I have cautioned her not to go out alone. Mr. Pym, what is to be done? This state of things cannot be allowed to go on. I call upon you, as a good and true man, to aid us, if it be in your power."

Mr. Pym made no reply. He walked on in his favourite

attitude, his hands clasped behind his back, just as he was walking in that sorrowful chamber, the evening you first beheld him ; and his face wore, to Mr. St. John's thinking, a strangely troubled look in the moonlight.

CHAPTER XXXV.

ON THE TERRACE.

MR. PYM went to the house alone. Frederick St. John met him in the hall as if by accident, and took him at once into the dining-room. Any suspicion that they had met before at the Rectory and come away from it together, was as far from the minds of the assembled company, as that they had both dropped from the clouds.

Mrs. St. John, who was better and had come down since dinner, Mrs. Beauclerc, Mrs. Carleton, and Sir Isaac, had sat down to whist. Mrs. Darling and Miss Denison were talking to each other at the centre table ; Miss Denison abusing Georgina as the wildest girl in Christendom, Mrs. Darling protesting that she could not be half so wild as her own daughter Rose. Mrs. Darling was all wonder and astonishment when Mr. Pym came in. What *could* have brought him to Lexington?—how very kind of him to call and see her. And it was she who took him up to introduce him to Sir Isaac.

One moment's recoil, one startled look at the face, and Mrs. Carleton held out her hand to the little surgeon, and was her own calm and gracious self. Seated at whist there, opposite to Sir Isaac, her voice low and sweet, her manner so gentle and collected, it would never have entered into any one's mind to imagine that *she* had been gliding about stealthily in the moonlight like a ghost, or a female poacher on forbidden ground : and perhaps the surgeon might have been excused his momentary doubt whether it was really Mrs. Carleton that they had seen.

"How well you are looking!" he exclaimed, as he shook hands with her.

And it was no hollow compliment. The woman he saw before him now, radiant in beauty, was no more like the distressing shadow he had visited at Ypres, than he himself was

like a lamp-post. Mrs. Carleton laughed. Yes, she said, she
was quite well now.

Mr. Pym begged he might not interrupt the game, and drew
away. Close upon that, the dean and his daughter came in,
and then came tea. Ere the surgeon had well swallowed his,
he was pacing the terrace outside with Mrs. Darling, no one
paying attention to them.

"You see I have obeyed your summons, Mrs. Darling," he
began; "have called at Castle Wafer by accident, as you
desired. What is the business that you wish to consult me
upon?"

Mrs. Darling had caught up her daughter's black lace shawl
as she left the room, and put it over her head; just as Charlotte
had so recently worn it upon hers. She pulled it tightly round
her silk gown as she answered—

"I wish to speak to you about my daughter: I fear she is
ill."

"In body, or in mind?"

A moment's struggle with herself ere she should answer.
But no; even now, although she had summoned the surgeon,
at a great cost and trouble, to her aid, she *could* not bring her
lips to admit a hint of the fatal malady.

"In mind!" she echoed, rather indignantly. "I don't
know what you mean, Mr. Pym. What should be wrong with
Mrs. Carleton's mind?"

"As you please," he said, with indifference. "I can go
back to-night if I am not wanted."

They had come to the end of the gravel walk, and Mrs.
Darling stood still, apparently contemplating the lovely prospect to be seen from Castle Wafer. How anxious looked her
face in the moonlight; but for those betraying beams the surgeon might not have read the struggle that was going on within
her breast.

"Why should you think anything was wrong with her mind?"
she again asked, but this time the tones were of pain, not of
resentment.

"Mrs. Darling, it may be as well that we should understand
each other," said he. "I did not come here to be trifled with.
Either let there be confidence between us, or let me go back
whence I came. It may facilitate matters if I tell you *I* have
cause to suspect your daughter's mind to be at present not
altogether in a healthy state. If I do go back, I fear it will

be my duty to intimate as much beforehand to Sir Isaac St.
John."

She looked perfectly aghast. "What do you mean, Mr.
Pym?"

"I mean just what I say, and no more. Oh, Mrs. Darling,
what nonsense this is—you and I to play at bo-peep with each
other! We have been doing it all the years of your daughter's
life. You cannot forget how much I know of the past: do
you think I have drowned my memory in a draught of Lethe's
waters? Surely if there is one man on earth whom you might
consult confidentially, it is myself. I know as much as you
know."

Mrs. Darling burst into tears, and sobbed for some minutes.
"I shall be better now," she said; "it will do me good.
Heaven alone knows what the tension has been."

"And now just tell me the whole, from beginning to end,"
said Mr. Pym, in a more kindly tone, "you ought to have
done it years ago. You may be sure I will do what I can for
the best: and there may be safety in counsel."

Now that the ice was broken, she entered pretty freely into
details, and soon experienced that relief, and it may also be
said that satisfaction in talking, which this confidential disclosure of some long-secret trouble is sure to bring. She told Mr.
Pym how, ever since Benja's death, she had had her doubts of
Charlotte's perfect sanity: and she freely confessed that her
hasty return to Castle Wafer was caused by a telegraphic message from Prance, who was growing alarmed at her mistress's
symptoms.

"What symptoms were they?" inquired the doctor.

"I don't know that I can enumerate them to you; they were
little odds and ends of things that Prance has noticed. Not
much, taken separately, but curious in the aggregate. Of
course the message did not contain them: I have learnt them
since I arrived. One thing I disliked more than all the rest—
Prance awoke one night and found her mistress was out of the
room. She was hastening away in search of her, and saw her
coming out of Miss Beauclerc's chamber. Now, for some
reason or other, Charlotte has taken a prejudice against Miss
Beauclerc——"

"A moment, Mrs. Darling. If I am to help you with advice,
you must speak without disguise. Do not say 'for some reason
or other;' tell the reason, if you know it."

Another struggle with herself: *must* she confess? Mrs. Darling clasped her hands in pain.

"Oh, how cruel it is to have to say these things! And of Charlotte, who has always been so reticent, so honourable, whatever her other failings. There! let me speak out and have done with it. I believe she is jealous of Miss Beauclerc : of Miss Beauclerc and of Sir Isaac St. John."

"Your daughter would like to remain here for ever—mistress of Castle Wafer, and Sir Isaac's wife?"

"Yes, I do believe it is so. And I could have believed such planning of any one in the world rather than of Charlotte. I have striven to persuade her to leave with me, and it is of no use. I would not for the world that she should marry again."

"She ought not to have married at all," remarked the surgeon.

"I could not help it. I did my best. You don't know what a care Charlotte has always been to me!"

"To return to Miss Beauclerc. Do you fear Mrs. Carleton might injure her?"

"Not if she retains her reason. But—should that leave her, even momentarily,—Mr. Pym," she broke off, "it was because I found myself incompetent to deal with these troubles that I wrote for you."

"You must take her away from Castle Wafer without delay."

"But she will not be taken away. In all ordinary matters she is as sane as I am; as capable of judging, of arguing, and of sensibly acting. It is only now and then that a sort of paroxysm comes over her. It may be only violent passion, to which you know she has ever been subject; but, it may be something worse. She is then, as I believe, incapable of controlling her actions; and should she find an opportunity of doing an injury at these times she might do it. There are two people in this house against whom I can see she is desperately incensed : Miss Beauclerc and Honour Tritton. Should she find herself alone with either of them in one of these paroxysms——"

Mrs. Darling stopped. The subject was too painful to continue. But the surgeon took up the thread in a quiet tone.

"We might have a second edition of the Alnwick tragedy."

Mrs. Darling—he could see it in the bright night—seemed to recoil a step. But she strove to answer with more than customary calmness.

"The Alnwick tragedy! I do not understand."

"When Alnwick's heir was—killed."

"Oh, Mr. Pym, Mr. Pym! you *cannot* think that was anything but a miserable accident?" cried the unfortunate mother. "It was nothing else. Honour alone was in fault."

"It may be that we shall never know," he answered. "My impression—nay, my belief—you and I had better be outspoken now, Mrs. Darling—always was, that Mrs. Carleton *had* something to do with that. I think at the time you entertained the same opinion."

Mrs. Darling made no answer. She walked on, her scared face raised in that tell-tale moonlight; her very lips white.

"I thought the probabilities, knowing what you and I know, were greatly against her at the time," repeated the surgeon; "I think them greater now. You are aware, I presume, that the imaginary image of Benja and the lighted church haunted her for months? And in that show of lanterns in France, on St. Martin's Eve——"

"How did you hear of that?" interrupted Mrs. Darling.

"Oh, I get to hear of many things," was the reply. "It does not matter how. I fear this terror, in one so cold and impassive as your daughter has always been, is rather suggestive of a guilty conscience."

"Why recall this?" asked Mrs. Darling, with a sob. "I think you are wrong in your suspicions.",

"I do not recall it to give you pain. Only to impress upon you how essential it is, with these doubts upon our minds, that Mrs. Carleton should be removed from Castle Wafer."

"Indeed, I see it as strongly as you do. But you know what her *will* has always been. And if our suspicion of her state of mind is wrong, and she is really sane, we are not justified in forcing her actions. Can you remain a few days and watch her, so as to form an opinion of her state? There's a plain, comfortable inn at hand, the Barley Mow, and you could be here very much in the daytime."

"For the matter of that, I could contrive to get invited to stay here," observed the surgeon, with a cough. "That good-natured brother of Sir Isaac's is sure to ask me. And, to tell you the truth, Mrs. Darling, if I undertake to watch her at all, it must be a close and uninterrupted watch."

"Close and uninterrupted!" repeated Mrs. Darling, whom the words did not altogether please. "I am so very fearful of any suspicion being excited abroad as to Charlotte's state."

"That suspicion already exists," remarked the doctor. "Your daughter's manners—these paroxysms that you speak of—have been observed and commented on. It was only a post or two before I got your summons, that I received a letter from this neighbourhood, implying doubts of Mrs. Carleton's state of mind, and inquiring if I could inform the writer whether insanity had been in her family."

Mrs. Darling's breath was nearly taken away with astonishment. "Who could have sent the letter? Surely, not Sir Isaac!"

"The letter was a confidential letter, and I cannot name the writer."

"If it was not Sir Isaac, it must have been Frederick St. John. Why need *he* meddle?"

"It was neither Frederick St. John nor Sir Isaac: I may tell you that much. I only mention this to prove to you that even were we willing to allow matters to go on as they have been going, it is now impossible. A weighty responsibility lies upon me, Mrs. Darling: and something must be done in one shape or another. Had I received no summons from you, I think I should still have come to Lexington."

Mrs. Darling walked to the end of the terrace before replying. Matters seemed to be growing complicated. Was the time of exposure really come? It had always lain upon her with an awful dread.

"But what can you do?" she asked. "Suppose, after watching Charlotte, you come to the conclusion that there's nothing really the matter with her——"

"But I should not come to that conclusion," he interrupted. "Were I to remain in the house a month, and see no proof whatever of insanity, I could not be sure that it did not exist. We know how cunning these people are, and——"

"Oh, Mr. Pym, how cruelly you speak!"

"I am sorry to do so. What I was about to say, in answer to your question, is this. Allowing that I perceive no present grounds for alarm, I must still assume that such grounds do exist; in short, both you and I know they do: and there will be one of two courses to pursue. Either you must remove your daughter from Castle Wafer before I quit it: or I must get rid of my responsibility by disclosing my fears to Sir Isaac St. John."

"No, no; not to him—not to any one if it can be pre-vented," implored Mrs. Darling. "I will get Charlotte away. Anything rather than make the dread public. Think how long I have succeeded in concealing it."

"To speak to Sir Isaac would not be to make it public. And I have already told you, Mrs. Darling, it is not so entirely a secret as you have supposed. However, if you remove Char-lotte, undertaking that she does not return, there will be no cause for my speaking to any one."

"I'll do it all; I'll try and do it," said Mrs. Darling. "And now about your own stay at Castle Wafer. How shall you manage it?"

"Leave it to me," replied Mr. Pym. "We medical men often possess a pass-key in an emergency. I think Mrs. Carle-ton will not like my staying. She did not seem pleased to see me."

"No?"

"It struck me that she did not. I observed a strange sort of shiver, a look of terror, pass over her face when she saw me."

"How observant you are!" was Mrs. Darling's comment. "*I* saw nothing of it."

"It is our business to be observant."

"Of course. And very useful I dare say you find the habit."

"You spoke of Honour Tritton," resumed the surgeon, pass-ing by the other remark. "Why do you suppose——"

"Hush!" breathed Mrs. Darling in a warning voice, and she laid her hand upon his arm to enforce the caution more em-phatically. "Is that Charlotte?"

Some one had cautiously raised the window of an upper room, and was peeping out. Mr. Pym's quick eyes saw at once that it was not Charlotte, but Prance. Mrs. Prance had her share of curiosity as well as more demonstrative people.

"We had better go in, Mrs. Darling," remarked the surgeon. "Should Mrs. Carleton come out and see us talking together, she might fancy my visit here had reference to her, and be forthwith on her guard accordingly. As she was—I know she was—on her guard when I went to Ypres."

The evening was not quite over, when the anxious pacers on the terrace re-entered the drawing-room; the whist players were just rising. Mrs. Carleton came over at once to Mr. Pym. Handsome and stately did she look, her rich dress sweeping the ground; her face calm, her manner gracious, she seemed just as sane as Mr. Pym himself. He happened to be looking with some interest at Miss Beauclerc; a fair, lovely, attractive girl, in her pretty white dress, and with her grey-blue honest eyes.

"When did you come to Lexington, Mr. Pym?"

The question proceeded from Mrs. Carleton, who had slipped into a seat beside him. He answered that he had arrived only that evening; had been sent for to see a patient.

"Who is it?" she asked.

"A young man suffering from heart disease," promptly responded Mr. Pym, deeming this positive evasion justifiable under the circumstances.

"And so you took the opportunity to call at Castle Wafer!" she said. And there might have been the slightest possible resentment perceptible in the tone, though not to an ear less quick than the surgeon's.

"Just so," he answered. "When we have nothing particular to do with ourselves, we are apt to make use of any past civilities that may be available. I remembered that Mr. Frederick St. John, when I met him at Alnwick, proffered me an invitation to call at Castle Wafer, should I ever travel to its vicinity."

"Oh!" she said. "Fred St. John's rather fond of those impromptu invitations. Do you go back to-morrow?"

"Not unless my patient shall have done with me."

Mr. Pym remained at Castle Wafer, a temporary guest. In the most natural manner conceivable, Frederick St. John, without being suspected of any ulterior motive, pressed the invitation on the little surgeon. Castle Wafer would be a more comfortable roof for him than the Barley Mow, and his sojourn there would afford him, Frederick, an opportunity of improving the acquaintance begun at Alnwick, he graciously observed, when they had met at the funeral of Mr. Carleton St. John. Mr. Pym suffered himself to be persuaded. And thus the surgeon took up his task of watching Mrs. Carleton, a very private-detective; installed thereunto by two anxious parties, neither of whom suspected the connivance of the other. What wheels within wheels there are in this world!

In one sense of the word, the step might have been dispensed with, for it did not serve to prevent the disclosure to Sir Isaac St. John. Mrs. Darling's great hope from the respite of the two or three days' watching, was, that she should in the meanwhile succeed in inducing Charlotte to bid adieu to Castle

Wafer, and thus obviate the necessity for any appeal to Sir Isaac. It might have proved so, so far as Mr. Pym was concerned; but the initiative was taken by the dean.

Very disagreeably impressed by the fresh doubts of Mrs. Carleton's sanity, acquired during the evening visit of Mr. Pym to the Rectory, the dean considered that there was now sufficient matter to justify a communication to Sir Isaac. He resolved to make it himself; and on the following morning, the one succeeding Mr. Pym's arrival, he went up for that purpose to Castle Wafer, and procured a private interview with Sir Isaac in his sitting-room.

A very different story, this, from the one sought to be told the other evening by Frederick. As the dean, calm, sensible, reliable, went through the whole, point by point, concluding with the fact that Mr. Pym was at Castle Wafer for no other purpose than to watch Charlotte Carleton, Sir Isaac listened with increasing wonder.

"And you say Frederick knew of this!" he exclaimed. "Why did he not tell me?"

"He did attempt to tell you; but failed. I suppose his ultra self-consciousness and the fear that even you might misconstrue his motives, withheld him from saying more."

"How could I be likely to misconstrue them?"

The dean said how. Which certainly did not tend to decrease the wonder of Sir Isaac.

"He has been assuming that Mrs. Carleton was looking after me! That she had designs upon me! *Me!* You must be mistaking me for Frederick."

"Certainly not for Frederick. Frederick's private opinion is, that the young woman hates him. I fancy there's not much doubt that she would have no objection to your making her Lady St. John."

When Sir Isaac fully comprehended this hypothesis as to himself, which he had little difficulty in doing, he burst into an uncontrollable fit of laughter. The dean saw how it was: Isaac St. John had been so firmly fixed in his resolution never to marry, had *lived* so in it, that the very notion of his breaking it, or of any woman's thinking she could induce him to break it, seemed to him nothing less than an impossibility.

"Then you never had an idea of Mrs. Carleton?" observed the dean.

"I never had an idea of Mrs. Carleton in that sense of the word, or of any one else," answered Sir Isaac. "I should as soon think of getting hanged as of getting married. And I do believe you must be wrong in supposing she has entertained such a notion. A young and pretty woman want to tie herself to me! Why, look at me; at what I am. No, no: it is not likely. And it was only the other day she lost her husband and her child; her heart must be buried with them for some time yet to come."

"Well, there lay the cause of Frederick's hesitation," said the dean. "With this idea upon him, no wonder he was tenacious of speaking. I confess I did not agree with him. I thought you were no more likely to take a wife than I am—who possess one already.

"It will be a joke against Frederick for the rest of my days," said Sir Isaac. "*I* marry? I wish, by the way, *he* would marry! But about poor Mrs. Carleton? I should like to see Mr. Pym."

The surgeon was summoned to the conference. And after the dean's departure, he disclosed to Sir Isaac the fear of her attempting some injury to Miss Beauclerc or to Honour: of which the dean remained in ignorance.

"There is only one thing to do," was the conclusion come to by Sir Isaac. "Inhospitable though any such measure may seem, Mrs. Carleton must this day quit Castle Wafer."

CHAPTER XXXVI.

LOCKED IN.

MR. PYM appeared to make himself at home at Castle Wafer. One of the best chambers had been assigned him, its door opening exactly opposite to the room occupied by Mrs. Carleton and by Prance. And that gentleman retired to rest with his door propped back, and his gaze on the corridor. Perhaps he slept with his eyes open.

In the morning he was up betimes. Going downstairs, he sought Honour, and sat in the housekeeper's room while he talked to her. He had really no ulterior motive in this; but he was a sociable man, and he merely wished to be civil to the girl, whom he had once seen so much of as Benja's nurse.

Honour was excessively gratified. In the first place at seeing the surgeon again ; in the next at indulging her gossiping propensities. She had heard little or nothing of Alnwick since she quitted it : Mrs. Tritton having left the Hall and the neighbourhood soon after herself. Question after question did she ask Mr. Pym of the changes, and would probably have gone on for an hour of her own good will, but that Mr. Pym, who was remarkably quick of sight and hearing, and why he wore glasses no one ever could make out—detected some faint sound or movement at the partially closed door, as if somebody were listening at it.

" Is any one wanting to come in, Honour ? "

Honour pulled the door open, and saw nothing. But a faint rustling, as of some person turning from the door as soon as he spoke, had caught Mr. Pym's ears.

" Look out," said he, sharply.

Honour looked out, and was just in time to see the petticoats of a lady disappearing round the corner of the passage, and to recognize them as Mrs. Carleton's.

" Mrs. Carleton, was it ? " observed the surgeon carelessly, as she made the remark. " Does she often pay you a visit here, Honour ? "

" I never saw her here before, sir. Perhaps she was coming in search of you."

" Ah, perhaps so," replied Mr. Pym, carelessly. " What were you saying, Honour ?—that you heard I went over to Germany to see the boy ? Well, it's true. Whether it was Germany or France, or any other habitable part of the globe, though, I can't take upon myself to say. I could not do him any good. He was at death's-door then. How did you hear it ? "

" From Mrs. Darling, sir. She often said a word to me when she was staying here the last time, and she mentioned that you had been had over to Master George, but it was of no use. What a sad thing it was that the child could not be cured ! "

" Ay. There are many sad things in the world, Honour ; sadder even than that. Well, I must go, or I shall keep breakfast waiting. You'll see me again before I leave."

He made his way to the breakfast-room, and sat down to

breakfast with the rest. Mrs. Carleton's face was impassive as usual: but the surgeon saw that she watched him just as keenly as he did her. After breakfast, as if to defeat the purpose for which he was staying at Castle Wafer, she shut herself up in Mrs. St. John's room, and no one could get near her. It was during this time that the interview took place between the dean and Sir Isaac.

"I entrust it all to you, Mr. Pym," Sir Isaac had said. "Perhaps speaking to Mrs. Darling will be sufficient: but—you know the laws of hospitality—I would rather not appear at all in this matter if I can help it. Let the departure be your doing—you understand. Only in case of necessity bring in my name."

Mr. Pym's first step was to seek Mrs. Darling. *She* was shut up in her room too; so, after waiting for some time, he sent a message to her, and she came to him. The observant surgeon saw that there was a blank, disappointed look in her face.

"I can do nothing with Charlotte," she exclaimed. "She refuses most positively to quit Castle Wafer: and when I urged it, she put an end to the colloquy by leaving me. What is to be done?"

The surgeon could not say what was to be done. Only that to get away Mrs. Carleton that day was indispensable.

Mrs. Darling, poor woman, began to temporize. Charlotte was perfectly well now, she was sure, and a day or two's delay could make no difference. To-morrow, perhaps, or the next day, she might be induced to hear reason. At length Mr. Pym—for Mrs. Darling seemed inclined to become obstinate in her turn—was obliged to hint at the commands of Sir Isaac.

Mrs. Darling was bitterly incensed, believing that Mr. Pym had been the informant. "I did not think you would have been so treacherous," she exclaimed. "You promised me not to speak to Sir Isaac until all means had been tried to get Charlotte away."

"I did not speak to him. He spoke to me."

"He spoke to you! First?"

"Yes. He sent for me into his room, and entered upon it."

"Who could have told him?" cried Mrs. Darling, after a mortified pause. And Mr. Pym remained silent: it was not his business to speak of the dean.

" The less we discuss this matter the better, Mrs. Darling. It would bring no profit. All we have to do is to remove your daughter. And if I were you I would let this hint about Sir Isaac be as if it had not been spoken. It would be painful to you to show consciousness of it ; doubly painful to him. He is a true gentleman : but tales have been carried to him of Mrs. Carleton's state of mind, and he deems it necessary that she should not remain."

" I would give half I am worth to know who it is that has been meddling ! " exclaimed Mrs. Darling. " What is to be done ? Will you speak to Charlotte ? "

" Of course I will. If you cannot persuade her, I must try my powers. It will be a very awkward thing if we have to get her away by force or stratagem."

" By stratagem we shall never accomplish it," said Mrs. Darling. " Charlotte is too keen to be imposed upon."

He waited until luncheon-time. He thought it better to lead to an interview with Mrs. Carleton, than to send and demand it. She came down with Mrs. St. John, and the luncheon passed off as usual, every one being at table except Sir Isaac. Mr. Brumm said his master was taking luncheon in his room, but offered no other apology for his absence, and Georgina went boldly in to him.

But Mr. Pym was destined to be defeated, at least in a degree. He whispered to Mrs. Carleton to come and walk with him on the terrace as they rose from table, and drew her hand within his arm and went out with her. It was a dull lowering day, threatening rain, and she looked up at the skies with rather a vacant look. Mr. Pym told her as gently as he could, that it was deemed necessary she should have change of air ; that he and Mrs. Darling were both anxious on the score of her health, and thought immediate change of scene essential. She laughed in his face ; she set him and her mother at defiance ; she spoke of appealing to Sir Isaac : and then Mr. Pym hinted—as he had done to her mother—that Sir Isaac acquiesced in the measure.

No sooner had the words left his lips, than a change passed over her face. Medical man though he was, Mr. Pym shrank from it : never had its aspect been more livid, its expression so wildly terrible. He caught her arm, put it within his, and began to speak words of soothing kindness. But she broke from him ; muttered something incoherently about the plot

against her, which those in the house had been planning to
carry out, and escaped indoors. Mr. Pym had little doubt
that by "those in the house," she meant Miss Beauclerc and
Honour. It is very likely she included himself and Mrs.
Darling.

He followed her; he called Mrs. Darling to his aid. That
she had secreted herself in her own room, they found at once,
since the door was fastened inside, and no reply was given to
their knocks. The surgeon grew alarmed. This state of
things was more than likely to end in a paroxysm of insanity.
By-and-by mutterings were heard inside; violent pacings of
the room; short derisive laughs; and one shrill scream. Mrs.
Darling was nearly beside herself; and Prance—Prance the
impassive—for once betrayed terror.

"I shall break open the door," said Mr. Pym.

But he went first of all to apprise Sir Isaac of what he was
going to do. Sir Isaac gave him *carte blanche* to do what he
pleased; but urged that poor Mrs. Carleton's comfort should
be studied as much as was practicable. And under the circumstances he did not press for her departure; only stipulating
that Mr. Pym should undertake the charge of her until she did
leave.

When Mr. Pym got back to the corridor, he found the dismayed watchers and waiters outside it, Mrs. Darling and Prance,
had been joined by another—Honour Tritton.

It is not possible for a commotion such as this to occur in
a house without its sounds transpiring to the household.
Quietly as these knockings and callings had been carried on,
news of them penetrated to the servants below. "Mrs. Carleton
had bolted herself in her chamber, and could not be got at."
Honour, in her interest, it may be in her curiosity, went upstairs at once. Perhaps she deemed she had a sort of right
to do so, from her former relations with Mrs. Carleton.

Mr. Pym scarcely noticed her. The noise inside the room
had increased; that is, the pacings to and fro were louder and
quicker. Mrs. Darling clasped her hands in helpless dismay:
she lifted her imploring face to the surgeon; she put her lips
to the key-hole for the twentieth time.

"Charlotte! my darling Charlotte! I want to come in. I
must come in. I—I have left a key in your room. It will
soon be time to dress for dinner."

There was no response. But the pacings increased to a run.

The dull day had become darker, and Honour turned into Miss Beauclerc's room, and brought out a tall wax candle, lighted, in a silver candlestick.

"Mrs. Carleton, I must beg of you to unlock the door," cried out the surgeon. "If you do not, I shall be compelled to break it open. Pray undo it."

It was of no avail. A mocking laugh was again heard, but there was no other response.

"Take care of yourselves," said Mr. Pym.

The door flew open with a burst. The first object they saw was Mrs. Carleton, standing against the opposite wall and glaring at them. Glaring! the word has been used often in regard to her eyes at times, but there is no other so applicable. Mr. Pym went straight up to her. She eluded him with a spring, pounced upon the unsuspecting and terrified Honour, and in another moment was grappling with her, a fight for dear life.

Poor lady! What her thoughts had been during that self-imprisonment she alone knew. That they had tended rapidly to increase the mind's confusion, to speed her on to the great gulf of insanity, already so near at hand, perhaps to have been its very turning-point, there could be no doubt of. And it may be that the sight of Honour amidst her enemies, of Honour bearing a lighted candle, recalled her mind to that dreadful night not yet two years gone by.

Whatever it may have been, whether any single cause, or many causes combined: the mortification of being turned from Castle Wafer, the visit of Mr. Pym, the seeing him that morning with Honour, or the opposition and confusion of this one afternoon: certain it was, that the moment her mother and Prance had been dreading in secret so long, had come. Mrs. Carleton was insane.

It took all three, the surgeon, Mrs. Darling, and Prance, to secure her in her violence: just as it had taken more than one to secure her father in the years gone by. Honour was released, terrified nearly to death, bruises on her arms, and a bite on her cheek, of which she would never lose the mark.

When she was secured from doing harm to herself or others, Mr. Pym touched Prance, and motioned her to a room apart. Had Prance been capable of astonishment at anything, she might have felt it then. He closed the door and pointed to a chair.

"The time for evasion has gone by," he began. "To-morrow will see your mistress in an asylum, Prance, from which she can never more be released in safety. And—do you know for what cause I have brought you here?"

"No, sir," answered Prance; but in some hesitation, as if she half-divined what the cause might be.

"I am about to speak of that past night at Alnwick; the burning of Benja. I feel as sure"—and he raised his finger to her impressively—"that your mistress had something to do with that, and that you knew it, as I am that you are before me there. Few persons can deceive me; and your manner that night and subsequent to it, clever as you may have thought yourself, convinced me there was a tale to tell. I did not press for it then; I had my reasons; but I must hear it now."

"I had nothing to do with it, sir," replied Prance, not daring to equivocate; feeling perhaps, with him, that the time for suppression had gone by.

"I don't suppose you had," returned Mr. Pym. "But you were in that niche, where Honour saw you, for all that. Come! You must acquaint me with the particulars of that night: they may be a guide to my treatment of your mistress. I must know them, whether or not. Did she set the child on fire?"

"No, sir, I don't think she did. At least, not intentionally."

"At any rate, she was in the room at the time?"

"Yes, she was. But I think he caught fire accidentally. There was some scuffle, and I fancy his white pinafore set alight."

"But she bolted the door upon him?"

Prance actually for a moment looked distressed. "I'm afraid she did, sir: the one door. The other, I have always believed, and always shall believe, the child fastened himself."

"She bolted it on him when he was burning?"

"Ah, I don't know that, sir; I don't know it for certain."

"You have feared it."

"Yes; only that."

Mr. Pym sat down in a chair opposite Prance, the table being between them. "Begin at the beginning, Prance," he said. "This is a waste of time. How much of that night's occurrences did you see and hear?"

"You—you are not asking for the purpose of proving the crime against her, are you, sir?" demanded Prance.

"Of proving the crime against her, woman!" echoed Mr.

Pym, wrathfully. "Your mistress is past having anything of that sort proved against her : past its consequences, for that is, I presume, what you mean. Had I wished to bring it home to her, I should have stirred in it at the time. I have been as quiet and careful as you. Now then, begin. Let us hear what you had to do with it, and what brought you in the niche. You have not forgotten, I suppose?"

"No, indeed, sir! I have thought of it all a great deal too often to be pleasant," she said, leaning her head upon her hand. "The account I gave before had very much of truth in it : though not the whole of the truth," she added, after a pause.

"Then tell the whole now," said Mr. Pym, growing impatient at the delay.

The substance of Prance's communication was as follows. After she had been in the herb-room, she went upstairs to wash her hands, which had become soiled from picking the herbs. Whilst in her chamber, which was next to Mrs. Carleton's, she heard her mistress come up from the dining-room and go into her chamber, and she followed her in, to ask whether she wanted a light or anything, for it was getting quite dusk. Mrs. Carleton was not in her room, but had gone through the dressing-room, and was standing in the nursery, just inside the door, apparently gazing at something, as one transfixed : a dull sort of light came from the nursery, enabling Prance to see her distinctly. Being rather curious, she peeped in, and saw Master Benja slowly parading a lighted church about, which he carried before him : it was on this her mistress's eyes were fixed. It was really a pretty object, Prance said, lighted up in the dark room. The child was speaking; words calculated to irritate Mrs. Carleton——

"What were they!" interrupted Mr. Pym, when Prance had got thus far in her narrative. "Can you repeat them?"

"'I'll tell you what I shall do, Honour, when I am master of Alnwick,'" repeated Prance. "'You shall be mistress, and give all the orders, and we'll have a great wall built up, so that mamma can't come near us. But we'll have Georgy, and keep him to ourselves.'" Those were the words, Prance continued, and they seemed to irritate her mistress : she darted forward, and gave the child a sharp blow on the ear. She (Prance) went away, leaving a sound of noise and crying behind her. Declared, if it were the last word she had to speak, that she had no thought of real injury. She went through the dressing-

room, through the bedroom, which door she shut, and went
down into the dining-room. Georgy was asleep on the large
chair, his legs hanging down. A very short while—immediately, indeed—her mistress followed her down ; noticed, and
thought it very singular, that she bolted the dining-room door
after her. Seemed greatly excited ; walked about in a strange
manner ; Prance thought she must have been quarrelling with
Honour. Presently she sat down, and took Georgy's feet upon
her lap. This gave Prance an opportunity of slipping back
the bolt, and quitting the room. Had not liked to do so
before ; must have been there at least a quarter-of-an-hour.
Went up to her room ; heard no noise whatever ; never supposed but that Honour was in the nursery with Master Benja.
Stood a minute or two in the passage, listening ; thought she
might hear them speaking of the quarrel. Heard nothing—
all was quite still, and then supposed Honour had taken
Master Benja down to the servants' hall, which had been forbidden by Mrs. Carleton. Was stealing along the passage to
find this out, intending to tell of her, when Honour came
running up the back-stairs, and Prance, not to be seen, slipped
into the niche until Honour should have entered the nursery.
Found then that Master Benja was in the nursery. Honour
could not open the door, and called out to ask why he had
turned the button. Was peeping out of the niche, and saw
Honour drop a load of things from her apron, and come flying
past her into the dressing-room. Did not think at the time
she was seen ; passage was pretty dark. Took the opportunity to escape into her own room, and was lighting a candle
when Honour's cries startled her. Came out of her room, saw
Honour running down the front staircase, her cries awful. It
brought the servants from the kitchen, it brought Mrs. Carleton
and Georgy out of the dining-room ; and then she (Prance)
found out what had happened. That was all.

"And you mean to tell me you did not suspect anything
wrong until then ?" asked Mr. Pym, as she concluded.

"As I am a living, breathing woman, sir, I never suspected
it," answered Prance, showing for once some emotion. "I
don't think Honour herself was more shocked than I was."

"And why did you not tell the truth about your being in
the niche ?"

"Ah, sir, I did not dare. Might it not, in the questioning
that would have ensued, have directed suspicion to my mis-

tress? The moment I discovered that Honour was not in the room when my mistress attacked Master Benja, I felt frightened to death, fearing she had done it. I—— "

"Stay a minute. I don't understand," interrupted Mr. Pym. "You say you looked into the nursery. You must have seen that Honour was not there."

"Indeed, sir, I did not. I saw but a very small portion of the room; the door opens inwards to the wall, and obstructs the best part of the room to any one standing as I did. I never supposed but that Honour was present in her usual seat; otherwise I should not have left my mistress alone with the child. The boy himself helped to mislead me: those few words he said appeared to be spoken *to Honour.* I concluded afterwards, that when he heard his mamma enter, he must have thought it was Honour who had gone in, and was too much occupied with his toy to turn his head to look."

"It's an awful thing!" ejaculated Mr. Pym.

"It has driven my mistress mad," returned Prance. "But, sir—she did not purposely set him on fire: she did not. I have gathered a great deal from words she has let drop in her paroxysms, and I know it was not done purposely. 'The church fell and set fire to his pinafore, in blazing up,' she said one night when she was moaning : and I am sure it did."

"But she bolted the door on him."

"Ah, yes, she did that; bolted it upon him, knowing he was on fire; there's no doubt of it. I have gathered that much. I think at the moment she was mad, unconscious of what she did. She is not naturally cruel, only in these uncontrollable attacks. And then—and then—— "

"And then, what?" asked the surgeon.

"She had taken too much wine that afternoon," continued Prance, lowering her voice. "Not intentionally; not from the love of drinking: unthinkingly, as it were. You see, sir. she had dined at the hour when she usually took her luncheon, and she did not eat much, I noticed ; made a luncheon more than a dinner. But she seemed to have a great thirst upon her, and drank a good deal of wine ; champagne, and sherry, and port ; altogether, I think her head was a little confused ; indeed, I'm sure it was. She would not have beaten Benja in the dining-room, but for that. Oh, the remorse that has been hers ! "

"I suppose so."

"It is remorse that has turned her brain. I thought in Flanders it would come on then; it did in a measure; but she got over it. Over and over again would she have given her own life to recall the boy's; I think she would even have given Georgy's. What she did, she did in a moment of passion; of aberration; and she has repented it ever since, and lived in dread of detection. Her horror of Honour has arisen from the feeling that had the girl not left Benja alone, it could not have happened, and she had not had the sin upon her. Indeed, sir, she is to be pitied; to be pitied more than condemned."

"Let us think so, at any rate, Prance," remarked Mr. Pym. "Does Mrs. Darling know this?"

"Well, sir, no; not exactly. I have dropped a word or two, and I know she guesses the rest; but I have not said it."

"Best not, perhaps," said the surgeon. "It is a secret that may remain between you and me."

CHAPTER XXXVII.

A MEETING IN PARIS.

"I WONDER why I am kept a prisoner here?" exclaimed Georgina Beauclerc.

She stood at the open French window of the Rectory drawing-room as she said it, partly indoors, partly out, and her auditor was Frederick St. John, who was coming along the gravel path, in the twilight of the autumn evening, on his road from Castle Wafer. Georgina had happened to walk over to the Rectory early in the afternoon, and a message followed her from Sir Isaac, that she was not to go back to Castle Wafer until sent for. The young lady was surprised, indignant, and excessively curious. The message had arrived about three o'clock: it was now very nearly dinner-time, and she was not released. The dean, Mrs. Beauclerc, and their guest were at Lexington; consequently, Miss Georgina had passed the hours by herself, and very dull they had been.

He came up, taking off his hat as he approached, as if he were warm from fast walking. Georgina retreated inside the room, but waited for him at the window.

"I have come to release you," he said, in answer to her question. "I am glad you obeyed me, and stayed."

"Obeyed you! I obeyed Sir Isaac."

"It was I who sent the message, Georgina."

"I wish I had known that!" she exclaimed, after a breathless pause. "I never should have stayed."

He laughed. "That's why I used Isaac's name. I thought you might not be obedient to me."

"Obedient to you, indeed, Mr. St. John! I should think not. Things would have come to a pretty pass!"

She tossed back her shapely head, to show her indignation. Mr. St. John only laughed again.

"Are they all out, Georgina?"

"Yes, they are out, and I have been alone all these hours. I wonder you don't take contrition to yourself."

"I wonder at it too."

"I should like to know the reason of my having been kept here? In all the course of my experience I never met with so outrageous a thing."

"Your experience has been so long a one, Georgie!"

"Well, I am not going to be ridiculed. I shall go back to Castle Wafer: perhaps Sir Isaac will be able to enlighten me. You can stay behind here; they'll be home sometime."

She tied her bonnet, fastened her mantle—having stood in them all the afternoon, momentarily expecting to be released, as he had called it—and was hastening through the window. Frederick laid a detaining hand upon her.

"Not yet, Georgina. I have come to stop your return to Castle Wafer."

"I thought you said you had come to release me!"

"I meant release you from suspense—to satisfy your curiosity, which has, I suppose, been on the rack. You are not to come back to Castle Wafer at all: we won't have you."

"You can let things alone," returned Georgina, throwing off her bonnet. "But I think you might have told me before now —keeping me with my things on all these hours!"

"I could not conveniently come before. Well, shall I relieve that curiosity of yours?"

Again she threw up her face petulantly. "That's just as you like. I don't care to hear it."

"You know you do care to hear it," he said. "But indeed, Georgina"—and his half-mocking, half-tender tone changed to seriousness—"it is a subject that I shrink from entering upon. Mrs. Carleton is ill. That is the reason we are banishing you for the present from Castle Wafer."

Georgina's mood changed also: the past one had been all make-believe, not real.

"Ill! I am so sorry. Is it anything infectious?"

"I will tell you what it is, Georgina: it is insanity. That she was not quite sane, I have suspected some little time; but this afternoon she has become very much worse. She locked herself in her room, and Mr. Pym was obliged to burst the door open, and now she is—very excited indeed. Mr. Pym told me he feared some crisis was approaching. This was just after she fastened herself in her room; and I sent that message to you at once. Isaac agrees with me that you had better remain at home to-night: Castle Wafer will not be a very sociable place this evening; and we must respect Mrs. Darling's feelings."

"Oh, I see, I see!" impulsively interrupted Georgina, all her good qualities in full play. "Of course it would not be right for strangers to be there. Poor Mrs. Darling! But is it true, Frederick? *Insane!*"

"I fear so."

"Perhaps it is some temporary fever that will pass off?"

"Well—we must hope for the best. And now—will you regard this as a confidential communication?"

"Yes, certainly; if you wish it."

"I think it is better to do so. She may recover; and in that case it would be very sad for the report to have been spread abroad. I knew I might trust you; otherwise I should not have spoken. We have had secrets together before."

"Shall you not tell papa?"

"I shall tell him, because he knows of the matter already. No one else. Should her malady be confirmed, of course it will become generally known."

"Do you know, I thought you had bad news when I saw your face," resumed Georgina. "You looked so worn and anxious. But you have looked so for some days past."

"Have I? I've been tired, I suppose, from want of sleep. I have not been in bed for some nights. I have been watching."

"Watching! Where?"

"In the corridor at home."

Georgina looked at him in surprise. "What were you watching for?"

"Oh—for ghosts."

"Please be serious. Do tell me what you mean. I don't understand you in the least."

"It is so pleasant to share a secret that I think I must tell it you, Georgina. You remember your nightmare?"

"My nightmare? Oh yes, when I fancied some one came into my room. Well?"

"Well—I thought it just possible, that instead of a nightmare it might have been reality. That Mrs. Carleton, in her restlessness, had wandered out of her room. It was not an agreeable thought, so I have watched every night since, lest there should be a repetition of it."

Georgina was as quick as lightning at catching an idea. "You were afraid for me! You watched to take care of me!"

"Something of that sort. Did you lock your door as I desired?"

"Yes: all but one night, when I forgot to do it."

"Just so. Knowing what a forgetful, careless young lady I had to deal with, I concluded that I must depend upon myself, instead of her. A pretty thing, if Mrs. Carleton had run away with you!"

A few bright rays were perceptible in the western horizon, illumining the twilight of the hitherto dull day. Georgina Beauclerc was gazing straight out to them, a very conscious look in her face. Suddenly she turned it to Mr. St. John.

"Will you tell me—had your words to me last evening, warning me not to be abroad, anything to do with this?"

He nodded. "Suspecting Mrs. Carleton's malady, I did not know who might be safe from her, who not: and I saw her in the grounds then."

"Last night?"

"Last night. She was close to you."

A moment's thought, which was a revelation to Georgina, and she drew nearer to him with a start. "I see it all, Frederick. I remember what you said about her jealousy: you have been protecting me."

"Trying to do it."

"How shall I thank you? And I have been so impertinent and cross! Perhaps I owe even my life to you!"

"I have not done it for nothing, I can tell you, young lady. I have been thinking of my repayment all through it."

He put his arm round her before she could get away, and drew her close to him. His voice became low and tender; his face, bent to hers, was radiant with persuasive eloquence.

"I told you last night that I thought I had saved you from a great danger——"

"And you repaid yourself," interrupted Georgina, with a dash of her native sauciness, and a glow on her blushing cheeks.

"No, I did not. I—don't know whether it's this watching after your safety, or what else it may be; but I have arrived at the conviction, that I shall have to take care of you for life. Georgina, we might have known years ago that it would come to this."

"Known that! When you only hated me!"

"If I hated you then—which I did not—I love you now. I cannot part with you. Georgina, my darling, I shall never part with you. I don't think you would like to part with me."

Her heart beat as it had never beaten before in her life; her eyes were blinded with tears. Joy so great as this had never been foreshadowed, except in some rare dream. He kissed the tears away.

"But it cannot be that you love me," she whispered.

"I love you dearly; although I once told a friend of yours that I would not marry Georgina Beauclerc though there were not another English girl extant. He saw into the future, it may be also into my heart, more clearly than I did."

"You said that? To a friend of mine! Who was it?"

"One who lies buried in the cloisters at Westerbury."

Her eyes went far out again to that light in the west. The words carried her back again to those past days,—to the handsome boy who had so loved her.

"You never cared for him, poor fellow!" observed Mr. St. John.

"No; I never cared but for one in my life," she softly whispered.

"I know that. He was the first to tell me of it. Not that I —as I believe now—needed telling. Georgina, they say marriages are made in heaven; I think we might have seen, even then, that we were destined for each other—— What's the matter?"

Georgina darted away from him as if she had been shot.

Her ears were quicker than his. The dean's carriage was approaching; was close upon them.

"I suppose I may speak to him, Georgina?"

"Perhaps if I said no, you wouldn't listen to me. You always did contrive to have your own way, and I suppose you will take it still. But I think you are very unfeeling—very cruel; and I am as bad."

"I know what you mean: that we should allow—this—to ensue upon the news I came to tell you. Poor Mrs. Carleton! We shall have time and to spare, I fear, for all our best sympathies. Oh, child! you don't know what my anxiety on your score has been! But it has served to show me, what I was only half convinced of before: my love for you."

The dean came in. Georgina escaped to her mother and Miss Denison. The latter spoke crossly to her. "Ah," thought Georgina, "would she dare to abuse me if she only knew whose wife I am going to be?" and she actually kissed the astonished Miss Denison, in her great happiness.

Mr. St. John spoke to the dean. Of Mrs. Carleton first: and the dean was both shocked and surprised to find the crisis had come on so quickly. He then said that he and Sir Isaac thought it better that Georgina should for the moment quit Castle Wafer.

"Quite right," said the dean. "She ought not to have stayed there so long. Of course she should not, had I been aware of this. The fact is, she would not come home; you heard her; she has a great affection for Castle Wafer."

"Would you very much mind, sir, if she some time came back to it for good?"

"Eh?" said the dean, turning his surprised eyes sharply on Mr. St. John. "Who wants that?"

"I do. I have been asking her if she will do so."

"And what does she say?"

A smile crossed Mr. St. John's lips. "She said I generally contrived to have my own way, and she supposed I should have it now."

"Ah, well; I have thought it might come to that! But I cannot bear to part with her. Frederick St. John"—and the dean spoke with emotion as he wrung his hand—"I would rather you took her from me than any other man in the world."

It was a lovely day in the following spring, and Paris was gay and bright. In a handsome house in one of its best quarters, its drawing-rooms presenting that blended aspect of magnificence and lightness which you rarely see out of the French capital, were a group of three people; two ladies, both brides of a week or two, and a gentleman. Never did eye gaze on two more charming brides, than Madame de la Chasse, that house's mistress, and Mrs. Frederick St. John.

Are you prepared to hear that that mistress was Rose? She sat laughing gaily, throwing back, as was her wont of old, that mass of golden curls. Her marriage had taken many by surprise, Frederick St. John for one; and he was now joking her about it.

"It was quite impossible to believe it, you know, Rose. I thought you would not have condescended to marry a Frenchman."

"I'd rather have married you," freely confessed Rose, and they all laughed. "But he has changed now; he has become presentable, thanks to me; and I don't intend to let him lapse again."

"I am sure you are happy!" said Georgina. "I see it in your face."

"Well, the truth is, I do like him a little bit," answered Rose, with a shy sort of blush, which spoke more plainly than her words. "And then he is so fond and proud of me; and heaps such luxuries upon me. It all arose through my staying at the Castellas' last autumn; he was always coming there."

"You know, Rose"—and Mr. St. John took her hand and spoke in all seriousness,—"that I wish you both, from my very heart, every happiness."

"And I'm sure I wish it to you," she said. "And I think you might have told me when I used to tease you about Sarah Beauclerc, that I was wrong in the Christian name. I suspected it last year when I saw you both together at Castle Wafer."

"Not then," interrupted Georgina; "you could not have seen it then."

"I did, though; I'm clever in that line, Mrs. St. John. I used to see his eyes follow you about, and he would leave me at any moment for you. How is Sir Isaac?"

"Quite well," answered Mr. St. John, "and as happy in my marriage as a child. Our ostensible home, after all, is to be

Alnwick; but I dare say we shall spend with him eight months out of every year at Castle Wafer."

"And my ill-fated half-sister, Mrs. Carleton St. John?" asked Rose, a deep shade of sadness clouding her radiant face. "Is there *no* hope of her restoration?"

"I fear none," he replied.

. "I wonder sometimes whether they are quite kind to her in that private asylum?"

"There's no doubt they are. Mr. Pym sees her sometimes; your mamma often. But that of course you know better than I do."

"I wanted mamma to take me to see her before I left England for good; but she would not."

"And so much the better," said Mr. St. John. "It could not be well for you, Madame de la Chasse."

"'Madame de la Chasse!'" she echoed. "Well, it sounds curious to hear *you* call me so. Ah! how strange! that he should have married me; and you—Poor Adeline! Does your wife know about her?" suddenly questioned Rose, in her careless way.

"Yes," spoke up Georgina.

"Old loves go for nothing when we come to be married. We laugh at the past then, and think what love-sick silly children we were. I have settled down into the most sober wife living."

"It looks like it," cried Mr. St. John.

"I *have*," retorted Rose, "whether it looks like it or not. I shall be as good and steady a matron as your wife there, who loves you to her fingers' ends."

Georgina laughed and blushed as they rose to leave, promising plenty of visits to the young Baroness during their stay in Paris.

In going out, they met the Baron. Georgina was surprised to see so good-looking a man; for Mr. St. John had described to her his close-cut hair and his curled moustache. That was altered now; the hair was in light waves; the moustache reduced to propriety: Rose said she had made him presentable.

He was very cordial; had apparently forgotten old scores against Mr. St. John, and pressed the hospitality of his house upon them as long as they were in Paris. Their frequent presence in it, he said, would complete the bliss of himself and his wife.

"Frederick," exclaimed Georgina, thoughtfully, when they had returned to their hotel, "should you think the Baron ever loved Adeline as he does Rose? He is evidently very fond of her."

"Perhaps he did not. His intended marriage with Adeline was a *contract;* with Rose he had time to fall in love."

"And—perhaps—*you* never loved her so very, very deeply!" timidly rejoined Georgina, raising to him her grey-blue eyes."

"I must say one thing," he answered, smiling; "that if a certain young lady of my particular acquaintance is not satisfied with her husband's love—— "

She did not let him go on; she threw herself into his sheltering arms, the tears of emotion falling from her eyes.

"Oh, my husband, my darling; you know, you know! I think you must have loved me a little all through; even when we used to quarrel at Westerbury."

"I think I did, Georgina. Of one fact you may be very sure, that I would not exchange my wife for any other, living or dead. I hope, I believe, under Heaven's blessing, that I may so love her to the end."

"Amen," softly breathed Georgina.

THE END.

PRINTED BY WILLIAM CLOWES AND SONS, LIMITED, LONDON AND BECCLES.

MRS. HENRY WOOD'S NOVELS.

Sale between One and Two Million Copies.

EAST LYNNE. *400th Thousand.*

THE CHANNINGS. *140th Thousand.*

MRS. HALLIBURTON'S TROUBLES. *120th Thousand*

THE SHADOW OF ASHLYDYAT. *77th Thousand.*

LORD OAKBURN'S DAUGHTERS. *77th Thousand.*

VERNER'S PRIDE. *65th Thousand.*

ROLAND YORKE. *100th Thousand.*

JOHNNY LUDLOW. First Series. *50th Thousand.*

MILDRED ARKELL. *68th Thousand.*

ST. MARTIN'S EVE. *60th Thousand.*

TREVLYN HOLD. *54th Thousand.*

GEORGE CANTERBURY'S WILL. *50th Thousand.*

THE RED COURT FARM. *44th Thousand.*

WITHIN THE MAZE. *65th Thousand.*

ELSTER'S FOLLY. *35th Thousand.*

LADY ADELAIDE. *35th Thousand.*

OSWALD CRAY. *35th Thousand.*

JOHNNY LUDLOW. Second Series. *23rd Thousand.*

ANNE HEREFORD. *35th Thousand.*

DENE HOLLOW. *35th Thousand.*

EDINA. *25th Thousand.*

A LIFE'S SECRET. *38th Thousand.*

COURT NETHERLEIGH. *26th Thousand.*

BESSY RANE. *30th Thousand.*

JOHNNY LUDLOW. Third Series. *13th Thousand.*

THE MASTER OF GREYLANDS. *30th Thousand.*

ORVILLE COLLEGE. *33rd Thousand.*

POMEROY ABBEY. *30th Thousand.*

JOHNNY LUDLOW. Fourth Series. New Edition.

LONDON:

RICHARD BENTLEY & SON, New Burlington Street, W.

Publishers in Ordinary to Her Majesty the Queen.

CRITICISMS OF THE PRESS.

EAST LYNNE.

"'East Lynne' is so full of incident, so exciting in every page, and so admirably written, that one hardly knows how to go to bed without reading to the very last page."—THE OBSERVER.

"A work of remarkable power which displays a force of description and a dramatic completeness we have seldom seen surpassed. The interest of the narrative intensifies itself to the deepest pathos. The closing scene is in the highest degree tragic, and the whole management of the story exhibits unquestionable genius and originality."—THE DAILY NEWS.

THE CHANNINGS.

"'The Channings' will probably be read over and over again, and it can never be read too often."—THE ATHENÆUM.

MRS. HALLIBURTON'S TROUBLES.

"The boldness, originality, and social scrutiny displayed in this work remind the reader of Adam Bede. It would be difficult to place beside the death of Edgar Halliburton anything in fiction comparable with its profound pathos and simplicity. It is long since the novel-reading world has had reason so thoroughly to congratulate itself upon the appearance of a new work as in the instance of 'Mrs. Halliburton's Troubles.' It is a fine work ; a great and artistic picture."—THE MORNING POST.

THE SHADOW OF ASHLYDYAT.

"'The Shadow of Ashlydyat' is very clever, and keeps up the constant interest of the reader. It has a slight supernatural tinge, which gives the romantic touch to the story which Sir Walter Scott so often used with even greater effect ; but it is not explained away at the end as Sir Walter Scott's supernatural touches generally, and inartistically, were."—THE SPECTATOR.

LADY ADELAIDE.

"One of Mrs. Henry Wood's best novels."—THE STAR.

"Mme. Henry Wood est fort célèbre en Angleterre, et ses romans—très moraux et très bien écrits—sont dans toutes les mains et revivent dans toutes les mémoires. *Le serment de lady Adelaïde* donneront à nos lecteurs une idée très suffisante du talent si élevé de mistress Henry Wood."—INSTRUCTION PUBLIQUE.

ROLAND YORKE.

"In all respects worthy of the hand that wrote 'The Channings' and 'East Lynne.' There is no lack of excitement to wile the reader on, and from the first to the last a well-planned story is sustained with admirable spirit and in a masterly style."—THE DAILY NEWS.

VERNER'S PRIDE.

"'Verner's Pride' is a first-rate novel in its breadth of outline and brilliancy of description. Its exciting events, its spirited scenes, and its vivid details, all contribute to its triumph. The interest this work awakens, and the admiration it excites in the minds of its readers, must infallibly tend to the renown of the writer, while they herald the welcome reception of the work wherever skill in construction of no ordinary kind, or a ready appreciation of character, which few possess, can arouse attention or win regard."—THE SUN

OSWALD CRAY.

"Mrs. Wood has certainly an art of novel-writing which no rival possesses in the same degree and kind. It is not, we fancy, a common experience for anyone to leave one of these novels unfinished."—THE SPECTATOR.

BESSY RANE.

"The power to draw minutely and carefully each character with characteristic individuality in word and action is Mrs. Wood's especial gift. This endows her pages with a vitality which carries the reader to the end, and leaves him with the feeling that the veil which in real life separates man from man has been raised, and that he has for once seen and known certain people as intimately as if he had been their guardian angel. This is a great fascination."—THE ATHENÆUM.

LORD OAKBURN'S DAUGHTERS.

"The story is admirably told."—THE SPECTATOR.

DENE HOLLOW.

"Novel-readers wishing to be entertained, and deeply interested in character and incident, will find their curiosity wholesomely gratified by the graphic pages of 'Dene Hollow,' an excellent novel, without the drawbacks of wearisome digressions and monotonous platitudes so common in the chapters of modern fiction."—THE MORNING POST.

ELSTER'S FOLLY.

"Mrs. Wood fulfils all the requisites of a good novelist : she interests people in her books, makes them anxious about the characters, and furnishes an intricate and carefully woven plot."—THE MORNING POST.

MILDRED ARKELL.

"Mrs. Henry Wood certainly possesses in a wholly exceptional degree the power of uniting the most startling incident of supernatural influence, with a certain probability and naturalness which compels the most critical and sceptical reader, having once begun, to go on reading. . . . He finds himself conciliated by some bit of quiet picture, some accent of poetic tenderness, some sweet domestic touch telling of a heart exercised in the rarer experiences ; and as he proceeds he wonders more and more at the manner in which the mystery, the criminality, the plotting, and the murdering reconciles itself with a quiet sense of the justice of things ; and a great moral lesson is, after all, found to lie in the heart of all the turmoil and exciting scene-shifting. It is this which has earned for Mrs. Wood so high a place among popular novelists, and secured her admittance to homes from which the sensational novelists so-called are excluded."— THE NONCONFORMIST.

SAINT MARTIN'S EVE.

"A good novel."—THE SPECTATOR.

"Mrs. Wood has spared no pains to accumulate the materials for a curiously thrilling story."—THE SATURDAY REVIEW.

ANNE HEREFORD.

"Mrs. Wood's story, 'Anne Hereford,' is a favourable specimen of her manner ; the incidents are well planned, and the narrative is easy and vigorous."—THE ILLUSTRATED LONDON NEWS.

GEORGE CANTERBURY'S WILL.

"The name of Mrs. Henry Wood has been familiar to novel-readers for many years, and her fame widens and strengthens with the increase in the number of her books."—THE MORNING POST.

A LIFE'S SECRET.

"Now that the rights of capital and labour are being fully inquired into, Mrs. Wood's story of 'A Life's Secret' is particularly opportune and interesting. It is based upon a plot that awakens curiosity and keeps it alive throughout. The hero and heroine are marked with individuality, the love-passages are finely drawn, and the story developed with judgment."—THE CIVIL SERVICE GAZETTE.

THE RED COURT FARM.

"When we say that a plot displays Mrs. Wood's well-known skill in construction, our readers will quite understand that their attention will be enchained by it from the first page to the last."—THE WEEKLY DISPATCH.

TREVLYN HOLD.

"We cannot read a page of this work without discovering a graphic force of delineation which it would not be easy to surpass."—THE DAILY NEWS.

WITHIN THE MAZE.

"The decided novelty and ingenuity of the plot of 'Within the Maze' renders it, in our eyes, one of Mrs. Henry Wood's best novels. It is excellently developed, and the interest hardly flags for a moment."—THE GRAPHIC.

THE MASTER OF GREYLANDS.

"A book by Mrs. Wood is sure to be a good one, and no one who opens 'The Master of Greylands' in anticipation of an intellectual treat will be disappointed. The keen analysis of character, and the admirable management of the plot, alike attest the clever novelist."—JOHN BULL.

JOHNNY LUDLOW.

THE FIRST SERIES.

"We regard these stories as almost perfect of their kind."—THE SPECTATOR.

"Fresh, lively, vigorous, and full of clever dialogue, they will meet with a ready welcome."—THE STANDARD.

ORVILLE COLLEGE.

"Mrs. Wood's stories bear the impress of her versatile talent and well-known skill in turning to account the commonplaces of daily life as well as the popular superstitions of the multitude."—THE LITERARY WORLD.

PARKWATER.

"Mrs. Wood's pleasant style and vivid imagination were never more pleasantly manifested."—JOHN BULL.

EDINA.

"The whole situation of the book is clever, and the plot is well managed."—ACADEMY.

"Edina's character is beautifully drawn."—THE LITERARY WORLD.

POMEROY ABBEY.

"All the Pomeroys are very cleverly individualised, and the way in which the mystery is worked up, including its one horribly tragic incident, is really beyond all praise."—THE MORNING POST.

JOHNNY LUDLOW.

THE SECOND SERIES.

"The author has given proof of a rarer dramatic instinct than we had suspected among our living writers of fiction. It is not possible by means of extracts to convey any adequate sense of the humour, the pathos, the dramatic power and graphic description of this book."—THE NONCONFORMIST.

COURT NETHERLEIGH.

"We always open one of Mrs. Wood's novels with pleasure, because we are sure of being amused and interested."—THE TIMES.

"Lisez-le ; l'émotion que vous sentirez peu à peu monter à votre cœur est saine et fortifiante. Lisez-le ; c'est un livre honnête sorti d'une plume honnête et vous pourrez le laisser traîner sur la table."—LE SIGNAL (Paris).

www.ingramcontent.com/pod-product-compliance
Lightning Source LLC
Chambersburg PA
CBHW031819270326
41932CB00008B/467